Ownership and Inheritance in Sanskrit Jurisprudence

OXFORD ORIENTAL MONOGRAPHS

This series of monographs from the Faculty of Oriental Studies, University of Oxford, makes available the results of recent research by scholars connected with the Faculty. Its range of subject matter includes language, literature, thought, history, and art; its geographical scope extends from the Mediterranean and Caucasus to East Asia. The emphasis is more on specialist studies than on works of a general nature.

Ownership and Inheritance in Sanskrit Jurisprudence

CHRISTOPHER T. FLEMING
British Academy Postdoctoral Fellow at the University of Oxford

OXFORD
UNIVERSITY PRESS

OXFORD
UNIVERSITY PRESS

Great Clarendon Street, Oxford, OX2 6DP,
United Kingdom

Oxford University Press is a department of the University of Oxford.
It furthers the University's objective of excellence in research, scholarship,
and education by publishing worldwide. Oxford is a registered trade mark of
Oxford University Press in the UK and in certain other countries

First Edition published in 2020
Impression: 1

Published in the United States of America by Oxford University Press
198 Madison Avenue, New York, NY 10016, United States of America

British Library Cataloguing in Publication Data
Data available

Library of Congress Control Number: 2020941053

ISBN 978–0–19–885237–7

DOI: 10.1093/oso/9780198852377.001.0001

Printed and bound in Great Britain by
Clays Ltd, Elcograf S.p.A.

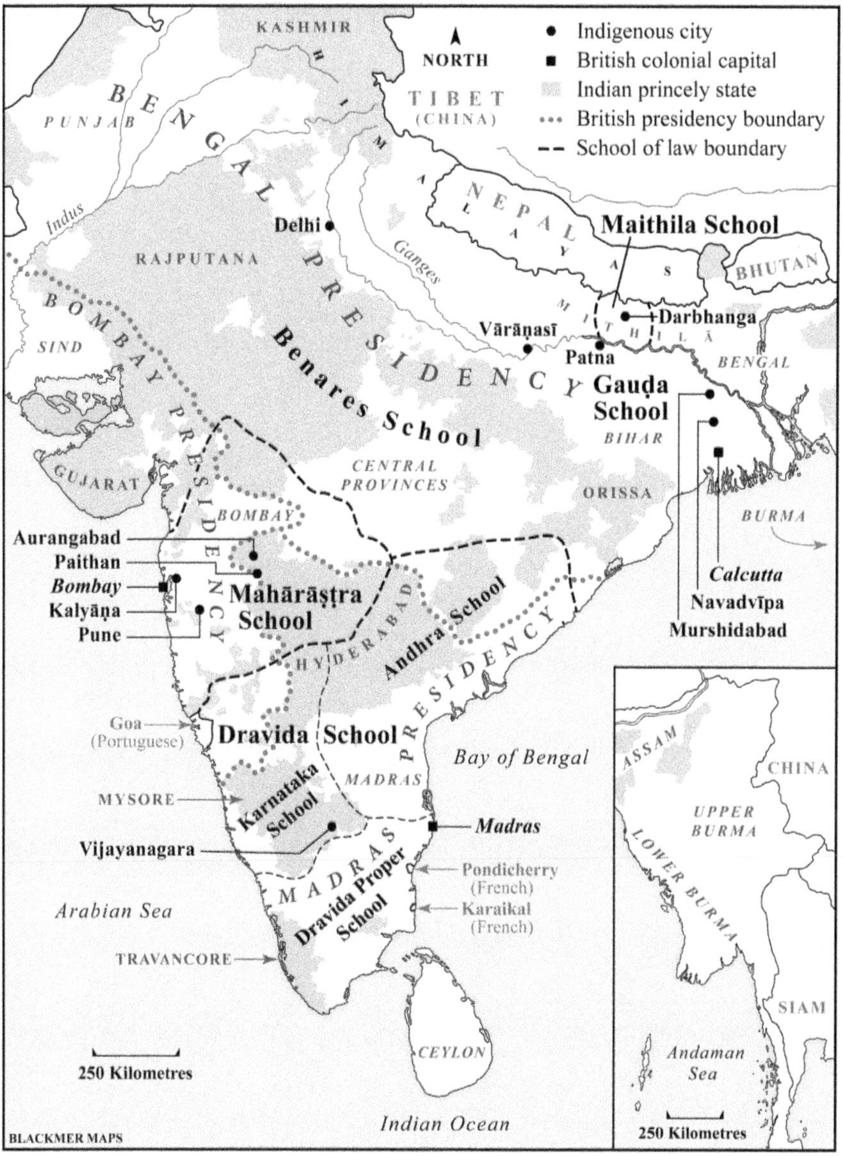

The Five Schools of Anglo-Hindu Law *c.*1868

vāgarthāviva saṃpṛktau vāgarthapratipattaye / jagataḥ pitarau vande pārvatīparameśvarau //1//
ākāśātpatitaṃ toyaṃ yathā gacchati sāgaram / sarvadevanamaskāraḥ keśvaṃ pratigacchati //2//

Acknowledgements

My Supervisors
(Oxford)
Christopher Z. Minkowski
James Benson, Rosalind O'Hanlon, Diwakar Acharya, Anand Venkatkrishnan
(Harvard)
Parimal Patil, Alex Watson, Francis Clooney, Charles Hallisey, Anne Monius
(Whitman)
Jonathan S. Walters, Daniel Kent, Walter Wyman, James Hanson

My Sanskrit Teachers
Satyanarayana Sharma, Madhura Godbole, Meenal Kulkarni, Katarzyna Pazucha

My Friends and Colleagues
(Los Angeles)
James McHugh, Lisa Bitel, Thomas Seifrid, Rebecca Lemon, Jessica Marglin, Stephanie Jamison, Kathryn Dickason, Sean Gibbons, Nicholas Wales, Scott Altman, Brian Horton (*Honoris Causa*)
(Oxford)
Vishal Sharma, Yiming Shen, Charles Foster, Tara (Fabienne) Hathaway, Bihani Sarkar, Stefano Zacchetti, Mark Howe, Glynis Price, The Oxford Centre for Hindu Studies, The Balliol College MCR, The Gardener's Arms
(Harvard)
Caley Smith, Tyler Richard, Alexander Forte, Jahnabi Barooah Chanchani, Adam Lyons, Rādhikā Blinderman, Parameśvara Rāmakṛṣṇa Cittūr Ayyar, John Fields, The Widener Library Sanskrit Reading Group, The Center for the Study of World Religions
(Whitman)
Carter Leblanc, Matthew Gwiazdoń, Aviv Bridge, Ash, Rick Mora, Nicholas Griffin, Olivia Molden, Kiet Vo, Anthony Woods, John-David Toren, Carly Johnson, The Whitman College Debate Team, Matt Gander (*Honoris Causa*)

My Family
Tim, Brenda, Michael, Anna, Margot, and Lucie Fleming.
Katherine Spencer. Joy Barkey. JGAD
Fide et Fiducia

Special thanks to Karen Raith at OUP, to Saranya Ravi and SPI, to Larry McCrea, to Elizabeth Stone, and to Rosane Rocher. I completed this book as a member of the Society of Fellows in the Humanities at the University of Southern California and as a British Academy Postdoctoral Fellow at the University of Oxford.

Contents

List of Figures and Tables

Figures

Tables

Glossary of Sanskrit Terms

Ācāra—Custom
Brāhmaṇa—Member of priestly caste
Brāhmaṇasabhā—Assembly of Brāhmaṇas
Dākṣinātya—Southern
Dāna—Gift
Dāya—Inheritance
    Apratibandhadāya—Unobstructed inheritance
    Sapratibandhadāya—Obstructed inheritance
Dāyavibhāga—Division of Inheritance (name of vivādapada)
Dhana/Dravya—Asset, property
Dharma—Law, justice, equity, righteousness
Dharmaśāstra—Sanskrit jurisprudential literature
Dharmaśāstrin—A scholar of Dharmaśāstra
Drāviḍa—Southern, Dravidian
Gauḍa—Eastern, Bengali
Janmasvatva—Ownership by birth
Kratvartha—Activities whose primary purpose is the support of the Vedic ritual
Laukika—Extra-śāstric (lit. 'worldly')
Maithila/Miśra—Pertaining to the Mithilā Region
Mīmāṃsā—Ritual hermeneutics
Mīmāṃsaka—A scholar of Mīmāṃsā
Navya-Nyāya—'New' Logic
Navya-Naiyāyika—A scholar of 'New' Logic
Nibandha—A digest (often accompanied by commentary)
Padārtha—Conceptual category
Paṇḍita—Traditional Sanskrit scholar of Brāhmaṇa heritage
Prabhutva—Dominion, possession
Puruṣārtha—Activities whose primary purpose is the pleasure of people
Pūrvapakṣin—Advocate of prima facie opinion
Ṣadr Dīwānī 'Adālat—Superior Civil Courts in the Company's Presidencies
Śakti—Causal capacity
Sapiṇḍa—Having the same piṇḍa, i.e. a kinsman.
    a. According the Bengal School: having the same funerary offering
    b. According to the *Mitākṣarā* and Maithila Schools: having a consanguineous relationship.
Śāstra—Traditional Sanskrit knowledge system
Śāstraikasamadhigamyatva—discernible from the śāstra alone
Śiṣṭācāra—Proper conduct
Smṛti—'Remembered Texts' (collections of primary legal rules)

Svatva—Property (the abstract state of being someone's property)
Sva—property (an asset that is someone's property)
Svāmitva/Svāmya—Ownership, Property
Śrāddha—Funerary ceremony
Uparamasvatva—Ownership by the cessation of the ownership of the previous owner
Vārāṇaseya—Pertaining to Vārāṇasī
Vibhāga—Division/partition
Vivādapada—Title of litigation
Yatheṣṭaviniyoga—Use as desired
Yatheṣṭaviniyojyatva—Usability as desired
Yatheṣṭaviniyogayogyatva—Fitness for use as desired
Yatheṣṭaviniyogārhatā—Entitlement for use as desired

Introduction

> Something is someone's property (when) someone is eligible to use it as desired.
> Śabarasvāmin, *Mīmāṃsābhāṣya* (fourth century CE).[1]

> There is nothing which so generally strikes the imagination, and engages the affections of mankind, as the right of property; or that sole and despotic dominion which one man claims and exercises over the external things of the world, in total exclusion of the right of any other individual in the universe. And yet there are very few, that will give themselves the trouble to consider the original and foundation of this right.
> William Blackstone, *Commentaries on the Laws of England* (1763).[2]

This monograph explores two related legal phenomena from classical India: ownership and inheritance. It attends to these phenomena within the Sanskrit text-traditions of jurisprudence (Dharmaśāstra), scriptural hermeneutics (Mīmāṃsā), and formal logic (Navya-Nyāya) and shows that the philosophical theories of ownership that emerged from hermeneutical and (later) logical literature were recalibrated and redeployed strategically by jurists to defend two competing models of inheritance—in which families held assets in joint trusts or in which family patriarchs exercised nearly unfettered control over ancestral assets.[3]

During India's long early modern period (1500–1800) these two juridical models of inheritance (and their attendant philosophical justifications) were adopted by Brāhmaṇa scholars (Paṇḍitas) who portrayed themselves as the embodiment of southern (Dākṣiṇātya) or eastern (Gauḍa) proper conduct (śiṣṭācāra). Ownership became a prominent topic in broader debates between southern and eastern Paṇḍitas regarding the just, Dharmic ordering of society. These debates resulted in the creation of regional 'schools' of pre-colonial Sanskrit jurisprudence in which one can identify consistent lines of argument that were

[1] *Mīmāṃsādarśana*, vol. 5, ed. V. G. Apte (Pune: Anandashrama Press, 1933), 1656: *Śābarabhāṣya* on *Mīmāṃsāsūtra* 9.1.9: yo yad abhipretaṃ viniyoktum arhati tat tasya svam.

[2] William Blackstone, *Commentaries on the Laws of England: Book the Second* (Oxford: Clarendon Press, 1766), p. 2.

[3] For the concept of 'text-traditions' in Sanskrit intellectual history, see Lawrence McCrea and Parimal Patil, *Buddhist Philosophy of Language in India: Jñānaśrīmitra on Exclusion* (New York: Columbia University Press, 2007), pp. 3–7.

Ownership and Inheritance in Sanskrit Jurisprudence. Christopher T. Fleming, Oxford University Press (2020).

DOI: 10.1093/oso/9780198852377.003.0001

strongly associated with specific academic institutions, scholastic lineages, and disciplinary techniques in different regions of India.

The advent of European colonialism and the codification of Dharmaśāstra as Hindu personal law through the administrative apparatuses of the British East India Company resulted in a novel development whereby the state enforced what were previously scholastic, meta-legal discourses as positive legal codes. Colonial, orientalist views of Dharmaśāstra as a record of the customary practices of the Hindus living in the Company's territories of Bengal, Bihar, Banaras, Bombay, and Madras, failed to capture much of Dharmaśāstra's theoretical, scholastic valence. Furthermore, the specific formulation of *five* 'schools of Hindu law' in Anglo-Hindu jurisprudence—Bengal, Mithila, Benares, Maharashtra, and Dravada—imposed the jurisdictional divisions of the Company's 'Adālat court system from the presidencies of Bengal, Bombay, and Madras onto Dharmaśāstric texts. An earlier, and different, formulation of *three* schools of Hindu jurisprudence—Gauḍa, Maithila, and Dākṣinātya—however, was as much an authentic representation of pre-colonial *intellectual* and *filial* patterns amongst Brāhmaṇa-jurists as it was a distortion generated by the idiosyncrasies, prejudices, and jurisdictional structure of the Company's courts.

Ownership, Property, and Svatva

This monograph provides an account of ownership in the intellectual history of Sanskrit jurisprudence. Before turning to the intricacies and controversies surrounding the discursive registers of law, Dharmaśāstra, and intellectual history, it is worth attending to what terms such as 'ownership' and 'property' mean in Western legal parlance and in traditional Sanskrit jurisprudence. The purpose of this section is twofold: (1) to introduce the reader to legal debates about ownership's metaphysics in the west and in India; and (2) to demonstrate that these arguments about property and ownership have been and remain deeply embedded in broader debates concerning the just and equitable organization of society. Ironically, in Anglo-American jurisprudence, 'property' is defined rather nebulously, if at all. Derrett notes that,

> fundamental concepts are often the more difficult to define because of their ubiquitous employment... [and] property is just such a concept, standing upon the frontiers of linguistics, law, and logic without deriving final shape from any of them... Many legal systems (which out of necessity employ the concept at every turn) contrive to dispense with a definition altogether.[4]

[4] J. Duncan Derrett, 'An Indian Contribution to the Study of Property', *Bulletin of the School of Oriental and African Studies* 18 (1956): 475–498, 475.

Joseph Singer summarizes a fairly standard view of property in Anglo-American jurisprudence as 'legal relations among people regarding control and disposition of valued resources'.[5] 'When we think of property,' writes Singer, 'we tend to think of ownership ... [and] an owner has the power to control the property she owns.'[6] One might think of this physicalist power 'to control' in Blackstone's or in Śabarasvāmin's terms: as despotic dominion (dominatio, prabhutva) or as use as desired (yatheṣṭaviniyoga).[7] However, 'ownership does not mean the absolute right to control what one owns; rather, it is the fullest bundle of rights that the law will recognize'.[8]

This realist view of property as a bundle of rights—possession, title, mortgage, lease, sale, and so forth—which amounts to a list of the incidents of property, has come under withering critique from two directions. On the one hand, legal anthropologists—taking the view of property as relations among people, as *in personam*—have deconstructed the bundle by disaggregating its 'sticks' (rights) into a nearly endless series of social relations.[9] On the other hand—a hand that this study of ownership in Sanskrit jurisprudence plays into—a series of Anglo-American legal scholars, who emphasize the distinctive *in rem*, affecting an item, quality of property, have argued persuasively for a unitary category of property (and ownership).[10]

[5] Joseph Singer, *Property*, 5th edn (New York: Wolters Kluwer, 2017), p. 2. The formulation of property as relations between people rather than as relations between people and objects traces its origins to a series of articles by Wesley Hohfeld. See 'Some Fundamental Legal Conceptions as Applied in Juridical Reasoning', *Yale Law Review* 23.16 (1913): pp. 28–59; and *Yale Law Review* 26.8 (1917): 710–70. See Henry Smith, 'Property Is Not Just a Bundle of Rights', *Econ Journal Watch* 8.3 (2011): 279–91, 280: 'Hohfeld's tendency to make fine distinctions was embraced and extended because the social planner or judge could tinker with the bundle, and given the Progressive and New Deal agenda of the Realists, this would allow sticks to be transferred from owners to others with the result still being "property"... This picture carried into the American Law Institute's Restatement of the Law of Property of 1938 (§ 7, § 10), which defines "real property" as one of a number of present possessory estates and an "owner" as the person who has one or more interests. Objections on the grounds that policy-driven innovations violated property rights could simply be defined away as naïve and superstitious formalism and conceptualism in the service of an anti-Progress agenda masquerading as objective reality.'

[6] Singer, *Property*, p. 2.

[7] For an account of earlier, 'Blackstonian', physicalist and absolute theories of ownership and property, see Kenneth Vandevelde, 'The New Property of the Nineteenth Century: The Development of the Modern Concept of Property', *Buffalo Law Review* 29 (1980): 325–68.

[8] Singer, *Property*, p. 3. For a list and description of the incidents of property, see A. M. Honoré, 'Ownership', in *Oxford Essays in Jurisprudence*, ed. Anthony G. Guest (Oxford: Oxford University Press, 1961), pp. 107–47.

[9] C. M. Hann, 'Introduction: The Embeddedness of Property', in *Property Relations: Renewing the Anthropological Tradition*, ed. C. M. Hann (Cambridge: Cambridge University Press, 1998), pp. 1–47.

[10] The canonical works from this position are those of Thomas Merrill and Henry Smith: 'Optimal Standardization in the Law of Property: the Numerus Clausus Principle', *Yale Law Journal* 110.1 (2000): 1–70; 'The Property/Contract Interface', *Columbia Law Review* 101 (2001): 773–852; *Property: Principles and Policies* (New York: Foundation Press, 2007); Henry Smith, 'Property as the Law of Things', *Harvard Law Review*, 125 (2012): 1691–1726. Also see Robert C. Ellickson, 'Two Cheers for the Bundle-of-Sticks Metaphor, Three Cheers for Merrill and Smith', *Econ Journal Watch* 8.3 (2011): 215–22.

Naturally, philosophical discussions concerning the definition and the nature of property and ownership have been and remain deeply embedded in various debates in political theory.[11] Hobbes and Locke's theories of ownership as an artificial creation of the state, or as a natural right that pre-existed the formation of sovereign states, were far more than mere observations on a ubiquitous facet of human commerce. Rather, these theories of ownership were part and parcel of broader arguments concerning British society in the wake of an emerging liberal economic order.[12] One can hardly forget that many of the most trenchant critiques of economic liberalism (and its human impact)—Marxist, feminist, or critical racial—use property, and private ownership in particular, as their point of departure for untangling the threads of power and ideology that bind injustice and power.[13] Similarly, property has become a central category for theorizing individuals' rights over their *own* bodies in an era of rapid technological advancement in medicine, or for advocating the cultivation of moral virtue in the face of the free market's commodification of human value.[14] Examples of property as a cipher for society are legion, but this survey should convey to the reader that in the West—as in classical India—technical, jurisprudential questions about ownership and broader, philosophical and political questions about how society ought to be organized are intimately linked.

In classical Sanskrit jurisprudential and philosophical texts, ownership and property are given more concrete definitions and more rigorous metaphysical accounts than in perhaps any other legal tradition. If Western jurists focused on ownership's incidents—to the neglect of its coherence as a unitary category—traditional Sanskrit scholars focused on the definition of ownership and property—to the neglect of a rigorous account of its incidents. In the earlier (roughly fifth century BCE to fifth century CE) strata of Sanskrit jurisprudential literature (for example, the Dharmasūtras of Āpastamba, Gautama, Baudhāyana, and Vasiṣṭha and the Dharmasmṛtis of Manu, Nārada, and Yājñavalkya) and in

[11] Alan Ryan, *Property and Political Theory* (Oxford: Blackwell, 1984).

[12] Benjamin Lopata, 'Property Theory in Hobbes', *Political Theory* 1.2. (1973): 203–18; James Tully, *A Discourse on Property: John Locke and His Adversaries* (Cambridge: Cambridge University Press, 1980).

[13] See, for example, Anthony Giddens, *Capitalism and Modern Social Theory: An Analysis of the Writings of Marx, Durkheim, and Max Weber* (Cambridge: Cambridge University Press, 1971); Jeane Schroeder, *The Vestal and the Fasces: Hegel, Lacan, Property, and the Feminine* (Berkeley: University of California Press, 1998); Gloria Billings and William Tate, 'Toward a Critical Race Theory of Education', *Teachers College Record*, 97.1 (1995): 47–68.

[14] See, for example, Imogen Goold, 'Property Rights in Bodily Material', in *Tensions and Traumas in Health Law*, ed. Ian Freckleton and Kerry Petersen (Annandale: Federation Press, 2017), pp. 367–83; Imogen Goold and Muireann Quigley, 'Human Biomaterials: The Case for a Property Approach', in *Persons, Parts and Property: How Should We Regulate Human Tissue in the 21st Century?*, ed. Imogen Goold, Jonathan Herring, Loane Skene, and Kate Greasley (Oxford: Hart Publishing, 2014), pp. 231–62; Jasper A. Bovenberg, *Property Rights in Blood, Genes and Data: Naturally Yours?* (Leiden: Brill, 2006); Michael Sandel, *What Money Can't Buy: The Moral Limits of Markets* (London: Allen Lane, 2012).

the epics (*Rāmāyaṇa* and *Mahābhārata*), one encounters a variety of terms used, more or less uncritically, to refer to ownership: īśā, prabhutva, svāmya, etc. Although theoretical speculation on the meaning of ownership and property is largely absent from this early material, by the sixth century CE, Indian scholars began to employ a relational pair of terms to denote proprietary relationships between owners and assets—svāmitva (sometimes svāmya) and svatva.[15] The scholastic use of Sanskrit's characteristic linguistic precision and arsenal of nominal and verbal suffixes produced a theory of ownership and property that escapes many of the definitional difficulties of the Anglo-American tradition.

In brief, Sanskrit scholars theorized ownership and property as a relation (sambandha) between an owner (svāmin) and something owned, i.e. something that is someone's property (svam). Sva, a reflexive pronoun, is used adjectivally in Sanskrit to denote things (not necessarily assets) with which one has a personal relation—as in 'my parents' (svapitarau), 'my knowledge' (svajñāna) or 'my duty' (svadharma). Svāmin (a possessive derivation from sva) denotes the person who possesses a relation to some sva. Svāmitva and svatva are suffixed words which denote the abstract state or condition of being an owner and being owned: ownerness and own-ness. With very few—and highly technical—exceptions, Sanskrit theorists used svatva and svāmitva almost interchangeably to describe 'ownership' and 'property' (the latter in the sense of Property rather than in the sense of property).[16] It is important, however, to distinguish between assets (dhana, dravya, artha, and so on) and property (sva, svam): the former denote the range of 'things' which can be owned, while the latter characterize particular assets as being owned.

The theorists initially argued that ownership could be defined as or be characterized in terms of 'use as desired' (yatheṣṭaviniyoga). In the course of time, Sanskrit scholars recalibrated aspects of this account of ownership: some emphasized its cognitive aspect (via saṃskāras, mental impressions), others described the relation between owner and owned as that of agent and object (kartṛkarman), while others—particularly logicians—assigned ownership to various ontological categories such as those of quality (guṇa), absence (abhāva) or even the distinct conceptual category 'ownership' (padārthāntara). Debates raged about the modes of acquiring ownership—and what role Sanskrit jurisprudence played in limiting the modes of acquisition available to members of various classes. The incidental characteristic of ownership evolved: from an unrestricted right to use an asset as

[15] Of course, svatva and svāmitva appeared far earlier in Sanskrit grammatical (Vyākaraṇa) literature to describe the meaning of the genitive case ending. See Ethan Kroll, 'A Logical Approach to Law' (PhD Dissertation, University of Chicago, 2010), pp. 24–9.

[16] For a discussion of svatva and svāmitva in terms of property and ownership, see Manomohini Dutta, 'Inheritance, Property and Women in the *Dāyabhāga*' (PhD Diss, University of Texas, 2016), pp. 78–93. For the interchangeability of svatva and svāmitva, see H. T. Colebrooke's marginalia in his copy of the *Svatvarahasya* (fol 13a): 'Propy [*sic*] & ownership is [*sic*] the same'. Cited in Kroll, 'A Logical Approach to Law', pp. 198–9.

desired to a more circumscribed *fitness* for use as desired (yatheṣṭaviniyogayogyatva). Through all of its historical vicissitudes, the Sanskrit theory of ownership remained 1) a relationship 2) between an owner and property 3) that afforded an owner some right (adhikāra) related to use as desired (though that did not necessarily entail the actual use as desired). This tradition of ownership was radically *in rem* and radically formal.

Naturally, these technical reflections on ownership and property were part of a broader scholastic discourse (śāstra) that sought to order society according to a very specific political theory—the Dharma of caste and stage of life (Varṇāśramadharma). The categories of Dharma and Śāstra are theorized in the following section, but to conclude this section, it is necessary to emphasize the importance of ownership and property in Western and Sanskrit jurisprudence. Talking about ownership and inheritance is a way of drawing attention to the ways that people relate to objects and relate to one another. These relations are notoriously difficult to settle conclusively but debates about ownership—however abstract and technical—are part of much larger projects that are concerned with ideas of morality, justice and 'law'. For many Indians, these ideas are denoted by the term Dharma, and the Sanskrit tradition that analysed Dharma is known as Dharmaśāstra.

Dharma, Dharmaśāstra, and Śāstra

This monograph tracks the development of the concept of ownership and inheritance within Dharmaśāstra, the expert Sanskrit tradition of jurisprudential thought. Although the relationship between Dharmaśāstra and other text-traditions (hermeneutics and formal logic) is analysed, the primary focus is on how these thought traditions' arguments concerning ownership and property inflected juridical debates about the problem of inheritance—and this problem's place in the development of regionally specific schools of Indian legal thought. This section adumbrates the history of the terms 'Dharma', 'Dharmaśāstra', and 'Śāstra', in order to convey to the reader the unique features of the moral and intellectual systems in which debates about ownership and inheritance occur. Before turning to questions concerning the relationship between Dharmaśāstra and Western 'law' in the next section, it is important to emphasize the far-reaching, totalizing semantic range of Dharma—and to sketch out a basic textual history of the Dharmaśāstric tradition.

Dharma, as Patrick Olivelle notes:

> constitute[s] the most central feature of Indian civilization..., irrespective of linguistic, sectarian, or regional differences...One has only to pick up any introduction to Hinduism or Buddhism to note the prominence given to this

> term by the authors... One is also left with the impression that, following the orientalist image of the 'unchanging' India, dharma has always been the central concept of Indian religion and culture.[17]

Dharma's ubiquity in Indian civilization is the product of a long historical process whereby the term was appropriated and recalibrated by successive waves of religious reformers and traditional scholars. Variations on the term Dharma-derived from the verbal root √dhṛ, to bear, to support—appear in the oldest Sanskrit text, the *Ṛgveda* (1200–800 BCE), and occasionally in the *Atharvaveda* (*c.*1000 BCE), but,

> dharma was not a central term in the ritual or theological vocabulary of the middle and late vedic texts. It occurs less frequently in the Brāhmaṇas and Upaniṣads than we would have predicted for a term that was to become the central concept of Indian civilization.[18]

Olivelle's thesis—shared by Alf Hiltebeitel and Wilhelm Halbfass—is that the term Dharma was appropriated by the śramaṇic movements of the fifth century BCE (Buddhism and Jainism) as a term for their visions of a universal moral good, and adopted in the third century BCE by Aśoka Maurya as a central feature of a pan-Indian political theology—one in many ways opposed to the social hierarchy of Vedic Brāhmaṇism.[19] In response, post-Mauryan Brāhmaṇas developed their own concept of Dharma: as 'the privileges, duties and obligations of a man [sic], his standard of conduct as a member of the Āryan community, as a member of one of the castes, as a person, in a particular stage of life [Varṇāśramadharma]'.[20] The end result of this shift—from universal, non-violent ethics to an all-encompassing series of duties—is a radically deontological Dharma which:

> encompasses the prescriptions for, the acts of, and the effects of ritual, purification, diet, statecraft, and penance in addition to rules for legal procedure, contracts, property, corporations and partnerships, inheritance, marriage, and crimes of various sorts.[21]

[17] Patrick Olivelle, 'Introduction', *Journal of Indian Philosophy* 32.5–6 (2004): 421–2.

[18] Patrick Olivelle, *Manu's Code of Law: A Critical Edition and Translation of the Mānava-Dharmaśāstra* (Oxford: Oxford University Press, 2005), p. 42. For the best historical overview of the concept of Dharma, see Patrick Olivelle (ed.), *Dharma: Studies in Its Semantic, Cultural and Religious History* (Delhi: Motilal Banarasidass, 2009).

[19] Olivelle, *Manu's Code of Law*, pp. 42–3; Wilhelm Halbfass, *India and Europe: An Essay in Understanding* (New York: SUNY, 1988), pp. 310–33; Alf Hiltebeitel, *Dharma* (Honolulu: University of Hawaii Press, 2010).

[20] P. V. Kāṇe, *A History of Dharmaśāstra*, vol. 1. part 1, 2nd edn (Poona: Bhandarkar Oriental Research Institute, 1968), p. 3. Cf. Olivelle, *Manu's Code of Law*, pp. 43–4. Also see Patrick Olivelle, *The Āśrama System: The History and Hermeneutics of a Religious Institution* (Delhi: Munishiram Manoharlal, 1993), esp. pp. 8–34.

[21] Donald Davis, 'Hinduism as a Legal Tradition', *Journal of the American Academy of Religion* 75.2 (2007): 241–267, 243.

Of course, this reformulated, radically social Dharma of the post-Mauryan Hinduism is not *merely* a list of obligations. Rather, it is a list of obligations that, taken together, form a model of righteous cosmic order to which moral human action ought to conform.[22] Indeed, this sense of Dharma informs virtually every subsequent Hindu theological system—those that rebel against it, those that embrace it enthusiastically and those that transcend it.

The expert Sanskrit scholastic tradition that transformed the śramaṇic vision of Dharma as a universal ethical good into Varṇāśramadharma is Dharmaśāstra, which, 'with an unbroken history of over two millennia . . . is undoubtedly the longest in Indian history'.[23] The first Dharmaśāstric texts, composed no earlier than the fourth century BCE, were a series of Dharmasūtras, the oldest being those of Āpastamba, Gautama, Baudhāyana and Vasiṣṭha. These short aphoristic codes of ritual and legal rules, along with household (gṛhya) and ritual (śrauta) sūtras, formed a category of literature known as Kalpasūtra.[24] By the second century CE, a new genre of Dharma literature emerged: Dharmaśāstra. The Dharmaśāstras, or Dharmasmṛtis, were versified digests of rules that greatly expanded the scope of topics and the depth of opinions on various issues from the Dharmasūtras.[25] Dharmaśāstra literature included, innovatively, political, commercial, and legal material from Kauṭilya's *Arthaśāstra*.[26] Dharmaśāstra treatises, beginning with the watershed *Mānavadharmaśāstra* (second to third centuries CE), adopted the *Arthaśāstra*'s scheme of eighteen titles of litigation (vyavahārapadas/vivādapadas). One title of litigation, the partition of inheritance (dāyavibhāga), became the site of hot-blooded debates amongst later Dharmaśāstrins.

Over the following centuries, a textual tradition of commentaries (bhāṣyas, ṭīkās), digests (nibandhas) and monographs (kutūhalas, nirṇayas, tattvas, rahasyas, etc.) emerged that attempted to synthesize the many conflicting passages of sūtra and smṛti (Dharmasūtra and Dharmasmṛti) into a coherent intellectual system—Dharmaśāstra. It was in this commentarial tradition, beginning with Bhāruci's sixth century CE commentary on the *Mānavadharmaśāstra*, that ownership (svatva) emerged as a category of legal analysis.[27] Svatva allowed commentaries to distinguish between legal ownership and mere possession—in cases of adverse possession, questionable title, and inheritance—and by the second

[22] Paul Hacker, 'Dharma in Hinduism', *Journal of Indian Philosophy* 34.5 (2006): 479–96.

[23] Patrick Olivelle, 'Dharmaśāstra: a Textual History', in *Hinduism and Law: An Introduction*, ed. Timothy Lubin, Donald Davis, and Jayanth Krishnan (Cambridge: Cambridge University Press, 2012), pp. 28–57, 28.

[24] Ibid., pp. 37–9. See Kāṇe, *History of Dharmaśāstra*, vol. 1. part 1, 2nd edn, pp. 19–22. For the Dharmasūtras, see Patrick Olivelle, *The Dharmasūtras: the Law Codes of Āpastamba, Gautama, Baudhāyana, and Vasiṣṭha* (Oxford: Oxford University Press, 1999).

[25] Olivelle, 'Dharmaśāstra', p. 41.

[26] Ibid., p. 41. Also see Olivelle, *Manu's Code of Law*, pp. 13–16. For the *Arthaśāstra* see Patrick Olivelle, *King, Governance, and Law in Ancient India: Kauṭilya's Arthaśāstra* (Oxford: Oxford University Press, 2013).

[27] See Kroll, 'A Logical Approach to Law', pp. 30–1.

millennium CE, discussions of svatva and inheritance were twinned in Vijñāneśvara's *Ṛjumitākṣarā* (eleventh to twelfth centuries), a commentary on the *Yājñavalkyasmṛti*.[28] One of Vijñāneśvara's innovations—analysed in depth in Chapter 1 of this monograph—dealt with a model of inheritance in which sons and grandsons obtain ownership in their father and grandfathers' assets merely by being born (janmasvatva). The problem for Vijñāneśvara was that the Dharmasūtras and the Dharmasmṛtis never mention birth as one of the canonical methods of acquiring ownership (svatvahetu).

Vijñāneśvara's solution—that ownership and property are extra-śāstric phenomena whose modes of acquisition are established according to custom (ācāra)—set off a long-running debate about the boundaries between Dharmaśāstra and the extra-śāstric, mundane world that cleft India's Dharmaśāstric community of scholars into at least two camps. For these two camps—which would crystallize in commentarial traditions that developed around the *Mitākṣarā* and Jīmūtavāhana's *Dāyabhāga* (twelfth to fifteenth centuries)—the essential questions were what śāstra was and where the boundaries between śāstra and the activities of the extra-śāstric world (lokavyavahāra) ought to be drawn. In answering these questions, scholars turned to two related śāstric traditions, scriptural hermeneutics (Mīmāṃsā) and formal logic (Navya-Nyāya).

Dharmaśāstra is not law, *per se*. Rather, it is a traditional Sanskrit knowledge system, a śāstra. Like other śāstras, Dharmaśāstra has two characteristic traits: 1) an elaborate, highly systematized series of rules—for analysing and organizing the many disparate and often contradictory injunctions of the Dharmasūtras and the Dharmasmṛtis—and 2) a highly abstracted, metadiscursive conceit that places it above and beyond extra-śāstric human behavior. Drawing on Sheldon Pollock's understanding of śāstras as 'a verbal codification of rules, whether of divine or human provenance, for the positive and negative regulation of particular cultural practices', this passage outlines the essential features of śāstra as a scholastic meta-tradition and introduces two śāstric traditions whose rules of interpretation influenced Dharmaśāstric debates about ownership and inheritance.[29] Beginning with the six Vedāṅgas, auxiliary disciplines (600–300 BCE)—grammar, prosody, phonetics, etymology, astronomy, and sacrificial liturgy—'ancillary disciplines that developed out of the perceived need to preserve and understand obsolescent Vedic texts', Sanskrit intellectual activity produced radically nomothetic śāstras pertaining to Dharma and dozens of other topics.[30] As Pollock notes,

[28] For Vijñāneśvara, see Kāṇe, *A History of Dharmaśāstra*, vol. 1. part 2, 2nd edn (Poona: Bhandarkar Oriental Research Institute, 1975), pp. 601–16.

[29] Sheldon Pollock, 'The Idea of Śāstra in Traditional India', in *The Shastric Traditions in Indian Arts*, ed. Anna Dallapiccola (Stuttgart: Steiner Verlag Wiesbaden, 1989), pp. 17–26, 18.

[30] Ibid.

> Classical Indian civilization... offers what may be the most exquisite expression of the centrality of rule-governance in human behavior... secular life as a whole was subject to a kind of ritualization, whereby all its performative gestures and signifying practices came to be encoded in texts. Śāstra, the Sanskrit word for these grammars, thus presents itself as one of the fundamental features and problems of Indian civilization in general and of Indian intellectual history in particular.[31]

The dependence of virtually all śāstric genres on the Vedas, however, as the transcendent, unchanging model of all human activity resulted in an intellectual culture in which,

> there can be for the thinker no originality of thought, no brand-new insights, notions, preceptions, [*sic*] but only the attempt better and more clearly to grasp and explain the antecedent, always already formulated truth. All Indian learning, accordingly, perceives itself and indeed presents itself largely as commentary on the primordial śāstras.[32]

As an intellectual science, Dharmaśāstra required sophisticated hermeneutical techniques to reconcile its vast corpus of conflicting injunctions.[33] The Mīmāṃsā, the most important śāstric system of hermeneutics, developed around the *Mīmāṃsāsūtras* of Jaimini (around the turn of the first millennium CE).[34] Anand Venkatkrishnan characterizes Mīmāṃsā as:

> a tradition that attempted to understand a corpus of texts, the Veda, by developing systematic interpretive principles. These principles both argued for the epistemological validity of the Veda, defined as distinct from competing scriptural traditions and possessing transcendental authority, and organized the Veda's internal components based on a hierarchy of meaningful language.[35]

The practitioners of the Mīmāṃsā, Mīmāṃsakas, developed a hermeneutical system whereby authoritative passages from the Vedas could be analysed in terms of a hierarchical set of injunctions (vidhis).[36] The Mīmāṃsakas'

[31] Sheldon Pollock, 'The Theory of Practice and the Practice of Theory in Indian Intellectual History', *Journal of the American Oriental Society* 105.3 (1985): 499–519, 500.

[32] Ibid., 515.

[33] For an account of contradictions within individual smṛtis, see Olivelle, *Manu's Code of Law*, pp. 29–36.

[34] For an introduction to Mīmāṃsā and its technical vocabulary, see Franklin Edgerton, *The Mīmāṃsā Nyāya Prakāśa; or Āpadevī: A Treatise on the Mīmāṃsā System* (New Haven, CT: Yale University Press, 1929).

[35] Anand Venkatkrishnan, 'Mīmāṃsā, Vedānta, and the Bhakti Movement' (PhD Dissertation, Columbia University, 2015), pp. 3–4.

[36] For the hierarchy of injunctions, see Lawrence McCrea, 'The Hierarchical Organization of Language in Mīmāṃsā Interpretive Theory', *Journal of Indian Philosophy* 28.5 (2000): 429–59.

hermeneutical arsenal—determining sentential meaning, classifying injunctions according to scope and time, separating optional and mandatory injunctions, distinguishing between transcendent and mundane effects, and so on—became the standard toolbox for Dharmaśāstrins, particularly by the turn of the second millennium CE.[37]

In addition to providing the hermeneutical techniques that Dharmaśāstric authors used to analyse jurisprudential problems, Mīmāṃsā authors developed an early theory of ownership that provided an essential support to the Dharmaśāstric theory of ownership by birth (janmasvatva). Beginning with Śabarasvāmin's (fourth century CE) commentary on the *Mīmāṃsāsūtras*, the *Śābarabhāṣya*, several Mīmāṃsakas argued that Dharmaśāstric restrictions (niyamas) regarding the acquisition of assets had moral, rather than legal, force (or, more precisely, affected the moral virtue of an individual rather than an asset's appropriateness for sacrificial use). Further, they argued that ownership, as a *fitness* for use as desired (yogyatva), did not always afford an owner the actual use of an asset as desired.

One argument that this monograph develops is that Dharmaśāstric arguments concerning the juridical model of ownership by birth evolved in tandem with Mīmāṃsā theories of ownership as an extra-śāstric phenomenon. This distinctive and consistent cluster of Mīmāṃsā and Dharmaśāstra arguments emerged in various commentaries on Vijñāneśvara's *Mitākṣarā* and coalesced into a characteristically 'southern' school of thought regarding property in the śāstric monographs of members of the Bhaṭṭa family of Paṇḍitas, who lived in Vārāṇasī during the sixteenth, seventeenth, and eighteenth centuries.

Another śāstric tradition that influenced Dharmaśāstra was Navya-Nyāya, the 'new epistemology' that developed in Mithilā in the thirteenth century.[38] These new logicians, Navya-Naiyāyikas, reformulated the earlier systems of Nyāya and Vaiśeṣika, which were interested in 'ascertaining correctly what people know' and in mapping 'the phenomenal world of experience' onto a series of conceptual categories (padārthas).[39] The Navya-Naiyāyikas employed a technical vocabulary—delimitation, conceptual category, invariable concomitance, and so on—that brought increased specificity to the use of language.[40] Ownership drew sustained

[37] Domenico Francavilla, *The Roots of Hindu Jurisprudence: Source of Dharma and Interpretation in Mīmāṃsā and Dharmaśāstra* (Turin: Comitato Corpus Iuris Sanscriticum et fontes Iuris Asiae Meridianae et Centralis, 2005); P. V. Kāṇe, *A History of Dharmaśāstra*, vol. 5. part 2 (Poona: Bandharkar Oriental Research Institute, 1962), pp. 1152–1351; Lawrence McCrea, 'Hindu Jurisprudence and Scriptural Hermeneutics', in *Hinduism and Law: An Introduction*, ed. Timothy Lubin, Donald Davis, and Jayanth Krishnan (Cambridge: Cambridge University Press, 2012), pp. 123–36; Kisori Sarkar, *The Mimansa Rules of Interpretation as Applied to Hindu Law* (Calcutta: Thacker & Spink, 1907).

[38] For work on this relationship, see Kāṇe, *A History of Dharmaśāstra*, vol 5, part 2, pp. 1468–82.

[39] Kroll, 'A Logical Approach to Law', pp. 3–6.

[40] Ibid., pp. 9–11. For overviews of Navya-Nyāya, see H. H. Ingalls, *Materials for the Study of Navya-Nyāya Logic* (Cambridge, MA: Harvard University Press, 1951); Jonardon Ganeri, *The Lost Age of*

attention from Navya-Naiyāyikas, particularly those who lived and worked at the university of Navadvīpa, Bengal, in the sixteenth, seventeenth, and eighteenth centuries.[41] Unlike the Mīmāṃsakas, these logicians defended a theory of ownership that depended on śāstra as the exclusive source of knowledge about how ownership is acquired. At the same time, and in the same university, several Dharmaśāstrins developed—via a commentarial tradition on Jīmūtavāhana's *Dāyabhāga*—a juridical model of inheritance diametrically opposed to that of the *Mitākṣarā* and its followers. The Bengali Dharmaśāstrins used a Navya-Nyāya-inflected idiom to argue that sons and grandsons acquired ownership in the father or grandfather's estate only after their father or grandfather's legal divestiture of ownership (uparamasvatva).

Dharmaśāstra is a technical, scholastic science (śāstra) that portrays itself as a comprehensive guide to Dharma, the various duties incumbent on individuals (whose archetype is an able-bodied Brāhmaṇa male). In this system, seemingly distinct activities ranging from making one's toilet to dividing one's estate among one's children are facets of a larger, transcendent model of how society ought to be organized according to caste and class. Ownership emerged as a category relatively late in the Dharmaśāstric tradition—initially in the sixth century CE, but largely after the turn of the second millennium. The appearance of ownership as an analytical category coincides with the Dharmaśāstric tradition's adaption of many of the intellectual tools of Mīmāṃsā. A core argument of this monograph is that Mīmāṃsā and later Navya-Nyāya theories of ownership had a direct impact on Dharmaśāstric approaches to ownership and inheritance.

Law, Legalism, and Schools of Hindu Law

One can speak meaningfully about the existence of regionally and methodologically distinct 'schools' of Hindu jurisprudence—built around commentaries on the *Mitākṣarā* and the *Dāyabhāga*—regarding ownership and inheritance in precolonial and early colonial India. This claim requires a descriptive account of 'law', 'jurisprudence', and 'schools of thought' that wades into heated debates in contemporary scholarship concerning where and how to draw the line between 'law', and 'Dharmaśāstra'.

Scholarly perspectives on the issue tend to fall into one of two camps. One camp, represented by Ludo Rocher, Donald Davis, and Patrick Olivelle, argues

Reason: Philosophy in Early Modern India 1450–1700 (Oxford: Oxford University Press, 2011). For an overview of Nyāya, see Stephen Phillips, *Epistemology in Classical India: The Knowledge Sources of the Nyaya School* (Oxford: Routledge, 2012).

[41] These logicians form the subject of Kroll's dissertation. For the history of Navadvīpa, see Ganeri, *The Lost Age of Reason*, pp. 42–59.

persuasively that Dharmaśāstra is, first and foremost, 'a meta-discourse', whose influence on practical affairs was indirect and indexed differently at different times.[42] For Ludo Rocher, 'the entire commentarial tradition [on Dharmaśāstra] is totally separated from reality; nor was it ever intended to intervene in the reality of practical law and jurisdiction'.[43] The other camp, inaugurated by early orientalist, British administrators such as William Jones (1746–1794) and Henry Colebrooke (1765–1837) and reconfigured by later scholars including J. Duncan Derrett (1922–2012), Robert Lingat (1892–1972), and P. V. Kāṇe (1880–1972), advances some variation of the hypothesis that Dharmaśāstra texts record the cultural and legal practices of Hindus in discrete temporal and geographical junctures.[44] For example, Lingat and Derrett argue that 'the appearance of the commentaries and digests marks a phase... it is no exaggeration to say that it was only with that interpretation that a true juridical science began in India'.[45]

I follow Rocher and Davis in identifying Dharmaśāstra as primarily a scholastic tradition whose intricate, hypothetical debates about property likely bore little direct resemblance to the operation of the law in pre-colonial India. It is difficult to imagine how anyone would be persuaded by the elaborate use of Navya-Nyāya terms such as 'delimitation', 'counterpositive-ness', and 'relational non-existence' to rule a particular way on a point of law. This monograph, however, employs the methodological lens of intellectual history to explore the importance of Dharmaśāstra as a primarily intellectual activity against the backdrop the inter-Brāhmaṇa competitions for power, prestige, and regional identity that characterized the practice of śāstra in early modern India.[46] My approach to Dharmaśāstra shifts the focus of analysis from criticisms of problematic colonial understandings of Dharmaśāstra as positive law—that is, that the operation of courts forms the baseline for understanding Hindu jurisprudence—to an intertextual study of Dharmaśāstric jurisprudence within the social and cultural contexts of scholarship in early modern and colonial India.

[42] Olivelle, *Manu's Code of Law*, p. 64. See Davis, 'Hinduism as a Legal Tradition': 241–67; Ludo Rocher, 'Schools of Hindu Law', in *Studies in Hindu Law and Dharmaśāstra*, ed. Donald Davis (London: Anthem, 2014), pp. 119–28; and 'The Historical Foundations of Ancient Indian Law', in *Studies in Hindu Law and Dharmaśāstra*, ed. Donald Davis (London: Anthem, 2014), pp. 59–82.

[43] Rocher, 'The Historical Foundations of Ancient Indian Law', p. 76.

[44] Bernard Cohn, *Colonialism and Its Forms of Knowledge: The British in India* (Princeton, NJ: Princeton University Press, 1996); Neeladri Bhattacharya, 'Remaking Custom: the Discourse and Practice of Colonial Codification', in *Tradition, Dissent and Ideology: Essays in Honour of Romila Thapar*, ed. R. Champakalakshmi and S. Gopal (New Delhi: Oxford University Press, 1996), pp. 20–51; Robert Lingat, *The Classical Law of India*, trans. J. Derrett (Berkeley: University of California Press, 1973); J. Duncan Derrett, *Dharmaśāstra and Juridical Literature*, (Wiesbaden: Harrassowitz, 1973); Kāṇe, *History of Dharmaśāstra*, vol. 1, part 1, 2nd edn.

[45] Lingat, *The Classical Law of India*, p. 143.

[46] For the use of intellectual history in early modern India, see Jonardon Ganeri, 'Contextualism in the Study of Indian Intellectual Cultures', *Journal of Indian Philosophy* 36.5 (2008): 551–62; Christopher Minkowski, Rosalind O'Hanlon, and Anand Venkatkrishnan, eds. *Scholar Intellectuals in Early Modern India* (London: Routledge, 2015).

The error of viewing Dharmaśāstra as a codification of Hindu law—rather than as a uniquely Sanskritic form of jurisprudence—is as old as the discipline of Western Indology. In 1772, Warren Hastings, the incumbent Governor-General of Bengal, devised 'A Plan for the Administration for Justice in Bengal' that established an integrated hierarchy of civil courts (dīwānī 'adālats) in the Bengal Presidency, culminating in the Ṣadr Dīwānī 'Adālat, to which Hindus and Muslims could appeal.[47] The key innovation in Hastings' 'Judicial Plan' was that 'in all suits regarding inheritance, marriage, caste, and other religious usages, or institutions, the laws of the Koran with respect to Mahometans and those of the *Shaster* with respect to the Gentoos shall be invariably adhered to'.[48] In 1793, Lord Cornwallis introduced a series of judicial reforms to the 'Adālat courts and this 'Cornwallis System' was adopted by the Bombay and Madras Governments in 1799 and 1802 (reformed 1827) respectively.[49] The introduction of the 'Adālat system to these presidencies and their respective territories produced a tremendous need to identify and to comprehend the 'laws of the *Shaster*'.

The core of the misunderstanding lay in the company officials' assumption of the relatively stable divisions between ecclesiastical and secular jurisdictions in Britain, where matters of inheritance, adoptions, marriage and the other 'religious' issues were resolved by biblical interpretation.[50] Christi Merrill notes that 'Hastings made the straightforward assumption that there were sacred texts in India that would offer a source for interpretation comparable to ecclesiastical authorities in British law.'[51] If a British distinction between secular and ecclesiastic jurisdictions set the stage for the creation of Hindu law, the emerging orientalist project, which 'saw ancient texts as the source of authentic knowledge about immemorial custom and tradition', ensured that, with regard to Hindus,

[47] Rosane Rocher, 'The Creation of Anglo-Hindu Law', in *Hinduism and Law: An Introduction*, ed. Timothy Lubin, Donald Davis, and Jayanth Krishnan (Cambridge: Cambridge University Press, 2012), pp. 79–88, 78–9; Atul Chandra Patra, *The Administration of Justice under the East India Company in Bengal, Bihar and Orissa* (New Delhi: Asia Publishing House, 1962); M. P. Jain, *Outlines of Indian Legal History*, 6th edn (Bombay: Tripathi, 2006). William Morley, *The Administration of Justice in British India: Its Past History and Present State* (London: Williams and Norgate, 1858), pp. 43–8. Islamic criminal law was administered through Ṣadr Faujdari Adālats.

[48] George Forrest, *Selections from the Letters, Dispatches and Other State Papers Preserved in the Foreign Department of the government of India, 1772–1785*, vol. 2 (Calcutta: Government Press, 1890), p. 290, cited in J. Duncan Derrett, 'The British as Patrons of the Śāstra', in *Religion, Law and the State in India*, ed. J. Duncan Derrett (London: Faber & Faber, 1968), pp. 225–273, p. 232 fn 2. Cf. Rocher, 'The Creation of Anglo-Hindu Law', p. 79.

[49] Morley, *The Administration of Justice in British India*, pp. 56–8 (Bengal); pp. 95–7 (Bombay); and pp. 82–3 (Madras).

[50] Christi Merrill, 'The Afterlives of Panditry: Rethinking Fidelity in Sacred Texts with Multiple Origins', in *Decentering Translation Studies*, ed. Judy Wakabayashi and Rita Kothari (Amsterdam: John Benjamin, 2009), pp. 75–94, 79. Also see Rachel Sturman, 'Property and Attachments: Defining Autonomy and the Claims of Family in Nineteenth-Century Western India', *Comparative Studies in Society and History* 47.3 (2005–07): 611–37.

[51] Merrill, 'The Afterlives of Panditry', p. 79.

Dharmaśāstra would serve as its script and Paṇḍitas—soon to be framed as 'jurists' and as 'lawgivers'—would be its actors.[52] Indeed, it seems that one of Hastings' primary motivations in commissioning 'a digest of Hindu Law' (the Sanskrit *Vivādārṇavasetu*) was to stave off British government interference in the legal affairs of the Company by proving that Hindus had legal codes of their own (and thus did not require the introduction of British civil law).[53]

A consequence of Hastings' Judicial Plan was that tremendous resources were invested in crafting digests of Dharmaśāstra texts that outlined the Hindu law of inheritance, contract, marriage, divorce, and adoption.[54] Orientalists, including William Jones and Henry Colebrooke, began a philological endeavor—to identify and translate the principal Hindu law books—that coincided with the expansion of a colonial judicial apparatus that was designed to enforce these Dharmaśāstric treatises as the statutory codes of Anglo-Hindu Law.[55] Henry Colebrooke, Julius Jolly and the jurists of the Anglo-Indian legal system developed and applied as law the theory that Dharmaśāstra literature could be divided into *Dāyabhāga* (of Jīmūtāvahana and his followers) and *Mitākṣarā* with Bihari, Benarsi, Mahārāṣṭrian, and Madrasi subgroups) schools.[56] According to this formulation, each school and sub-school encapsulated the customary practices of the Hindu inhabitants of its respective region. The core of this theory was the division of Dharmaśāstra into two principal schools of Hindu law regarding inheritance that supposedly developed as a result of a schism between the followers of Vijñāneśvara's *Mitākṣarā* and Jīmūtavāhana's *Dāyabhāga*. In 1810, Henry Colebrooke published a translation of the *Mitākṣarā* and the *Dāyabhāga*'s chapters on inheritance, where he listed the various Dharmaśāstras associated with different schools of Hindu law.[57]

Colebrooke attributed his model of two principal schools—based on the *Dāyabhāga* and *Mitākṣarā*—and four *Mitākṣarā* sub schools—Mithilā, Benares, Bombay and Madras—to a philosophical difference of opinion regarding ownership between the two schools. He wrote in 1825 that

[52] Bhattacharya, 'Remaking Custom', pp. 20–51, 22.

[53] Rosane Rocher, *Orientalism, Poetry, and the Millennium: the Checkered Life of Nathaniel Brassey Halhed, 1751–1830* (Delhi: Motilal Banarsidass, 1983), pp. 52–3.

[54] The *Vivādārṇavasetu*, compiled in 1773, was translated in 1776 as *A Code of Gentoo Laws*. The *Vivādabhaṅgārṇava*, compiled between 1788 and 1794, was translated between 1797 and 1798 as *A Digest of Hindoo Laws*.

[55] See Rosane Rocher, 'The Creation of Anglo-Hindu Law'; Ludo Rocher, 'Schools of Hindu Law'; Donald Davis, 'Law in the Mirror of Language: The Madras School of Orientalism on Hindu Law', in *The Madras School of Orientalism: Producing Knowledge in Colonial South India*, ed. Thomas Trautman (Oxford: Oxford University Press, 2009), pp. 288–309.

[56] Rocher, 'Schools of Hindu Law', p. 119. See P. V. Kāṇe, *A History of Dharmaśāstra*, vol. 3. 2nd edn (Poona: Bhandarkar Oriental Research Institute, 1973), pp. 544–5.

[57] Henry Colebrooke, *Two Treatises on the Hindu Law of Inheritance: Jimutavahana and Vijnaneshwara* (Calcutta: Hindoostanee Press, 1810), pp. ii–v.

> In the eastern part of India, viz. Bengal and Bahar, where the Vedas are less read, and the Mīmānsā [*sic*] less studied than in the south, the dialectic philosophy, or Nyāya, is more consulted, and is relied on for rules of reasoning and interpretation upon questions of law, as well as upon metaphysical topics. Hence have arisen two principal sects or schools, which, construing the same text variously, deduce upon some important points of law different inferences from the same maxims of law.[58]

Colebrooke's model of schools of law was not without its critics—many of whom doubted that scholastic Dharmaśāstra constituted an accurate record of the regional customary laws of various Hindu castes—but schools of Hindu law became an established feature of colonial and post-colonial Anglo-Hindu law.[59] A substantial body of case law that determined the legal contours of these schools developed in the courts and a number of Sanskritists and historians attempted to reconstruct the unique confluence of social trends that led medieval Paṇḍitas to adapt the Dharmaśāstric laws of inheritance to reflect the practices of Bengali, Dravidian or Mahārāṣṭrian custom. The views peculiar to Jīmūtāvahana's *Dāyabhāga* (the alienability of the share of an undivided coparcener, the near-absolute discretion of the patriarch in the division of inheritance and the legal validity of partitions enacted in contravention of the Dharmaśāstra) were attributed to Bengal's unique history.[60] For G. C. Sarkar, Brāhmaṇa immigrants from Kanauj needed to protect their wealth from the local Bengali families they intermarried with, while S. C. Mitra argues that Buddhism and 'Tantrism' contributed the strong patriarchy of the Bengali School of Inheritance.[61]

Colebrooke's formulation of schools of Hindu law has come under critique by Rocher and Davis, who emphasize the scholastic, śāstric features of Dharmaśāstra. They argue that Dharmaśāstra is not 'law' in the sense of 'rules backed by sanctions enforced by the state'.[62] For Rocher, 'that Dharmaśāstra is first and foremost a scholarly and scholastic tradition, not a practical legal tradition'.[63] He argues that British approaches to Dharmaśāstra as a record of positive law,

[58] Sir Thomas Strange, *Elements of Hindu Law: Referable to British Judicature in India*, vol. 1 (London: Payne and Foss, 1825), p. 314.

[59] For example, see J. H. Nelson, *Prospectus of the Scientific Study of the Hindu Law* (London: Kegan Paul & Co, 1881); A. C. Burnell, *The Law of Partition and Succession: from the MS. Sanskrit Text of Varadarāja's Vyavahāranirnaya* (Mangalore: Stolz, 1872). Sir Henry Maine wrote in 1861 that 'the Hindoo Code, called the Laws of Menu... does not, as a whole, represent a set of rules ever actively administered in Hindostan'. Cited in Ludo Rocher, 'Law Books in an Oral Culture: The Indian Dharmaśāstras', in *Studies in Hindu Law and Dharmaśāstra*, ed. Donald Davis (London: Anthem, 2014), pp. 103–117, 107.

[60] See Ludo Rocher, *Jīmūtavāhana's Dāyabhāga: The Hindu Law of Inheritance in Bengal* (Oxford: Oxford University Press, 2002), p. 31.

[61] Ibid.

[62] Donald Davis, *The Spirit of Hindu Law* (Cambridge: Cambridge University Press, 2010), p. 1.

[63] Donald Davis, 'Introduction', in *Studies in Hindu Law and Dharmaśāstra*, ed. Donald Davis (London: Anthem, 2014), pp. 18–19.

fundamentally misconstrue a 'scholarly' tradition as a 'legal' tradition.[64] If Dharmaśāstra is not law in the strict sense, what is it? For Rocher, 'the true nature of the Hindu lawbooks' is the product of 'pandits, who worked with a set of data which they tried... to arrange within a number of acceptable systems'.[65] The stability of these systems of interpretation 'is the remarkable element in Sanskrit technical literature [śāstra], and it is not restricted to law and Dharmaśāstra'.[66] For Rocher, Brahmanical discussions of ownership and inheritance represent the pinnacle of Brahmanical Dharmaśāstric debate (particularly when tinged with the vocabulary of the Navya-Nyāya). Referring to the existence of schools of law, Rocher writes that,

> there was plenty of room for argumentation, but argumentation that relies on factors of personal ability, such as the more or less extensive knowledge of the Mīmāṃsā rules, the sharpness of the mind of the author etc. The remarkable fact is that each author wanted to surpass the other, with the result being that these so-called juridical commentaries grew into one big academic tournament of subtle argument.[67]

Rocher's conclusion, echoed with vehemence by Davis, is that 'the *Dāyabhāga* may have become extremely successful and may have been the source of a regular school of thought on inheritance. We have no right, however, to accuse the author of dishonesty, and say that he used the ancient *smṛtis* as a pretext to lay down or codify the law of Bengal'.[68]

Rocher's characterization of Jīmūtavāhana's *Dāyabhāga* as the source of a regular 'school of thought on inheritance' has not received adequate attention. What do we call a śāstric school of legal thought if law is an inappropriate term? The answer lies in shifting our approach from Dharmaśāstra as law to Dharmaśāstra as jurisprudence—the theoretical study of the law. Davis offers the most sophisticated account of Dharmaśāstra as an expert jurisprudential tradition. Davis defines law as 'the theology of ordinary life', rather than 'rules backed by sanctions enforced by the state'.[69] Law, in his estimation, 'is both the instrument and rhetoric by which the most... quotidian of human acts are first

[64] Ibid., 19. [65] Rocher, 'Hindu Conceptions of Law', p. 53.

[66] Ibid. For the nature of śāstra, its apparent consistency of form and relationship to historical reality see Pollock, 'The Theory of Practice and the Practice of Theory in Indian Intellectual History', 'Playing by the Rules: Śāstra and Sanskrit Literature', in *Shastric Traditions in Indian Arts*, ed. Anna Dallapiccola (Würzburg: Ergon Verlag, 1989), pp. 301–12, and '"Tradition" as "Revelation": Śruti, Smṛti, and the Sanskrit Discourse of Power', in *Lex et Litterae: Essays on Ancient Law and Literature in Honour of Oscar Botto*, ed. S. Lienhard and I. Piovano (Turin: Edizioni dell'Orso, 1997), pp. 395–417.

[67] Rocher, 'The Historical Foundations of Ancient Indian Law', 78.

[68] Rocher, 'Schools of Hindu Law', p. 127. For Davis's more polemical repetition of the same argument, see *The Spirit of Hindu Law*, p. 97; 'Law in the Mirror of Language', p. 304, endnote 3.

[69] Davis, *Spirit of Hindu Law*, p. 1. For an introduction to legal pluralism, see John Griffiths, 'What Is Legal Pluralism', *Journal of Legal Pluralism* 24 (1986): 1–55.

placed in a system or structure larger than the individual experience'.[70] For Davis, Dharmaśāstras 'contain . . . Hindu jurisprudence, a way of thinking about law from a distinctly Hindu perspective'.[71]

Davis defines pre-colonial 'Hindu law' as 'a variegated grouping of local legal systems . . . that were united by a common jurisprudence or legal theory represented by Dharmaśāstra'. This definition aids scholars in understanding that the practical facets of India's 'local legal systems' were made 'more or less Hindu' by their 'correspondence' to Dharmaśāstric rules and categories.[72] Davis notes that this isomorphic relationship between 'law' and 'jurisprudence' is not limited to the Indian context,

> Dharmaśāstra contains the theological jurisprudence of Hindu law and the only reasonable basis upon which local legal systems in India can be called Hindu at all. Anyone familiar with American or European jurisprudence is well aware that the level of abstraction in jurisprudence and its use of hypotheticals, though drawn from legal practice, offers little help in the actual practice of law. Few would suggest, however, that jurisprudence is irrelevant for it is part of the training and disciplining of lawyers and judges in how to think legally. Dharmaśāstra served a similar purpose as its very name śāstra, which instructs or disciplines, tells us.[73]

Davis notes that Dharmaśāstric scholasticism constitutes 'a thought-world that stands apart from the practical world of culture' wherein śāstric 'rules instead construct an imagined "metacultural" domain that seeks to become the substitute for culture, to transcend it in the same way that culture is held to displace nature'.[74] Furthermore,

> the drive to protect an imagined world composed of and guarded by rules is found in all major traditions of religious law. This imaginative realm of rules accounts for the common phenomenon in scholastic traditions of rules that have no possible application in life but are nevertheless debated . . . with tremendous zeal. On Jewish and Roman jurists, Hezser writes, 'neither the rabbis nor Roman legal experts were interested in such distinctions [between reality and fiction in case-law] since they were not interested in historical accuracy . . . The legal world

[70] Ibid., 1. [71] Ibid., 13.

[72] See Donald Davis, 'Intermediate Realms of Law: Corporate Groups and Rulers in Medieval India', *Journal of the Economic and Social History of the Orient* 48.1 (2005): 92–117; and Timothy Lubin, 'The Theory and Practice of Property in Premodern South Asia: Disparities and Convergences', *Journal of the Economic and Social History of the Orient* 68.5–6 (2018): 803–50.

[73] Davis, 'Hinduism as a Legal Tradition': 246.

[74] Donald Davis, 'Rules, Culture, and Imagination in Sanskrit Jurisprudence', in *Legalism: Rules and Categories*, ed. Paul Dresch and Judith Scheele (Oxford: Oxford University Press, 2015), pp. 29–52, 44.

becomes a separate ontological sphere governed by its own rules and distanced from simple social reality'.[75]

We have arrived at an understanding of Dharmaśāstra as a form of jurisprudence, which: (1) constitutes an abstract, meta-discourse *about the law*; (2) involves technical interpretive rules; and (3) can be indexed to practical law in a variety of ways at a variety of times and places. The theory of Dharmaśāstra that shifts from law to legalism accurately captures many of the distinguishing features of the history of Dharmaśāstra.[76] While Davis's legalistic idea of Dharmaśāstra militates against Colebrooke's formulation of schools of Hindu *law*, *sensu stricto*, it militates in favour of Rocher's suggestive assertion that Vijñāneśvara and Jīmūtavāhana may have founded influential schools of Hindu *jurisprudence* whose different juridical conclusions were the result of philosophical, hermeneutical and institutional commitments—precisely as Colebrooke claimed in 1825.

What, however, is a 'school' of Hindu jurisprudence? How do we chart the development, interaction and competition between schools of jurisprudence and other Sanskrit text-traditions? How can an intellectual history of ownership and inheritance in these schools of Sanskrit jurisprudence contribute to broader projects concerning the effect of colonialism on India's traditional knowledge systems?

Intellectual History, the Scale of Texts, and Schools of Thought

Until then I had thought each book spoke of things, human or divine, that lie outside books. Now I realized that not infrequently books speak of books: it is as if they spoke among themselves. In the light of this reflection, the library seemed all the more disturbing to me. It was then a place of a long, centuries-old murmuring, an imperceptible dialogue between one parchment and another, a living thing, a receptacle of power not to be ruled by a human mind, a treasure of secrets emanated by many minds, surviving the death of those who had produced them or had been their conveyers. (Umberto Eco, *The Name of the Rose*)[77]

[75] Ibid., p. 45. Catherine Hezser, 'Roman Law and Rabbinic Legal Composition', in *The Cambridge Companion to Rabbinic Literature*, ed. Charlotte Fonrobert and Martin Jaffee (Cambridge: Cambridge University Press, 2007), pp. 144–163, 146.

[76] Davis's pluralistic approach to Dharmaśāstra, with its broad reading of law as a rules-based thought system is firmly grounded in the socio-legal and anthropological movement at Oxford known as 'legalism'. For an overview of the legalism's methodology, see Paul Dresch and Judith Scheele, 'Introduction', in *Legalism: Rules and Categories*, ed. Paul Dresch and Judith Scheele (Oxford: Oxford University Press, 2015), pp. 1–28, 1: 'The idea of legalism that we took from Lloyd Fallers was described in volume 1 of this series as involving an appeal to rules that are distinct from practice, the explicit use of generalizing concepts, and a disposition to address in such terms the conduct of human life.'

[77] Umberto Eco, *The Name of the Rose*, trans. William Weever (New York: Harcourt, 1983), p. 286.

This monograph employs an intellectual historical approach to the study of the development of Dharmaśāstric schools of jurisprudence concerning ownership and inheritance. A 'school of thought' entails two phenomena that are often, but not always, mutually concurrent: 1) a consistent and comprehensive line of argumentation, that, unlike a single concept, forms a comprehensive scale of texts that orients the author in relation to previous scholarship; and 2) a deliberate self-representation as a follower, defender, or revitalizer of a tradition with which one has a familial, regional, or disciplinary connection. The scale of texts forces us to ask how an individual author situates himself in relation to his intellectual tradition. When an author's relationship is framed as taking part in a shared cluster of opinions and in a shared lineage, then we may describe that author as participating in a 'school of thought'.

This section introduces the reader to three key terms: intellectual history, early modernity, and the scale of texts. Each of these terms informs the monograph's aim of charting the development of schools of jurisprudence in Indian intellectual history. Intellectual history is a contested term. On the one hand, as Anand Venkatkrishnan notes,

> The history of ideas . . . was for most of the twentieth century a Euro-American exercise in understanding intellectual shifts in their historical context . . . [and] its initial practitioners, such as R. G. Collingwood, were heir to a Hegelian idealism that viewed all history as the history of ideas.[78]

A different, less Hegelian, strand of intellectual history that 'understood texts as active expressions of language, or speech acts . . . [which] made interventions in a broader discourse or milieu within which they participated' informs contemporary research on Sanskrit knowledge systems.[79] A key feature of this 'Skinnerian' approach to intellectual is contextualism: namely, how 'a particular document or pronouncement [may be] situated in a biographical, social, political and literary context rich enough to enable an inference to be drawn about the nature of the illocutionary intervention the document embodies'.[80] Nevertheless, Ganeri highlights the difficulty of applying Skinner's technique to India, where Sanskrit scholasticism's penchant for verbosity and rhetorical pretences to a-historical

[78] Venkatkrishnan, 'Mīmāṃsā, Vedānta, and the Bhakti Movement', p. 13. The Hegelian approach to Indian intellectual history has been subject to a thorough critique from Ronald Inden. See *Imagining India* (Oxford: Blackwell, 1990).

[79] Venkatkrishnan, 'Mīmāṃsā, Vedānta, and the Bhakti Movement', pp. 13–14. Quentin Skinner, *Visions of Politics*, vol. 1: *Regarding Method* (Cambridge: Cambridge University Press, 2002). For an introduction to Indian Intellectual history, see Sheldon Pollock, 'Is There an Indian Intellectual History?', *Journal of Indian Philosophy* 36.5 (2008): 533–42.

[80] Ganeri, 'Contextualism', 553.

transcendence result in an intellectual milieu that often feels 'all text and no context'.[81]

Sanskrit intellectual history requires a rigorously intertextual approach, and the best work on this subject has come from an international collaborative project, 'Sanskrit Knowledge Systems on the Eve of Colonialism'.[82] The group, which 'aims to investigate the substance and social life of Sanskrit learning from about 1550 to 1750' deploys various techniques to 'illuminate our understanding of the scholarly production of intellectuals and social observers during India's early modern period'.[83] They argue that considerations of intellectual 'discipline, sect, lineage, and community' formed the context for literary interventions on the part of individual śāstric authors.[84]

One key problem for the working group is the extent to which pre-colonial India experienced a modernity analogous to that of the West.[85] For many, the distinguishing feature of early modernity in South Asia is a 'connectedness' between various areas of the subcontinent and the networks of royal patronage and śāstric knowledge production that accompanied it.[86] Rosalind O'Hanlon, drawing from the work of Christopher Bayly, argues that Mughal India's Brāhmaṇa 'ecumene' was characterized by intense, pan-Indian competition for the patronage of royal and imperial courts.[87] As a result, scholars working on the intellectual history of early modern India have reconstructed the intricacies of, among other things, the relationship between Mīmāṃsā hermeneutics and bhakti devotionalism, the social politics of using Dharmaśāstric texts to adjudicate regional caste disputes, or the intersecting lines of teacher–disciple knowledge transmission in Advaita Vedānta against the backdrop of political developments

[81] Ibid.

[82] Pollock, 'Is There an Indian Intellectual History'. Also see Sheldon Pollock, 'New Intellectuals in Seventeenth Century India', *The Indian Economic and Social History Review* 38.1 (2001): 3–31.

[83] Sheldon Pollock, 'The Languages of Science in Early Modern India', in *Forms of Knowledge in Early Modern Asia: Explorations in the Intellectual History of India and Tibet, 1500–1800*, ed. Sheldon Pollock (London: Duke University Press, 2011), pp. 19–48, 20. Christopher Minkowski, et al., 'Introduction', *Scholar Intellectuals in Early Modern India*, p. 1.

[84] Ibid., p. 2.

[85] For a general account of early modernity, see John Richards, 'Early Modern India and World History', *Journal of World History* 8.2 (1997): 198–203. For contrasting perspectives on the issue, see Sheldon Pollock, 'Pretextures of Time', *History and Theory* 46.3 (2007): 336–83; and Sheldon Pollock, *The Ends of Man at the End of Premodernity* (Amsterdam: Royal Netherlands Academy of Arts and Sciences, 2005); Parimal Patil, 'The Historical Rhythms of the Nyāya-Vaiśeṣika Knowledge-System', in *Periodization and Historiography of Indian Philosophy*, ed. Eli Franco (Vienna: Sammlung de Nobili, Institut für Südasien-, Tibet- und Buddhismuskunde der Universität Wien, 2009), pp. 91–126; and Dipesh Chakrabarty, 'The Muddle of Modernity', *American Historical Review* 116.3 (2011): 663–75.

[86] Rosalind O'Hanlon, 'Letters Home: Banaras Pandits and the Maratha Regions in Early Modern India', *Modern Asian Studies* 44:2 (2010): 201–40, 201. Cf. Sanjay Subrahmanyam, 'Connected Histories: Notes Towards a Reconfiguration of Early Modern Eurasia', *Modern Asian Studies* 31.3 (1997): 735–62.

[87] Rosalind O'Hanlon, 'Speaking from Śiva's Temple: Banaras Scholar Households and the Brahman "Ecumene" of Mughal India', *South Asian History and Culture* 2.2 (2011): 253–77, 254.

in early modern northern India.[88] A perennial favourite topic of analysis for studies of early modern śāstric intellectual history has been the Bhaṭṭa family of Benares.[89] The Bhaṭṭas, a family of Mahārāṣṭrian Brāhmaṇas who moved to Vārāṇasī in the sixteenth century, dominated the northern Indian intellectual scene of the sixteenth and seventeenth centuries. They seem to have influenced nearly every discipline of śāstra, from Mīmāṃsā, to Dharmaśāstra, Advaita-Vedānta, and Alaṅkāraśāstra.

R. G. Collingwood's theory of a 'scale of forms' offers a new analytical tool for describing these complex intertextual relationships between Sanskrit ideas across chronological, disciplinary, and sectarian lines. Collingwood observes that,

> if in philosophical thought every difference of kind is also a difference of degree, the specifications of a philosophical concept are bound to form a scale; and in this scale their common essence is bound to be realized differentially in degree as well as differentially in kind.[90]

Collingwood's argument is that a scale of forms reveals 'overlap and hierarchy' in philosophical thought, where 'concepts do not stand as autonomous units to each other, but as overlapping in a progressively developing series, each stage of which is related to its predecessor as advanced is to lower'.[91] The result is that 'the logical movement from one form to another is . . . an overlapping chain in which each successive stage both confirms and extends the one before'.[92]

The historian of India, Ronald Inden, recalibrates the scale of forms as a 'scale of texts' in order to shift the historical study of India from a Hegelian history of essentialized ideas to an empirical account of historical agents in time and place. He describes a scale of texts as the way in which,

> later agents and their texts overlap with those of their predecessors and contemporaries and, by engaging in a process of criticism, appropriation, repetition, refutation, amplification, abbreviation, and so on, position themselves in relation to them.[93]

[88] Anand Venkatkrishnan, 'Ritual, Reflection, and Religion: the Devas of Banaras', *South Asian History and Culture* 6.1 (2015): 147–71. Rosalind O'Hanlon, 'The Social Worth of Scribes: Brahmins, Kayasthas and the Social Order in Early Modern India', *Indian Economic Social History Review* 47.4 (2010): 563–95. Christopher Minkowski, 'Advaita Vedānta in Early Modern History', in *Religious Cultures in Early Modern India: New Perspectives*, ed. Rosalind O'Hanlon and David Washbrook. Special volume of *South Asian History and Culture* 2.2 (2011): 205–31.

[89] For the family in general, see James Benson, 'Śaṃkarabhaṭṭa's Family Chronicle: The *Gādhivaṃśavarṇana*', in *The Pandit: Traditional Scholarship in India*, ed. Axel Michaels (Delhi: Manohar Publishers, 2001), pp. 105–18.

[90] R. G. Collingwood, *An Essay on Philosophical Method* (Oxford: Clarendon Press, 1933), p. 77.

[91] Peter Johnson, *R. G. Collingwood: an Introduction* (Bristol: Thoemmes Press, 1998), p. 27.

[92] Ibid.

[93] Ronald Inden, J. Walters, and D. Ali, *Querying the Medieval: Texts and the History of Practices in South Asia* (Oxford: Oxford University Press, 2000), p. 12.

Inden, Daud Ali, and Jonathan Walters' use of the scale of texts to reconstruct the relationship between the textual artifacts of 'complex agents'—committees of scholars, monastic institutions, corporate guilds, and so on—and the 'imperial formations' of medieval South Asia has set a new paradigm for historical studies of pre-modern South Asia.[94]

While Inden focuses on elite, imperial arenas—the Rāṣṭrakūṭa, Cālukya, and Cola courts—this monograph employs the model of a scale of texts to analyse the works of individual scholars, scholar families and scholastic institutions within specific intellectual and social contexts. The scale of texts is ideally suited to the thickly intertextual milieu of early modern India and to the discipline of Dharmaśāstra. Furthermore, the scale of texts, when combined with the Sanskrit Knowledge Systems' account of early modern northern Indian social history, provides a method for theorizing 'schools of thought' because it encourages analysis of the architectural structures of thought. The scale of texts makes it possible to reconstruct the ways in which groups of scholars advance, refine, and reject various clusters of arguments—that are often associated with specific social and intellectual affiliations.

The project of demonstrating the existence of schools of Sanskrit jurisprudence is not limited to teasing out the complexities of Rocher and Davis's polemic against Colebrooke's misunderstanding of Dharmaśāstra as positive law. Rather, an analytical focus on how schools of jurisprudence developed in medieval and early modern India—and survived, albeit in a transformed way, into the colonial period—militates against a truism in the study of Indian: what Sudipta Kaviraj calls 'an epistemic rupture on the vastest possible scale, one of the greatest known in history'.[95] Rosane Rocher and Brian Hatcher have argued, persuasively, that with regard to Dharmaśāstra, the advent of European colonization did not spell the end of innovation in Paṇḍitic thought.[96] Between 1772 and 1864 (when the Crown's newly formed High Courts assumed epistemic authority over Sanskirt jurisprudence) Paṇḍitas from Bengal, Bihar, and Benares, who were hired by agents of the East India Company, compiled a series of some of the most sophisticated Dharmaśāstric works on contract, inheritance, adoption and the like. Intriguingly, the arguments in these colonial-era digests reflect the continuance

[94] For a similar project, see Velcheru Rao, David Shulman, and Sanjay Subrahmanyam, *Textures of Time: Writing History in South India, 1600–1800* (Delhi: Permanent Black, 2001).

[95] Sudipta Kaviraj, 'The Sudden Death of Sanskrit Knowledge', *Journal of Indian Philosophy* 33.1 (2005): 119–42, 132.

[96] Rosane Rocher, 'Weaving Knowledge: Sir William Jones and Indian Pandits', in *Objects of Enquiry: the Life, Contributions, and Influences of Sir William Jones, 1746–1794*, ed. Garland Cannon and Kevin Brine (New York: New York University Press, 1995), pp. 51–79; Rosane Rocher, 'The Career of Rādhākānta Tarkavāgīśa, an Eighteenth-Century Pandit in British Employ', *Journal of the American Oriental Society* 109.4 (1989): 627–33; Brian Hatcher, 'Sanskrit and the Morning After: The Metaphorics and Theory of Intellectual Change', *Indian Economic and Social History Review* 44.3 (2007): 333–61.

of the traditional, medieval, and early modern Dharmaśāstric schools of thought that developed in Vārāṇasī, Navadvīpa and Mithilā.

Viewing schools of Sanskrit jurisprudence purely as a 'phony' colonial invention elides the contributions of a generation of Paṇḍitas to an ancient system by attributing their insights and interests to the will of their colonial suzerains. A recent work on ownership and property in colonial-era Dharmaśāstra digests commits the deeply ironic error of castigating several novel Sanskrit arguments concerning the nature of property—arguments that may well prove that India exercised a greater influence on Anglo-American jurisprudence than previously thought—as foreign impositions.[97]

Outline of the Chapters

Each chapter traces the connection between a Dharmaśāstric model of inheritance and a philosophical (Mīmāṃsā or Navya-Nyāya) theory of ownership. Chapter 1 examines the development of the concept of ownership in Mīmāṃsā and Dharmaśāstra writings between roughly the first millennium CE and the fifteenth century CE. The chapter focuses on the framing of ownership as an extra-śāstric phenomenon in Mimāṃsā commentarial literature and connects these Mīmāṃsā arguments to the development of the juridical model of ownership-by-birth (janmasvatva) articulated in Vijñāneśvara's eleventh- to twelfth-century commentary on the *Yājñavalkyasmṛti*, the *Ṛjumitākṣarā*. The *Mitākṣarā* delineates a watershed moment at which pre-existing, but nascent theories of ownership-by-birth that had appeared in early Dharmaśāstra commentaries were melded with a theory of ownership as an extra-śāstric phenomenon that appears in Prābhākara-Mīmāṃsā writings. Vijñāneśvara's combination of Mīmāṃsā theories of ownership and Dharmaśāstric models of inheritance formed a distinctive pattern of argument—a scale of texts. This combination of recalibrated Prābhākara-Mīmāṃsā-derived arguments about ownership and a consolidated series of Dharmaśāstric passages forms the distinctive feature of a discernible *Mitākṣarā* school of jurisprudence. The chapter concludes that Vijñāneśvara is a founder of a school of legal thought in the sense that he *consolidated* earlier Dharmaśāstrins' theories of ownership and inheritance and established the parameters for future debate about the issue. The chapter does not, however, argue that the early *Mitākṣarā* school—a primarily academic school—was associated with distinct geographical regions or teacher-disciple lineages.

The second chapter examines Maithila and Bengali (Gauḍa) schools of jurisprudence that developed in the Mithilā region and at the university of Navadvīpa

[97] An error typified in Nandini Bhattacarya-Panda's *Appropriation and Invention of Tradition: The East India Company and Hindu Law in Bengal* (New Delhi: Oxford, 2008).

(founded in 1514) in Bengal during the fourteenth and sixteenth centuries respectively. In fourteenth-, fifteenth-, and sixteenth-century Mithilā, successive generations of munificent, Brāhmaṇa-friendly rulers (of the Karṇāṭa, Oinīvāra/Kāmeśvara, and Khaṇḍavalā dynasties respectively) produced a distinctive, largely insular intellectual culture. Mithilā-based scholars were keen to emphasize their roles in the administration of the Kingdom of Mithilā, their connection to Mithilā's official Brāhmaṇa lineages (mūlas), and to distinguish Maithila texts and traditions from those of Bengal (Gauḍa). The most authoritative Maithila Dharmaśāstra treatises—Caṇḍeśvara Ṭhakkura's *Vivādaratnākara* (active 1314–70), Vācaspatimiśra II's *Vivādacintāmaṇi* (1425–80), and Misarumiśra's *Vivādacandra* (mid-fifteenth century)—neither reference the *Mitākṣarā*'s Mīmāṃsā-inflected theory of ownership-by-birth, nor connect Maithila philosophical, Navya-Nyāya theories of ownership, with their juridical models of inheritance directly.[98]

In the sixteenth century, several Mithilā-trained Paṇḍitas of Bengali extraction returned home to found the university of Navadvīpa. The Dharmaśāstrins and Naiyāyikas who lived and worked together in Navadvīpa's colleges (ṭols) shared a cluster of philosophical and jurisprudential propositions, many pertaining to ownership and inheritance. Navadvīpan Dharmaśāstrins, including Śrīnāthācārya Cūḍāmaṇi (1475–1525), Rāmabhadra I (1510–70), and Acyutacakravartin (1510–70), and logicians, such as Raghunātha Śiromaṇi (1460–1540), and Jayarāma Nyāyapañcānana (seventeenth century), began to speak of themselves, their ritual practices, and their intellectual opinions, as being part of a Bengali (Gauḍa), rather than a Maithila school of thought. Navadvīpa's jurists and logicians focused on the *Dāyabhāga* of Jīmūtavāhana (twelfth to fifteenth centuries), an obscure, previously unknown treatise on inheritance, as the central text of their new school of jurisprudence: dozens of commentaries on the *Dāyabhāga* were written in a Navya-Nyāya idiom and dozens of Navya-Nyāya treatises on ownership defend arguments from the *Dāyabhāga*. In their commentaries on the *Dāyabhāga*, Dharmaśāstrins such as Śrīnāthācāryacūḍāmaṇi, Rāmabhadra and Acyutacakravartin deployed Navya-Nyāya theories of ownership to defend Jīmūtavāhana and reject Vijñāneśvara's theory of ownership-by-birth and the arguments of Maithila Dharmaśāstrins such as Caṇḍeśvara and Vācaspatimiśra II. Likewise, Navadvīpan-trained Navya-Naiyāyikas, including Rāmabhadra Sārvabhauma and Jayarāma Nyāyapañcāna, developed metaphysical accounts of ownership that accepted the conclusions of the *Dāyabhāga*, *a priori*, and that rejected the opinions of Maithila authors, *a priori*.

The third chapter examines the reception of this upstart *Dāyabhāga* school of jurisprudence, and its Navya-Nyāya theories of ownership, in the competitive, pan-Indian—and heavily Mīmāṃsā—university city of Vārāṇasī in the sixteenth and seventeenth centuries. For the Bhaṭṭa family of Vārāṇasī, an influential family

[98] For Caṇḍeśvara, Misarumiśra, and Vācaspatimiśra II, see P. V. Kāṇe, *A History of Dharmaśāstra*, vol. 1, part 2, 2nd edn, pp. 763–75, 842–44, and 844–54, respectively.

of Mahārāṣṭrian Mīmāṃsakas and Dharmaśāstrins who identified themselves as exemplary southern (Dākṣinātya) Brāhmaṇas, Gauḍa Dharmaśāstrins and their Navya-Nyāya philosophy constituted a significant threat. The Bhaṭṭas characterized Vijñāneśvara's *Mitākṣarā* as the paradigmatic southern, Mīmāṃsā-compliant treatise on inheritance. They incorporated the *Mitākṣarā* and Mīmāṃsā theories of ownership into a comprehensive southern school of jurisprudence—whose opinions they contrasted with those of the Gauḍas. This school of thought, developed in the commentarial writings of successive members of the Bhaṭṭa family, including Rāmakṛṣṇabhaṭṭa (sixteenth century), Kamalākarabhaṭṭa (active 1610–40), Nīlakaṇṭhabhaṭṭa (mid-seventeenth century) and Gāgābhaṭṭa (late seventeenth century) deployed Mīmāṃsā theories of ownership and inheritance against Navya-Nyāya ones. The Bhaṭṭas' polemic against the Navadvīpan, Navya-Nyāya-inflected school of jurisprudence marks a watershed moment when the *Mitākṣarā* and its Mīmāṃsā-derived theory of ownership were incorporated into a broader, distinctively southern scale of Dharmaśāstra texts that framed the *Mitākṣarā/Dāyabhāga* divide as a debate between Mīmāṃsā and Navya-Nyāya theories of ownership.

The fourth chapter turns to the British encounter with traditional Sanskrit learning in the late eighteenth and early nineteenth centuries and traces the construction of Hindu Schools of Law in colonial India between 1772 and 1827. The chapter examines three digests of Sanskrit Dharmaśāstra that were compiled at the behest of the East India Company and whose English translations were utilized by British jurists in colonial courts: the *Vivādārṇavasetu* (translated in 1776 as *A Code of Gentoo Laws*), the *Vivādabhaṅgārṇava* (translated in 1795–6 as *A Digest on Contracts and Succession*), and the *Dharmaśāstrasaṃgraha* (which probably served as an impetus for Colebrooke's *Two Treatises*). These treatises recapitulate the eastern and southern scales of Dharmaśāstra texts that developed originally in Navadvīpa and Vārāṇasī in the sixteenth and seventeenth centuries. On the one hand the *Vivādārṇavasetu* and the *Vivādabhaṅgārṇava*, compiled by teams of Bengali logicians, synthesize and defend the *Dāyabhāga*'s Bengali (Gauḍa) theories of ownership-by-the cessation-of-the-ownership-of-the-previous-owner (uparamasvatva), ownership as discernible-from-the-śāstra-alone (śāstraikasamadhigamyatva), and *factum valet* against the opinions of Maithila rivals (often utilizing the formal techniques of Navya-Nyāya philosophy). On the other hand, the *Vyavahārabālambhaṭṭī*—compiled by a Mahārāṣṭrian Mīmāṃsaka—defends the *Mitākṣarā*'s southern (Dākṣinātya) theories of ownership-by-birth (janmasvatva) and of ownership as extra-śāstric (laukika) against the *Dāyabhāga* and logicians identified as Bengali (Prācya, Gauḍa, and so on.).

The Paṇḍitas who assisted British orientalists and jurists in the compilation of Dharmaśāstra digests and in the construction of Anglo-Hindu law replicated early modern classificatory schemes that portrayed arguments from the *Dāyabhāga* and the *Mitākṣarā* as belonging to Gauḍa, Maithila, and Dākṣiṇātya schools. Although these Paṇḍitas' opinions justified Colebrooke's broad distinction between the *Mitākṣarā* and *Dāyabhāga* schools of jurisprudence (and between Maithila, Gauḍa, and southern Paṇḍitas), Colebrooke appears to have been equally motivated by the expansion of the Company's sovereignty—and its 'Adālat system of courts—to Bengal, Bihar, and Benares. Furthermore, distinctions between 'Benares' and 'Bombay' schools of law, while partly attributable to the great prestige in which the writings of the Bhaṭṭa family were held in the Marāṭhā Confederacy (1680–1818), were largely a product of the introduction of the 'Adālat system to portions of the Bombay Presidency in 1799. Finally, the construction of a 'Madras' school of Dharmaśāstra—along with its 'Andhra', 'Dravada Proper', and 'Karnata' sub-schools—was the unwarranted creation of Orientalist scholars who imposed the paradigm of other provinces onto sundry Dharmaśāstra texts in order to provide the newly created (1802) Madrasi 'Adālat system with sources of personal law for Hindu litigants.

Consequently, the division of Dharmaśāstric discussions of inheritance into Gauḍa, Vārāṇasī, Maithila, Dākṣinātya and Drāviḍa schools was not *entirely* alien to Dharmaśāstra as a discipline. Rather, the Dharmaśāstra compendia of the eighteenth century and the earlier intellectual history of ownership and inheritance support a model of Sanskrit schools of legal thought—albeit ones that do not neatly align with the territorial and jurisdictional boundaries of the colonial state. Indigenous considerations of regional identity, pedagogical lineage, and disciplinary commitments were as important in the emergence of Anglo-Hindu law as foreign, British notions of religion, law, and property.

The book concludes by exploring the evolution of Anglo-Hindu law in the late nineteenth and in the early twentieth centuries. Chapters 1 to 4 reconstructed the development of theories of ownership and inheritance in pre-colonial Sanskrit jurisprudence and charted the reception (and contortion) of Sanskrit jurisprudence in early Anglo-Hindu law. The missing portion of the story involves how these Sanskrit juridical theories of property and personhood, once established concretely in colonial law, served as the basis for wide-reaching changes in the political economy of South Asia. The dismissal of court Paṇḍitas in 1864, when the High Courts assumed judicial knowledge over Hindu law, occurred in concert with the emergence of a liberal 'market governance', involving liberal legal reform, the distinction (and adjudication) between 'private' and 'public' spheres of commercial activity, and the flattening of communal identities.[99] Shifting juridical understanding of the 'Hindu Undivided Family' (HUF) from a commercial, profit-oriented firm into a highly restricted, extra-commercial endowment occurred alongside a homogenization of 'Hinduism' as a religious and legal category.

[99] Ritu Birla, *Stages of Capital: Law, Cultures, and Market Governance in Late Colonial India* (Durham, NC: Duke University Press, 2009).

Ownership and Property—however dull they might appear to be—ought not be viewed in the same light in which Kafka grimaced at Austrian law—as 'sawdust... chewed by a thousand mouths before'.[100] Rather, property law—or the Sanskrit theoretical reflection thereon—was inflected by the intellectual dynamism, hot-blooded polemic, and diversity of thought of the many Paṇḍitas who dedicated their lives to the śāstric study of property.

[100] Robert Kaplan, 'Joseph K. Claims Compensation: Franz Kafka's Legal Writings', *Advances in Historical Studies* 3 (2014): 115–21, 116.

1
Mīmāṃsā and the *Mitākṣarā* School of Jurisprudence

This chapter traces the development of the concept of ownership in Mīmāṃsā and Dharmaśāstra texts from approximately the first millennium CE to the fifteenth century CE—or from the *Śābarabhāṣya* to the *Madanaratnapradīpa*.[1] The chapter is concerned with the framing of ownership as extra-śāstric (laukika) in Mimāṃsā writings and the importance of an extra-śāstric theory of ownership in the development of the juridical model of ownership-by-birth (janmasvatva) articulated in Vijñāneśvara's *Ṛjumitākṣarā*.[2] Towards that end I draw attention to two linked trends in Indian jurisprudential history: (1) the development of a philosophical concept of ownership that occurred in the Mīmāṃsā tradition centuries before the earliest logicians (Naiyāyikas); and (2) the recalibration and redeployment of several arguments concerning this Mīmāṃsā-derived concept by medieval Dharmaśāstra commentators who self-consciously framed their approaches to the jurisprudence of inheritance as further refinements of Vijñāneśvara's *Ṛjumitākṣarā*.

The central object of enquiry of the chapter is Vijñāneśvara's eleventh-to twelfth-century commentary on the *Yājñavalkyasmṛti*, the *Ṛjumitākṣarā* (commonly referred to as the *Mitākṣarā*).[3] The *Mitākṣarā* served as the touchstone for virtually every subsequent Dharmaśāstrin. As P. V. Kāṇe notes:

> The Mitākṣarā holds a position similar to that of the Mahābhāṣya of Patañjali in Grammar or the Kāvyaprakāśa of Mammaṭa in Poetics. It embodies in itself the results of centuries of legal speculation that preceded it and becomes in its turn a source of further exegesis and improvements.[4]

[1] For Mīmāṃsā and Dharmaśāstra, see Domenico Francavilla, *The Roots of Hindu Jurisprudence: Source of Dharma and Interpretation in Mīmāṃsā and Dharmaśāstra* (Turin: Comitato Corpus Iuris Sanscriticum et fontes Iuris Asiae Meridianae et Centralis, 2005).

[2] See Donald Davis, *The Spirit of Hindu Law* (Cambridge: Cambridge University Press, 2010), and Ethan Kroll, 'A Logical Approach to Law' (PhD Dissertation, University of Chicago, 2010).

[3] For Vijñāneśvara, see P. V. Kāṇe, *A History of Dharmaśāstra*, vol. 1, part 2, 2nd edn (Poona: Bhandarkar Oriental Research Institute, 1975), pp. 601–16; Günter-Dietz Sontheimer, *The Joint Hindu Family: Its Evolution as a Legal Institution* (New Delhi: Munshiram Manoharlal, 1977), pp. 120–39; and J. Duncan Derrett, 'The Relative Antiquity of the Mitāksharā and the Dāyabhāga', *Madras Law Journal* (1952): 9–15.

[4] P. V. Kāṇe, 'The Predecessors of Vijñāneśvara', *The Journal of the Bombay Branch of the Royal Asiatic Society* (1925): 193–221.

Ownership and Inheritance in Sanskrit Jurisprudence. Christopher T. Fleming, Oxford University Press (2020).

DOI: 10.1093/oso/9780198852377.003.0002

The *Mitākṣarā* was also the essential text for H. T. Colebrooke's theory of regional schools of Dharmaśāstric law of inheritance. As Colebrooke declares in the preface to his *Two Treatises*:

> The range of its authority and influence is far more extensive than that of Jimutavahana's treatise; for it is received in all the schools of Hindu law, from Benares to the southern extremity of the peninsula of India, as the chief groundwork of the doctrines which they follow, and as an authority from which they rarely dissent.[5]

How and *why* did the *Mitākṣarā* attain its remarkable prominence in the history of Sanskrit jurisprudence—and, in particular, legal debates concerning the question of ownership-by-birth? The *Mitākṣarā* marks a crucial juncture at which earlier, inchoate *legal* theories of ownership-by-birth—that had appeared in previous Dharmaśāstra commentaries—were consolidated and combined with a Mīmāṃsā-derived, *philosophical* theory of ownership as an extra-śāstric phenomenon. For the *Mitākṣarā* and for Vijñāneśvara's followers in Dharmaśāstra, ownership is theorized as a quality (guṇa) of an asset (dhana, dravya), produced by extra-śāstrically established acts of acquisition (lokasiddhārjanopaya) and characterized as a fitness for use as desired (yatheṣṭaviniyogayogyatva).

Furthermore, this chapter tackles three problematic assumptions concerning the place of the *Mitākṣarā* in the history of the jurisprudence of ownership in Sanskrit. The first assumption concerns the relationship between Vijñāneśvara and earlier Dharmaśāstra commentators such as Viśvarūpa, Bhāruci, and Medhātithi. Rocher and Davis, for example, point out that ownership-by-birth—the argument most strongly associated with Vijñāneśvara—had proponents and opponents in earlier Dharmaśāstra commentaries and they warn that projecting a *Mitākṣarā/Dāyabhāga* debate into the strata of Dharmaśāstra commentary immediately before and after the composition of the *Mitākṣarā* is anachronistic.[6]

The second assumption concerns the relationship between Mīmāṃsā/ *Mitākṣarā* theories of ownership as extra-śāstric and the proprietary interests of the Paṇḍitas who developed these theories. J. Duncan Derrett, for example, frames these extra-śāstric theories of ownership as morally regressive—as the cynical move of Brāhmaṇas who were 'pathetically keen' to prove the validity of their community's rights in assets acquired through deplorable methods.[7] One problem with this position is that it assumes, wrongly, that arguments in Mīmāṃsā and

[5] H. T. Colebrooke, *Two Treatises on the Hindu Law of Inheritance* (Calcutta: Hindoostanee Press, 1810), iv.

[6] See Davis, *The Spirit of Hindu Law*; Ludo Rocher, 'Schools of Hindu Law', in *Studies in Hindu Law and Dharmaśāstra*, ed. Donald Davis (New York: Anthem Press, 2014), pp. 119–41.

[7] J. Duncan Derrett, 'The Right to Earn in Ancient India: A Conflict between Expediency and Authority', *Journal of the Economic and Social History of the Orient* 1.1 (1957): 66–97, 84, fn 1.

Dharmaśāstra bear a one-to-one resemblance to social realities outside of the śāstric tradition. Furthermore, this orientalist attribution of a legal development to the longstanding stereotype of Brāhmaṇa venality ignores the long series of arguments in Mīmāṃsā and Dharmaśāstra writing where the theory of property as an extra-śāstric phenomenon is subjected to ethical considerations of moral propriety and societal equity.

The third assumption concerns the extent to which Mīmāṃsā writings articulate a philosophically robust model of ownership and its incidental qualities. Ethan Kroll, for example, postulates that,

> The first sophisticated definition of svatva comes not from the Dharmaśāstra or Mīmāṃsā, but from a seemingly random passage in the Nyāyavārttikatātparyaṭīkā... of the 9th c. [Nyāya] scholar Vācaspatimiśra.[8]

A careful review of Mīmāṃsā texts, particularly those from the Prābhākara school of Mīmāṃsā, reveals that Mīmāṃsā ideas about property were far more complex than previously thought. Furthermore, these ideas about property were integral to the development of Dharmaśāstric theories of inheritance, particularly amongst those śāstrins who followed Vijñāneśvara's arguments. It is this centuries-long reliance on philosophical ideas about property—developed largely by Prābhākara-Mīmāṃsā authors—which can be identified as the distinctive feature of a *Mitākṣarā* school of jurisprudence.

This chapter argues three points: (1) that the Mīmāṃsā developed the earliest Sanskrit theories concerning ownership and property; (2) that Vijñāneśvara's treatment of inheritance marks a turning point because he combined Mīmāṃsā theories of ownership with the ethical dimensions of Dharmaśāstric legal problems; and (3) that subsequent Dharmaśāstrins in the late medieval period followed the further philosophical developments in Prābhākara-Mīmāṃsā concerning ownership when they commented on, expanded, or criticized Vijñāneśvara's model of inheritance. Vijñāneśvara is a founder in the sense that he *consolidated* earlier Dharmaśāstrins' theories of ownership and inheritance and established the parameters for future debate about the issue. Vijñāneśvara fashioned a distinctive, influential scale of Dharmaśāstra and Mīmāṃsā texts.

Consolidating Earlier Dharmaśāstra

In the waning centuries of the first millennium of the common era, ownership grew in importance as an analytic tool for Dharmaśāstra commentators such as

[8] Kroll, 'A Logical Approach to Law', pp. 34–5.

Bhāruci, Viśvarūpa and Medhātithi. Nevertheless, the question remains: to what extent do these earlier authors' approach to ownership and inheritance anticipate the unique arguments of the *Mitākṣarā*?[9] The best answer to this question—that the *Mitākṣarā* marks a sea-change in the Dharmaśāstric approach to ownership and inheritance—contrasts with the standard account in contemporary Dharmaśāstra studies. Two eminent scholars of Dharmaśāstra, Ludo Rocher and Donald Davis, for example, argue against the idea that Vijñāneśvara founded a '*Mitākṣarā* school of law'.[10] As Davis notes:

> The characterization of the jurisprudential distinction between ownership by birth (janmasvatvavāda) and ownership by the father's death (uparamasvatvavāda) as a debate between the Mitākṣarā and the Dāyabhāga 'schools of Hindu Law' is a phony, artificial creation of [H. T.] Colebrooke . . . I state this so boldly primarily to encourage future scholars . . . to stop repeating this mischaracterization of the classical Hindu law.[11]

Davis's admonition stems from his detailed knowledge of medieval Dharmaśāstra, wherein 'both of these texts [the *Mitākṣarā* and the *Dāyabhāga*] articulated their own version of these two legal positions', but 'both positions also had earlier advocates and later critics'.[12] Davis's argument appears to be supported by a passage from the sixteenth-century *Sarasvatīvilāsa* of Pratāparudra in which various perspectives on inheritance are attributed to pre-Vijñāneśvara Dharmaśāstrins—such as Asahāya, Bhāruci and Medhātithi—and to Vijñāneśvara.[13] Jīmūtavāhana's *Dāyabhāga* is conspicuously absent from Pratāparudra's summary of various Dharmaśāstric models of inheritance.

On closer examination, the matter is a bit more complicated than Davis's bold assertion of phony-ness on Colebrooke's part would suggest. Although earlier Dharmaśāstrins debated whether sons acquired ownership-by-birth (janmasvatva) or by partition (vibhāga), Vijñāneśvara inaugurated a new epoch in the intellectual history of Dharmaśāstra by compiling an inchoate, but recognized (by Viśvarūpa and Medhātithi), theory of sons' coparcenary property rights in their father's estate and then transforming it into a comprehensive model of inheritance. The crucial element of Vijñāneśvara's system—the distinction between apratibandhadāya and sapratibandhadāya (unobstructed and obstructed

[9] Kroll, 'A Logical Approach to Law', pp. 17–23.

[10] See, for example, Rocher, 'Schools of Hindu Law'.

[11] Davis, *The Spirit of Hindu Law*, p. 97.

[12] Ibid.

[13] *Sarasvatīvilāsa*: *Vyvahārakāṇḍaḥ*, ed. R. S. Sastry (Mysore: Oriental Library Sanskrit Series, No. 71, 1927), p. 347: **asahāyavijñānayogiprabhṛtīnām** tu yat svāmisambandhād eva nimittād anyasya svam bhavati tad dāyaśabdenocyate iti, tan na sahante **bhārucyaparārkaprabhṛtayaḥ** svatvahetūnām krayādīnām tallakṣaṇāsambhavāt . . . tarhi strīṇām dāyānarhatvāt. Earlier in the chapter, p. 344, Prataparudra defines daya as 'paternal assets fit for partition': **bhārucyaparārkādīnām** lakṣaṇam—vibhāgārham pitṛdravyam dāyam iti tad eva samyak.

inheritance, respectively)—was a synthetic combination of a customary theory of birth as a cause of ownership (articulated in Medhātithi's *Manubhāṣya*) and a legal theory of sons' pre-partition proprietary rights in their father's estate (advanced by Viśvarūpa in the *Bālakrīḍā*). This twofold definition of inheritance, that elevated custom to the status of śāstric law, forced Vijñāneśvara to free the concept of ownership from its śāstric constraints and to argue against the *Smṛtisaṃgraha* and Dhāreśvara's theory of ownership as mere possession.

The Definition of Inheritance (Dāya)

Vijñāneśvara opens his discussion of inheritance in a lengthy preamble to *Yājñavalkyasmṛti* 2.114. Given the importance of ownership as a framing analytic for his *Dāyaprakaraṇa*, it is striking that Vijñāneśvara does not define svatva or svāmya in this section of the *Mitākṣarā*. Later in the *Vyavahārādhyāya*, Vijñāneśvara defines property (svam) as 'an asset in connection to one's self'.[14] On the other hand, Vijñāneśvara defines inheritance (Dāya) as an 'asset which becomes the property of another, solely on account of (that person's) relation to the (asset's) owner'.[15] Furthermore, according to Vijñāneśvara:

> Inheritance is twofold: unobstructed (apratibandha) and obstructed (sapratibandha). Unobstructed Inheritance is when the assets of fathers and grandfathers become the property of sons and grandsons by virtue of their being sons and grandsons. But, obstructed inheritance is (when these same assets) become the property of paternal uncles, brothers, etc in the absence of the owner and in the absence of (their) sons.[16]

According to Pratāparudra, the first element of Vijñāneśvara's definition of inheritance was coined first by Asahāya, the author of a partially lost commentary on the *Nāradasmṛti*.[17] Although Asahāya may well have originated this definition two facts are worth noting: 1) Asahāya's commentary has not been preserved in its

[14] *Yājñavalkyasmṛti: with the Mitākṣarā of Vijñāneśvara*, ed. R. K. Panda (Delhi: Bharatiya Kala Prakashan, 2011), 2.168, 335: svam ātmasambandhi dravyam.

[15] Ibid., prelude to 2.114, 280: tatra dāyaśabdena yad dhanam svāmisambandhād eva nimittād anyasya svam bhavati tad ucyate.

[16] Ibid., 280: sa ca dvividhaḥ apratibandhaḥ sapratibandhaś ca. tatra putrāṇām pautrāṇām ca putratvena pautratvena ca pitṛdhanam pitāmahadhanam ca svam bhavatīty apratibandho dāyaḥ. pitṛvyabhrātrādīnām tu putrābhāve svāmyabhāve ca svam bhavatīti sapratibandho dāyaḥ. For a translation of this passage in the *Mitākṣarā*, see Rosane Rocher and Ludo Rocher, 'Ownership by Birth: The *Mitākṣarā* Stand', *Journal of Indian Philosophy* 29 (2001): 241–55. Generally, I've tinkered with the Rochers' translations to maintain conformity of technical terms throughout this monograph.

[17] For Asahāya's date, textual history and positions in Dharmaśāstra, see P. V. Kāṇe, *A History of Dharmaśāstra*, vol. 1, part 1, 2nd edn (Poona: Bhandarkar Oriental Research Institute, 1968), pp. 546–51.

totality; and 2) with the exception of the *Sarasvatīvilāsa*, Asahāya is never invoked as an authority for the purposes of defining inheritance. One can infer from these two facts that even if Vijñāneśvara took his cue from Asahāya, the *Mitākṣarā* was this definition's chief representative in later years. Although earlier commentators, such as Bhāruci and Medhātithi, offered alternative definitions of inheritance, there is no evidence that their definitions were connected with a theory of ownership-by-cessation—typically as a result of legal or biological death—of the ownership of the previous owner (uparamasvatva).[18]

Vijñāneśvara is the first known Dharmaśāstrin to combine Asahāya's definition of inheritance with a theory of inheritance in which a proprietary right exists but is obstructed by the existence of a nearer cognate. Vijñāneśvara's characterization of inheritance as being obstructed or unobstructed may be connected to a theory of ownership which had its antecedents in earlier Dharmaśāstric debates concerning mortgages (ādhi). Variations on the term obstruction (bandha) appear frequently in earlier and later Dharmaśāstric discussions of mortgage.[19] The sūtras and smṛtis forbid a mortgager or mortgagee from alienating mortgaged assets.[20] This put Dharmaśāstrins in a double bind—if a mortgager's ownership were extinguished by the act of mortgage, what would prevent a mortgagee from selling the mortgaged asset? Conversely, if a mortgager retains ownership of a mortgaged asset, what would prevent him from selling or mortgaging it again to someone else? The solution lay in theorizing an obstructed form of ownership.[21] Thus, the *Mitākṣarā's* division of inheritance into obstructed and unobstructed subtypes is an example of Vijñāneśvara's synthesis of pre-existing Dharmaśāstric ideas about ownership, that had little to do with inheritance.

Vijñāneśvara's twofold definition of inheritance dovetails neatly with his definition of kinship (sāpiṇḍya) as a blood relation.[22] The *Mānavadharmaśāstra* (9.186–7) defines sāpiṇḍya relations in terms of offering piṇḍa (rice balls) to

[18] For various definitions of dāya, see J. Duncan Derrett, 'The Development of the Concept of Property in India, *c.* AD 800–1800', in *Essays in Classical and Modern Indian Law*, vol. 2, ed. J. Duncan Derrett (Leiden: E. J. Brill, 1977), pp. 8–130, 54.

[19] See *Bṛhaspatismṛti* 1.10.38 in Patrick Olivelle, *A Sanskrit Dictionary of Law and Statecraft* (Delhi: Primus Books, 2015), p. 81: ādhir bandhaḥ samākhyātaḥ sa ca proktaś caturvidhaḥ. Cf. J. Duncan Derrett, 'The Development of the Concept of Property in India, *c.* AD 800–1800', 8–130, 81 fn 299; I. S. Pawate, *Dāyavibhāga: or the Individualization of Communal Property and the Communalization of Individual Property in the Mitakhsara Law* (Dharwar: Karnatak University Press, 1975), pp. 41–3.

[20] For example, see *Yājñvalkyasmṛti* 2.23 and *Mānavadharmaśāstra* 8.143.

[21] Pawate, *Dāyavibhāga*, pp. 41–3. While Vijñāneśvara fails to mention the idea that a mortgagor's is *obstructed*, he generally follows Aparārka's conclusion about the second mortgage being void. The passage from Aparārka, a comment on Yāj. 2.23–4, reads: yathā—kṣetrādikam ādhim kṛtvā vikrīya dattvā vā punas tasyaiva kṣetrasya puruṣāntaram praty adhamarṇena ādhir dānam vikrayo vā kriyate. tadā pūrvakriyā satyottarā mithyā. pūrvakṛtābhyām dānavikrayābhyām svāmitvanivṛttau punar asvāminā kriyamāṇau dānavikrayau na sidhyataḥ. ādhikaraṇena tu yady api svāmibhāvo na nivartyate tathāpi pratibadhyate. tataś ca tasya kṣetrasya ādhitvānivṛttau puruṣāntaram pratyādhitvam kartum naiva śakyate.

[22] For Sapiṇḍa relations in Sanskrit Jurisprudence, see J. R. Gharpure, *Sāpiṇḍya, or, The Law of Sapiṇḍa Relationship* (Bombay: Office of the Collection of Hindu Law Texts, 1943).

one's ancestors at funerary ceremonies (śrāddhas) and correlates this spiritual benefit with the right to inherit property:

> Three generations shall be given water, three generations must be offered piṇḍas. It is the fourth generation that offers these. The fifth generation is not entitled (to make an offering). Assets always go to the one who is closest to the deceased sapiṇḍa.[23]

Vijñāneśvara offers an alternative definition of kinship that dovetails with his broader project of linking consanguinity and inheritance:

> Sapiṇḍa-relationship arises between two people through their being connected by particles of one body. Thus the son stands in sapiṇḍa-relationship to his father because of the particles of his father's body (having entered his) . . . Therefore one ought to know that wherever the word sapiṇḍa is used, there exists . . . a connection with one body, either immediately or by descent.[24]

Does Ownership Precede Partition?

Vijñāneśvara's distinction between unobstructed and obstructed inheritance, built on the intellectual scaffolding of mortgaged property, is contingent on the assumption that sons acquire a proprietary right in their fathers' and paternal grandfathers' estates during their lifetime. Viśvarūpa argued that ownership must precede partition for reasons of logical coherence, and Medhātithi argued that although *customary* aphorisms might acknowledge ownership-by-birth on the part of a son, *legally* speaking, one should not follow such dicta in practice. Vijñāneśvara consolidated these two positions by expanding Viśvarūpa's relatively sparse comments to address a more robust body of smṛti law and by framing Medhātithi's customary practices as śāstric law.

Viśvarūpa (ninth century), a southerner who wrote the *Bālakrīḍā*, an influential commentary on the *Yājñavalkyasmṛti*, is probably the first śāstrin to argue that ownership precedes partition. Without explicitly advancing a theory of ownership-by-birth, he argues that in regard to grand-paternal assets, ownership

[23] *Manubhāṣya of Medhātithi*, vols 2–3, ed. Ganganatha Jha (Calcutta: Asiatic Society of Bengal, 1939), p. 298: trayāṇām udakaṃ kāryaṃ triṣu piṇḍaḥ pravartate / caturthaḥ saṃpradātaiṣāṃ pañcamo nopapadyate //9.186// anantaraḥ sapiṇḍādyas tasya tasya dhanaṃ bhavet /9.187 / For differing theories of sapiṇḍa-ship and their relation to inheritance, see Ludo Rocher, 'Inheritance and Śrāddha: The Principle of "Spiritual Benefit"', in *Studies in Hindu Law and Dharmaśāstra*, ed. Donald Davis (New York: Anthem Press, 2014), pp. 267–78. Rocher's translation.

[24] *Mitākṣarā* on *Yājñavalkyasmṛti* 1.52, 22–3: sapiṇḍatā ca ekaśarīrāvayavānvayena bhavati. tathā hi putrasya pitṛśarīrāvayavānvayena pitrā saha ekapiṇḍatā . . . evaṃ yatra yatra sapiṇḍaśabdas tatra tatra sākṣāt paramparayā vā ekaśarīrāvayavānvayo veditavyaḥ.

on the part of male children and grandchildren precedes partition. The discussion hinges on an interpretation of Yāj. 2.124: 'the ownership of both the father and the son is the same in land, trusts, and assets which were acquired by the grandfather'.[25] In a phrase that would be echoed later by Vijñāneśvara, Viśvarūpa asks 'now, does ownership (arise) after partition, or does partition (occur) when ownership already exists?'[26] Viśvarūpa argues that Yāj. 2.124 indicates that sons and fathers *both* have dominion (prabhutva) in grand-paternal assets.[27] Viśvarūpa's only warrant is that Yāj. 2.125 states explicitly that sons born after a partition are entitled to a portion of the partitioned estate.[28] Consequently, ownership would not be produced for a son born after partition if partition were the cause of the production of ownership.[29]

Viśvarūpa acknowledges an objection: if sons had ownership in their father's assets before partition, a father could not perform sacrifices (a duty incumbent on able-bodied males) without the consent of their sons.[30] If a son already possesses a proprietary right in the ancestral estate, how could a father obtain the permission of his neonatal son to conduct a sacrifice?[31] Viśvarūpa's only response is that a father can perform sacrifices with *his* self-acquired assets (assets in which a son does *not* have svatva) and a father can divide those assets (unlike grand-paternal assets) as *he* wishes.[32]

While Viśvarūpa's comments are remarkable because they frame his analysis of *Yājñavalkyasmṛti* 2.124–125 through the lens of ownership and because he argues, implicitly, for ownership-by-birth (or something close to it), they are noticeably thin. Viśvarūpa's arguments are confined to two verses and are not connected to his comments on any other verses pertaining to inheritance. He is content to use the term in his discussion of inheritance, as in other locations in the *Bālakrīḍā*, as a short-hand for a connection to an asset.[33] Indeed, Viśvarūpa never explicitly ties a theory of pre-partition ownership with a theory of birth as a cause

[25] *Yājñavalkyasmṛti:* with the *Bālakrīḍā of Viśvarūpācārya*, vol. 1, ed. Gaṇapati Śāstrī (Trivandrum: Trivandrum Sanskrit Series, No. 74, 1922), *Yājñvalkyasmṛti* 2.124 (121 in Bharatiya Kala Prakashan edition), p. 244: bhūr yā pitāmahopāttā nibandho dravyam eva vā / tatra syāt tādṛśam svāmyam pituḥ putrasya cobhayoḥ //

[26] Ibid.: atha kiṃ vibhāgāt svatvam, uta svatve sati vibhāga iti.

[27] Ibid.: bhūr yā pitāmahopāttā nibandho vā akṣayanidhiḥ anyad eva vā dravyam, tatra pitāputrayos tulyam prabhutvam syāt pratyetavyam nirvicikitsam evety arthaḥ. ubhayor ity avibhaktasyaiva svatvajñāpanārtham.

[28] Ibid., 2.125 (122 in Bharatiya Kala Prakashan edition), p. 245: vibhakte 'pi savarṇāyāḥ putro jāto vibhāgabhāk /.

[29] Ibid.: tasmāt svatve saty eva ity uktam. yadi hi vibhāgena svatvasambandho 'bhaviṣyat, tato vibhaktajasya [putrasya] dravyasambandho nopāpatsyata.

[30] Ibid., intro to 2.124, p. 244: vibhāgāt svatvam ity āhuḥ. anyathā jātaputrasyādhānādiśrutir dravyasādhāraṇyāt svatyāgāsambhavād virudhyate.

[31] Ibid.: na ca tadanujñānād anuṣṭhānam iti yuktam, jātamātrasyānujñānāśakteḥ.

[32] Ibid., 2.125, p. 245: yat tv anuṣṭhānavirodhādi codyam, tat svayam ārjitenāpi tat siddher na kimcit ... yā tv icchayā vibhāgasmṛtiḥ sā svayamupāttadravyavato draṣṭavyā.

[33] For Viśvarūpa's other references to svatva, see Kroll, 'A Logical Approach to Law', pp. 31–3.

of ownership—precisely the framing issue for the *Mitākṣarā's* model of inheritance.

Vijñāneśvara adopts most of Viśvarūpa's arguments from YS 2.124–125 (121–2 in the *Mitākṣarā*), but he embeds them within a broader argument that seeks to accomplish two things: 1) foreground the implications of YS 2.124 as a warrant for ownership-by-birth (and apratibandhadāya); and 2) demonstrate the compatibility of such a view with several seemingly contradictory smṛti passages. For example, Vijñāneśvara concludes his comments on ownership-by-birth by undertaking a careful, line-by-line analysis of smṛti passages pertaining to joint family possessions. An opponent might argue that: 1) a father could not perform sacrifices enjoined after the birth of a son because the son would have svatva in the father's possessions from birth;[34] and 2) rules exempting affectionate gifts made by father to his sons or wives from partition would be redundant if sons were owners from birth because such gifts (of joint assets) could only be made with the consent of all members of the family.[35] Vijñāneśvara responds to the first objection by arguing that the force of the Vedic injunction is sufficient to empower a father to perform a sacrifice with joint family assets.[36]

Furthermore, a father *does* have the ability to act independently with regard to his movable, self-acquired assets and to perform sacrifices with it.[37] With reference to the *Viṣṇusmṛti's* verse on affectionate gifts, Vijñāneśvara states that the exemption of affectionate gifts from partition refers to instances of either the father making gifts of self-acquired movable assets (over which sons presumably have no proprietary interest) or of immovable assets given with the consent of all the sons with a proprietary interest in it.[38] Consequently, Vijñāneśvara argues that one cannot deny that sons acquire ownership in paternal and grand-paternal assets as a result of birth.[39] A further example of Vijñāneśvara's thoroughness is

[34] *Mitākṣarā* on *Yājñāvalkyasmṛti* 2.114, p. 282: vibhāgāt svatvam iti tāvaty uktam. jātaputrasyādhānavidhānāt. yadi janmanaiva svatvam syāt tadotpannasya putrasyāpi tatsvam sādhāraṇam iti dravyasādhyeṣv ādhānādiṣu pitur anadhikāraḥ syāt. See note 30 for a parallel passage in the *Bālakrīḍā*.

[35] Ibid., pp. 282–3: tathā vibhāgāt prāk pitṛprasādalabdhasya vibhāgapratiṣedho nopapadyate. sarvānumatyā dattatvād vibhāgaprāptyabhāvāt. yathāha śauryabhāryādhane cobhe yac ca vidyādhanam bhavet / trīṇy etāny avibhājyāni prasādo yaś ca paitṛkaḥ // Nārada 13.6 // iti tathā bhartrā prītena yad dattaṃ striyai tasmin mṛte 'pi tat / sā yathākāmam aśnīyād dadyāt vā sthāvarād ṛte // Nārada 1.28 // iti prītidānavacanam ca nopapadyate janmanaiva svatve.

[36] Ibid., p. 283: yad apy arthasādhyeṣu vaidikeṣu karmasv anadhikāra iti, tatra tad vidhānabalād evādhikāro gamyate.

[37] Ibid.: tasmāt paitṛke paitāmahe ca dravye janmanaiva svatvam, tathāpi pitur āvaśyakeṣu dharmakṛtyeṣu vācanikeṣu prasādadānakuṭumbabharaṇāpadvimokṣādiṣu ca sthāvaravyatirikta dravyaviniyoge svātantryam iti sthitam.

[38] Ibid., p. 283: yat tu 'bhartrā prītena' ity ādi **viṣṇuvacanam** sthāvarasya prītidānajñāpanam tat svopārjitasyāpi putrādyabhyanujñayaiveti vyākhyeyam. pūrvoktair maṇimuktādivacanaiḥ sthāvaravyatiriktasyaiva prītidānayogyatvaniścayāt. The verses involving 'gems and pearls' read: maṇimuktāpravālānām sarvasyaiva pitā prabhuḥ / sthāvarasya tu sarvasya na pitā na pitāmahaḥ // pitṛprasādād bhujyante vastrāṇy ābharaṇāni ca / sthāvaram tu na bhujyeta prasāde sati paitṛke //.

[39] Ibid.: tasmāt paitṛke paitāmahe ca dravye janmanaiva svatvam.

his introduction of an exception (apavāda) to the general rule that fathers may not alienate immovable assets without the consent of their agnatic families.[40] Viśvarūpa's comments were obviously an inspiration for Vijñāneśvara, but the *Mitākṣarā* tests Viśvarūpa's theory against a broader body of Dharmaśāstric passages.[41]

Vijñāneśvara elevates the theory of ownership-by-birth from an extra-legal custom to the status of law. In doing so he is probably indebted to Medhātithi's (ninth-to-eleventh-century) commentary on the *Mānavadharmaśāstra*, the *Manubhāṣya*.[42] The *Bhāṣya*, often lauded for its balance between brevity and subtlety, represents the first substantial discussion of theories of ownership-by-birth in Dharmaśāstra.[43] In contrast to Davis's assertion that Medhātithi was an opponent of janmasvatva, Medhātithi explicitly testifies to a son's proprietary right as a result of his birth as a matter of custom (ācāra). Like Viśvarūpa, Medhātithi applies the concept of pre-partition ownership as an analytical tool to address thorny issues in inheritance, but he doesn't advocate a distinctive position. Medhātithi serves as an index of the state of inheritance before Vijñāneśvara: there are statements concerning ownership-by-birth that are attributed to teachers (ācāryas), but they are neither recognized as smṛti nor are they applied consistently to a comprehensive model of inheritance.

In a discussion of whether a son's qualities or his caste should determine his relative worth in relation to inheritance, Medhātithi argues that caste is the most important factor because 'the teachers say that one is born into the ownership of assets'.[44] On Manu 9.212, Medhātithi argues that separated, co-uterine sons might still partake of a partition when their father dies because 'one who is born is called an owner'.[45] Medhātithi immediately limits this description of ownership-

[40] Ibid.: eko 'pi sthāvare kuryād dānādhamanavikrayam / āpadkāle kuṭumbārthe dharmārthe ca viśeṣataḥ //.

[41] Vijñāneśvara acknowledges Viśvarūpa's influence in an introductory verse. See *Mitākṣarā* on *Yājñāvalkyasmṛti* 1.1, p. 1: **yājñavalkyamunibhāṣitam** muhur **viśvarūpavikaṭoktivistṛtam** / dharmaśāstram **ṛjubhir mitākṣarair bālabodhaye** vivicyate //.

[42] For Medhātithi's date and works, see Kāṇe, *History of Dharmaśāstra*, vol. 1, part 2, 2nd edn, pp. 573–83.

[43] J. Duncan Derrett, 'The Concept of Law According to Medhātithi, a Pre-Islamic India Jurist', in *Essays in Classical and Modern Hindu Law*, vol. 1, ed. J. Duncan Derrett (Leiden: Brill, 1976), pp. 174–97.

[44] *Manusmṛti: with the Manubhāṣya of Medhātithi*, vols 2–3, ed. Ganganatha Jha (Calcutta: Asiatic Society of Bengal, 1939), p. 291; samavarṇāsu vā jātāḥ sarve putrā dvijanmanām / uddhāram jyāyase dattvā bhajeran itare samam //Manu 9.156// jāter atyantamānyatvāt. 'utpanno vārthasvāmyam ity ācāryā' iti.

[45] Ibid., pp. 302–3: sodaryā vibhajeraṃs tam sametya sahitāḥ samam / bhrātaro ye ca saṃsṛṣṭā bhaginyaś ca sanābhayaḥ // Manu 9.212 // yata uktam—samutpanno vācyaḥ svāmīti. The logic here is subtle: Medhātithi argues that because Manu 9.212 mentions co-uterine (sodaryā) and un-separated (saṃsṛṣṭa) brothers *separately*, separated co-uterine brothers must have a proprietary right. 'The Ācāryas...' is one of the most hotly contested *smṛti* passages in the history of Indology. See, for example Julius Jolly, *Outlines of an History of the Hindu Law of Partition, Inheritance and Adoption* (Calcutta: Thacker, Spink and Co., 1883), p. 110, where he argues that: 'Vijnāneśvara or his predecessors, from whom he may be supposed to have borrowed his theory, came to fabricate a text, in which the doctrine that property is by birth is attributed to the holy teachers... and to attribute this text to the Sage Gautama, who was looked to as the principal authority in regard to the sources of ownership.'

by-birth—referring the reader back to an earlier verse of Manu (9.104)—which describes sons as 'powerless/non-independent' in regard to paternal assets during the lifetime of their parents—and explains that Manu 9.104 shows that ownership (svāmya) accrues to sons immediately after the death of their father.[46]

Manu 9.209 states that 'if a father recovers lost ancestral assets, he shall not, unless he so wishes, share it with his sons, being as it is his self-acquired assets'.[47] The assumption underlying Manu's comment appears to be that in other circumstances, a father must share it with his sons. Medhātithi argues that:

> If, for so long as they are minors (lit. not full-grown), sons are owners (of ancestral assets), then (when they are adults), because sons are in no way different (than fathers with respect to those ancestral assets), all (fathers and sons) partake of the assets of the grandfather (during a division of assets) because the division of inheritance is preceded by ownership.[48]

Medhātithi admits that sons have a proprietary right in ancestral assets and argues that a father, upon the birth of his son, should not mortgage or sell his assets with the exception of using said assets to support the family properly.[49] Medhātithi adds a cautionary note, relating that:

> In actual practice (ācāreṇa), even though, in this stage of (their) life, sons have ownership (in ancestral assets), sin (on the part of sons) dividing (these assets), is inferred on the strength of seeing (in smṛti) admonitory verses (such as) 'and divided by an unwilling father'.[50]

Medhātithi is clearly aware of the moral hazard of emphasizing the coextensive proprietary rights of fathers and sons in paternal assets. Indeed, he argues that because exercising one's proprietary right against the will of one's father is not dharmic, a son should obtain assets through means other than from paternal assets.[51] If sons were to force their father to partition paternal assets, then that would be like someone who receives improper gifts—there would be ownership, but there would also be sin on the part of the son.[52]

[46] *Manubhāṣya*, p. 302: anīśās te hi jīvatoḥ iti tatra pitur ūrdhvam samanantaram eva putrāṇām svāmyam darśayati.

[47] Ibid., p. 301: paitṛkam tu pitā dravyam anavāptam yad āpnuyāt / na tat putrair bhajet sārdham akāmaḥ svayam arjitam //9.209//.

[48] Ibid., p. 302: saty api ca putrasya svāmye yāvad apraptās tāvat sarvathā viśeṣābhāvāt sarve pitāmahadhanabhājaḥ svatvapūrvakatvād vibhāgasya.

[49] Ibid.: bandhakrayādikriyāsu pitṛdhanam jātaputreṇa na viniyoktavyam. yogakuṭumbabharaṇādau tu viniyogo darśitaḥ.

[50] Ibid.: ācāreṇa saty api cāsyām avasthāyām putrāṇām svāmye 'pitrā cākāmena vibhaktān', iti nindādarśanād balād vibhājayantaḥ pāpā ity anumīyate.

[51] Ibid.: ataḥ sambhavaty upāyāntare na pitārthanīyaḥ. adharmo hi tathā syāt.

[52] Ibid.: yāthāsakṛta[sat]pratigraheṇa bhavati svāmyam doṣas tu puruṣasya.

In contrast to Medhātithi, Vijñāneśvara elevates this morally ambiguous custom of ownership-by-birth to the status of law by linking a theory of unobstructed and obstructed inheritance with the sūtras of Gautama outlining śāstric means of acquiring assets. Vijñāneśvara quotes a passage from the *Gautamadharmasūtras*: 'one becomes an owner by inheritance, purchase, partition, garnering, or discovering'.[53] For Vijñāneśvara, inheritance (riktha) means unobstructed inheritance and partition (samvibhāga) means obstructed inheritance.[54] Furthermore, according to Vijñāneśvara, 'the following Gautama [Dharmasūtra] text proves the point: the teachers say that one obtains ownership of assets right from birth'.[55] The difference between Medhātithi and Vijñāneśvara might seem trivial—the former quotes what might well be a popular maxim while the latter places this maxim within the *Gautamadharmasūtras* which list the ways in which one becomes an owner. Vijñāneśvara's *Mitākṣarā*, however, abandons Medhātithi's moral uncertainty: for Vijñāneśvara ownership-by-birth is not an undesirable, but acknowledged practice—it is the central pillar of his model of inheritance. Virtually every Dharmaśāstrin after Vijñāneśvara would characterize the phrase 'the teachers say that one obtains ownership of assets right from birth' as 'that sūtra of Gautama which appears in the *Mitākṣarā*'.[56]

The (Extra)Śāstric Nature of Ownership

Vijñāneśvara's attempts to elevate a custom—that does not appear in any known version of the *Gautamadharmasūtras*—to the status of law forced him to justify an extra-śāstric theory of ownership. As Derrett notes, 'had he and his followers seriatim been convinced of the genuineness of this text and its interpretation it would have been quite unnecessary for them to consider... whether Property might be extra-śāstric and capable of causes apart from the methods of acquisition

[53] Rocher, 'Ownership by Birth': 245; *Dharmasūtras Parallels: Containing the Dharmasūtras of Āpastamba, Gautama, Baudhāyana, and Vasiṣṭha*, ed. Patrick Olivelle (Delhi: Motilal Banarsidas, 2005), p. 211: svāmī rikthakrayasaṃvibhāgaparigrahādhigameṣu brāhmaṇasyādhikam labdham kṣatriyasya vijitam nirviṣṭam vaiśyaśūdrayoḥ.

[54] *Mitākṣarā* on Yāj. 2.114, p. 282: tatrāpratibandho dāyo riktham... samvibhāgaḥ sapratibandho dāya.

[55] Ibid., p. 283: tathotpattyaivārthasvāmitvam labhetety ācāryāḥ iti **gautamavacanāt**. Cf, *Smṛticandrikā*, vol. 3.2, ed. L. Śrīnivāsācārya (Mysore: Government Oriental Library, Government Oriental Library Series, Bibliotheca Sanskrita, 1916), p. 603: tathā ca paitṛkadhanalābhahetutvenoktam **gautamenaiva**—'utpattyaivārthasvāmitvam labhetety ācāryaḥ'.

[56] Raghunandana refers to the phrase attributed to Gautama as 'the text of Gautama... cited in the *Mitākṣarā*' probably to indicate its lack of complete authenticity and Śrīkṛṣṇa (in his commentary on the *Dāyabhāga*, 2.21) states that it is spurious (amūla). P. V. Kāṇe, *A History of Dharmaśāstra*, vol. 3, 2nd edn (Poona: Bhandarkar Oriental Research Institute, 1973), pp. 557–8, fn 1041. Cited in the apparatus to *Vivādatāṇḍava*, 1949, 2: **mitākṣarādhṛtagotamavacanam** amūlaṃ. Also, see Sontheimer, *The Joint Hindu Family*, p. 93. For Aparāditya's defence of a similar position see Kāṇe, *History of Dharmaśāstra*, vol. 3, 2nd edn, p. 557, fn 1040.

laid down in the smṛti-texts'.[57] Although Medhātithi refers very sparingly to ownership and to the acquisition thereof as extra-śāstric, Vijñāneśvara's is probably the first Dharmaśāstrin to tie an extra-śāstric theory of ownership to the problem of inheritance. Vijñāneśvara introduces the issue by asking: 'is ownership discernible from the śāstra alone, or is it discernible from other sources?'[58]

Vijñāneśvara's opponent objects to an extra-śāstric theory of ownership on the grounds that it would render the smṛtis, which list various means of acquiring assets, superfluous; it would legally recognize the ownership of thieves and other undesirables; and it would reduce ownership to a matter of mere possession.[59] Consequently, Vijñāneśvara's opponent makes a convincing case that ownership should be discernible from the śāstra alone (śāstraikasamadhigamyatva).[60] Vijñāneśvara's opponent is probably the Saṃgrahakāra or Dhāreśvara.[61] Dhāreśvara and the Saṃgrahakāra's views first (and only) appear in the *Smṛticandrikā* of Devaṇṇabhaṭṭa, a thirteenth-century follower of Vijñāneśvara, who records a passage from the *Smṛtisaṃgraha* that makes the argument clearer:

> It is surely not the case that the owner of an asset is the one in whose hand it lies. For is it not the case that one's property can be in the hands of others because of theft and the like? Therefore, ownership should be (known) from śāstra alone, not also from experience.[62]

Devaṇṇabhaṭṭa records a verse from the Saṃgrahakāra which states: 'One cannot say that one's property is whatever he uses as he desires, for the use of everything is restricted by the śāstra.'[63] The opponent attempts to argue that even if the production of ownership were established extra-śāstrically, the use of one's

[57] J. Duncan Derrett, 'The Right to Earn': 81, fn 1.

[58] *Mitākṣarā*, p. 280: kim śāstraikasamadhigamyam svatvam uta pramāṇāntarasamadhigamyam iti.

[59] *Mitākṣarā*, p. 281: **gautamavacanāt** 'svāmī rikthakrayasaṃvibhāgaparigrahādhigameṣu brāhmaṇasyādhikam labdham kṣatriyasya vijitam nirviṣṭam vaiśyaśūdrayoḥ' [Gautama 10.39–42] iti pramāṇāntaragamye svatve nedam vacanam arthavat syāt; For recognizing theft and reprobated acquisition... adattādāyinaḥ sakāśād yājanādidvāreṇāpi dravyam arjayatām daṇḍavidhānam anupapannam syāt svatvasya laukikatve... api ca laukikam cet svatvam mama svam anenāpahṛtam iti na brūyād, apahartur eva svatvāt. anyathānyasya svam tenāpahṛtam iti nāpahartuḥ svam. evam tarhi survarṇarajatādisvarūpavad asya vā svam anyasya vā svam iti śaṃśayo na syāt.

[60] Ibid., p. 242; *Mitākṣarā*, 281: tatra śāstraikasamadhigamyam iti tāvad ukam...

[61] For the Saṃgrahakāra and Dhāreśvara, see Kāṇe, *History of Dharmaśāstra*, vol. 1, part 2, pp. 537–41 and 585–91 respectively. Vijñāneśvara refers to the views of the Saṃgrahakāra and Dhāreśvara, but not in the context of ownership. Indeed, it is only from Devaṇṇabhaṭṭa onwards that the *Smṛtisaṃgraha* and the *Mitākṣarā* are placed in apposition.

[62] For Devaṇṇabhaṭṭa's date and context, see Kāṇe, *History of Dharmaśāstra*, vol. 1, part 2, pp. 737–41; *Smṛticandrikā*, vol. 3.2, p. 600: vartate yasya yad dhaste tasya svāmī sa eva na / anyasvam anyahasteṣu cauryadyaiḥ kim na vartate // tasmāc chāśtrata eva syāt svāmyam nānubhavād api /.

[63] Ibid., p. 601: na ca svam ucyate tadvat svecchayā viniyujyate / viniyogo 'pi sarvasya śāstreṇaiva niyamyate //.

property is regulated by the śāstras and consequently one cannot define ownership in terms of use as desired.

Vijñāneśvara's response is that ownership is extra-śāstric because 'people living in foreign lands' (pratyantavāsins) engage in commerce without any knowledge of the śāstras and because ownership allows people to engage in practical, extra-śāstric activities.[64] Indeed, as Vijñāneśvara notes:

> Ownership is extra-śāstric because, like rice, etc., it accomplishes activities whose goals are extra-śāstric. The Āhavanīya and other (fires), discernible from the śāstras, do not accomplish activities whose goals are extra-śāstric. For, in this case, (such fires) do not accomplish (extra-śāstric activities) such as cooking by means of their (śāstric) forms such as Āhavanīya, but, rather, by means of (extra-śāstric) forms such as a fire, being perceived through direct perception, etc.[65]

Furthermore, Vijñāneśvara points out that theft is never recognized as a source of ownership in an extra-śāstric society.[66] Ownership is determined by an activity which is recognized in the extra-śāstric world as a valid act of acquisition, not by a śāstric passage.[67] Vijñāneśvara's point is that:

> (A piece of gold, etc.) does not accomplish purchase, etc., by means of its golden form, etc., but, rather, only by means of ownership. For, that which is not someone's property cannot accomplish an activity such as purchase for him.[68]

For Vijñāneśvara, because ownership was earlier proved to be established extra-śāstrically, 'it is said that ownership is certainly established extra-śāstrically. In the (extra-śāstric) world, one cannot deny that the ownership of sons, etc., by birth alone is even more established.'[69] Vijñāneśvara is the first Dharmaśāstrin to have addressed those objections to an extra-śāstric theory of ownership that would be identified later with the Saṃgrahakāra. Vijñāneśvara is also the first Dharmaśāstrin to use that theory to answer an opponent who argues that, in

[64] *Mitākṣarā*, p. 281: api ca pratyantavāsinām apy adṛṣṭaśāstravyavahārāṇām svatvavyavahāro dṛśyate.

[65] Ibid.: laukikam eva svatvam laukikārthakriyāsādhanatvāt vrīhyādivat. āhavanīyādīnām hi śāstragamyānām na laukikakriyāsādhanatvam asti…na hi tatrāhavanīyādirūpeṇa pākādisādhanatvam. kiṃ tarhi pratyakṣādiparidṛśyamānāgnyādirūpeṇa.

[66] Ibid.: na caitāvatā caurādiprāptasyāpi svatvam syād iti mantavyam. loke tatra svatvaprasiddhyabhāvāt vyavahāravisaṃvādāc ca.

[67] Or, *via negativa*, if the act is dubious, the ownership is dubious. Ibid., p. 282: yad api svam anenāpahṛtam iti na brūyāt svatvasya laukikatva iti tad apy asat svatvahetubhūtakrayādisaṃdehāt svatvasaṃdehopapatteḥ.

[68] Ibid., p. 281: iha tu suvarṇādirūpeṇa na krayādisādhanatvam api tu svatvenaiva. na hi yasya yat svam na bhavati tat tasya krayādyarthakriyām sādhayati.

[69] Ibid., p. 283: lokaprasiddham eva svatvam ity uktam. loke ca putrādīnām janmanaiva svatvam prasiddhataram nāpahnavam arhati.

reference to inheritance, 'ownership does not (come about) by birth, but, rather, ownership (comes about) by the death of the owner or by partition'.[70]

From a purely juridical standpoint, Vijñāneśvara's *Mitākṣarā* marks a turning point. One can argue that bits and pieces of the *Mitākṣarā*'s theory of ownership-by-birth and of the *Dāyabhāga*'s theory of ownership-by-cessation existed before Vijñāneśvara. This, rather than an absence of institutional appendices, is the essence of Rocher and Davis's opposition to identifying Vijñāneśvara as a 'founder' of a 'school of thought' about inheritance and ownership. The evidence suggests that such opposition is anachronistic: it is difficult to see how Medhātithi and Viśvarūpa offer anything more than stray, largely unconnected comments. Such an anachronistic perspective is also contrary to the basic fact that great, influential thinkers such as Vijñāneśvara, Mammaṭa, or Patañjali were not influential because they invented their systems *ex nihilo* but because they consolidated the fragmented ideas of earlier thinkers—that they set the boundaries of the scale of texts within which later authors would develop the tradition. In combining the definition of inheritance with a theory of mortgages and by linking the resulting theory of obstructed and unobstructed inheritance with a select series of smṛti passages, Vijñāneśvara set the general boundaries within which the debate about inheritance would unfold for several centuries, until the emergence of the *Dāyabhāga* in the sixteenth century.

Consolidating Mīmāṃsā Theories of Ownership

This section takes up the relationship between the *Mitākṣarā*'s legal model of inheritance and its recalibration of Mīmāṃsā-derived, philosophical theories of ownership. The distinction between law and philosophy is notoriously ill-defined, but here it draws the reader's attention to the difference between *what* the smṛtis say regarding ownership and inheritance and *how* one ought to characterize the smṛtis in relation to the other śāstric disciplines.[71] Vijñāneśvara's *Mitākṣarā* marks a turning point in the Dharmaśāstric approach to ownership and inheritance—by tying Vijñāneśvara's legal defence of ownership-by-birth with a theory of ownership as an extra-śāstrically established eligibility for use as desired (yatheṣṭaviniyogārhatā) that was developed primarily in Prābhākara-Mīmāṃsā texts.

In positing the efficacy of extra-śāstric modes of acquiring assets, Vijñāneśvara found convenient allies in two Prābhākara-Mīmāṃsā treatises: the *Bṛhatī* of Prabhākara and, possibly, the *Ṛjuvimalāpañcikā* of Śālikanātha. The earliest Dharmaśāstras (the smṛtis and sūtras), like the *Mīmāṃsāsūtras,* say little to

[70] Ibid.: na janmanā svatvam kintu svāminā śād vibhāgād vā svatvam.

[71] For a basic introduction to the topic of law and philosophy, see Mark Tebbit, *Law and Philosophy: An Introduction* (London: Routledge, 2017).

nothing about the nature of ownership. It was only with the Mīmāṃsā commentaries of Śabara, Prabhākara and Śālikanātha that ownership and its relationship to the sacrifice and to the extra-śāstric world was interrogated. Their theory of ownership—as that which is fit to be used according to its acquirer's intentions—was surely not the morally suspect 'what I hold I own' model advanced by Kroll and Derrett.[72] Furthermore, even at so early a stage of development as Śabara's *Mīmāṃsābhāṣya*, there was a concern about the moral rectitude of an act of acquisition. These early Mīmāṃsā theories of ownership were applied, increasingly as time wore on, by early Dharmaśāstra commentators such as Viśvarūpa and Medhātithi to solve thorny legal concerns such as adverse possession, the ownership of land, and joint family inheritance. What sets Vijñāneśvara's *Mitākṣarā* apart from its predecessors is the depth of its recalibration of certain arguments from the Prābhākara-Mīmāṃsā and its use of Mīmāṃsā-reasoning to tackle concerns about the moral propriety of placing the question of legal ownership outside of śāstric regulation.

This section makes three arguments which relate to the way in which Mīmāṃsā theories of ownership influenced the development of a *Mitākṣarā* school of jurisprudence: 1) that as early as Śabara (fourth century CE) Mīmāṃsakas began to wrestle with the metaphysics of ownership; 2) that the Prābhākara-Mīmāṃsakas Prabhākara and Śālikanātha argued that ownership was characterized by moral *propriety* rather than practical *possession*; and 3) that although Viśvarūpa and Medhātithi sporadically employed these theories of ownership to address thorny legal conundrums, Vijñāneśvara was the first Dharmaśāstrin to extend their dual vision of ownership as puruṣārtha and extra-śāstric to the defence of ownership-by-birth.

Ownership in Śabara's *Bhāṣya*

A close examination of Śabarasvāmin's commentary on the *Mīmāṃsāsūtras*, the *Śābarabhāṣya*, militates against Kroll's assertion that:

> Śabara provides little insight into the meaning of svatva, and references to svatva by early commentators on his work are equally spare . . . the difficulty for him lies in ascertaining whether, and how, that saṃbandha should be created when the donee is not a real human being.[73]

Śabara mentions svatva explicitly in six places in the *Śābarabhāṣya*—all in relation to giving (dāna) or to sacrificing (yāga/tyāga)—but he never provides a

[72] See Kroll, 'A Logical Approach to Law', p. 37, where he identifies Pārthasārathimiśra as making 'a regressive move'.

[73] Kroll, 'A Logical Approach to Law', p. 29.

clear definition of the term.[74] We can, however, reconstruct a consistent understanding of the conceptual content of Śabara's theory of ownership—as a fitness for use as desired—through a reading of how Śabara analyses three instances of ownership; the acquisition of assets, divine ownership, and the limits of 'giving all' in the Viśvajit sacrifice. Śabara is the earliest known śāstrin to understand ownership in terms of an extra-śāstrically established fitness for use as desired, and that Śabara laid the foundation for the subsequent development in Prābhākara-Mīmāṃsā treatises of a theory of ownership that served as the cornerstone of the *Mitākṣarā* school of inheritance.

Śabara hints at his understanding of svatva in the fourth adhyāya of the *Mīmāṃsāsūtras*, where he examines the distinction between those activities whose primary purpose is the support of the Vedic ritual (kratvartha) and those activities whose primary purpose is the pleasure of people (puruṣārtha).[75] Śabara's most important argument in defence of the acquisition of assets as puruṣārtha—that if ownership existed merely for the purpose of conducting sacrifices, there would be no ownership outside of a ritual context—concerns, implicitly, the issue of the fundamental nature of ownership itself.[76] In brief, one might wonder whether ownership is inherently a ritual activity given that the performance of the ritual itself depends on (owned) assets.[77] Śabara flips the script on his opponent and argues that if the acquisition of assets were kratvartha then there could be no sacrifice at all:

[74] Ibid., pp. 28–9: According to Kroll the six places are: ŚB on MS 2.2.1, 3.3.44, 4.1.30, 4.2.28, 6.7.1–2, and 10.3.50.

[75] *Mīmāṃsādarśana*, vol. 4, ed. V. G. Apte (Pune: Anandashrama Press, 1932), p. 1193, Ms 4.1.1: athātaḥ kratvarthapuruṣārthayor jijñāsā. Śabara frames this distinction as a question of *motive*, i.e. why an individual would choose to carry out a particular Vedically prescribed command (vidhi). Ibid., p. 1194, Ms 4.1.2, defines puruṣārtha as: yasmin prītīḥ puruṣasya tasya lipsārthalakṣaṇāvibhaktatvāt. Ganganatha Jha, in *Śābarabhāṣya*, vol. 2 (Baroda: Baroda Oriental Institute, 1934), p. 709, translates this as: 'that upon which follows the happiness of man; because its undertaking is due to the man's desire to obtain happiness and [the man's purpose] is not different [from happiness]'. Śabara adds that such actions proceed exclusively from an (extra-śāstric) desire for benefit rather than from a śāstric injunction. Śabara defines kratvārtha as the opposite to puruṣārtha and argues that kratvartha activities are known *only* from the śāstra, i.e. the Vedas. See *Mīmāṃsādarśana*, vol. 4, p. 1194, Śb on MS 4.1.2: tasya lipsārthalakṣaṇā. tasya lipsārthenaiva bhavati, na śāstreṇa. kratvartho hi śāstrād avagamyate, nānyathā . . . puruṣārthe lakṣite, tadviparitaḥ kratvartha iti kratvarthasya lakṣaṇaṃ siddham. The basic distinction is that some actions, such as pouring ghee into a fire at a particular time or invoking a particular devatā in a ritual, are enjoined by the Veda without reference to a particular 'fruit' (phala). Sometimes a sacrificer is ordered to invoke a devatā or press Soma at a specific juncture *merely because it is enjoined by the Veda*. At other times, an activity—such as acquiring assets or having children—has a patently obvious reward for the person who performs it.

[76] *Mīmāṃsādarśana*, vol. 4, p. 1197: Śb on Ms 4.1.2.2: atha yad uktam, niyamavacanam anarthakam, puruṣārthe dravyaparigrahe satīti. ucyate . . . na ca parokṣam pratyakṣasya bādhakam bhavati. The issue for Śābara is that the pūrvapakṣin must indirectly postulate (parokṣam yuktibuddhyā) a reason for the acquisition of assets. This is, in Śābara's estimation, insufficient to displace the visible pleasure which assets bring to individuals.

[77] Ibid., pp. 1195–6: tasmād yajatiśrutigṛhītaṃ dravyārjanaṃ yena vinā yāgo nivartate, sa yāgasya śrutyā parigṛhīta iti gamyate. tasmāt kratvartha iti.

> And further, if the acquisition of assets is for the sake of the sacrifice because of the śāstra, then it (a given asset), so acquired, could not be used (viniyujyeta) anywhere else (i.e. in any non-ritual way). Then there would be the complete elision of all sacrifices.[78]

Śabara's comments imply a connection between ownership and use—where the key word is the optative of the root √yuj, 'to use'. Śabara makes this connection explicit in the ninth adhyāya of the *Mīmāṃsāsūtras* where he argues against the view that the Gods might have ownership.[79] Śabara argues that phrases such as 'the deity's village' or 'the deity's field' must be understood as figurative usages of the word 'the deity's'.[80] Śabara invokes what appears to be a maxim concerning what qualifies as one's property:

> Something is someone's property (when) someone is eligible to use it as desired. And a deity does not use a village or a field as it desires. Therefore, one can't say 'he bestows (ownership on the deity)'. That which is abandoned, having been offered to the deity, however, becomes the wages of the deity's attendants.[81]

One might argue that deities can make use of their assets through temple priests who act in accordance with the deity's wishes.[82] Śabara's response offers the most concrete definition of what constitutes a proprietary relation:

> This is not right; what is vouched for by direct Perception is that the things are used according to the wish of the Temple-priests themselves... In fact, even those who speak of the Deities as possessing the things, do not deny the will of the Priests (as determining the actual use of the things); in fact, they themselves say that 'the Deity does as the attendant priests desire'; and that person who

[78] Ibid., p. 1196: api ca, yadi śāstrāt karmārtham dravyārjanam, tan nānyatra viniyujyeta tathārjitam. tatra sarvatantraparilopaḥ syāt.

[79] *Mīmāṃsādarśana*, vol. 5, p. 1651: Śb on Ms 9.1.7: ārthapatyā ca. evaṃ hi smaranti. arthānām īṣṭe devateti. tathā, devagrāmo devakṣetram ity upacāras tām eva smṛtim draḍhayati. Cf, S. C. Bagchi, *Juristic Personality of Hindu Deities* (Calcutta: University of Calcutta, 1931), p. 70. For Mīmāṃsā theories of God, see Francis X. Clooney, 'Why the Veda Has No Author: Language as Ritual in Early Mīmāṃsā and Post-Modern Theology', *Journal of the American Academy of Religion* 55.4 (1987): 659–84; and Francis X. Clooney, 'What's a God? The Quest for the Right Understanding of *Devatā* in Brāhmaṇical Ritual Theory (*Mīmāṃsā*)', *International journal of Hindu Studies* 1.2 (1997): 337–85.

[80] *Mīmāṃsādarśana*, vol. 5, p. 1656: Śb on MS 9.1.9: upacāro 'pi devagrāmo devakṣetram ity upacāramātram.

[81] Ibid.: yo yad abhipretam viniyoktum arhati tat tasya svam. na ca grāmam kṣetram vā yathābhiprāyam viniyuṅkte devatā. tasmān na saṃprayacchatīti. devaparicārakāṇāṃ tu tato bhṛtir bhavati, devatām uddiśya yat tyaktam.

[82] Ganganatha Jha, trans., *Śābarabhaṣya*, vol. 5, p. 1436; *Mīmāṃsādarśana*, vol. 5, p. 1656: Śb on Ms 9.1.9: yad eva lokā arthān viniyuñjate, tad devatābhiprāyād evety adhyavasyāma iti.

follows the will of another and who cannot make use of the things according to his own desire cannot be the owner of those things.[83]

In the seventh pāda of the sixth adhyāya of the *Mīmāṃsāsūtras*, Śabara discusses the Viśvajit sacrifice, in which one is enjoined to give away all one's property without exception.[84] Śabara argues that proprietary svatva extends only to that which one has under their dominion (prabhutva).[85] Although one could not give one's parents as parents to another person—in the sense of ending his filial relationship and creating another's filial relationship—one could give one's parents as servants.[86] Śabara concedes the alienability of one's relatives in the capacity of a servant, but he argues that such a practice is 'illegal', or 'inappropriate' (na nyāyya).[87] Śabara's comments imply a distinction between two kinds of svatva—that svatva which denotes a filial relationship and that svatva which denotes a proprietary relationship. Śabara's distinction between family as family and family as property would have been relevant in ancient India in which epigraphical and Dharmaśāstra records suggest that fathers sometimes sold their wives, sons, and daughters as property, but not the other way around.[88]

Śabara's thoughts on ownership illuminate four essential points that are significant for the later intellectual history of ownership that developed in Mīmāṃsā and Dharmaśāstra literature. First, Śabara is probably the first śāstrin to introduce a comprehensive, if often implicit, understanding of ownership as a relationship (sambandha) between an owner (svāmin) and property (sva), characterized as an eligibility (arhatā) to be used (√yuj) as desired (yadabhipreta). Second, usability is subject to practical and moral limitations: one cannot give away a familial relationship and one should surely not give away one's family members in the capacity of slaves. Third, śāstric rules governing the acquisition of ownership have an invisible, moral force rather than a visible, legal force. All three concepts received extended treatment by later Mīmāṃsakas and were of great utility in

[83] Ganganatha Jha, trans., *Śābarabhāṣya*, vol. 4, p. 1436; *Mīmāṃsādarśana*, vol. 5, p. 1656: Śb on Ms 9.1.9: tan na. pratyakṣāt pramāṇād devatāparicārakāṇāṃ abhiprāya ity avagamyate. sa na śakyo bādhitum. ye 'pi devatām īśānām varṇayanti, te 'pi nāpahnuvate paricārakāṇām abhiprāyo bhavatīti. na ceśāno bhavati yaḥ parābhiprāyam anurudhyate, yasya na svābhiprāyād viniyogo bhavati.

[84] *Mīmāṃsādarśana*, vol. 4, p. 1492, MS 6.7.1: svadāne sarvam aviśeṣāt.

[85] Ibid. p. 1493, MS 6.7.2: yasya vā prabhūḥ svād itarasyāśakyatvāt.

[86] Ibid. p. 1492: nanu dānam ity ucyate svatvanivṛttiḥ, parasvatvāpādanam ca. tatra pitrādīnām aśakyam svatvam nivartayitum. na hi kathaṃcit pitā na pitā bhavati. ucyate. satyam nāsau na pitā bhavati. śakyate tu paravidheyaḥ kartum. parasvatvāpādanam ca dānam dadāter arthaḥ.

[87] Ibid. p. 1493: na caitan nyāyyam, yat pitrādīnām paricārakatvam.

[88] See Nirmal Chandra Chatterjee, 'Patria Potestas in Ancient India', *Proceedings and Transactions of the All-India Oriental Conference* (AIOC), vol. 2 (Calcutta: University of Calcutta, 1922): pp. 365–7; J. Duncan Derrett, 'Prohibition and Nullity: Indian Struggles with a Jurisprudential Lacuna', *Bulletin of the School of Oriental and African Studies* 20 (1957): 203–15, 206, fn 1; and J. Duncan Derrett, 'An Indian Contribution to the Study of Property', *Bulletin of the School of Oriental and African Studies* 18 (1956): 475–98, 492, fn 4.

the unfolding of the Dharmaśāstra debate concerning ownership in general and inheritance in particular.

Even if Śabara does not offer an explicit definition of ownership or svasvāmisambandha in the *Bhāṣya*, his formulation, 'yo yadabhipretam viniyoktum arhati tat tasya svam' is, in practice, a definition of ownership. If so, Śabara's proto-yatheṣṭaviniyoga understanding of svatva is the earliest attested instance of such a concept in Sanskrit. Kroll supposes that the earliest formulation of such a theory is found in the work of Vācaspatimiśra the first (ninth century CE), but Śabara's comments push such a date back by at least four centuries—and indicate that Vācaspatimiśra I may well have borrowed his definition from the Mīmāṃsā tradition.[89]

Theories of Ownership in Prābhākara-Mīmāṃsā Writings

A survey of the next layer of Mīmāṃsā discussion concerning ownership—Prabhākara's *Bṛhatī* and Śālikanātha's *Ṛjuvimalāpañcikā*—addresses two of Kroll and Derrett's largest misconceptions about the development of the Miṃāṃsā theory of ownership.[90] Derrett and Kroll characterize the Mīmāṃsā as advocating a regressive theory of ownership as mere possession. Derrett frames Vijñāneśvara's theory of ownership as the move of a Brāhmaṇa 'pathetically keen' to prove the validity of his community's often questionable titles to assets.[91] Derrett states boldly:

> Following Prabhākara . . . Vijñāneśvara and his followers, with slight demur, in their eagerness to quieten anxiety as to titles commit themselves to the proposition that the ultimate source of information on the validity of acquisitions is popular recognition: a conclusion which we cannot but deplore, especially when we bear in mind specific instances of the conflict between justice, law and common practice in such matters as tax evasion.[92]

[89] Kroll, 'A Logical Approach to Law', pp. 36–7: Kroll admits that Vācaspatimiśra, 'provides no indication as to the source of yatheṣṭaviniyogayogyatva, and it is entirely possible his usage reflects a phrase common to contemporary scholarly parlance'. I suggest that the earliest attestation of such scholarly parlance is Śabara's *bhāṣya*.

[90] For an overview of the difference between these schools, see Ganganatha Jha, *Pūrvamīmāṃsā in its Sources* (Benares: Benares Hindu University, 1942); and Ganganatha Jha, *The Prābhākara School of Pūrva Mīmāṃsā* (Allahabad: University of Allahabad, 1911). For an overview of the historical evolution of Mīmāṃsā, see Jean-Marie Verpoorten, *Mīmāṃsā Literature* (Wiesbaden: O. Harrassowitz, 1987). For more recent work on the school, see Elisa Freschi, *Duty, Language and Exegesis in Prābhākara Mīmāṃsā: Including an Edition and Translation of Rāmānujācārya's Tantrarahasya Śāstraprameyaparicchedа* (Leiden: Brill, 2012).

[91] Derrett, 'The Right to Earn': 66–97, 84.

[92] Ibid., 85–7.

Kroll supports such a view implicitly when he contrasts Pārthasārathimiśra's definition of svatva as yatheṣṭavinijojyatva with Vācaspatimiśra I's definition of svatva as yatheṣṭaviniyogayogyatva.[93] Kroll argues that there is a:

> subtle, but vital, distinction. The term yogyatva (fitness) implies, as Vācaspati Miśra suggests, a notion of aucitya (propriety). Aucitya implies a system of laws, governance, or moral precepts to which action should conform. The risk, as Pārthasārathi would presumably acknowledge, is that aucitya inevitably restricts the use of assets to a particular sphere, namely, that sphere of activity deemed ucita (proper).[94]

Kroll foregrounds moral propriety (aucitya) as the primary concern of Nyāya and he identifies usability (yojyatva) as the primary concern of Mīmāṃsā.

Admittedly, the Bhāṭṭa school of Mīmāṃsā *appears* to take a morally regressive view of ownership as possession. While Kumārilabhaṭṭa has relatively little to say about the nature of ownership, his commentator, Pārthasārathimiśra (tenth century), offers a definition of ownership as an asset's usability as desired (yatheṣṭaviniyojyatva).[95] Pārthsārathimiśra argues that if we accept that ownership is an asset's usability as desired, and if the acquisition (and use) of assets existed solely for the sake of sacrifices, there would be no ownership because one could not use an asset as desired outside of the sacrificial context.[96] If there is no ownership, then there could not be a sacrifice because one could not give one's own assets.[97] Consequently, says Pārthasārathimiśra, a śāstric restriction on how one acquires assets is subordinate to the act of acquisition itself and it is fair to postulate sin on the part of a man who acquires assets through a non-śāstric means and oversteps said restriction.[98] Pārthasārathimiśra's definition is more ambiguous than Kroll might assert. Vijñāneśvara's followers argued that yatheṣṭaviniyojyatva and yatheṣṭaviniyogayogyatva amount to the same thing: an asset's moral fitness to be used by its owner.[99] Furthermore, the issue of ownership's philosophical nature does not seem to have become a point of contention between Prābhākara and Bhāṭṭa-Mīmāṃsakas in the centuries following Pārthasārathimiśra.

[93] Kroll, 'A Logical Approach to Law', pp. 37–9. [94] Ibid., p. 40.

[95] *Tantraratnam*, vol. 5, ed. Ganganatha Jha (Benares: Princess of Wales Sarasvati Bhavan Texts, No. 31, Part 1, 1930), p. 19: Tr on Tṭ on Ms 4.1.2: yatheṣṭaviniyojyatvam hi svatvam. Cf. Kroll, 'A Logical Approach to Law', p. 38. For the date of Pārthasārathimiśra, see Kroll, 'A Logical Approach to Law', p. 37; and Jean-Marie Verpoorten, *Mīmāṃsā Literature*, pp. 41–2.

[96] *Tantraratnam*, vol. 5, p. 19: Tr on Tṭ on Ms 4.1.2: kevalakratvarthatve tv anyatrāviniyogād yatheṣṭaviniyojyatvābhāvāt svatvābhāva iti. Cf. Kroll, 'A Logical Approach to Law', pp. 38–9.

[97] *Tantraratnam*, vol. 5, p. 19: Tr on Tṭ on Ms 4.1.2: svīyadravyābhāvāt parityāgo nāstīti kratuvighātaḥ syāt.

[98] Ibid.: Tr on Tṭ on Ms 4.1.2: evam ca niyamasyārjanāṅgatvāt tadatikrame puruṣasyopāyāntareṇārjane pratyavāyaḥ kalpyate. Cf. Kroll, 'A Logical Approach to Law', p. 39.

[99] See Madanasiṃha's arguments in 'Vijñāneśvara's Successors', below.

In either case, a definition of ownership in terms of eligibility (arhatā) arose in the commentarial tradition of the Prābhākara school of Mīmāṃsā. Prabhākara himself says little about of ownership.[100] Prabhākara makes two contributions: a statement that '"acquisition does not produce ownership" is incoherent', and a defence of ownership as a singular entity.[101] Like Pārthasārathimiśra, Prabhākara insists that overstepping śāstric restrictions on how one acquires assets will create a blemish for the acquirer but will not create a blemish for the sacrifice (that requires legal ownership on the part of the sacrificer/acquirer).[102]

Śālikanātha (tenth century), author of the *Ṛjuvimalāpañcikā*, a commentary on Prabhākara's *Bṛhatī*, presents one of the first comprehensive models of ownership in Mīmāṃsā literature.[103] The *Ṛjuvimalāpañcikā* is probably the missing link between Śabara's nascent definition of ownership as a fitness for use as desired and Bhavanātha's definition of ownership in the *Mīmāṃsānayaviveka* as an eligibility for use as desired. Śālikanātha's innovations are threefold: he defines ownership as eligibility for use as desired (yatheṣṭaviniyogārhatā); he introduces the theory of ownership-by-birth; and he applies his theory of ownership to the problem of the Viśvajit sacrifice. Śālikanātha provides, arguably the first proper definition of ownership when he notes that 'it has been stated by the blessed commentator (Śabarasvāmin)—"yo yad yathābhiprāyam viniyoktum arhati tat tasya svam"'.[104] Śālikanātha argues that what Śabara means to say is that ownership is an eligibility (arhatā) for use as desired and not the mere use of an object as desired. After all, such a definition would over-extend to objects obtained through violent force, and would fail to extend to the assets of infants, lunatics and others who lack the legal capacity to engage in commercial transactions.[105]

Śālikanātha gives the earliest account of the doctrine of ownership-by-birth in Mīmāṃsā literature. He states that 'acquisition is of manifold form, sometimes (for example) birth, as in the case of paternal assets'.[106] Śālikanātha's defence of ownership-by-birth is linked to a theory of ownership in which the modes of

[100] For Prabhākara, see Verpoorten, *Mīmāṃsā Literature*, pp. 31–4.

[101] *Bṛhatī of Prabhākaramiśra with the Ṛjuvimalā of Śālikanātha*, vol. 4, ed. S. Subrahmanyan Shastri (Madras: University of Madras Press, 1964), p. 962, Bṛ on Śb on Ms 4.1.2: arjanam svatvam nāpādayatīti vipratiṣiddham; ibid., pp. 961–2: atrocyate neme adhikāraśūnyā niyamavidhayaś śakyante vaktum. jīvanāya pravṛttā adhikṛtā bhaviṣyanti. na ca śabdād evādhikāraḥ adhikārād eva hy adhikāraḥ. sa tu kvacit chabdāvagamyaḥ kvacit pramāṇāntarāvagamyaḥ. ataḥ svatvasyāviśeṣāt sarvapuruṣārthanirvṛttau na viśeṣaś śakyate 'vadhārayitum. Prabhākara's pūrvapakṣin argues that there might be two svatvas because there are two reasons why one might be qualified to acquire assets: for personal support and for sacrifices. Prabhākara says that this is untenable.

[102] Ibid., p. 965: tasmāt puruṣārthā dravyārjananiyamā iti sthitam. ato niyamātikramaḥ puruṣasyānarthaḥ na kratoḥ.

[103] On Śālikanātha, see Verpoorten, *Mīmāṃsā Literature*, pp. 38–9.

[104] *Ṛjuvimalā*, p. 962: uktam hi **bhagavatā bhāṣyakāreṇa** yo yad yathābhiprāyam viniyoktum arhati tat tasya svam.

[105] Ibid., p. 962: atrāyam bhāvaḥ—na yatheṣṭaviniyoganibandhanam svatvam balātkārahṛteṣu atiprasaṅgat. bālādidhaneṣu aprasaṅgāc ca.

[106] Ibid.: arjanam ca nānārūpam kvacij janma, yathā paitṛkeṣu.

acquiring assets are known from extra-śāstric usage: 'eligibility exists for someone when acceptance and the like, which are the means of obtaining ownership and which are established in the extra-śāstric world, are undertaken'.[107] Śālikanātha adds that one should infer that sometimes marriage is the cause of the production of ownership in the case of the joint assets of a husband and wife.[108] It is likely that Śālikanātha was aware of Dharmaśāstric texts or of floating maxims which assume such a theory of acquisition (from birth or marriage) and that his inference in the *Ṛjuvimalāpañcikā* is an attempt to explain the apparent existence of a proprietary relationship in those instances without recourse to the formal lists of modes of acquisition in Gautama or Manu.

For example, when Śālikanātha comments on the giving of 'the earth' in the Viśvajit sacrifice in the sixth adhyāya of the *Mīmāṃsāsūtras*, he argues that one cannot possibly give the entire globe, endowed with pastures, highways, water and the like.[109] However, ownership is extra-śāstric and people *can* give a village and when they give a village, they are really giving the houses and fields which are delimited by the phrase, 'a village'.[110] Śālikanātha does not elaborate on the significance of his phrase 'laukikam ca svatvam'. What the phrase seems to imply, in the context of the debate concerning the giving of 'the earth', is that local convention dictates that people have a right to come and go (and draw water, etc.) in common, public spaces.

This raises the question: what is the purpose of śāstric restrictions on ownership if the ways of acquiring ownership are determined from extra-śāstric practice? For Śālikanātha, Dharmaśāstrins use the modes of acquiring assets that are established from extra-śāstric usage in order to ward off confusion 'as in the case of Vyākaraṇa and the like'.[111] Śālikanātha seems to imply that, like grammar, Dharmaśāstra draws upon the collective practices of people outside of the Veda and selects some of these practices for particular praise and some of these practices for censure.

Śālikanātha's *Ṛjuvimalāpañcikā* marks a decisive change in the scale of Mīmāṃsā texts addressing ownership: he frames Śabara's comments on ownership in term of *eligibility*—moral propriety—and he introduces extra-śāstric convention as the standard by which legal ownership is determined. Śālikanātha's comments are sparse and their implications would be developed by later Dharmaśāstrins and Mīmāṃsakas.

[107] Ibid.: tena yatheṣṭaviniyogārhatayā svatvam, tadarhatā ca tatra tasya yatra pratigrahādayo loke prasiddhā upāyāḥ pravṛttāḥ.

[108] Ibid.: kvacit pariṇayaḥ yathā daṃpatyoḥ dhanam ity evamādiṣūhanīyam. For the idea that ownership is equal between husbands and wives, see Sontheimer, *The Joint Hindu Family*, pp. 11–14.

[109] *Ṛjuvimalā of Śālikanātha*, vol. 5, p. 194: Ṛj on Bṛ on Śb on Ms 6.7.2: bhūgolakam gopatharājamārgajalādisamanvitam kṛtsnam eva dātum na śakyate...

[110] Ibid.: laukikam ca svatvam. ye tu grāmādikam dadati te 'pi vāstukṣetrādikam eva dadatīti mantavyam. grāmas tu tadavacchedaka iti niravadyam.

[111] *Ṛjuvimalā*, vol. 4, p. 962, Ṛj on Bṛ on Śb on Ms 4.1.2: **smṛtikārāś** ca lokaprasiddhopāyam eva kurvate vyāmohanivṛttaye **vyākaraṇādivat**.

Mīmāṃsā in Pre-*Mitākṣarā* Dharmaśāstra Commentary

One of the most distinctive elements of the *Mitākṣarā*'s defence of ownership-by-birth is its foregrounding of Prabhākara's arguments that śāstric restrictions governing the acquisition of assets are puruṣārtha and that the sources of ownership (including birth) are established by extra-śāstric practice. While Viśvarūpa and Medhātithi make sporadic but non-negligible references to Mīmāṃsā, Vijñāneśvara's invocation of Prabhākara (and implicitly Śālikanātha) ties into the broader argument that the *Mitākṣarā* marks a turning point in history of Dharmaśāstra. Rather than cite the odd aphorism, Vijñāneśvara foregrounds the Mīmāṃsā theory of ownership as extra-śāstric, follows the *Ṛjuvimalāpañcikā*'s considerations of theft and implicitly adopts the definition of ownership as an eligibility for use as desired. Vijñāneśvara's innovation of reading Prābhākara commentaries on M.S. 4.1.2 in conjunction with discussions of inheritance became the standard approach for most subsequent Dharmaśāstrins.

Viśvarūpa invokes Śabara's characterization of the rules governing the acquisition of assets as puruṣārtha in a comment on Yāj. 2.144. Yāj 2.144 gives a list of persons excluded from inheritance: the impotent, outcasts, an outcast's son, the lame, lunatics, an idiot and those suffering from incurable diseases.[112] Viśvarūpa comments that some would argue that 'lame' and other terms figuratively denote all individuals who are ineligible to perform Vedic rites such as the Agnihotra.[113] Viśvarūpa argues that this cannot be correct because assets are puruṣārtha.[114] Indeed, we can observe that even unlearned, ritually ineligible individuals are capable of (using) assets.[115] The opponent's argument—that a deformed person is not entitled to a share of inheritance because he is not eligible to perform sacrifices—relies on an implicit assumption that ownership is limited to the sphere of ritual activity. Viśvarūpa hints at how this theory of ownership might apply to inheritance. He records 'the traditional belief' (sampradāya) is that there is a relationship (sambandha) between un-outcast but ritually ineligible sons and the assets of their grandfathers.[116] However, Yāj. 2.144 must be taken as an illustration of the inappropriateness of such sons using those assets for anything other than their maintenance.[117]

Medhātithi's *Bhāṣya* demonstrates a more developed use of Mīmāṃsā than Viśvarūpa's *Bālakrīḍā*. Medhātithi argues that if sons were to force their father to

[112] *Bālakrīḍā*, p. 253: klībo 'tha patitas tajjaḥ paṅgur unmattako jaḍaḥ / andha 'cikitsyarogādyā bhartavyāḥ syur niraṅśakāḥ //Yājñavalkya 2.144//.

[113] Ibid.: paṅgavādivacanāny agnihotrādyanadhikṛtānām sarveṣām upalakṣaṇārthānīti kecit.

[114] Ibid.: tad asat puruṣārthatvād dravyasya.

[115] Ibid.: avaidyasya cānadhikṛtasyaiva dravyārhatvadarśanāt.

[116] Ibid.: pitāmahadravyasambandhas tv apatitānām andhādīnām asty eveti sampradāyaḥ.

[117] Ibid.: samarthyenaiva tu bharaṇamātrātirikthadravyaviniyogāśakter aucityānuvādo 'yam ity avaseyam.

partition paternal assets, then that would be like someone who receives improper gifts—there would be ownership, but there would also be sin on the part of the son.[118] The phrase 'there would ownership but there would also be a moral blemish on the part of the person' might well reflect an awareness of Prabhākara on Medhātithi's part.[119] In a series of verses delineating the rights and duties of individuals in regard to slaves (śūdras and dāsas), Medhātithi draws a contrast between *independence* (svātantrya) and *ownership* (svāmya) and argues that 'since it is called "*their* assets" (svadhana) slaves (and sons and wives) *do* have ownership in their own assets'.[120] The core of Medhātithi's argument is Prabhākara's statement in the *Bṛhatī* that '"acquisition does not produce ownership" is incoherent'.[121] For, as Medhātithi argues, such a proposition would be as ridiculous as saying 'the woman whose son I am is not my mother'.[122]

Medhātithi displays an awareness of Śabara's views on ownership in two passages which delimit the legal facts of property: discussions of 'gods' property' (devasva) and the gift of earth (bhūdāna). Medhātithi argues that one might concede that popular usage might speak of some assets as 'gods' property', but it is not possible for these assets to exist in a proprietary relationship with a particular god because:

> of the impossibility of the gods' svasvāmisambandha in the primary sense (of the word). For the gods do not use an asset as they please. Nor are they seen to guard (their property). And such (use and protection) is how property is defined in extra-śāstric usage.[123]

Medhātithi's reference to the lack of use as desired refers clearly to the *Śābarabhāṣya*.[124] Medhātithi's repeated use of the word 'sambandha', particularly the svasvāmisambandha, may well reflect an awareness of Śālikanātha's explicit use of that term to characterize ownership. Medhātithi also appears to rely on Śālikanātha's *Ṛjuvimalāpañcikā* when the former discusses private ownership of

[118] See notes 50, 51, and 52. [119] See note 102.

[120] *The Laws of Manu with the Bhāṣya of Medhātithi*, vol. 5, p. 434; *Manubhāṣya*, vols 2–3, p. 239: bhāryā putraś ca dāsaś ca traya evādhanāḥ smṛtāḥ / yat te samadhigacchanti yasya te tasya tad dhanam //Manu 8.416// asti tāvad dāsānāṃ svadhane svāmyam, yadā svadhanam iti vyapadiśyate. atrocyate. pāratantryavidhānam etat. asatyām bhartur anujñāyām na strībhiḥ svātantryeṇa yatra kvacid dhanam viniyoktavyam. evam putradāsayor api draṣṭavyam.

[121] See note 101.

[122] *The Laws of Manu with the Bhāṣya of Medhātithi*, vol. 5, p. 434; *Manubhāṣya*, vols 2–3, 8.416, p. 239: yathā kaś cit brūyād yasyā aham putraḥ sā na mama jananīti tādṛg etat.

[123] *Manubhāṣya*, vols 2–3, pp. 375–6 (on 11.25): atha samācārato devasvam bhavatu, svasvāmibhāvas tāvan nāsti... devān uddiśya yāgādikriyārtham dhanam yad utsṛṣṭam tad devasvam. mukhyasya svasvāmisambandhasya devānām asambhavāt. na hi devatā icchayā dhanam niyuñjate. na ca paripālanavyāpāras tāsām dṛśyate. svam ca loke tādṛśam ucyate. tasmād devoddeśena yad uktam nedam mama devatāyā idam iti tad devasvam; Cf. S. C. Bagchi, *The Juristic Personality of Hindu Deities* (Calcutta: University of Calcutta Press, 1933), pp. 71–4.

[124] See note 81.

'the earth'. The question for Medhātithi concerns what precisely is entailed in land ownership. Much of Medhātithi's argument occurs in the *Bṛhatī* as read through the *Ṛjuvimalāpañcikā* rather than through Śabara or Kumārila.[125] Medhāthti writes:

> As for the Mīmāṃsakas' statement that one cannot give the earth in the Viśvajit sacrifice, namely, 'the earth is not (to be given) because it is common to all', that applies to the globe (rather than fields and the like). For the earth is common to all people in the sense that they can do such things as walk about on it.[126]

Vijñāneśvara's Consolidation of Prābhākara-Mīmāṃsā Theories

One of Vijñāneśvara's boldest innovation is his explicit invocation of Prabhākara's *Bṛhatī*. Prabhākara, following Śabara, concludes that the restrictions on the acquisition of assets (listed in Gautama, Manu and other smṛtis) are puruṣārtha and that overstepping those restrictions will harm a person, but not the ritual act (in which said asset is used).[127] Vijñāneśvara—defending the position that ownership-by-birth accords with an extra-śāstric theory of ownership—notes that 'the Mīmāṃsakas [lit. Nyāyavids] believe that ownership acquired through restricted methods is established extra-śāstrically'.[128] Vijñāneśvara invokes the opinion of 'the master' (guru) Prabhākara:

> For it has been said in the *Lipsāsūtra* in the third varṇaka: 'if restrictions on the acquisition of assets were kratvartha, there would be no ownership because ownership would be śāstric (or, established in a non-wordly way)'. Having entertained this objection to the very possibility of the prima-facie opinion [expressed in the Lipsasutra], the Guru vindicates it in the following way: 'that the acquisition of assets through acceptance, etc., brings about ownership is established extra-śāstrically'. (The Guru) says: 'if the acquisition of assets were kratvartha, there would certainly be no ownership, and the ritual would certainly not occur. As someone has said: "acquisition does not produce ownership" is incoherent'.[129]

[125] See notes 109 and 110.

[126] *Manubhāṣya of Medhātithi*, vols 2–3, pp. 115–16 (on 8.99): kṛtsnagolakābhiprāyam eva cādeyatvam bhūmer viśvajiti mīmāṃsakair uktam, 'na bhūmiḥ syāt sarvān pratyaviśiṣṭatvād iti (*Śābarabhāṣya* on 6.3.3)'. sarvān puruṣān praticaṅkramaṇādiyogyatayāviśiṣṭatā bhūmir.

[127] See note 102.

[128] *Mitākṣarā*, 2.168, p. 281: niyatopāyakam svatvam lokasiddham eveti nyāyavido manyante.

[129] *Mitākṣarā*, 2.114, p. 281: tathāhi **lipsāsūtre tṛtīye varṇake** dravyārjananiyamānām kratvarthatve svatvam eva na syāt svatvasyālaukikatvād iti pūrvapakṣāsaṃbhavam āśaṅkya dravyārjanasya pratigrahādinā svatvasādhanatvam lokasiddham iti pūrvapakṣaḥ samarthito **guruṇā**—nanu ca dravyārjanasya kratvarthatve svatvam eva na bhavatīti yāga eva na samvarteta pralapitam idam kenāpi 'arjanam svatvam nāpādayati' iti vipratiṣiddham iti vadatā. Cf. note 101.

Vijñāneśvara uses this argument to support his contention that because ownership is an extra-śāstric matter and, because, lay convention recognizes birth as a source of acquiring ownership, sons must have a proprietary interest in their patrilineal estate from birth. The second argument from the *Bṛhatī*, which Vijñāneśvara lifts verbatim, is the conclusion (siddhānta): that 'a breach of a restriction (on acquisition) affects the individual, not the ritual'.[130] Indeed, Vijñāneśvara's next argument, identified as an 'elaboration' (vivṛta) of the previous opinion cuts to the core of the issue:

> In the prima-facie opinion, when restrictions on the acquisition of assets are kratvartha, then rituals would be accomplished only through assets acquired according to these restrictions (and) not through assets acquired in contravention of these restrictions. Nor would there be sin for a man who oversteps these restrictions. But, in truth, because a restriction on acquisition is puruṣārtha, a ritual becomes complete even through assets acquired in contravention of that restriction (and) there is indeed the blemish of violating a restriction on the part of the person (who acquired assets in contravention of the restriction). Thus, ownership is accepted even for someone who acquired (some property) in contravention of restrictions.[131]

For Vijñāneśvara, unlike Viśvarūpa and Medhātithi, the twinned theories of ownership as extra-śāstric and the restrictions governing its acquisition as puruṣārtha are central to the case which he has been building about inheritance: even if birth as a source of ownership is extra-śāstric, there is no problem because the śāstra does not have sole authority over how one acquires ownership.

Prabhākara, however, only claims that the restrictions regulating the acquisition of assets are puruṣārtha, i.e., performed with a motivation regarding the individual. A restriction being puruṣārtha and ownership being extra-śāstric are not synonymous. Vijñāneśvara goes far beyond Prabhākara's sparse comments in the *Bṛhatī*. Indeed, scholars, noting that Vijñāneśvara's elaboration (vivṛta) does not appear in Prabhākara's *Bṛhatī*, have wondered from where it might have come.[132] Given Śālikanātha's endorsement of ownership-by-birth, it seems likely that Vijñāneśvara relies on the view of the first known Mīmāṃsaka who also endorses

[130] *Mitākṣarā*, p. 281: tathā siddhānte 'pi svatvasya laukikatvam aṅgīkṛtyaiva vicāraprayojanam uktam ato niyamātikramaḥ puruṣasya na kratoḥ iti. Cf. Bṛ on Śb on Ms 4.1.2 cited in note 102.

[131] *Mitākṣarā*, p. 281: asya cārtha evam vivṛtaḥ . . . yadā dravyārjananiyamānām kratvarthatvam tadā niyamārjitenaiva dravyeṇa kratusiddhir na niyamātikramārjitena dravyeṇa na puruṣasya niyamātikramadoṣaḥ pūrvapakṣe. rāddhānte tv arjananiyamasya puruṣārthatvāt tadatikrameṇārjitenāpi dravyeṇa kratusiddhir bhavati, puruṣasyaiva niyamātikramadoṣa iti niyamātikramārjitasyāpi svatvam aṅgīkṛtam.

[132] Rosane Rocher and Ludo Rocher, 'Ownership by Birth' p. 253 fn 24: 'Although this 'elaboration' does not appear in the *Bṛhatī*, the *Subodhinī* and the *Bālambhaṭṭī* attribute it the guru (vivṛto guruṇeti śeṣaḥ). Mitramiśra's digest, the *Vyavahāraprakāśa*, which cites the passage, attributes it to a commentator (ṭīkākṛt). It is not part of the *Ṛjuvimalāpañcikā*, Śālikanātha's commentary on the *Bṛhaṭī*'.

the view that the accomplishment of ownership is extra-śāstric—Śālikanātha. Vijñāneśvara appears to assume Śālikanātha's interpretation of this passage of the *Bṛhatī*.[133] This may seem to be a small distinction, but Vijñāneśvara's defence of ownership as extra-śāstric—in conjunction with an interpretation of the restrictions on acquisition as puruṣārtha—allows us to locate him neatly within a specific level of commentarial development in the Mīmāṃsā tradition: namely, in Śālikanātha's dramatic expansion of Prabhākara's ideas in the *Bṛhatī*.

Furthermore, Vijñāneśvara expands on both of these topics in the inheritance section of the *Mitākṣarā*.[134] What is noticeably absent from the *Mitākṣarā* is any definition of ownership. The closest Vijñāneśvara gets to defining ownership are his comments that 'if the way in which an item is acquired—by purchase, etc.—is in question, the person who owns it is in question as well' and that '(a piece of gold, etc.) does not accomplish purchase, etc., by means of its golden form, etc., but, rather, by means of ownership. For, that which is not someone's property cannot accomplish an activity such as purchase for him'.[135] One might suspect that in arguing that ownership accomplishes sale Vijñāneśvara adopts Pārthasārathimiśra or Śabara's view of ownership as possession, yatheṣṭaviniyojyatva. This would be incorrect, however, because Vijñāneśvara is concerned, explicitly, with distinguishing between possession and ownership—between usability and moral propriety. Vijñāneśvara's specific phrasing, 'na hi yasya yat svam na bhavati tat tasya krayādyarthakriyām sādhayati', evokes Śabara and Śālikanātha's definition of ownership as an eligibility for use as desired when extra-śāstrically established acts of acquisition such as acceptance are undertaken. For Vijñāneśvara, as for Śālikanātha, it is an extra-śāstrically recognized act of acquisition which makes an asset one's property and that asset fit for use in transactions.[136] It appears that Vijñāneśvara implicitly draws on Śālikanātha's definition of ownership as yatheṣṭaviniyogārhatā—a definition which Vijñāneśvara's followers make explicit.

Vijñāneśvara's theory that the causes of ownership are not restricted to śāstric passages depends, either implicitly or explicitly, on a series of arguments from Prābhākara-Mīmāṃsā texts concerning ownership and there are indications that Vijñāneśvara was working from Śālikanātha's *Ṛjuvimalāpañcikā* (the first Mīmāṃsā text known to explicitly mention birth as an extra-śāstrically established cause of ownership). Vijñāneśvara appears to have drawn on a quite sophisticated Mīmāṃsā theory of ownership which did not conceive of ownership as mere practical possession. Indeed, Vijñāneśvara was aware of the issue of moral propriety (evidenced by his discussion of theft) and was not content to free ownership from any legal constraints. Although Vijñāneśvara was not the first Dharmaśāstrin to use Śabara, Prabhākara and Śālikanātha's theories of ownership, he was the first to tie these theories to a model of inheritance. Vijñāneśvara's

[133] See notes 106–7. [134] See note 65. [135] See notes 67 and 68. [136] See note 107.

successors—those for and against ownership-by-birth—would frame their discussion of ownership by using Mīmāṃsā material from the Prābhākara school. In short, just as Vijñāneśvara marks a turning point in his *legal* approach to *inheritance* he also marks a turning point in the *pre-legal* approach to *ownership*.

The Medieval *Mitākṣarā* School

This section turns to the reception of the *Mitākṣarā* amongst later Dharmaśāstrins, examining how Vijñāneśvara's followers such as Devaṇṇabhaṭṭa (*Smṛticandrikā*, 1150–1225), Viśveśvara (*Subodhinī*, 1360–1390) and Madanasiṃha (*Madanaratnapradīpa* 1425–1450) copy an increasingly sophisticated philosophical analysis of svatva in Bhavanātha's *Mīmāṃsānayaviveka* (eleventh century). Devaṇṇabhaṭṭa, Viśveśvara, and Madanasiṃha augment Vijñāneśvara's arguments concerning ownership and inheritance by drawing on new arguments from the Prābhākara-Mīmāṃsā tradition. Specifically, they recalibrate the *Mīmāṃsānayaviveka*'s theory of ownership as yatheṣṭaviniyogārhatā to defend Vijñāneśvara's theories of ownership-by-birth and unobstructed inheritance. These later commentators pushed Vijñāneśvara's jurisprudence forward and placed the *Mitākṣarā* at the center of a distinctive cluster or legal and philosophical arguments—a school of thought.

Bhavanātha's *Mīmāṃsānayaviveka* systematizes earlier Mīmāṃsā theories of ownership and offers an early and sophisticated treatment of ownership that anticipates several arguments that defined Navya-Nyāya approaches to ownership. Furthermore, reading the *Mīmāṃsānayaviveka* in concert with earlier treatises from the Prābhākara-School reveals that, far from creating the definition of yatheṣṭaviniyogārhatā ex nihilo, Bhavanātha was merely expanding a consistent line of argumentation that traced its genesis to the *Śābarabhāṣya*. The *Mīmāṃsānayaviveka's* extensive discussion of moral propriety also dispels the cynicism with which the extra-śāstric theory of ownership is typically received in modern scholarship. Indeed, what Derrett sees as the fundamental flaw of Bhavanātha and Vijñāneśvara—namely, opening the potential sources of valid ownership to the norms of one's community without enabling thieves and other scoundrels—constitutes the framing question that defines the *Mitākṣarā*'s followers of Dharmaśāstra as a coherent school of jurisprudence.

Bhavanātha's *Mīmāṃsānayaviveka*: Mīmāṃsā's First Metaphysics of Ownership

Bhavanātha's eleventh-century *Mīmāṃsānayaviveka*, a commentary on the *Mīmāṃsāsūtras*, refines arguments developed in the Prābhākara school during the early medieval period. We know little about Bhavanātha's life and historical context. While a few arguments concerning ownership from the *Mīmāṃsānayaviveka* have received scholarly attention from Derrett, Kāṇe, and Rocher, these authors have limited their treatment to passages which appear in Dharmaśāstranibandhas such as the *Smṛticandrikā* and the *Madanaratnapradīpa*.[137] Bhavanātha's key arguments are expansions of Śālikanātha's sparse comments from the *Ṛjuvimalāpañcikā*. Bhavanātha defines ownership as 'eligibility for use as desired' (yatheṣṭaviniyogārhatā); theorizes that ownership is a relationship (sambandha) between an acquirer and an acquired asset; and supports an extra-śāstric theory of ownership with an appeal to śāstric grammar (Vyākaraṇa).

Bhavanātha argues that 'according to Śabara, ownership is not use as desired, but, rather, eligibility for use as desired (yatheṣṭaviniyogārhatā)'.[138] Bhavanātha quotes a maxim that the fact that 'whatever one has acquired is for his purposes'.[139] Glossing Śālikanātha, Bhavanātha explains that if acquisition was subordinate to the purposes of the sacrifice, then there would be no ownership, i.e., usability as desired (yatheṣṭaviniyojyam).[140] For Bhavanātha, this eligibility for use as desired is not produced from the śāstra or from sacrificial activities, but from manifold acts of acquisition, such as birth, that are established in the extra-śāstric world.[141]

While Śabara and Śālikanātha seem content with placing ownership outside the purview of sacrificial regulations and with leaving considerations of whether one is a legal owner to the Dharmaśāstrins, Bhavanātha engages in a lengthy discussion concerning the nature of ownership—employing various ontological categories. Bhavanātha argues that ownership is the relationship between an owner and their property (svasvāmisambandha) which is created, destroyed and transferred through legally valid acts of acquisition and alienation. Furthermore, he argues that his metaphysics are logically consistent and able to protect the ownership of children, the mentally infirm and other lawful owners from usurpation -arguments that may have diminished Derrett's dissatisfaction with the medieval Mīmāṃsā/Dharmaśāstra approach to ownership if he had been aware of them.

Bhavanātha introduces the metaphysical nature of ownership through an opponent who argues that 'there is no essential dharma dependent on an act of acquisition that can be properly understood (with epistemic certainty)'.[142] This is wrong, says Bhavanātha, because ownership is merely the relationship between an acquirer and an acquired object which is brought about by an act of acquisition.[143]

[137] Kāṇe, *History of Dharmaśāstra*, vol. 3, p. 550; Derrett, 'The Right to Earn': 66–97.

[138] *Mīmāṃsānayaviveka*, vol. 3, ed. S Subrahmanya Shastri (New Delhi: Rashtriya Sanskrit Sansthan, 2004), p. 44: na yatheṣṭaviniyogaḥ svatvam, kiṃtu yatheṣṭaviniyogārhatety uktam śābare.

[139] Ibid., p. 45: tac ca tasya tadarthatvam yad yenārjitam.

[140] Ibid.: nanu kratvaṅgatve dhanam na yatheṣṭaviniyojyam iti svam eva na bhavati.

[141] Ibid.: lokasiddham cārjanam janmādiḥ. Cf. notes 106 and 107.

[142] Ibid.: nanu nārja[n]ādhīnaḥ ko [']pi dharmo mānagamyaḥ.

[143] Ibid.: arjanād arjakārjyasambandha eva hi svasvāmisambandhaḥ.

In fact, it is established in the extra-śāstric world that the relationship between agent and object is brought about by action.[144] Consequently, with regard to property, one need not depend on a separate source of knowledge (other than knowledge of acquisition).[145] It would not be possible to argue that this relationship would be destroyed at the end of the act of acquisition because the loci of the two things having that relationship would not be destroyed.[146] For example, when a father concludes the act of 'fathering' he does not cease to be a father, but when a father dies one might metaphorically speak of 'father' in the sense of his previous state.[147] Bhavanātha recognizes that although acquisition is multifaceted, one cannot say that the use of the word 'sva' in reference to an asset is not singular.[148] This is because of the use of the word sva is something delimited by acquisition.[149] As for the word 'acquisition', it delimits through a reckoning/counting which is brought about through the sequence of memory.[150] Furthermore, an old man might use the word sva, in the sense of ownership, to refer to something he has held in the same possessive relationship since he was young.[151]

An opponent might argue that such a relationship between owner and an asset could never be destroyed through an act of abandonment (or sale) because the state of being an acquirer, like the state of being a father, would be indestructible.[152] Bhavanātha responds by arguing that when the cause of the destruction of the relationship occurs there cannot be the relationship—just as there is the destruction of the state of being a wife when someone commits one of the five great sins (mahāpātaka).[153] Bhavanātha explores another 'clever' (dhīra) theory of what svatva might be: that with regard to property (sva), ownership (svāmitva) is a particular peculiar condition of the soul (independent of the svasvāmisambandha) which is knowable through the mind.[154] Bhavanātha, however, responds that (svāmitva) would be knowable by the mind of people such as thieves or not knowable by the mind by children and the like.[155] Bhavanātha concludes by warning that inferring eligibility (for the use of an asset as desired) from the

[144] Ibid.: kriyāgarbho hi kartṛkarmaṇoḥ sambandho lokasiddhaḥ.

[145] Ibid., p. 46: na svam prati pṛthaṅmānam apekṣate.

[146] Ibid.: na caivam arjanakriyāpaye tajjanyasambandhasyāpy apāyaḥ sambandhiṇoḥ āśrayayor anapāyāt.

[147] Ibid.: na hi pituḥ kriyāpāye 'pi pitṛtvam apaiti pitur abhāve tu bhūtapūrvagatyopalakṣaṇam pitā.

[148] Ibid., p. 47: na cārjananānātve dhanaviṣayasvaśabd[a]syāpy anekārthatā.

[149] Ibid., pp. 47–8: svaśabdasyārjanopādhinā pravṛtteḥ.

[150] Ibid., p. 48: arjanaśabdas tu smṛtiparamparāgatā gaṇanopādhita eva.

[151] Ibid.: evam yaunādisambandhatulyayogakṣeme svatve svaśabdo vṛddhavyavahārasiddhaḥ. This portion of the *Nayaviveka* appears to be corrupt. My reading reflects the connection between memory and the example.

[152] Ibid., p. 46: nanv evam yāvaddravyaṃ sambandhasyānapagamāt tyāgo na syāt ... nanu pitṛtvavad aśakyahānārjakatā.

[153] Ibid.: maivam. sambandhāpāyahetūpanipāte kathaṃ sambandhaḥ ... mahāpātakādau bhāryātvāder api hānāt.

[154] Ibid., p. 50: yat tu dhīreṇoktam. svaṃ prati svāmitvam ātmadharmo manovedyam iti, tan na.

[155] Ibid.: corāder api tanmanovedyatayā syāt. bālasya ca na syāt.

observation of the use of an asset as one desired is foolish, and that consequently, that eligibility is merely the state of being the subject of an act of acquisition.[156]

Bhavanātha addresses the moral implications of an extra-śāstric theory of ownership by comparing smṛti to grammar. Bhavanātha reiterates that 'the destruction of the state of sva and svāmi as a result of a mental intention to relinquish (one's svatva) is established from extra-śāstric usage'.[157] An opponent frets—as Derrett would object eight hundred years later—that because extra-śāstric usage might wrongly assume there to be ownership in an asset acquired through theft or through force, one cannot determine the existence of ownership from extra-śāstric practice.[158] Bhavanātha writes:

> Smṛti (i.e. Dharmaśāstra), like smṛtis such as Vyākaraṇa, has as its purpose the construction of fixed rules concerning things that are not the subject of people's thoughts (i.e., known) for the first time. The smṛti is meaningful because it establishes the meaning of the śāstra (i.e., the Vedas) without giving up the essential meaning.[159]

An obvious objection is that in that case, Vedic injunctions to carve a sacrificial post, Vedic recitation and the like (yūpācāryādi), would be extra-śāstric acts that would be accomplished merely through extra-śāstric actions such as carving and teaching (laukikacchedanādhyāpanādi).[160] Bhavanātha counters this objection by arguing that even in the absence of a Vedic restriction people have known, not for the first time, that yūpas and the like are not accomplished merely through visible acts of acquisition (such as extra-śāstric carving or teaching).[161] A post, if carved through extra-śāstric carving alone, does not become a sacrificial post. It becomes a sacrificial post only if undertaken in conjunction with a Vedic injunction. As for the fact that there are such things as restrictions concerning the acceptance of

[156] Ibid.: yatheṣṭaviniyogadarśanād eva tadarhatādhīr iti tu mandam... arjanaviṣayatayaiva tadarhatety uktam.

[157] Ibid., p. 46: tad evaṃ lokasiddhas tyāgasaṅkalpād apāyo 'pi svasvāmitāyāḥ.

[158] Ibid.: nanu lokato 'pi balātkāracauryārjite 'pi svatvābhimānān na lokataḥ vyavasthā.

[159] Ibid., p. 47: ata evānidaṃprathamalokadhīviṣayavyavasthitinibandhanārthā smṛtiḥ **vyākaraṇādismṛtivat**. tāttvikatyāgācchāstrārthasiddher arthavattā smṛteḥ. The phrase tāttvikatyāgācchāstrārthasiddher appears to be corrupt. I am grateful to Diwakar Acarya for the useful emendation: tāttvik[ā]tyāgāc cchāstrārthasiddher arthavattā smṛteḥ. The *Madanaratna* refers to a sūtra from Patañjali 6.2.162, 'sadanvākhyānāc chāśtrasyeti'—because the śāstra explains (words) that are (already) existing. See note 111 for Śālikanātha's similar thoughts.

[160] Ibid.: nanv evam yūpācāryādiḥ laukikacchedanādhyāpanādikriyāsādhya eva laukika syāt. Alternatively, if we read anidaṃprathama as a gloss of apūrva, then the translation of the passage would be: '(Vedic Injunctions) to carve a sacrificial post, recite and the like, which are accomplished through extra-śāstric actions such as carving and teaching, would be extra-śāstric injunctions (and not Dharmic injunctions).'

[161] Ibid.: maivam. niyamamantrādivirahe saty api sāṃdṛṣṭikārjanakriyāmātrād yūpādyasiddher anidaṃprathamatayābhyupagamāt. Again, reading anidaṃprathama as apūrva would produce a different translation: 'Even in the absence of a restricting Vedic passage, one doesn't understand the injunction of the yūpa as an apūrva-vidhi just by seeing a yūpa acquired.'

gifts, these restrictions are for the sake of accomplishing a Vedically enjoined act of giving and not for the purpose of producing ownership.[162] Similarly, the varamaṅgala (enjoined by the Veda during weddings) is enjoined for a purpose pertaining to good fortune (abhyudaya), not for the purpose of making someone a wife.[163] The point is that even if legal ownership is an extra-śāstric matter, the religious rectitude of the act of acquisition that produced said ownership is still governed by the śāstra.

Bhavanātha's comments concerning Vyākaraṇa implicitly evoke a lengthy discussion of the relationship between śāstric and extra-śāstric activity (lokavyavahāra) which occurs in the opening sections of Patañjali's *Paspaśāhnika.*[164] For the grammarians, a grammatically incorrect word will convey meaning in a non-ritual context provided that it is intelligible to the community in which it is spoken.[165] Similarly, according to Bhavanātha, one acquires an unseen (adṛṣṭa) merit in following the restrictions offered the smṛti, but the smṛti does not have exclusive authority over the production of ownerhsip.

Bhavanātha does not equate possession with ownership. He goes to great lengths to prove that one cannot infer the existence of the latter when observing the former. Furthermore, Bhavanātha is keen to scrutinize his definition of ownership (and the definitions of others) through a test of its moral implications. The issue that Bhavanātha takes up and the Dharmaśāstrins examine at length is precisely the one that Derrett identifies as a failing in the system—the tension between ownership being overdetermined or underdetermined by śāstric injunctions. Bhavanātha informs the reader about the strengths and limits of śāstra as a source of knowledge about ownership.

When considering the level of sophistication in the Prābhākara-Mīmāṃsakas' attention to ownership it seems obvious why Vijñāneśvara would have used their arguments to defend an extra-śāstric theory of ownership. Śālikanātha and Bhavanātha give philosophically sophisticated and ethically complex accounts of ownership. Few have given Śabara the credit he deserves for being the first author to explore ownership in terms of eligibility for use as desired. Moreover, Bhavanātha's interest in the metaphysics of ownership—how it is created, maintained and destroyed and where it is located—antedates similar discussions amongst the Naiyāyikas by at least two centuries.

[162] Ibid.: yad api pratigrahe niyamādidarśanam tad api vihitadānasiddhyartham na svatvotpattyartham.

[163] Ibid.: varamaṅgalaniyamādaro 'pi na bhāryotpattyarthaḥ. kintv abhyudayāntarārthaḥ.

[164] *Vyākaraṇamahābhāṣya: Paspaśāhnika* ed. and trans. S. D. Joshi and J. A. F. Roodbergen (Pune: University of Pune, 1986).

[165] Ibid., 26 and 125–6: Varttika 4: samānāyām iti. yady api sākṣād apabhraṃśā na vācakās tathāpi smaryamāṇasādhuśabdavyavadhānenārtham pratyāyayanti. kecic cāpabhraṃśāḥ paramparayā nirūḍhim āgatāḥ sādhuśabdān asmarayanta evārtham pratyāyayanti. anye tu manyante sādhuśabdavad apabhraṃśā api sākṣād arthasya vācaka iti.

Vijñāneśvara's Successors

The cohort of post-Vijñāneśvara Dharmaśāstrins who defended the *Mitākṣarā*—typified by Devaṇṇabhaṭṭa (1150–1225), Viśveśvara (1360–1390) and Madanasiṃha (1425–1450)—relied on the *Mīmāṃsānayaviveka*'s definition of ownerhsip as yatheṣṭaviniyogārhatā to argue against the opinions of Dhāreśvara (1000–1055) and the Saṃgrahakāra (800–1000). This suggests that Vijñāneśvara did indeed found an influential school of thought—in which Dharmaśāstric discussions of inheritance took their cue from Mīmāṃsā—and that said school of thought continued to develop in tandem with Prābhākara-Mīmāṃsā theories of ownership. Three ways in which the medieval followers of the *Mitākṣarā* apply Bhavanātha's contributions to the concept of svatva warrant careful attention: 1) how they define ownership as yatheṣṭaviniyogārhatā to refute Vijñāneśvara's probable opponents from the *Mitākṣarā*—the Saṃgrahakāra and Dhāreśvara; 2) how they appeal to Bhavanātha's metaphysical arguments about ownership to account for how birth can lead to ownership; 3) how they expand the connection between smṛti and Vyākaraṇa to flesh out the moral implications of an extra-śāstric theory of ownership. In each case the core structure of the *Mitākṣarā*'s theory of unobstructed inheritance is retained.

Devaṇṇabhaṭṭa's *Smṛticandrikā*, one of the earliest extant Dharmaśāstra-nibandhas, defends the *Mitākṣarā* against the Saṃgrahakāra and Dhāreśvara's theory of ownership being discernible-from-the-śāstra-alone (śāstraikasamadhigamyatva) by appealing to the *Mīmāṃsānayaviveka*'s definition of ownership as eligibility for use as desired.[166] Devaṇṇabhaṭṭa is an explicit follower of the *Mitākṣarā*. The few places where he differs from Vijñāneśvara—such as the definition of inheritance—are typically small improvements framed using the concept of moral propriety.[167] Remarkably, the arguments of the only pre-Jīmūtavāhana opponents of Vijñāneśvara who wrote about ownership in any depth are preserved exclusively in a scale of texts fashioned by Vijñāneśvara's followers.

The context of the debate is a verse from the *Devalasmṛti* that describes sons as 'having non-ownership' (asvāmya) so long as the father is alive and free from

[166] Vijñāneśvara refers to the views of the Saṃgrahakāra and Dhāreśvara, but not in the context of ownership. Indeed, it is only from Devaṇṇabhaṭṭa onwards that the *Smṛtisaṃgraha* and the *Mitākṣarā* are placed in opposition.

[167] For example, Devaṇṇabhaṭṭa refines Vijñāneśvara's definition of dāya as 'asset which becomes the property of another, solely on account of (that person's) relation to the (asset's) owner'. Such a definition would allow women to be inheritors (dāyada). Rather, says Devaṇṇabhaṭṭa, dāya is 'an asset *eligible for partition* which becomes the property of another, solely on account of (that person's) relation to the (asset's) owner'. The idea of *eligibility* probably comes from the *Nayaviveka*. *Smṛticandrikā*, vol. 3.2, p. 623: na ca dāyaśabdena yad dhanaṃ svāmisambandhād eva nimittād anyasya svaṃ bhavati tad ucyata iti dāyādiśabdanirūpaṇārthaṃ **mitākṣarāyām** uktam yuktam. evaṃ hi patyuḥ svam patisambandhād eva nimittāt patnīsvam bhavatīti tasyāpi dāyatvāpattiḥ. tataś ca adāyāḥ striya iti śrutivirodho durvāraḥ syāt. asman mate tu vibhāgārham svam svāmisambandhād eva nimittād anyasya svam bhūtam dāyaśabdārthe iti vibhāgānarham patnīsvam na dāya.

fault.[168] Devaṇṇabhaṭṭa argues that this verse should be construed as establishing a lack of independence rather than ownership on the part of the sons.[169] Even when a father is alive and free from fault, it is established extra-śāstrically that sons have ownership in their father's assets.[170] Devaṇṇabhaṭṭa's framing question concerns whether ownership can exist without independent control over individual assets. An opponent (the Saṃgrahakāra/Dhāreśvara) argues that because svatva and svāmya are alike in referring to the acquisition and preservation (of assets), if one is proved to be discernible only from the śāstra, the other must be as well.[171] Consequently, ownership cannot be extra-śāstric and the ownership of sons (by birth) is not established in the extra-śāstric world because that would render Devala's explicit mention of 'not owners' worthless.[172] The opponent cites a passage from the *Smṛtisaṃgraha* which asserts that if one were to assume that the owner of some asset is the person in whose possession the asset is observed, then one could not (rightly) say 'he has stolen my property' because he is the owner since the asset has been seen in his possession.[173]

The debate centres on the proper definition of ownership. The Saṃgrahakāra argues that one could not say that one is able to use an asset as one likes because one is a legal owner (and not a thief).[174] Indeed, even if the production of ownership were established extra-śāstrically, the use of one's assets is regulated by the śāstras and consequently, the Saṃgrahakāra states: 'One cannot say that one's property is whatever one uses as desired, for the use of everything is restricted by the śāstra.'[175] Dhāreśvara, according to Devaṇṇabhaṭṭa, argues against the idea that because something is the property of the person who uses it as desired, and because something stolen should not be used as desired, there is no over-extension of the definition of ownership as yatheṣṭaviniyojytva.[176] This is because, according to Dhāreśvara, there is no such thing as usability as desired when the use of an asset, even when the subject of a transaction as one's property, is restricted by the śāstra to things such as supporting one's family and gurus.[177]

[168] *Smṛticandrikā*, vol. 3.2, p. 600: pitary uparate putrā vibhajeran pitur dhanam / asvāmyam hi bhavet eṣām nirdoṣe pitari sthite //

[169] Ibid.: iti, tatrāsvāmyavacanam asvātantryapratipādanārtham iti mantavyam.

[170] Ibid.: nirdoṣe pitari sthite 'pi pitṛdhane putrāṇām janmanā svāmyasya lokasiddhatvāt.

[171] Ibid., p. 601: yasmāt svāmyasvatvayos tulyayogakṣemayor ekataram adhikṛtya sādhite 'pi śāstraikasamadhigamyatve dvayor eva sādhitam bhavati.

[172] Ibid., p. 600: nanv alaukikam svāmyam na putrāṇām lokasiddham iti vṛdhaiva 'asvāmyaṃ hi bhavet' iti vacanasvārasyabhaṅgaḥ kriyate.

[173] Ibid., pp. 600–1: vartate yasya yad dhaste tasya svāmī sa eva na / anyasvam anyahasteṣu cauryadyaiḥ kiṃ na vartate // tasmāc chāstrata eva syāt svāmyaṃ nānubhavād api / kim ca yadi yad yasyāntike dṛṣṭam tasyaiva svāmī tarhy asya svam etenāpahṛtam iti na brūyāt, yasyaivāntike dṛṣṭam tasyaiva svāmitvāt.

[174] For Vijñāneśvara's arguments to that effect, see note 66.

[175] See note 63.

[176] *Smṛticandrikā*, vol. 3.2, p. 602: kim tu yad vastu yena yatheṣṭam vinijujyate tat tasya svam ity ucyate. tataś ca nātiprasaṅgādidūṣaṇam, apahṛtāder ayatheṣṭaviniyojyasya svavyavahārāprasaṅgād iti vācyam.

[177] Ibid.: yatas sarvasya svavyavahāraviṣayasyāpi dhanasya viniyogaḥ śāstreṇaiva gurubhṛtyāder bharaṇādau niyamyata iti yatheṣṭviniyojyam kim api nāstīti. prapañcitam caitat sarvam **dhāreśvarasūriṇā**.

The thrust of Dhāreśvara's argument is that the very nature of ownership as a śāstrically regulated phenomenon precludes the possibility of an extra-śāstric theory of ownership-by-birth.

Devaṇṇabhaṭṭa defends the *Mitakṣarā*'s theory of ownership-by-birth by appealing to the *Mīmāṃsānayaviveka*'s theory of ownership as eligibility for use as desired. Vijñāneśvara implicitly adopts this theory of ownership, but Devaṇṇabhaṭṭa states explicitly that 'we do not say that property is (something) to be used as desired but rather we say that property is what is eligible to be used as desired'.[178] An opponent argues that as śāstric obligations to support one's family or elders render the idea of 'use as desired' meaningless—because nothing is really available to be used as desired—but Devaṇṇabhaṭṭa quotes the *Mīmāṃsānayaviveka* to the effect that 'that which someone acquires is eligible to be used by him as desired' and argues that even in the absence of use as desired, an asset is eligible to be used as desired (by virtue of being acquired).[179] Devaṇṇabhaṭṭa explains, paraphrasing Bhavanātha, that 'acquisition is established extra-śāstrically as in the case of birth and the like' means that 'the acquisition of assets through means such as birth, purchase, division and the like, but not theft and the like, is established extra-śāstrically without a beginning'.[180]

Devaṇṇabhaṭṭa explains that because acquisition, which produces ownership, is established extra-śāstrically since time immemorial, people should certainly know that acquisition produces ownership so that they can accomplish extra-śāstric and Vedic activities.[181] Indeed, writes Devaṇṇabhaṭṭa, 'the Gautama-authored Dharmasmṛti (10.39–41) was written to constrain the means of acquisition that are established as being the content of extra-śāstric understanding without a begining, just as Vyākaraṇa and other smṛtis have as their purpose the delimitation of good words'.[182] Devaṇṇabhaṭṭa argues that the term inheritance (riktha) in the *Gautamadharmasūtras* actually means 'the acquisition of inheritance, i.e. the birth of the son and the like which produces ownership in the father's assets'.[183] This, says Devaṇṇabhaṭṭa, is how Gautama states that birth is a cause of obtaining

[178] Ibid.: atrocyate—na brūmo yatheṣṭam viniyojyam svam iti, kim tu yatheṣṭaviniyogārham svam iti brūmahe.

[179] Ibid.: nanu śāstreṇa gurubhṛtyāder bharaṇādau viniyoganiyamād yathā yatheṣṭaviniyojyaṃ durnirūpam tathā yatheṣṭaviniyogārhatvam api yatheṣṭaviniyogābhāvād eva durnirūpam. maivam, yatheṣṭaviniyogābhāve 'pi yad yenārjitam tat tasya yatheṣṭaviniyogārham ity evaṃ nirūpyate. tathā ca **nayaviveke bhavanāthenaivam** nirūpitaṃ 'tac ca tasya tadarham yad yenārjitam' iti granthena. Cf. *Mīmāṃsānayaviveka* in note 139.

[180] *Smṛticandrikā*, vol. 3, p. 603: sa eva 'lokasiddham cārjanam janmādi' iti. janmakrayasamvibhāgaparigrahādhigamādy evānidaṃprathamalokasiddhaṃ dhanārjanaṃ na punaś cauryādikam ity arthaḥ. For Bhavanātha's similar argument, see note 159.

[181] Ibid.: yata evānidaṃprathamalokasiddhārjanam eva svatvāpādakam tataś ca tad eva laukikavaidikavyavahārasiddhyartham avaśyam jñeyam.

[182] Ibid.: ata evānidaṃprathamalokadhīviṣayatayā vyavasthitārjanānām svagranthe nibandhanārthā 'svāmī rikthakrayasaṃvibhāgaparigrahādhigameṣu'... ityādikā **gautamādipraṇītā** dharmasmṛtiḥ sādhuśabdanibandhanārthavyākaraṇādismṛtivat kṛtety arthaḥ.

[183] Ibid.: riktham rikthārjanam pitrādidhane svāmitvāpādakam putrādijanmeti yāvat.

(ownership) in paternal assets: 'the teacher says that one obtains ownership of assets right from birth'.[184]

The rest of Devaṇṇabhaṭṭa's discussion of ownership-by-birth follows the *Mitākṣarā* closely. The *Smṛticandrikā*, like all of the *Mitākṣarā*'s followers, adheres tightly to this remarkable continuity of form that came to be identified as a specific school of thought. The *Smṛticandrikā*, however, is also notable in that it introduces two key arguments to the scale of texts: a citation of, and rejoinder to, the Saṃgrahakāra and Dhāreśvara's defence of ownership as being discernible-from-the-śāstra-alone and the *Mīmāṃsānayaviveka*'s analogy between Vyākaraṇa and Dharmaśāstra. The latter testifies to the shared trajectory of the development of the concept of ownership in Prābhākara-Mīmāṃsā texts and the increasing sophistication of the *Mitākṣarā* school of thought in medieval Dharmaśāstra digests. Devaṇṇabhaṭṭa's use of the *Mīmāṃsānayaviveka* is innovative, particularly his insistence that ownership is not merely established extra-śāstrically, but also not contingent on the ability to use one's property as desired.

Viśveśvarabhaṭṭa's fourteenth-century *Subodhinī* appears to be the oldest surviving commentary on the *Mitākṣarā*.[185] Viśveśvara typically glosses Vijñāneśvara without offering much further elaboration, but when discussing Vijñāneśvara's paraphrase of Prabhākara, Viśveśvara quotes the *Mīmāṃsānayaviveka* at length. Viśveśvara does not name Bhavanātha or the *Mīmāṃsānayaviveka*, but Viśveśvara defends ownership-by-birth by turning to Bhavanātha's arguments concerning the metaphysics of ownership.[186] Viśveśvara explores how the relationship between an owner and an asset is created and destroyed. Viśveśvara rejects the argument that there is no essential dharma, produced by acquisition and capable of being understood with epistemic certainty, which can be designated 'ownership'.[187] For Viśveśvara, ownership is merely that relationship between owner and property which is the relationship between acquirer and acquired brought about through an act of acquisition.[188]

Viśevśvara's point is that because it is established in the extra-śāstric world that the relationship between agent and object is brought about by action, one need not depend on a different source of knowledge (other than acquisition in order to know that someone is an owner of an asset).[189] The essential metaphysical

[184] Ibid.: tathāca paitṛkadhanalābhahetutvenoktam **gautamenaiva**—'utpattyaivārthasvāmitvam labhetety ācāryaḥ'. Devaṇṇabhaṭṭa explains that this means 'by the arising of the body in the mother's womb alone:' utpattyaiva mātur garbhe śarīrotpattyaivety arthaḥ. Cf. note 55.

[185] For the dating of Viśveśvarabhaṭṭa, see Kāṇe, *History of Dharmaśāstra*, vol. 1, part 2, pp. 792–804.

[186] *Mitākṣara: With Viśvarūpa and Commentaries of Subodhini and Bālambhatti*, ed. S.S. Setlur (Madras: Brahmavadin Press, 1912), p. 597, Introduction to Yāj. 2.114: janmanā pratigrahādibhiś cārjitasya dhanasya lokasiddham iti loke vṛddhavyavahārasiddhatvāt.

[187] Ibid.: nanu nārjanotpannaḥ ko 'pi dharmo mānagamyo yat svatvam iti vyavahriyate. maivam; Cf. *Mīmāṃsānayaviveka* in note 142.

[188] Ibid.: arjanād arjakārjyasambandho yaḥ svasvāmibhāvasambandhas tad eva svatvam.

[189] Ibid.: tac ca pṛthaṅmānam nāpekṣate; yataḥ kriyāgarbhaḥ kartṛkarmaṇoḥ sambandho lokasiddhaḥ. Cf. *Mīmāṃsānayaviveka* in note 144.

question turns on how an ephemeral action such as acquisition could bring about a relationship which is enduring. Viśveśvara, drawing on Bhavanātha, argues that there is no destruction of the relationship having the form of ownership produced by that (act of acquisition) when the act of acquisition terminates because the loci of the two things possessing that relation (acquirer and acquired) are not destroyed.[190] After all, a father does not cease to be a father when he has ceased the act of fathering.[191] Although brief, Viśveśvara's use of the *Mīmāṃsānayaviveka* confirms that the Dharmaśāstrins who followed Vijñāneśvara's theories of ownership-by-birth and unobstructed inheritance followed novel arguments that emerged in Prābhākara-Mīmāṃsā treatises and buttressed the legal implications of the *Mitākṣarā* with a pre-legal inquiry into the philosophical dimensions of ownership as an extra-śāstric phenomenon.

While Devaṇṇabhaṭṭa's *Smṛticandrikā* and Viśveśvara's *Subodhinī* leave several questions concerning ownership unanswered, Madanasiṃha's mid-fifteenth-century *Madanaratnapradīpa,* the most developed Dharmaśāstra digest of the *Mitākṣarā* school before the rise of the *Dāyabhāga* school, provides great detail about the relationship between Dharmaśāstra, Vyākaraṇaśāstra, and extra-śāstric custom.[192] The treatment of inheritance follows the *Smṛticandrikā* closely, but innovates in its interpretation of Pārthasārathimiśra's *Tantraratna* in accordance with Bhavanātha's *Mīmāṃsānayaviveka*. The *Madanaratnapradīpa* was probably the model for post-*Dāyabhāga Mitākṣarā* adherents -including Mitramiśra and Kamalākarabhaṭṭa. Furthermore, the *Madanaratnapradīpa* offers a series of novel elaborations on the *Mīmāṃsānayaviveka*'s arguments concerning ownership.

In the explanation of the division of inheritance, the *Madanaratnapradīpa,* following Devaṇṇabhaṭṭa, defines inheritance as 'an asset connected to the father and the like which is eligible for partition'.[193] Like Devaṇṇabhaṭṭa, Madanasiṃha introduces Saṃgrahakāra and Dhāreśvara as opponents who attack the theory of extra-śāstrically established ownership from both ends—svāmitva and svatva. The Saṃgrahakāra argues that ownership must be discernible-from-the-śāstra alone because an extra-śāstrically established ownership would extend even to thieves and the like.[194] The Saṃgrahakāra makes many of the same arguments which appear in the *Smṛticandrikā*: the inability to sue for stolen possessions, the irrelevance of śāstric restrictions regarding acquisition and the absence of birth

[190] Ibid.: na cārjanakriyāpaye tajjanyasvatvarūpasambandhasyāpāyaḥ sambandhiṇor āśrayayor anapāyāt. Cf. *Mīmāṃsānayaviveka*, vol. 3, p. 46: na caivam arjanakriyāpāye tajjanyasambandhasyāpy apāyaḥ, sambandhinoḥ āśrayayor anapāyāt.

[191] *Mitākṣara: With Viśvarūpa and Commentaries of Subodhini and Bālambhatti*, p. 597: na hi pituḥ kriyāpāye pitṛtvam apaiti. Cf. *Mīmāṃsānayaviveka* in note 147.

[192] *Madanaratnapradīpa: Vyavahāravivekoddyota*, ed. P. V. Kāṇe (Bikaner: Anup Sanskrit Library, Ganga Oriental Series; no. 6, 1948). For the background and context of the *Madanaratnapradīpa*, see Kāṇe's introduction to the edition.

[193] Ibid., p. 321: dāyo nāma vibhāgārham pitrādisambandhi dravyam.

[194] Ibid., p. 323: na hi yatsamīpe yad dhanam dṛṣyate tasya tad dhanam svam sa ca tasya svāmīti cauryādilabdhadhane 'pi svasvāmibhāvaprasaṅgāt.

in śāstric lists of means of acquiring ownership. Dhāreśvara argues that there could be no extra-śāstric understanding of ownership. Dhāreśvara's assertion is that one could not get out of Saṃgrahakāra's argument by saying that what is used by someone as they please is their property because even the use of lawfully acquired assets is regulated (niyamita) by śāstra.[195] Consequently, one could never use ownership (i.e. yatheṣṭaviniyojyatva) to defend an extra-śāstric theory of ownership.[196]

Madanasiṃha responds, like Devaṇṇabhaṭṭa, by appealing to the *Mīmāṃsānayaviveka*. First, in response to Dhāreśvara's concern about thieves and the obsolescence of smṛti, the *Madanaratnapradīpa*, following the *Mīmāṃsānayaviveka*, argues that 'acquisition, such as by birth, is established extra-śāstrically, and consequently, Dharmaśāstra, like Vyākaraṇaśāstra, merely compiles [for the sake of propriety] activities which are the subject of people's everyday usage without a beginning'.[197] The *Madanaratnapradīpa* explains that Vyākaraṇaśāstra teaches the meanings of words established in extra-śāstric usage in order to instruct people in the appropriate use of those words and cites a vārtika quoted in Patāñjali's *Mahābhāṣya* (1.1.62), 'śāstra explains words that exist'.[198] The thrust of the *Madanaratnapradīpa's* argument is that Vyākaraṇa selects particular forms of extra-śāstric linguistic usage for praise or censure depending on their śāstric correctness but doesn't determine what words are actually used in the world. Dharmaśāstra, like Vyākaraṇaśāstra, might praise or censure particular means of acquisition (recognized in the extra-śāstric world) for the sake of moral propriety, but such restrictions do not determine what the extra-śāstric world recognizes as legally valid means of acquisition.

A Brāhmaṇa might earn money in defiance of śāstric restrictions by farming (which he is prohibited from doing except in emergencies) but he will still have svatva in his ill-gotten gains. He may have to perform a penance in the form of abandonment of these assets or reciting mantras, but his children may divide said assets without incurring a moral blemish. A thief, however, who breaks a śāstric injunction not to steal will not have ownership because unlike farming, theft is not

[195] Ibid., p. 324: na ca yena yad yatheṣṭaṃ viniyujyate sa tasya svāmī tac ca tasya svaṃ caurādilabdhaṃ tu na tatheti vācyam. sarvasya nyāyopārjitasyāpi dhanasya kuṭumbapoṣaṇādau viniyogaḥ śāstreṇa niyamita iti svecchānusāreṇa viniyogaviṣayatvābhāvād iti. etat **saṃgrahakāramataṃ dhāreśvarabhaṭṭenāpy** āśritam. Cf. *Smṛticandrikā*, vol. 3.2, part II, p. 602: kiṃ tu yad vastu yena yatheṣṭaṃ vinijujyate tat tasya svam ity ucyate. tataś ca nātiprasaṅgādidūṣaṇam, apahṛtāder ayatheṣṭaviniyojyasya svavyavahārāprasaṅgād iti vācyam. yatas sarvasya svavyavahāraviṣayasyāpi dhanasya viniyogaḥ śāstreṇaiva gurubhṛtyādeḥ bharaṇādau niyamyata iti yatheṣṭviniyojyam kim api nāstīti. prapañcitam caitat sarvam **dhāreśvarasūriṇā**.

[196] Ibid., p. 324: tasmāc chāśtraikasamadhigamyatvāt katham svasvāmibhāvasya lokasiddhatvam.

[197] Ibid., pp. 324–5: uktaṃ caitan **nayaviveke prābhākaramatāmbujaprabhākareṇa bhavanāthena**—lokasiddhaṃ vārjanaṃ janmādi, ata evānidaṃprathamalokadhīviṣayatā sthite nibandhanārthā smṛtir **vyākaraṇādismṛtivad** iti. Cf. notes 159 and 180.

[198] Ibid., p. 325: yathā **vyākaraṇaśāstre** siddhā eva śabdāḥ sādhutvajñānārtham anukhyāyante tathety arthaḥ. **vyākaraṇaśāstrasya** lokasiddhaśabdānvākhyāpakatvam uktam **mahābhāṣye** 'sadanvākhyānāc chāśtrasyeti'. sadanvākhyānāt siddhaśabdānvākhyāpakatvād ity arthaḥ.

a locally recognized method of acquisition. His children, if they divide the assets, would incur a moral blemish and may be punished by the king.[199] In short, Madanasiṃha distinguishes between moral faults with an unseen effect (sin and the need for ritual purification) and extra-śāstric illegality which has a seen effect (in the form of state-sponsored punishment).

Madanasiṃha also offers a comprehensive theory of ownership for medieval Dharmaśāstra and he ties together two theories of ownership (yatheṣṭaviniyogārhatā and yatheṣṭaviniyojyatva) which he identifies with the Prābhākara and Kaumārila schools of Mīmāṃsā respectively. The *Madanaratnapradīpa*, invoking the *Mīmāṃsānayaviveka*, argues that ownership is not an asset's usability as desired, but, rather, its fitness for use as desired.[200] Using the metaphor of a seed in a granary, the *Madanaratnapradīpa* argues that although one might not be able to use an asset as one would like because of a śāstrically enjoined necessity such as supporting one's family, one is still the legal owner of the asset by virtue of having acquired it (through a valid method of acquisition). Similarly, while a seed stored in a dry granary may not produce sprouts, it is fit to produce sprouts by virtue of its being a seed.[201]

Interestingly, Madanasiṃha turns to Pārthasārathimiśra's *Tantraratna* and argues that this is the case 'even in the *Tantraratna* which follows the opinions of (Kumārila) Bhaṭṭa'.[202] Madanasiṃha parrots Pārthasārathimiśra's argument that if we accept that ownership is an asset's usability as desired, and if the acquisition (and use) of assets existed solely for the sake of sacrifices, there

[199] Ibid., pp. 325–6: yathā siddhaśabdānuśāsanārthe **vyākaraṇaśāstre** ye lokasiddhāḥ śabdās te sarve sāmānyato viśeṣato vānuśiṣṭā eveti yas tatra nānuśiṣṭo yo vā—na ṅisambuddhyoḥ—ityevamādivākyaiḥ sambuddhau luptanakāro 'sādhur ity evaṃrūpeṇa prakāreṇāsādhutayopadiṣṭaḥ sa lokasiddha eva na bhavatīti na prayogārhas tathā lokasiddhasya svatvahetunibandhanārthe **gautamādiśāstre** sarvo 'pi svatvahetur upadiṣṭa eveti yas tatra nopadiṣṭho yo vā cauryādivat svatvāsādhakatvenoktaḥ sa laukiko 'pi svatvahetur na bhavatīty ato 'satpratigrahavāṇijyādilabdhasya yadi śāstre svatvam niṣiddham tarhi loke 'pi cauryādilabdhavat tatsvatvasyānaṅgīkartavyatvāt. tasmād yad garhiteneti vākyam asatpratigrahasvayaṃkṛtakṛṣivāṇijyādīnāṃ svatvahetutve saty api brāhmaṇasya... **yājñavalkyabṛhaspatyādivākyair** āpadvṛttitvenoktānām teṣām anāpady āśrayaṇe doṣasambandhāt tadupāyalabdhadravyaparityāgajapataporūpam prāyaścittam vidadhāti na tu tadupāyalabdhasya svatvam niṣedhatīty āstheyam. ata evāsatpratigrahādinārjayitur na corādidaṇḍaviśeṣaḥ smaryate. evaṃ cānāpady api asatpratigrahādinārjitasya svatvam asty eveti tatputrāṇām tadvibhājyam eva. arjayitur eva doṣasambandhāt prāyaścittācaraṇam cauryādilabdhasya tu na tādṛktvam iti na tadvibhājyam. The analogy to Vyākaraṇaśāstra is thus: Pāṇini 8.2.8. 'na ṅisambuddhyoḥ' (one should retain the nasal ending in the vocative—i.e. bho rājan but not bho rāja) tells us to prefer one linguistic usage over another, but if one *were* to drop the nasal in the vocative case, it would be improper, but intelligible for the purpose of communication. Such a position would *not* mean that nonsense words are intelligible for the purpose of conveying meaning.

[200] Ibid., p. 325: na ca yatheṣṭaviniyojyatvam svatvam iti vayam brūmaḥ. kiṃ tarhi? yatheṣṭaviniyogayogyatvam. The *Madanaratnapradīpa* seems to have Pārthasārathimiśra's definition from the *Tantraratna* in mind. See Kroll, 'A Logical Approach to Law', p. 39, quoting *Tantraratna*, p. 19: yatheṣṭaviniyojyatvaṃ hi svatvam. kevalakratvarthatve tv anyatrāviniyogād yatheṣṭaviniyojyatvābhāvāt svatvābhāva iti.

[201] Ibid., p. 325: taç ca [svatvam] śāstreṇa kuṭumbabharaṇādiviniyoganiyamanena viniyogāntaraviṣayatām alabhamānasyāpy arjitatvaprayuktam asty eva. yathā kutaś cid dhetor aṅkurotpādanam akurvato 'pi kuśūlādisthitasya bījasya bījatvaprayuktam aṅkurotpādanayogyatvam.

[202] Ibid., p. 325: **bhaṭṭamatānusāriṇi tantraratne** 'pi...

would be no ownership because one could not use an asset as desired outside of a sacrificial context.[203] Derrett and Kroll view Pārthasārathimiśra's definition of ownership as being at odds with Bhavanātha's definition of ownership. Madanasiṃha, however, argues, on the basis of Pāṇini 3.3.169, that the gerundive yojya (from the root √yuj) is used in the sense of eligibility (arha).[204] The *Madanaratnapradīpa* thus attempts to bring Bhāṭṭa and Prābhākara theories of ownership into alignment. The other possibility—which appears to be borne out in the Mīmāṃsā tradition itself—is that the difference between yatheṣṭaviniyojyatva and yatheṣṭaviniyogārhatā amounted to far less than it has been made out to be in secondary scholarship. It seems that Vijñāneśvara and his followers drew from the Prābhākara-Mīmāṃsakas—rather than from the Bhāṭṭa-Mīmāṃsakas—largely because the former had far more to say about these issues.

Madanasiṃha's comments in the *Madanaratnapradīpa* support the broader argument that the development of the theory of ownership-by-birth was connected intimately with the theory of extra-śāstric ownership as developed in Mīmāṃsā generally, and in Prābhākara-Mīmāṃsā in particular. On the one hand, Vijñāneśvara took an inchoate, but recognized (by Viśvarūpa and Medhātithi) theory of sons' coparcenary property rights in their father's estate and transformed it into a comprehensive model of inheritance. In doing so, he was working against a more literal reading of the smṛtis and sūtras. In order to elevate custom to the status of śāstric law, Vijñāneśvara had to free the concept of ownership from its śāstric constraints. It is clear that the *Smṛtisaṃgraha* and Dhāreśvara had already opposed such an idea, but Vijñāneśvara found a convenient ally in the *Bṛhatī* and possibly the *Ṛjuvimalāpañcikā*. Ownership, they said, could not be limited to the sphere of ritual propriety because it was an extra-śāstric phenomenon. While Vijñāneśvara can be called, rightly, the founder of a school of jurisprudence for innovating this bold connection between dāya and Mīmāṃsā, it was left to those Dharmaśāstrins who inherited his theories to follow the implications of the *Mitākṣarā* systematically and to work out a definition of ownership. Devaṇṇabhaṭṭa and Madanasiṃha turned to a later Prābhākara-Mīmāṃsaka, Bhavanātha, to accomplish this task. For them, ownership could be defined as an asset's fitness for use as desired, and ownership could be acquired through any means not reprobated in the extra-śāstric world.

Conclusion

The rise of the *Mitākṣarā* as a discernible school of legal thought parallels the development of the Prābhākara school of Mīmāṃsā—without necessarily indicating

[203] Ibid.,: yatheṣṭaviniyojyatvam hi svatvam kevalakratvarthatve 'nyatrāviniyogād yatheṣṭaviniyogābhāve. Cf. note 95.

[204] Ibid.: viniyojyam atra viniyogārham—arhe kṛtyatṛcaś ca iti **pāṇinismaraṇāt**.

that Prābhākara-Mīmāṃsakas favoured the *Mitākṣarā* or that all Dharmaśāstrins who followed Vijñāneśvara favoured Prābhākara-Mīmāṃsā ideas on other legal issues. The earliest Dharmaśāstras (the smṛtis and sūtras), like the *Mīṃāṃsāsūtras*, say little to nothing about the nature of ownership. It was only with the Mīmāṃsā commentaries of Śabara, Prabhākara, Śālikanātha, and Pārthasārathimiśra that ownership and its relationship to the sacrifice and extra-śāstric world was interrogated. Their theory of ownership as that which is fit to be used according to its acquirer's intentions was surely not the 'what I hold I own' theory advanced by Kroll and Derrett. It is apparent that even at so early a stage of development as the *Mīmāṃsābhāṣya*, there was a concern about the moral rectitude of an act of acquisition. These early Mīmāṃsā theories of ownership were applied, increasingly as time wore on, by early Dharmaśāstra commentators such as Viśvarūpa and Medhātithi to solve thorny legal concerns such as adverse possession, the ownership of land and inheritance. Vijñāneśvara represents a sea-change in the history of the application of Mīmāṃsā reasoning to Dharmaśāstra.

The passage from the age of Dharmaśāstra commentaries to Dharmaśāstra-nibandhas saw the application of new arguments from the next stage of Prābhākara-Mīmāṃsā commentary as represented by the *Mīmāṃsānayaviveka*. Between the twelfth and the fifteenth centuries, Dharmaśāstric debates about ownership and inheritance took their cue from the *Mīmāṃsānayaviveka*. Madanasiṃha, however, brought a possible divergence between the Prābhākara and Bhāṭṭa-Mīmāṃsā school—on this issue of ownership—to a close, at least for the early modern adherents of the *Mitākṣarā*-school of jurisprudence. The well-known nexus between Dharmaśāstra and Mīmāṃsā was at the heart of the emergence and subsequent expansion of the *Mitākṣarā* school. Jīmūtavāhana, conspicuously absent from any of the texts in this chapter, was drawn later into a Nyāya-based attack on the theories of ownership articulated in the Mīmāṃsā.

This survey of ownership and inheritance in classical and medieval Dharmaśāstra and Mīmāṃsā treatises suggests that Davis and Rocher's reticence in identifying Vijñāneśvara as the founder of a school of law—in the sense that he originated the idea of ownership-by-birth, that he wrote in opposition to an eastern, Bengali, or Nyāya-inflected rival, or that he established an academic institution with students, disciples and discernible political applications—is prudent. It is difficult, however, to discount the demonstrable evidence of Vijñāneśvara's profound impact on the discipline of Dharmaśāstra centuries after the compilation of the *Mitākṣarā*. When one asks why Colebrooke would identity the *Mitākṣarā* as 'the chief groundwork' of Dharmaśāstra 'from *Benares* to the southern extremity of the peninsula of *India*' it is obvious that one reason is, as Kāṇe notes, that the *Mitākṣarā* is the Dharmaśāstric analogue to the *Mahābhāṣya* of Patañjali or the *Kāvyaprakāśa* of Mammaṭa.[205] This chapter has

[205] Colebrooke, *Two Treatises*, iv; P. V. Kāṇe, 'The Predecessors of Vijñāneśvara'.

explored the salient features of the *Mitākṣarā* school—the twofold definition of inheritance, the legal implications of ownership-by-birth, the theory of extra-śāstric ownership, the metaphysics of the Prābhākara school of Mīmāṃsā—in relation to Vijñāneśvara's predecessors and successors. The picture that emerged was stark: before Vijñāneśvara, Dharmaśāstrins made stray comments about ownership and Mīmāṃsā here and there, but they very clearly did not *follow* any discoverable pattern closely. After Vijñāneśvara many Dharmaśāstrins followed a pattern which was clearly based on the *Mitākṣarā*. We shall see in Chapter 2 that the ubiquity of the *Mitākṣarā* school made it an exceptionally strong opponent *against which* to develop an opposing, regional, Nyāya-inflected school of jurisprudence—complete with educational institutions, teacher–student transmissions, and polemical tendencies.

2
Navya-Nyāya and the Maithila and Gauḍa Schools of Jurisprudence

This chapter examines two schools of jurisprudence that emerged in eastern India between the fourteenth and the sixteenth centuries CE: that of Mithilā (Maithila/Miśra) and Bengal (Gauḍa). These schools of jurisprudence, in contrast to the school of thought that developed around Vijñāneśvara's *Ṛjumitākṣarā,* were neither strictly academic nor pan-Indian. Rather, they were isolated almost completely from Vijñāneśvara's *Mitākṣarā* and its Mīmāṃsā-derived theories of ownership, highly competitive, and influenced by Navya-Nyāya philosophical discourse. During the ascendency of three Brāhmaṇa-friendly dynasties, the Karṇāṭa (eleventh century–1324), Oinīvāra/Kāmeśvara (1353–1526), and the Khaṇḍavalā (1577–1947), the Mithilā region 'provided a very fertile climate for the growth and development of Dharmaśāstra and Nyāya'.[1] In Dharmaśāstra, scholars such as Caṇḍeśvara Ṭhakkura (active 1314–70), Vācaspatimiśra II (1425–1480), Misarumiśra (mid-fifteenth century), and Maheśa Ṭakkura (who founded the Khaṇḍavalā dynasty in 1556/7) developed a novel juridical approach to inheritance which largely avoided the theoretical issues of ownership and inheritance that occupied the attention of Vijñāneśvara and his followers. One explanation for these Dharmaśāstrins' disinterest in ownership-by-birth is that in their Navya-Nyāya writings, authors such as Vardhamāna Upādhyāya (fourteenth century), Vācaspatimiśra II, and Śaṃkara Miśra (fifteenth century) developed a theoretical account of ownership as a quality (guṇa) of an asset which is regulated strictly by Dharmaśāstric injunctions.

A sea-change occurred with the emergence of Navadvīpa, a now-famous university town in Bengal, during the late fifteenth century. For scholars at this institution, the most important treatise regarding inheritance was Jīmūtavāhana's *Dāyabhāga* (twelfth to fifteenth centuries). In the late fifteenth century, Navadvīpa's ṭols, śāstric instructional institutions, rose from obscurity to fame as centres of learning, particularly in two śāstric disciplines: jurisprudence

[1] Karin Preisendanz, 'The Production of Philosophical Literature in South Asia during the Pre-Colonial Period (15th–18th Centuries): the Case of the "Nyāyasūtra" Commentarial Tradition', *Journal of Indian Philosophy* 33.1 (2005): 55–94, 73. For more on the political and intellectual history of Mithilā, see R. M. Chakravarti, 'History of Mithilā during the Pre-Mughal Period', *Journal of the Royal Asiatic Society of Bengal* (New Series) 11 (1915): 407–31.

Ownership and Inheritance in Sanskrit Jurisprudence. Christopher T. Fleming, Oxford University Press (2020).

DOI: 10.1093/oso/9780198852377.003.0003

(Dharmaśāstra) and the 'new epistemology' (Navya-Nyāya).[2] By the end of the 16th century, a closely-connected community of Dharmaśāstrins (such as Raghunandana Bhaṭṭācārya 1510–1580) and Navya-Naiyāyikas (such as Raghunātha Śiromaṇi 1460–1540), who described themselves proudly—and who were described derisively by their opponents—as Bengali (Gauḍa) became (in)famous in pan-Indic scholarly debates, particularly with reference to inheritance and the philosophy of ownership. One of the more intriguing aspects of Navadvīpa's rise to prominence in Sanskrit intellectual history are the close pedagogical and intellectual connections between Gauḍa Dharmaśāstrins and Gauḍa Navya-Naiyāyikas. This chapter draws attention to the relationship between Navya-Nyāya theories of ownership as discernible-from-the-śāstra-alone (śāstraikasamadhigamyatva) and the Dharmaśāstric theory of ownership-by-the-cessation-of-the-ownership-of-the-previous-owner (uparamasvatva) articulated in Jīmūtavāhana's *Dāyabhāga*. I advance two lines of argumentation: (1) that Navadvīpan Dharmaśāstrins incorporated Jīmūtavāhana's *Dāyabhāga* in a self-consciously Gauḍa assemblage of Dharmaśāstra texts; and (2) that Navadvīpan commentaries on the *Dāyabhāga* and Navya-Nyāya discussions of ownership reflect a deliberate and mutually influential attempt to articulate an internally consistent cluster of Gauḍa theories of ownership and inheritance—a school—in opposition to a Maithila school of thought.

This chapter's object of enquiry is Jīmūtavāhana's *Dāyabhāga*, a Dharmaśāstric monograph on inheritance written sometime between the twelfth and fifteenth centuries. With the exception of Vijñāneśvara's *Mitākṣarā*, the *Dāyabhāga* is the most influential Sanskrit text on the division of inheritance (dāyavibhāga). The *Dāyabhāga* is remarkable for its polemic against the theory of ownership-by-birth and for its veneration in Bengal. When Colebrooke selected the *Dāyabhāga* as a counterpart to the *Mitākṣarā* in his formulation of schools of Hindu Law he notes that:

> The Bengal school alone, having taken for its guide Jīmūta-vahana's treatise, which is on almost every disputed point, opposite in its doctrine to the Mitācsharā ... the preference appeared decidedly due to the treatise of Jīmūta-vāhana himself ... because he was the founder of this school, being the author of the doctrine which it has adopted ...[3]

[2] For the history of Navadvīpa, see Jonardon Ganeri, *The Lost Age of Reason: Philosophy in Early Modern India 1450–1700* (Oxford: Oxford University Press, 2011), pp. 39–61. For the activities of Navadvīpan ṭols, see E. B. Cowell, 'Report on the Tolls of Nudea', *Proceedings of the Asiatic Society of Bengal* (1867): 86–102.

[3] H. T. Colebrooke, *Two Treatises on the Hindu Law of Inheritance* (Calcutta: Hindoostanee Press, 1810), p. v. Cf. Ludo Rocher, *Jīmūtavāhana's Dāyabhāga: The Hindu Law of Inheritance in Bengal* (Oxford: Oxford University Press, 2002), p. 23.

Although Ludo Rocher argues against the coherence of Colebrooke's formulation of schools of Hindu Law, he acknowledges that the *Dāyabhāga*'s prominence in colonial Bengal might mitigate the severity of Colebrooke's error:

> It is easy to understand why Colebrooke was advised to study and translate Jīmūtavāhana's Dāyabhāga. The Dāyabhāga had become very important in Bengal; it can be said without exaggeration that most later works [on inheritance] produced in Bengal were directly or indirectly commentaries on Jīmūtavāhana's text.[4]

We know virtually nothing about Jīmūtavāhana as an historical individual. That the *Dāyabhāga* can be dated no more precisely than somewhere in a nearly 400-year window is remarkable when we consider the relatively tight chronology for contemporaneous Dharmaśāstrins. Despite occasional references to Jīmūtavāhana's other two known works (the *Kālavivkea* and *Vyavahāramātṛkā*)[5] the *Dāyabhāga* was completely unknown until Śrināthācāryacūḍāmaṇi, a prominent Navadvīpan Navya-Nāyaiyika, wrote a commentary on it at the end of the fifteenth century.[6] The *Dāyabhāga*, a text diametrically opposed to the *Mitākṣarā* in matters of ownership-by-birth, went from total obscurity to become the second most important Dharmaśāstra treatise on inheritance, despite the fact that it was studied only by a relatively small number of Paṇḍitas in a handful of ṭols in and around Navadvīpa that were associated strongly with Navya-Nyāya philosophy. Rather than *expressing* a pre-existing, essential Bengali-ness—be it of family structure, of commercial pertinacity, or of idiosyncratic religious sentiment—the Paṇḍitas who commented on the *Dāyabhāga* and who developed distinctive ideas about ownership and inheritance were actively engaged in *creating* an appellation—Gauḍa—for themselves vis-à-vis more established rivals.

How and why did the *Dāyabhāga*—and its theory of heirs' ownership-by-the-cessation-of-the-ownership-of-the-previous-owner—come to be connected with the study of Navya-Nyāya in Bengal? The chapter corrects three misconceptions about the *Dāyabhāga* and the Gauḍa school of jurisprudence. One misconception, advanced by Ludo Rocher, is that 'from a historical point of view Jīmūtavāhana cannot have been 'the founder of the Bengal school . . . ' [because] in fact, the legal principles that have become characteristic traits of the Bengal school of inheritance were not even typically Bengali before Colebrooke translated the *Dāyabhāga*, in 1810'.[7] Rocher's skepticism about some aspects of Colebrooke's arguments are warranted, but Rocher ignores the incorporation of Jīmūtavāhana's *Dāyabhāga*

[4] Ludo Rocher, 'Schools of Hindu Law', in *Studies in Hindu Law and Dharmaśāstra*, ed. Donald Davis (New York: Anthem Press, 2014), pp. 119–41, 125.

[5] For Jīmūtavāhana's biography and bibliography, see Rocher, *Jīmūtavāhana's Dāyabhāga*.

[6] Rocher, 'Schools of Hindu Law', p. 125.

[7] Rocher, *Jīmūtavāhana's Dāyabhāga*, p. 32.

into a self-consciously Gauḍa scale of Dharmaśāstra texts that: a) consolidated the opinions of earlier authors such as Śūlapāṇi; and b) was oriented against a regional rival—the logicians and jurists of Mithilā and their particular configuration of Dharmaśāstra and Navya-Nyāya treatises.

Another misconception, also advanced by Rocher, asserts that Colebrooke was mistaken to argue that 'the Bengal school was greatly influenced by the nyāya system of philosophy'.[8] Rocher errs in focusing on the *Dāyabhāga* at the expense of the vast commentarial tradition that developed around the text (and led to its prominence). The Bengal school was influenced, profoundly, by Navya-Nyāya techniques and the *Dāyabhāga* became the darling of Bengali logicians in large part due to its ability to be read in congruity with fundamental Nyāya concepts of ownership as developed in the ṭols of Navadvīpa.

The third misconception belongs to Kroll. In his translation of much of the Navya-Nyāya archive on ownership, Kroll argues that:

> Significantly, neither Vardhamāna nor Raghunātha (nor any of the other post-Gaṅgeśa naiyāyika-s) appears to be arguing that the conception of svatva is not, as both Vijñāneśvara and Pārthasārathi Miśra contend, independent of dharmaśāstra.[9]

The thrust of Kroll's triple-negative argument is that Gauḍa Navya-Naiyāyikas accept Vijñāneśvara's Prābhākara-Mīmāṃsā-inflected theory of ownership as an extra-śāstric phenomenon, implicitly, *because they never reject that theory explicitly.* This *argumentum ad ignorantiam* fails to take into account three distinguishing features of Navya-Nyāya debates concerning the philosophy of ownership: (1) that Maithila Dharmaśāstrins crafted a juridical model of inheritance—one in which sons' entitlement to ancestral assets is protected legally—which was congruent with Maithila Navya-Naiyāyikas' view that Dharmaśāstric injunctions circumscribe the exercise of ownership; (2) that the shift of Navya-Nyāya from Mithilā to Bengal in the sixteenth century coincided with an increasing focus on inheritance (particularly uparamasvatva) as a topic of debate; and 3) that Gauḍa Navya-Naiyāyikas explicitly invoke Jīmūtavāhana and the *Dāyabhāga*-commentators' arguments about ownership and inheritance when exploring the legal implication of various metaphysical accounts of ownership.

Three key arguments substantiate the claim that the *Dāyabhāga* was foundational to a school of jurisprudence that emerged amongst various Bengali ṭols in the fifteenth century: (1) that Śrīnāthācāryacūḍāmaṇi (1475–1525) used the *Dāyabhāga* to fill a conspicuous gap in a Gauḍa scale of Dharmaśāstra texts that developed in opposition to a Maithila scale of Dharmaśāstra texts

[8] Ibid., p. 41.

[9] Ethan Kroll, 'A Logical Approach to Law' (PhD Dissertation, University of Chicago, 2010), p. 42.

and that coalesced around the work of Śūlapāṇi (1375–1460); (2) that Śrīnāthācāryacūḍāmaṇi and subsequent commentators on the *Dāyabhāga* such as Raghunandana Bhaṭṭācārya (1510–1580) and Acyutacakravartin (1510–1570) utilized Navya-Nyāya analytical techniques to defend a theory of ownership as discernible-from-the-śāstra-alone (śāstraikasamadhigamyatva, etc.), to reject the theory of ownership-by-birth, and to advance the Bengali Navya-Nyāya theories of ownership (of, for example, Raghunāthaśiromaṇi) against the Maithila Navya-Nyāya theories of ownership; and (3) that subsequent Nyāya debates about the philosophical nature of ownership: a) implicitly defend a theory of uparamasvatva; and b) employ arguments from Bengali *Dāyabhāga* commentators to analyse ownership in relation to inheritance.

This chapter argues for a stronger understanding of a 'school' in relation to Mithilā and to the *Dāyabhāga* than that which developed in relation to the *Mitākṣarā* in medieval India. As Navadvīpa and other centres of Nyāya and Dharmaśāstric learning in Bengali grew in prominence—and began to rival the more established intellectual community of scholars in Mithilā—in the sixteenth century, its Paṇḍitas developed a scale of texts that involved a Nyāya/Dharmaśāstra nexus, that used the term Gauḍa, self-consciously, to distinguish its members and opinions from those of Mithilā, and that followed the transmission of lines of argumentation from distinct teacher-disciple lineages in Navadvīpa and other Bengali ṭols. These Paṇḍitas developed a theory of ownership as a distinct conceptual category (padārtha) or as a syncopated pair of qualified absences (viśiṣṭābhāva) that, in either case, is produced by śāstrically determined methods of acquisition and that affords an owner a largely unrestricted right for use as desired (yatheṣṭaviniyoga). This view constrasted with the Maithila view in which ownership's *effects* were limited by Dharmaśāstra. Although the Gauḍa adherents of the *Dāyabhāga* school of jurisprudence reject the *Mitākṣarā*'s theory of ownership-by-birth—primarily for reasons of philosophical accuracy—they direct their polemic towards Mithilā primarily.

Maithila and Gauḍa Scales of Dharmaśāstra Texts

This section attends to the formation of Maithila and Gauḍa scales of Dharmaśāstra and Navya-Nyāya texts in Mithilā during the fourteenth century and in the ṭols of Bengal during the sixteenth century. It explores the roles of key thinkers and texts in both locations, including Vācaspatimiśra II in Mithilā and Śrīnāthācāryacūḍāmaṇi in Navadvīpa. Key questions include: to what extent did Mithilā-based Dharmaśāstrins and logicians develop a distinctive approach to ownership and inheritance; when did the *Dāyabhāga* become a quintessentially 'Gauḍa' text; how did the incorporation of the *Dāyabhāga* within a new, Gauḍa textual formation reflect broader trends in an emergent Gauḍa/Maithila rivalry; to what extent did the creation of a Gauḍa scale of Dharmaśāstra texts antedate Jīmūtavāhana; and what was the relationship between the terms Gauḍa and Maithila and 'Bengal' and Mithilā as geographic, political and cultural entities? The evidence suggests that Śrīnāthācāryacūḍāmaṇi's *Dāyabhāgaṭippanī* marks the juncture at which the *Dāyabhāga* became *the* emblematic Gauḍa treatise on inheritance and at which a clear distinction between rival Gauḍa and Maithila schools of jurisprudence emerged.

Even if Jīmūtavāhana was not himself a Bengali author, the *Dāyabhāga*'s appropriation by commentators such as Śrīnāthācāryacūḍāmaṇi who lived and worked in Bengal—and who began to apply Bengali appellations to many of the opinions found in the *Dāyabhāga*—ensured that future authors would link him with Bengal. Rocher observes that Jīmūtavāhana cannot 'have codified Bengali customs' because 'Śrīnātha's [and other commentators'] interest in the *Dāyabhāga* was not that of a practicing lawyer... [but was rather] confined to his *ṭol* in Navadvīpa'.[10] He asks, rhetorically:

> How can it, then, be explained that a text with the express purpose of giving local customs their place within the framework of the Dharmaśāstra remained practically unnoticed for four centuries [between the twelfth and fifteenth centuries]?[11]

The skewed view that the *Dāyabhāga* represents an attempt to bring the Dharmaśāstric jurisprudence of inheritance into alignment with local Bengali customs or to defend Bengali customs from the influence of the *Mitākṣarā*, led generations of scholars to 'look for elements that would explain why the law of inheritance was 'different' [in Bengal] from that of other parts of India as represented primarily by the chapter on inheritance in the *Mitākṣarā*'.[12] These explanations for the *Dāyabhāga's* extension of more inheritance rights to cognatic descendants than the *Mitākṣarā* range from the implausible to the absurd. G.C. Sarkar argues that Jīmūtavāhana's ancestors moved to Bengal from Kanauj and sired offspring from many local women (of similar caste but of lower rank) who grew up in their maternal grandfathers' houses.[13] S.C. Mitra, 'by contrast, emphasized the impact of Buddhism' and the importance it places on "natural affection" or the impact of 'Tantrism and the role it accords to various forms of the goddess' to account for the *Dāyabhāga*'s model of inheritance.[14] To account

[10] Rocher, 'Schools of Hindu Law', p. 125. [11] Ibid.
[12] Rocher, *Jīmūtavāhana's Dāyabhāga*, p. 29.
[13] Ibid. Cf. G. C. Sarkar, *Dāyatattva*, 2nd Edition (Calcutta: Cambray and Co., 1904), pp. xxxviii–xlii.
[14] Rocher, *Jīmūtavāhana's Dāyabhāga*, p. 29. Cf. S. C. Mitra, 'Origin and Development of the Bengal School of Hindu Law', *Law Quarterly Review* 21 (1905): 380–92; 22 (1906): 50–63.

for Jīmūtavāhana's apparent defense of ownership as usability as desired (yatheṣṭaviniyojyatva), S. Setlur appeals to Bengal's status 'from time immemorial, [as] a leading centre of trade'. For Setlur, 'because any clog on the free transfer of property is... inconvenient' to a commercial community, 'Jīmūtavāhana... made the [joint Hindu] family... to be a tenancy-in-common'.[15] Alternatively, J.C. Ghose argues that because—according to him—the *Dāyabhāga* was composed under the patronage of Jalāl-ud-dīn Muhammad Shāh (1415–1433) of Bengal, the *Dāyabhāga* is clearly 'the old Hindu Law modified by Muhammadan ideas about individual property'.[16]

Rocher admits that 'the *Dāyabhāga* may have become extremely successful and may have been the source of a regular school of thought on inheritance', and he hints that this may be due to Śrīnāthācāryacūḍāmaṇi and his disciples' commentarial efforts, but he does not follow the implications of such a view.[17] My argument follows R. M. Chakravarti, who notes that Śūlapāṇi, in attempting to establish a systematic Bengali approach to Dharmaśāstra—against that of Mithilā—'had not treated of the Vyavahāra and... Vivāda sections of smṛti... [and] this omission... might have influenced... [Śrīnāthācārycūḍāmaṇi] in selecting the subject of Dāya-bhāga... which had... [been] well studied in the Hindu courts of Mithilā'.[18] Śrīnātha and his pupil Raghunandana, 'backed by keen reasonings, strong prejudices, vigorous criticisms of the predecessors, specially the Maithilas... dominated the field of smṛti learning in Bengal'.[19]

An examination of the chronological development of several layers of the Bengali scale of Dharmaśāstric texts—Jīmūtavāhana, Caṇḍeśvara, Śūlapāṇi, Vācaspatimiśra II, Śrīnāthācāryacūḍāmaṇi, Raghunandana and Acyuta, demonstrates: (1) that medieval Bengali Dharmaśāstra was virtually unknown outside of Mithilā; (2) that Śūlapāṇi, Śrīnātha and Raghunandana attempted to offer a comprehensive, explicitly Bengali rejoinder to Mithilā in Dharmaśāstra; and (3) that Bengali commentators read the *Dāyabhāga*, anachronistically, according to this geographical division of Dharmaśāstra. In so doing, these commentators recast the *Dāyabhāga* as a foundational text of a Gauḍa school of jurisprudence that was based in Navadvīpa and other ṭols in Bengal.

[15] Ibid., 31. Cf. S. Setlur, 'Bengal School of Hindu Law', *Law Quarterly Review* 23 (1907): 202–19.

[16] Ibid., 31. Cf. J. C. Ghose, *The Principles of Hindu Law*, 3d ed., Vol 2, (Calcutta: S.C. Auddy & Co., 1917), xv.

[17] Rocher, 'Schools of Hindu Law', p. 127.

[18] R. M. Chakravarti, 'Contributions to the History of Smṛti in Bengal and Mithilā', *Journal of the Asiatic Society of Bengal* (1915): 311–406, 344. Śrīnātha's father, one Śrīkara, is—*pace* Chakravarti—*not* the author of a commentary on the *Dāyabhāga*, *Dāyabhāgavinirṇaya*. See R. C. Hazra, 'Śrīnāthācāryacūḍāmaṇi of Bengal: His Works and Legacy', *Indian Historical Quarterly* 26 (1950): 277–92, 287–9.

[19] Ibid., 357.

Inheritance and Ownership in Maithila Dharmaśāstra and Navya-Nyāya

The development of mutually influential (and antagonistic) Maithila and Gauḍa schools of Dharmaśāstra and Navya-Nyāya began in Mithilā (modern Tirhut). Mithilā was 'the principal seat of Hindu learning in the thirteenth, fourteenth, and fifteenth centuries' and a centre of Dharmaśāstra and Navya-Nyāya to which students from across India came in order to study.[20] Karin Preisendanz, discussing the emergence of Mithila's distinctive medieval intellectual culture observes that,

> Mithilā or Tirhut, [was] a region which was much more removed from the direct political and cultural impact of the Delhi Sultanate than other parts of northern India. Already the Karṇāṭa dynasty, from the eleventh century onwards until the invasion of Mithilā by the Tughluqs in 1324, and afterwards the rulers of the Kāmeśvara-Oinīvāra dynasty provided a very fertile climate for the growth and development of especially Dharmaśāstra and Nyāya in Mithilā . . . the late medieval and early modern non-Muslim rulers of regional kingdoms in northern India turned to promotion of Sanskritic scholarship in general to assert their cultural identity.[21]

This close connection between Sanskritic scholarship, territory, cultural identity, and political overeignty helps to account for the intimate relationship between Mithilā's leading Dharmaśāstra scholars and its ruling dynasties. Mithilā's relative isolation explains, perhaps, Maithila Dharmaśāstrins' insular tendencies as well as the unusual fact that Vijñāneśvara's theory of ownership-by-birth does not appear in their treatises. The great Maithila Dharmaśāstrin, Caṇḍeśvara Ṭhakkura (1314–1370), author of a series of sevenfold 'Jewel Mines' of Dharmaśāstra, the *Smṛtiratnākara*, 'was a powerful individual in the Karṇāṭa court and served as the *Mahāsāndhivigrahika*, or the 'Minister of Peace and War', of king Harisiṃhadeva'.[22] In his *Gṛhastharatnākara*, Caṇḍeśvara defends Vijñāneśvara's definition of sapiṇḍa-ship (as blood-relation rather than as funerary obligation) in order to build a juridical model of the Brāhmaṇa family that is consistent with King Harisiṃhadeva's *Pañjī Prabandha* (the official,

[20] S. C. Vidyabhusana, *A History of Indian Logic: Ancient, Medieval and Modern Schools* (Delhi: Motilal Banarsidass, 1971), pp. 521–2.

[21] Preisendanz, 'The Production of Philosophical Literature': 73.

[22] Anushan Pandey, 'Recasting the Brahmin in Medieval Mithilā: Origins of Caste Identity among the Maithil Brahmins of North Bihar' (PhD Dissertation, University of Michigan, 2014), p. 53. For Caṇḍeśvara, see P. V. Kāṇe, *A History of Dharmaśāstra*, vol. 1, part 2, 2nd edn (Poona: Bhandarkar Oriental Research Institute, 1975), pp. 763–75.

state-sponsored census of Maithila Brāhmaṇa lineages, mūlas).[23] Vācaspatimiśra II, who served as an advisor (pariṣad) to two Kāmeśvara kings, was part of a Brāhmaṇa lineage with royal and scholarly connections.[24]

In contrast to Vijñāneśvara and his followers' interlocking scale of Dharmaśāstra and Mīmāṃsā texts, Caṇḍeśvara, Misarumiśra, and Vācaspatimiśra offer strikingly similar descriptions of inheritance that mention neither ownership-by-birth, philosophical accounts of ownership (and its incidents), nor Vijñāneśvara's *Ṛjumitākṣarā*. Rather, they provide a relatively straightforward, twofold juridical model of inheritance: of partition made after the death of the father (called simply dāyabhāga); and of partition made during the lifetime of the father (jīvatpitṛkavibhāga). Although these Mithilā-based authors make no mention of the *Mitākṣarā*, their discussion of jīvatpitṛkavibhāga argues, either explicitly or implicitly, that Dharmaśāstric injunctions prohibit fathers and grandfathers from alienating ancestral assets without the consent of their sons and grandsons. These authors do not argue *for* or *against* the existence of sons' pre-partition rights of ownership in ancestral assets. Rather, they restrict a father's rights of ownership in ancestral assets (on the basis of Dharmaśāstra) to produce a juridical model of inheritance that is strikingly similar to that of Vijñāneśvara, but that also accords with Maithila Navya-Nyāya theories of ownership.

In the *Vivādaratnākara*, Caṇḍeśvara quotes *Yājñavalkyasmṛti* 2.121, 'the ownership of both the father and the son is the same in land, trusts, and assets which were acquired by the grandfather', and argues that '"similar ownership" (means that a father) is not (entitled to) a surplus share in this case, nor (can there be) a gift (of these properties) according to a father's desire'.[25]

Misarumiśra construes a variant reading of *Yājñavalkyasmṛti* 2.121 in a similar light:

> In reference to grand-paternal assets, a division is certainly proper for grandsons even when the father is alive. 'In assets obtained by the grandfather, movable and immovable, both fathers and grandsons are declared to have equal shares.' Because of this statement, a partition, while the father is alive, is certainly proper even in reference to (assets) acquired using grand-paternal (assets).[26]

[23] Ibid., pp. 53–5. Pandey's major contribution is to delineate the overlap Maithila Brāhmaṇa identity and Mithilā as a sovereign political territory. See, for example, Pandey's second chapter, 'The Making of a Maithil'. Also see Ugra Jha, *The Genealogies and Genealogists of Mithila* (Varanasi: Kishor Vidya Niketan, 1980), esp. pp. 36–54. For Vijñāneśvara and Jīmūtavāhana's differing theories of sapiṇḍaship and their relation to inheritance, see Ludo Rocher, 'Inheritance and Śrāddha: The Principle of "Spiritual Benefit"', in *Studies in Hindu Law and Dharmaśāstra*, ed. Donald Davis (New York: Anthem Press, 2014), pp. 267–78.

[24] Preisendanz, 'The Production of Philosophical Literature': 73–5.

[25] *Vivādaratnākara*, ed. Kamalakṛṣṇa Smṛtitīrtha (Calcutta: Asiatic Society of Bengal, 1931), p. 463: bhūr yā pitāmahopāttā nibandho dravyam eva vā / tatra syāt sadṛśaṃ svāmyaṃ pituḥ putrasya cobhayoḥ //Yāj. 2.121// sadṛśaṃ svāmyaṃ nātrāṃśādhikyaṃ na vā pitur icchayā dānaṃ.

[26] *Vivādacandra*, ed. Ram Krishna Jha (Benares: Vidya Vilasa Press, 1931), p. 69: paitāmahadhane pautrasya jīvaty api pitari vibhāgo 'rhaty eva. dravye pitāmahopātte sthāvare jaṅgame tathā / samam

Vācaspatimiśra II's implicit defense of coextensive property between grandfathers, fathers, and sons in ancestral assets occurs during a discussion of a father's absolute rights in self-acquired property. Vācaspatimiśra II begins by defending a father's absolute right to self-acquired assets: 'according to Viṣṇu, 'in reference to self-acquired assets, if a father divides (with his) sons, (it should be) according to (his) desire'.[27] On the basis of Manu 9.209 (if a father recovers lost ancestral assets, he shall not, unless he so wishes, share it with his sons, being as it is his self-acquired assets),[28] Vācaspatimiśra II reveals his support for the commonality of ownership between fathers and sons in all other ancestral assets:

> In like manner, (being 'self-acquired assets') is also recovered ownership (in ancestral assets) because of its conformity with the statement of Manu (9.209). And in this case the rule is (that it is must be) without the aid of (his) father's assets. But, in like manner, there is certainly commonality (between fathers and sons) for (ancestral assets) acquired by means of that (other ancestral assets). Therefore, the father alone is the master in reference to an equal and an equal division of those assets which the father has acquired without the aid of the assets of a previous person (in the family). Here also, the division is only by force of his (the father's) will. Here also sons are certainly powerless.[29]

The implication of Vācaspatimiśra's argument is that, excepting self-acquired and self-recovered assets, a father's control over grand-paternal and paternal assets is limited by the force of Dharmaśāstric injunctions. Furthermore, even though a father has ownership in these assets, he is prohibited from making an unequal distribution of assets except in reference to a series of carefully-designated categories of assets. In fact, sons are prohibited from forcing a father to partition only those (self-acquired) assets over which he is legally independent.[30]

aṃśitvam ākhyātam pituḥ pautrasya cobhayoḥ // iti vacanāt paitāmahopaśleṣeṇārjite 'pi jīvati pitari vibhāgo 'rhaty eva.

[27] *Vivādacintāmaṇi*, ed. Khemarāja Śrīkṛṣṇadāsa (Mumbai: Śrīveṅkaṭeśvara Press, 1955), p. 193: tad āha **viṣṇuḥ** pitā cet putrān vibhajet tasya svecchā svayamupātte 'rthe.

[28] *Manu-Smṛti: with the 'Manubhāṣya' of Medhātithi*, ed. Gaṅgānātha Jhā, Vol. 2 (Calcutta: Royal Asiatic Society of Bengal, 1939), p. 301: paitṛkaṃ tu pitā dravyam anavāptaṃ yad āpnuyāt / na tat putrair bhajet sārdham akāmaḥ svayam arjitam //9.209//

[29] *Vivādacintāmaṇi*, p. 196: tadvat svāmyuddhṛtam api **manuvacanānurodhāt**. atra ca pitṛdravyān-upaśleṣas tantram. tadupaśleṣārjitasya tu tadvat sādhāraṇyād eva. tathā ca pitrā pūrvapuruṣa-dravyānupaśleṣeṇa yad arjitaṃ tasya samavibhāge viṣamavibhāge ca pitaiva prabhuḥ. atra vibhāgo 'pi tadicchābalād eva. anīśatāpy atraiva putrāṇām.

[30] Ibid., p. 193: yad dhanaṃ pituḥ svātantryaviṣayas tasya tatsattve tadicchayaiva vibhāgaḥ. The implication is that a father's consent is *not* necessary for a partition of assets over which he does *not* have independent control.

Maithila Dharmaśāstra writings on inheritance show a continuity of argument that goes hand-in-glove with the durability of the nexus between regional sovereignty, Maithila Brāhmaṇa lineage formation, and Navya-Nyāya scholarship. In the *Dāyasāra* section of his *Dharmaśāstrīyanibandhāvalī*, Maheśa Ṭhakkura, writing at the onset of the Khaṇḍavalā Dynasty, copies the *Vivādacintāmaṇi*'s model of a partition performed during the lifetime of the father (jīvatpitṛkavibhāga) verbatim, and follows Vijñāneśvara's definition of kinship (sāpiṇḍya) as a biological relation.[31]

The simplicity of these Mithilā-based authors' Dharmaśāstra writings on inheritance is striking, particularly given their discussions of ownership in their Navya-Nyāya treatises. Although Misarumiśra's *Padārthacandrikā* is currently lost, Vācaspatimiśra's *Nyāyatattvāloka* offers an extremely detailed account of ownership, reflective of broader trends in Maithila approaches to the philosophical problem of ownership. The *Nyāyatattvāloka* assumes two points: (1) that Dharmaśāstra (rather than custom) is the epistemic authority for establishing the existence of ownership; and (2) that the ownership of fathers, sons, wives, is limited by Dharmaśāstric injunctions. In the *Nyāyatattvāloka*, Vācaspatimiśra II defines ownership as,

> fitness for use as desired (yatheṣṭaviniyogayogyatva)... [that] has the form of an opposition to the prior absence of purchase or some similar valid means of acquisition, which motivates use of an asset in a manner unopposed by law. A thing's identity as 'sva', is its being the site of the destruction of the prior absence of a valid means of acquisition such as purchase, which enables the use of the legitimately acquired asset in a manner not contradictory to śāstra.[32]

Maithila Dharmaśāstrins defend a *Mitākṣarā*-esque model of inheritance by employing Dharmaśāstric injunctions to restrict a father's independent control over ancestral assets, rather than by legitimizing customary notions of sons' ownership-by-birth. By avoiding the question of janmasvatva altogether, Maithila Dharmaśāstric models of inheritance do not contradict Maithila Navya-Nyāya theories of ownership.

[31] *Dharmaśāstrīyanibandhāvalī*, ed. S.C. Miśra and S. Bhattācārya (Darbhanga: Mithilāvidyāpīṭha, 1978), pp. 128–9. For the sapiṇḍa relation, see Pandey, 'Recasting the Brahmin', pp. 55–7 and *Dharmaśāstrīyanibandhāvalī*, 127: samānaṃ piṇḍo yeṣāṃ te sapiṇḍā...saptaśarīraṃ tad uktaṃ **garbh[o]p[a]niṣadi**...asthisnāyumayyānaḥ pitṛtas tvaṅmāṃsarudhirāṇi mātṛta iti pitṛmātryaṃśaśarīraṃ bhavati. Those who have the same kinship are kin...seven bodies...It is said in the *Garbhopaniṣad*: 'Bones, tendons, and mayyānaḥ(?) come from the father. Skin, flesh, and blood come from the mother. Thus, one possesses a body which contains particles of the father and the mother.' I am immensely grateful to Radha Blinderman for the emendation and translation.

[32] Kroll, 'A Logical Approach to Law', p. 63, fn 41; *Nyāyatattvāloka*: śāstr[ā]viruddhaviniyogaprayojakībhūtakrayādiprāgabhāvavirodhitvarūpaṃ yatheṣṭaviniyogayogyatvaṃ svatvam. śāstrāviruddho yo viniyogaḥ sāgamasya tatprayojako yaḥ krayādiprāgabhāvasya dhvaṃsaḥ tadvattvaṃ vastunaḥ svatvam. I am grateful for Larry McCrea's assistance with this passage. I have changed Kroll's translation of 'property' to 'asset' to maintain consistency throughout this monograph.

In the *Nyāyalīlāvatīprakāśa*, Vācaspatimiśra's Mithilā-based predecessor, Vardhamāna Upādhyāya (fourteenth century) defends the Maithila Dharmaśāstra argument that fathers, despite *their* ownership in ancestral assets, are contained in their exercise of that ownership by śāstric injunctions. Vardhamāna writes that,

> For example, the smṛti author Vyāsa writes: 'Heirs, whether separated or members of a joint family, are equal with respect to immoveable assets, and no one member should make a [sale] or gift [of that property] without the consent of the others'. Through this śloka (verse), Vyāsa recalls (smaryate) a Vedic prohibition on giving away, selling, or otherwise disposing of immoveable assets without the consent of one's sons.[33]

Furthermore, in the *Nyāyatattvāloka*, Vācaspatimiśra II hints at the existence of sons' pre-partition rights of ownership that would be consistent with his definition of ownership,

> Although svatva yielding use in a manner unopposed by law does exist for sons, wives, and other dependents, these individuals may nonetheless be unable to use an asset entirely as they wish, and may, for example, be unable to alienate that asset, based on a prohibition of Vedic [Dharmaśāstric] authority.[34]

Caṇḍeśvara's invocation of the *Mitākṣarā*'s definition of kinship notwithstanding, the Maithila school of jurisprudence appears united largely by its disinterest in non-Maithila Dharmaśāstric writings on the subject of inheritance. Maithila Dharmaśāstrins treated inheritance as a purely legal, Dharmaśāstric problem, and this approach dovetails, almost perfectly, with Navya-Nyāya theories of ownership as a purely Dharmaśāstric phenomenon. Coincidentally, these Mithilā-based scholars supported many of Vijñāneśvara's conclusions concerning a father's limited powers of alienation in ancestral assets, but Caṇḍeśvara, Vācaspati, Misarumiśra, and Maheśa Ṭhakkura arrived at these conclusions using a markedly different, non-Mīṃāmsā approach. In any case, all of the components of a school of jurisprudence—consistent lines of argumentation, deliberate self-representation as a follower, defender, or revitalizer of a tradition, and regional and disciplinary connections—are present in in the Navya-Nyāya and Dharmaśāstra writings of these Mithilā-based scholars.

[33] Ibid., pp. 52–3, fn 23; *Nyāyalīlāvatīprakāśa*: ata eva svatve saty api yatheṣṭaviniyoganiṣedho 'pi śābda eva yathā—vibhaktā vāvibhaktā vā dāyadāḥ sthāvare samāḥ / naikaḥ kuryāt krayaṃ dānaṃ parasparamataṃ vinā. ity anena sutānām asammatau dānavikrayādiniṣedhaḥ smarryate.

[34] Ibid., p. 65, fn 44; *Nyāyatattvāloka*: putradārādau tu yathoktaviniyogasvatvasattve 'pi śabdaniṣedhād vikrayādiyatheṣṭaviniyogābhāvaḥ.

A Walled Garden in Mithilā and Bengal

Despite their highly insular proclivities, Mithilā-based logicians and jurists tend to refer to—and to define themselves against—the opinions of their Bengali (Gauḍa) neighbours. Although Maithila authors take no notice of Bengali ideas concerning inheritance or property, the seeds of the Gauḍa/Maithla split on inheritance appear to have been sown in the shared soil of cultural and ritual practices.[35] R.C. Chakravarti argues that due to the Islamic conquest of Bengal in the twelfth century:

> until Sanskrit learning began to revive in the fifteenth century, Gauḍīya scholarship and composition remained dormant, and the outside world of Sanskrit knew very little of the older scholarship in Gauḍa except by vague and generally nameless traditions. Even in Mithilā, which had not lost all connection with Bengal, the references run vaguely Gauḍāḥ, Gauḍa-vākyāni, Gauḍā-smṛti, Gauḍa-nibandha, or still more vaguely as prāñcāḥ.[36]

Chakravarti's polite communalism notwithstanding, he highlights an important feature of the development of a Gauḍa school of Dharmaśāstra: before Śrīnāthācāryacūḍāmaṇi, Mithilā-based Dharmaśāstrins used the term 'Gauḍa', sparingly, as an appellation for treatises and cultural practices emanating from Bengal. Maithila Dharmaśāstrins display an awareness of Jīmūtavāhana and Śūlapāṇi's texts and arguments, and they occasionally identify these authors as Gauḍa, but they certainly not to describe an interlocking scale of texts or a school of thought. Caṇḍeśvara Ṭhakkura was one of the first Maithila scholars to attest to Bengali Dharmaśāstra.[37] Chakravarti notes that, based on a 'great similarity' between Caṇḍeśvara's *Kṛtyaratnākara* and Jīmūtavāhana's *Kālaviveka*, it is 'reasonable to infer that the *Kṛtyaratnākara* had borrowed... from the *Kālaviveka*... indirectly as Gauṛīya-smṛti'.[38] Moreover, Caṇḍeśvara refers to the ślokas detailing the celebration of the '*Durgotsava*, the great festival of Bengal' and 'Dasāharā' that appear in the *Kālaviveka* as 'Bengali statements accepted by the populace' (mahājanaparigṛhīta gauḍavākyāni).[39]

Chakravarti uses this reference to establish a *terminus ante quem* for Jīmūtavāhana, but if, as Bihani Sarkar argues, Jīmūtavāhana was 'the earliest smārta to proselytize the Durgā Pūjā' in the *Durgotsavanirṇaya* of the *Kālaviveka*, then Caṇḍeśvara's apparent reference to Jīmūtavāhana represents a

[35] Joydev Ganguly, *Dharmaśāstra in Mithilā* (Calcutta: Calcutta Sanskrit College, 1972), offers a synoptic account of the similarities and influences between Maithila and Gauḍa Dharmaśāstra. See, especially, chapter 5, 'Maithila Smṛti as Influenced by the Smṛti Writers of Bengal and other Provinces'.

[36] Chakravarti, 'Smṛti in Bengal': 325. The majority of Chakravarti's examples are taken from a manuscript of Caṇḍeśvara's *Kṛtyaratnākara*. Cf. fn 1.

[37] Chakravarti, 'Smṛti in Bengal': 382–4. [38] Ibid.: 326. [39] Ibid.

foundational moment in the development of a Bengali scale of Dharmaśāstra: the acknowledgement in Mithilā of specifically Gauḍa Dharmaśāstra texts.[40] Caṇḍeśvara's *Kṛtyaratnākara* inaugurated a pattern that characterized medieval Bengali Dharmaśāstra: an oscillating exchange between Bengali and Maithila authors in which Dharmaśāstra became identified, gradually, with regional opinions about certain topics. Similarly, Vācaspatimiśra II, records the views of 'easterners' (prāncāḥ) in the *Vyavavahāracintāmaṇi*.[41] In his *Nyāyasūtroddhāra*, Vācaspati refers to himself as 'a paṇdit of the Mithilā king' (Mithileśvarasūriṇā).[42] Vācaspati was the first Dharmaśāstrin to refer to the views of Śūlapāṇi and he was the second or third Dharmaśāstrin (after Caṇḍeśvara or Śūlapāṇi) to refer to the works of Jīmūtavāhana (but not to the *Dāyabhāga*).[43]

In light of these Mithilā-based Dharmaśāstrins' identification of Śūlapāṇi and Jīmūtavāhana as Gauḍa, one might be tempted to view Śūlapāṇi or Jīmūtavāhana as the founders of a Bengal school. Although Śūlapāṇi's works would become ubiquitous touchstones for Bengali and non-Bengali Dharmaśāstrins, Śūlapāṇi never identifies himself as Gauḍa nor does he frame his arguments as rejoinders to a Mithilā school of thought.[44] Neither Śūlapāṇi nor Jīmūtavāhana ever speak about their geographical location and only subsequent self-identified Gauḍa authors labelled them as Gauḍa and framed their arguments as attacks on a Maithila school.[45] Chakravarti argues that Śūlapāṇi was 'among the earliest stars of the Hindu Revival [in Bengal because]...he reorganized the Bengal School of Smṛti'.[46] Caṇḍeśvara's possible reference to Jīmūtavāhana's *Kālaviveka* aside, there is no evidence to support Chakravarti's assertion that a discernible Bengal school of Dharmaśāstra antedated Śūlapāṇi (or, more properly speaking, Śrīnāthācāryacūḍāmaṇi). Nor does Śūlapāṇi refer to Caṇḍeśvara or Vijñāneśvara on matters on inheritance. Śūlapāṇi refers once to the views of 'the *Ratnākara*' in the *Sāṃkrāntiviveka*, but he does not label Caṇḍeśvara a Maithila or contrast Caṇḍeśvara with a Gauḍa perspective.[47] Śūlapāṇi seems to have conceived of his many nibandhas on individual topics as a corporate whole: an investigation into smṛti (*Smṛtiviveka*), but not as a codification of 'Gauḍa Smṛti'. Moreover, Śūlapāṇi did not write a treatise on inheritance per se. He composed a commentary on the *Yājñavalkyasmṛti*—the *Dīpakalikā*, but in his comments on Yājñavalkya's section on inheritance (2.114–149), he gives a

[40] Bihani Sarkar, 'The Rite of Durgā in Medieval Bengal: An Introductory Study of Raghunandana's *Durgāpūjātattva* with Text and Translation of the Principal Rites', *Journal of the Royal Asiatic Society*, Series 3, 22.2 (2012): 325–90, 330. doi:10.1017/S1356186312000181.

[41] Chakravarti, 'Smṛti in Bengal': 396.

[42] Ibid., 399. For Vācaspatimiśra, see Kāṇe, *History of Dharmaśāstra*, vol. 1, part 2, pp. 844–54.

[43] Ibid., 315–16.

[44] For Śūlapāṇi, see Kāṇe, *History of Dharmaśāstra*, vol. 1, part 2, pp. 823–40.

[45] Chakravarti, 'Smṛti in Bengal': 340–1.

[46] Ibid.: 343.

[47] Ibid.: 342, fn 1. evam eva **kalpataru-ratnākara-parijātādayaḥ**.

perfunctory account of inheritance without articulating an explicit theory of uparamasvatva or śāstraikasamadhigamyasvatva.

Śūlapāṇi's most famous treatises—the *Dattakaviveka* (adoption), *Durgotsavaviveka* (Durgā festival) and the *Śrāddhaviveka* (funerary rites)—attracted commentary from self-styled Navadvīpan logicians. That juncture—at which Navadvīpan logicians and Dharmaśāstrins produced a commentarial corpus that combined Śūlapāṇi and Jīmūtavāhana's works and framed them as a Gauḍa alternative to Vācaspatimiśra II and Caṇḍeśvara—marks the founding of a Gauḍa school of jurisprudence.[48]

Śrīnāthācāryacūḍāmaṇi: The Founder of the Bengal School

The production of commentarial literature on Jīmūtavāhana and Śūlapāṇi's treatises in Navadvīpa in the late fifteenth century marks the emergence of a Bengal school of thought with regard to ownership and inheritance. At this time, many Bengali logicians and Dharmaśāstrins who trained in Mithilā, the regional centre of śāstric learning, migrated home to establish their own educational institutions. These ṭols, many of which were located in Navadvīpa, would coalesce into the 'University of Nadia'. In Dharmaśāstra, the central figure of this new school of thought was Śrīnāthācāryacūḍāmaṇi. He, rather than Jīmūtavāhana or Śūlapāṇi, ought to be viewed as the founder of a Bengali school of jurisprudence because: (a) his work (and that of his followers) identified self-consciously as Bengali, Navadvīpan, etc; (b) he created a comprehensive commentarial tradition that synthesized the *Dāyabhāga*'s model of inheritance with Śūlapāṇi's theory of śrāddha (spiritual benefit); and (c) inaugurated a pedagogical chain of transmission (paramparā) in which commentators read Jīmūtavāhana polemically against Caṇḍeśvara, Vācaspatimiśra II and other Maithila Paṇḍitas (as well as against Vijñāneśvara).

We know relatively little about Śrīnātha, other than that he established a ṭol in Navadvīpa at the time that that city was emerging as a major centre of commerce and of śāstric learning in the early sixteenth century.[49] Chakravarti notes that:

> It would seem that in Navadvīpa (the admitted home of his son Rāmabhadra) his ṭol was one of the most important and influential, where brilliant students [such as Raghunandana . . . were carefully trained. To Śrīnātha belongs the credit of popularizing the study of Jīmūtavāhana's difficult Dāyabhāga. In fact, by their commentaries he, his son, and . . . Raghunandana, established the reputation of Jīmūtavāhana for all time to come.[50]

[48] Ibid.: 337–40.
[49] See, Kroll, 'A Logical Approach to Law', p. 14; Ganeri, *The Lost Age of Reason*, pp. 57–9.
[50] Chakravarti, 'Smṛti in Bengal': 351.

Śrīnātha authored commentaries on Jīmūtavāhana's *Dāyabhāga* (*Dāyabhāgaṭippanī*) and Śūlapāṇi's *Śrāddhaviveka.*[51] He also compiled a series of 'oceans' of Dharmaśāstra covering purification (śuddhi), rites (kṛtya) and discernments (vivekas) on topics including the Durgā festival (based on Jīmūtavāhana's *Kālaviveka*).[52] In the introduction to his commentary on the *Dāyabhāga*, Śrīnātha identifies himself, modestly, as the son of Śrīkara and as '[a] jewel of the east' (prācīratna).[53] Śrīnātha's son, Rāmabhadra, who writes in the colophon of his *Vyavasthāsaṃgraha* that he is a 'resident of Navadvīpa', helps us to place Śrīnātha in this particular city in Bengal.[54] A remarkable feature of Śrīnātha's writing is his self-awareness as an 'eastern' author and his apparent interest in attacking Maithila authors. For example, his *Śuddhitattvārṇava,* which names Vācaspatimiśra's *Śuddhicintāmaṇi*, 'refers occasionally to Gauḍas . . . [and] quotes often the customs of Maithilas (more than seventeen times), and has . . . criticized them with such remarks' as *tan-na yuktaṃ, tac-cintyaṃ, matam-apāstaṃ, tan-mandaṃ*'.[55]

Śrīnātha founded a school of Gauḍa Dharmaśāstra not only because he began a tradition of identifying as Bengali and of criticizing the 'Miśras' of Mithilā. He left an indelible imprint on the shape of the scale of Dharmaśāstra texts that Bengali Dharmaśāstrins would follow. Śrīnātha developed a commentarial pattern that focused on synthesizing three texts of his illustrious forebears: Jīmūtavāhana's *Dāyabhāga*, Śūlapāṇi's *Śrāddhaviveka*, and Jīmūtavāhana and Śūlapāṇi's *Kālaviveka* and *Durgāpūjāviveka*. Taken together, Śrīnātha's commentaries attack Vācaspatimiśra and Caṇḍeśvara on matters of inheritance, the principle of spiritual benefit (for which the *Śrāddhaviveka* was the principal text) and the Durgotsava.[56] In linking Śūlapāṇi's *Śrāddhaviveka* with Jīmūtavāhana's *Dāyabhāga*, Śrīnātha and his Bengali successors advanced a distinctly Gauḍa alternative to the *Ṛjumitākṣarā*-derived theory of kinship (sapiṇḍa-ship) as blood relation that was *de rigueur* in Maithila juridical writings. The Gauḍa authors drew on Jīmūtavāhana's understanding of kinship as a funerary relationship and on Śulapāṇi's model of funerary relationships to establish a model of inheritance based on 'the criterion of being *upakārika* "of service" to the deceased by offering *piṇḍas*'.[57]

Śrīnātha inaugurated the *Dāyabhāga* and the *Śrāddhaviveka* commentarial traditions. His *Arṇava* texts—and the proselytization of a Gauḍa version of

[51] Ibid.: 345–6. [52] Ibid.: 348–9.

[53] *Dāyabhāga*, ed. Heramba Chatterjee (Howrah: Howrah Saṃskṛta Sāhitya Samāja, 1978), p. 1. *Dāyabhāgaṭippaṇī* on DBh 1.1: **śrīkarācāryaputreṇa prācīratnena** dhīmatā / ṭippanī **śrīnāthena** vidhīyate //

[54] Chakravarti, 'Smṛti in Bengal': 350: **navadvīpanivāsī.** [55] Ibid.: 346.

[56] For the question of the 'Spiritual Benefit' from śrāddha and the preference for various heirs in the *Dāyabhāga*, see Rocher, 'Inheritance and Śrāddha'.

[57] Ibid., 268–70. Also see Manomohini Dutta, 'Upakāra: The Theory of Spiritual Service and Women's Inheritance in the Dāyabhāga', *The Journal of Hindu Studies* 11.3 (2018): 260–84.

Durgāpūjā therein—proved popular among later Bengali commentators such as Raghunātha Sārvabhauma (*Smārtavyavasthārṇava*) and Gopāla Nyāyapañcānana (*Ācāranirṇaya*) and among southern Paṇḍitas such as Kamalākarabhaṭṭa (*Nirṇayasindhu*—where the *Arṇavas* are identified as Gauḍanibandhas).[58] Śrīnāthācāryacūḍāmaṇi's work marks the founding of a Bengal school of Dharmaśāstric thought because it combines a self-consciously 'eastern' self-identification with an attempt to organize disparate texts by eastern authors into a comprehensive rejoinder to Mithilā-based opponents. Śrīnātha was preoccupied with defending Śūlapāṇi's legacy. He acknowledges his indebtedness to Śūlapāṇi in an introductory verse to his commentary on the *Śrāddhaviveka* and he claims that he wrote a commentary on the *Śrāddhaviveka* because Śūlapāṇi's arguments 'were often misrepresented by the people through jealousy or ignorance or fondness for bad logic'.[59] Rāmabhadra Nyāyālaṅkāra Bhaṭṭācārya, however, names contemporary Dharmaśāstra authors on inheritance only when defending Śrīnātha—whom he identifies as his father and guru—from the attacks of Acyuta Cakravartin.[60]

Raghunandana and Acyuta: Jīmūtavāhana as an Opponent of Mithilā and the *Mitākṣarā*

Śrīnātha and Rāmabhadra incorporated the *Dāyabhāga* into an explicitly Gauḍa scale of Dharmaśāstra texts—built around Śūlapāṇi. However, Śrīnātha's most prominent pupil, Raghunandana Bhaṭṭācārya and Śrīnātha's most vocal critic, Acyutānanda Chakravartin, first read Jīmūtavāhana, anachronistically, as rejecting the views of Vijñāneśvara, Caṇḍeśvara and Vācaspatimiśra.[61] Acyuta and Raghunandana's commentaries on the *Dāyabhāga* mention, polemically, the opinions of Caṇḍeśvara, Miśra, the Maithila[62] and the *Mitākṣarā*.[63] Raghunandana Bhaṭṭācārya, was a pupil in Śrīnātha's ṭol. His commentary on the *Dāyabhāga*, the

[58] *Dāyabhāga*, ed. H. Chatterjee, xix, fn 29. Cf. Sarkar, 'The Rite of Durgā': 332.

[59] Hazra, 'Śrīnātha Ācārya-cūḍāmaṇi': 291, fn 58: kva **śūlapāṇer** vacanaṃ durūhaṃ [kva] dhīmadīyālpatamā tathāpi / bravīmi tātparyalavaṃ tadīyaṃ yad atra tan me sudhiyaḥ kṣamadhvam //292, fn 63: kecit kutarkādhyavasāya + + nye dveśāt (? dveṣāt) pare gaḍḍarikāpravāhān / ajñānataḥ kecana **śūlapāṇer** bhāṣyanti siddhāvapathādapetāḥ //

[60] Chakravarti, 'Smṛti in Bengal', 348. Cf. *Dāyabhāga*, ed. H. Chatterjee, xx. Cf. also *Dāyabhāga*, ed. Bhāratacandra Śiromaṇi (Calcutta: Vidyāratna Press, 1863), p. 89, on Dbh, 2.53.

[61] For Raghunandana's identification of Śrīnātha as his Guru, see Hazra, 'Śrīnātha Ācārya-cūḍāmaṇi': 290.

[62] Chakravarti, 'Smṛti in Bengal': 324; Rocher, *Jīmūtavāhana's Dāyabhāga*, pp. 18 and 22. Acyuta (and Śrīkṛṣṇa) on Dbh 2.27: iti **caṇḍeśvarādyanumataditam** apakārtum āha; on Dbh 4.3: atra **caṇḍeśvarādisvahastitam prācīnamatam** adhikṣeptum āha; on Dbh 9.1.31: iti **ratnākarāmatam** api niṣpramāṇam ity anyathā siddhāntayati sampratītam; and Raghunandana on Dbh 12.4: iti **ratnākaramiśrādimatapratyuktam**.

[63] Rocher, *Jīmūtavāhana's Dāyabhāga*, p. 22; Raghunandana on Dbh 1.7, 1.39, and 1.42; Acyuta and Śrīkṛṣṇa on Dbh 1.39, 2.18 and 4.2.27.

Dāyabhāgavyākhyā, 'quotes, among other[s]...the *Cintāmaṇi*...the Miśrāḥ (often), the *Ratnākara*' and often criticizes 'Vācaspati Miśra and his followers'.[64] Raghunandana wrote an overview of the essence of Smṛti in 28 sections, called the *Aṣṭāviṃśati-tattva*.[65] For Raghunandana, the polemic against Maithila Dharmaśāstrins are in the same vein as Śrīnātha's: part of a broader competition over Dharmaśāstra generally in which inheritance formed a small, but important facet. Acyuta and Śrīkṛṣṇa, on the other hand, appear far more invested in the *Dāyabhāga* and in arguing against Śrīnātha *and* the Maithila Dharmaśāstins. Acyuta was a far keener logician than either Śrīnātha or Raghunandana and his interest in the *Dāyabhāga* extended beyond the merely legal to the logical.

Chakravarti argues that although famous Maithila Dharmaśāstrins 'agree generally with those ideas of the North Indian School' it was 'in fact the later Gauṛiyas [who] by frequently criticizing and discussing these Maithilas suggested the idea that they formed a separate school'.[66] Śrīnātha's *Dāyabhāgaṭippanī* marks the moment when the *Dāyabhāga* was incorporated into a scale of Dharmaśāstra (and Navya-Nyāya) texts that was connected intimately with the rise of Navadvīpa as a centre of śāstric learning. It is understandable, then, that as Navadvīpa's importance grew, its leading Paṇḍitas such as Raghunandana and Acyuta Cakravartin came to read the *Dāyabhāga* increasingly against prominent Maithila texts, and to usher in an apparent schism between Bengali and Maithila schools of thought. As Rocher notes, 'Gauḍa' and 'Maithila' appellations appear commonly in the writings of eighteenth-century eastern Indian Dharmaśāstrins.[67]

Table 2.1 charts the Gauḍa scale of Dharmaśāstra texts that emerged in sixteenth-century Navadvīpa. The table is arranged vertically in descending chronological order. The table is arranged horizontally by each author's date, location, and principal treatise on inheritance and Durgāpūjā/śrāddha. At each horizontal layer, a given text incorporates arguments from texts that appear lower in the same column. The founding of Navadvīpa in 1514 marks the emergence of a Gauḍa scale of Dharmaśāstra texts. Gaps (in inheritance and in śrāddha), filled in by later authors, attest to the deliberate mapping of the Gauḍa scale of texts onto the Maithila scale of texts.

Avacchedakas, Nirūpakas, and Padārthas in *Dāyabhāga* Commentaries

By the end of the sixteenth century Bengali Dharmaśāstrins began to assemble a distinctively Gauḍa scale of texts, vis-à-vis Mithilā, that incorporated Jīmūtavāhana's *Dāyabhāga* as its paradigmatic treatise on inheritance. Almost

64 Chakravarti, 'Smṛti in Bengal': 352. 65 Ibid. 66 Ibid.: 377.
67 Rocher, 'Schools of Hindu Law', p. 121.

Table 2.1 The Gauḍa Scale of Dharmaśāstra Texts

Author Name, Location, Date	Treatise on Inheritance	Treatise on Śrāddha	Treatise on Durgāpūjā
Rāmabhadra I (Navadvīpa, 1510–70)	Dāyabhāgavivṛti	Śrāddhavyavasthā	Smṛtitattvavinirṇaya
Acyutacakravartin (Navadvīpa, 1510–70)	Dāyabhāgasiddhānta-kumudacandrikā	Śrāddhavivekaṭippaṇī	N/A
Raghunandana Bhaṭṭācārya (Navadvīpa, 1510–80)	Dāyatattva/ Dāyabhāgavyākhyāna	Śrāddhatattva	Durgāpūjātattva
Śrīnāthācāryacūḍāmaṇi (Navadvīpa, 1475–1525)	Dāyabhāgaṭippaṇī	Śrāddhacandrikā/Śrāddhadīpikā	Kṛtyatattvārṇava
1514: Emergence of Navadvīpa (Raghunātha Śiromaṇi Founds 'Chair' in Nyāya)			
Vācaspatimiśra II (Mithilā, 1425–80)	Vivādacintāmaṇi/ Vyavahāracintāmani	Śrāddhacintāmaṇi	Kṛtyacintāmaṇi
Śūlapāṇi (Bengal, 1375–1460)	**N/A Śrīnātha fills with Dāyabhāga**	Śrāddhaviveka	Durgāpūjāviveka
Caṇḍeśvara (Mithilā, 1314–70)	Vivādaratnākara	**N/A Vācaspatimiśra fills with Śrāddhacintāmaṇi**	Kṛtyaratnākara
Jīmūtavāhana (Bengal? 12–14th centuries)	Dāyabhāga	N/A Śrīnātha fills with Śrāddhaviveka	Kālaviveka

simultaneously, Vasudeva Sārvabhauma and Raghunātha Śiromaṇi, two Bengali Brahmans who probably studied Navya-Nyāya in Mithilā, returned to Navadvīpa and set about training a new generation of Gauḍa logicians.[68] Vidyabhushana argues that Raghunātha 'founded... a special Chair of Logic' in the 'University of Navadvīpa' where 'in Smṛti there is a chair of the Senior Smārta (Jurist), which was inaugurated by Raghunandana'.[69] Ownership was a popular topic for Maithila Navya-Naiyāyikas and Raghunātha Śiromaṇi and Rāmabhadra Sārvabhauma, wrote on the topic extensively. Considering the centrality of theories of ownership to Dharmaśāstric models of inheritance, and considering the fact that sixteenth-century Bengali Dharmaśāstrins and logicians lived and worked in the same ṭols in Navadvīpa, some measure of influence between these two disciplines seems likely.

Although the *Dāyabhāga* became the darling of legions of logicians, 'in reality', Rocher notes, there is little *nyāya* in the *Dāyabhāga*'—but of course, this observation does not necessarily invalidate 'Colebrooke's statement to the effect that the Bengal school was greatly influenced by the *nyāya* system of philosophy'.[70] Indeed, Colebrooke 'could not help facing *Navya-Nyāya* firsthand while reading the commentaries on the *Dāyabhāga*' and 'in the *ṭols*... in Bengal, the two main topics of instruction were *Navya-Nyāya* and *dharmaśāstra*'.[71] Rocher's observation, 'that, in Colebrooke's opinion... [the *Mitākṣarā* and the *Dāyabhāga*] were accepted as the laws of Benaras and Bengal, respectively, at a later stage only', invites an examination of the historical processes by which the geographical and intellectual connections between the *Dāyabhāga*, Navya-Nyāya philosophy, and Bengali Paṇḍitas arose.[72]

Although Navya-Nyāya terminology does not appear in the *Dāyabhāga*, the *Dāyabhāga*'s commentators, particularly Śrīnāthācāryacūḍāmaṇi, Rāmabhadra I, Acyutacakravartin and Śrīkṛṣṇatarkālaṅkāra articulate an interpretation of the *Dāyabhāga* that hinges on Navya-Nyāya techniques and theories.

This section unpacks three instances where the commentators use Navya-Nyāya terminology to frame the *Dāyabhāga* as a rejoinder to the Maithila and the *Mitākṣarā* schools of jurisprudence. First, the commentators use Navya-Nyāya terminology (avacchedaka, vyāpyatva) to explain Jīmūtavāhana's derivation of inheritance (dāya) as an object noun from the root √dā, (to give) and thereby to defend Jīmūtavāhana's theory of uparamasvatva (ownership-by-the-cessation-of-the-ownership-of-the-previous-owner). Second, when summarizing Jīmūtavāhana's pūrvapakṣin (an advocate of janmasvatva), the commentators advocate three different philosophical theories of ownership that draw from and argue against Maithila Navya-Nyāya theories of ownership and support Gauḍa-Nyāya theories of ownership. Third, when the commentators reject ownership-by-birth and the *Mitākṣarā's* adage that sons become owners by birth, they rely on Navya-Nyāya

[68] See Ganeri, *The Lost Age of Reason*, pp. 42–5; H. H. Ingalls, *Materials for the Study of Navya-Nyāya Logic* (Cambridge, MA: Harvard University Press, 1951), pp. 9–19; Kroll, 'A Logical Approach to Law', pp. 100–2.

[69] S. C. Vidyabhusana, *A History of Indian Logic*, pp. 525–7.

[70] Rocher, *Dāyabhāga*, p. 41.

[71] Ibid., pp. 40–1.

[72] Rocher, 'Schools of Hindu Law', p. 122.

theories of ownership as discernible-from-the-śāstra-alone (śāstraikasamadhigam yatva). Śrīnāthācārya and Acyuta's commentaries transform the *Dāyabhāga* into a Nyāya-based text that attacked the *Mitākṣarā* school's theory of ownership-by-birth and the Maithila school's Dharmaśāstra/Navya-Nyāya nexus.

Delimiting Dādhātvarthatā: Navya-Nyāya Techniques in *Dāyabhāga* Commentaries

Śrīnātha, Rāmabhadra and Acyuta employ two characteristically Navya-Nyāya terms: delimiter (avacchedaka) and pervaded-ness (vyāpyatva) when commenting on Jīmūtavāhana's definition of inheritance.[73] As the *Dāyabhāga* commentarial tradition developed, it grew increasingly inflected by a technical Navya-Nyāya idiom. In Dbh 2.4–5, Jīmūtavāhana defines dāya as 'something given' (dīyate).[74] Jīmūtavāhana notes that:

> and the use of 'to give' (in this case) is secondary because of the similarity of result (between the primary and secondary meanings): namely, the production of ownership for someone else preceded by the extinction of the svatva of people who have died or 'gone forth' or the like'.[75]

But, relates Jīmūtavāhana, 'dead people and the like do not (formally) abandon that (ownership)'.[76] Consequently, 'the word dāya is used in a secondary sense to refer to assets in which there is ownership (for another), contingent on a connection with the previous owner, when that (previous owner's) ownership expires'.[77] Whether or not Jīmūtavāhana refers deliberately to Vijñāneśvara's definition of inheritance as an 'asset which becomes the property of another, solely on account of (that person's) relation to the (asset's) owner', the *Dāyabhāga's* definition of dāya as derived from √dā precludes ownership-by-birth *a priori*.[78] Jīmūtavāhana's theory of inheritance as a conventional (nirūḍha) object noun derived from a secondary meaning feels strained: Mitramiśra (1610–1640) and Derrett found it cumbersome.[79] The burden of logically explicating Jīmūtavāhana's views fell to his commentators.

Śrīnātha's introduction to the *Tātparyadīpikā* states that he envisioned himself as writing his commentaries 'for the sake of my students because those who

[73] Ingalls, *Navya-Nyāya Logic*, pp. 28–9 and 47–9.

[74] Rocher, *Dāyabhāga*, p. 250: dīyata iti vyupattyā dāyaśabdaḥ.

[75] Ibid.: dadātiprayogaś ca gauṇaḥ mṛtapravrajitādisvatvanivṛttipūrvakaparasvatvotpattiphalasāmyāt. See also Manomohini Dutta, '*Dāya*: The Conceptual Understanding of Inheritance and Gift in the *Dāyabhāga*', *Journal of Indian Philosophy* 47 (2019): 111–31.

[76] Rocher, *Dāyabhāga*, p. 250: na tu mṛtādīnāṃ tatra tyāgo 'sti.

[77] Ibid.: tataś ca pūrvasvāmisambandhādhīnaṃ tatsvāmyoparame yatra dravye [svatvaṃ] tatra nirūḍho dāyaśabdaḥ.

[78] *Mitākṣarā*, prelude to 2.114, 280: tatra dāyaśabdena yad dhanaṃ svāmisambandhād eva nimittād anyasya svam bhavati tad ucyate.

[79] Rocher, *Dāyabhāga*, p. 54, fn 5.

know the essence of philosophy, as if feigning not to look at an elephant, do not pay attention to smṛti, and others are too stupid to ponder words and their meanings'.[80] Similarly, Śrīnātha relates in his *Vivekārṇava* that 'this effort of mine is [intended] to ward off the stream of lemmings [who hold] untruths with regard to that which is partial to nyāya, the path of the wise that agrees with the meaning of the Vedas'.[81] Śrīnātha, commenting on Dbh 2.4–5, characterizes the artificiality of Jīmūtavāhana's derivation of dāya as an issue of pervasion (vyāpti). He argues that it is implausible for an asset in which ownership is produced upon the extinction of the ownership of a relative to be the object (of the verb √dā) because it is impossible for there to be invariable concomitance (vyāpyatva) between an asset of a (dead) relative and the secondary meaning of 'to give' that is derived from 'it is given'.[82] Consequently, explains Śrīnātha, "it is given' means, figuratively, the state of possessing the result produced by the meaning of the verbal root (√dā)'.[83] Śrīnātha's son, Rāmabhadra, summarizes his father's argument using the Navya-Nyāya concept of delimitation:

> My father argued that the verbal root and nominal suffix (of dāya) are (both) secondary:[84] (1) because 'to give' cannot mean, in its primary sense, the death of a relative or the like, as will be derived from 'it is given'; and (2) because of the absence of logical concomitance between that (figuratively derived meaning) and the assets and the like (of the relative). In truth, however, √dā means (in its primary sense) an intention 'this (this asset) is not mine', whose result is the production of ownership for another, and because of the impossibility of that [meaning of the verbal root] in the present circumstances, 'to give' means, figuratively, the set of things beginning with the death of a relative and the like, which are merely activities whose result is the production of ownership for someone else (preceded by the destruction of the previous owner's ownership). Consequently, the nominal suffix is certainly primary because there exists invariable concomitance (between it and) an action in the form of possessing the fruit brought about by that (death and the like) which is the delimiter of (√dā) verbal root-meaning-ness.[85]

[80] Hazra, 'Śrīnāthācāryacūḍāmaṇi of Bengal', 291, fn 57: gajanimīlanavan na manaś ciraṃ dadhati darśanatattvavidaḥ smṛtau / padapadārthavicārajaḍāḥ [pare] tad aha śiṣyahitāya mama śramaḥ //

[81] R. C. Hazra, 'Śrīnātha Ācārya-Cūḍāmaṇi: A Smṛti-Writer of Bengal', *ABORI* 32 (1951): 34–52, 46, fn 1: śrutyarthasaṃvādini yo budhānāṃ naiyāyike vartmani pakṣapātaḥ / tatrāsatāṃ gaḍḍarikā pravāhabhramāpanodāya mama śramo 'yam //

[82] *Dāyabhāga*, ed. H. Chatterjee, p. 28; *Dāyabhāgaṭippaṇī* on Dbh 2.4–5: dīyata ityādi vakṣyamāṇalakṣaṇayā dadātyarthasya sambandhidhanavyāpyatvāsambhavāt sambandhisvatvoparamajanyasvatvakadravyasya karmatvāghaṭanāt ity āha dīyata ityādi.

[83] Ibid.; *Dāyabhāgaṭippaṇī* on Dbh 2.4–5: dīyate iti dhātvarthajanyaphalabhāgitvopalakṣito 'rtha ityāha dīyata ityādi.

[84] Secondary in the sense of having a non-literal, non-etymological meaning.

[85] Ibid.; *Dāyabhāgavivṛti* on Dbh 2.4–5: dīyata iti vakṣyamāṇadadātyarthasya sambandhinidhanāder dadātyaśakyatvāt dhanādeś ca tadvyāpyatvābhāvāt prakṛtipratyayau gauṇav iti **guravaḥ**. vastutaḥ parasvatvāpattiphalakasya 'na mamedam' iti saṅkalpasya dadātyarthatvāt tasya ca prakṛte 'sambhavāt

Delimitation to establish logical concomitance is a quintessentially Navya-Nyāya technique, but Śrīnātha and Rāmabhadra employ this technique to support a characteristically Gauḍa theory of Dharmaśāstra: uparamasvatva. It would be difficult for someone like Vijñāneśvara to defend a theory of ownership-by-birth if inheritance were derived from the verbal root √dā, because 'to give',—in its primary or in its secondary meaning—presupposes the extinction of prior ownership before the arising of subsequent ownership.

Acyuta, critical of Śrīnātha, gives a more revealing account of the derivation of inheritance and its legal implications that is framed in terms of the delimitation of the state of being the verbal root √dā. Acyuta states 'it is fair to use dāya in the technical sense—of something given—because there is evidence (of the use of) the ghaṅvidhi (an object noun derived from √dā) in the *Manusmṛti*'.[86] Acyuta explains that the reason that Jīmūtavāhana uses √dā in a secondary sense is that the primary meaning of √dā—which involves a 'relinquishing' (tyāga) conditioned by the cessation of ownership, and is the (mental) intention "this is not mine"—is inappropriate (because dead people do not have mental intentions)'.[87] Acyuta concludes by stating:

> As for the delimiter of the range of the secondary usage (of the verbal root √dā), provided it is not relinquishment, the delimiter is merely the state of being an activity that serves as the cause of the ownership of another preceded by the extinction of the ownership (of the previous owner). Consequently, there is no lack of invariable concomitance, nor is it inappropriate to say that (a relative's) assets are the object (of the verbal action 'to give'). Therefore, Ācāryacūdāmaṇi's opinion—that the nominal suffix (in dāya) is secondary because it is merely the state of having the result produced by the meaning of the verbal root (death and the like), because: (1) if death and the like have the meaning 'to give', then the verbal root √dā is secondary; (2) in that case the asset (of a relative) is not the object (of the verbal root √dā) inasmuch as

parasvatvāpattiphalakavyāpāramātraṃ sambandhimaraṇādikaṃ dadātinā lakṣyate. dhātvarthatāvacchedakatajjanyaphalaśālitvarūpakriyāvyāpyatvasattvāt pratyayo mukhya eva.

[86] Ibid.; *Kumudacandrikā* on Dbh 2.4–5: tathā ca saṃjñāyām api dāyo datta iti vācyam **manusmṛtau ghañvidhāv** udāhṛtatvāt. Cf. *Manusmṛti: with the Sanskrit Commentary Manvarth-Muktāvalī*, ed. J. L. Shastri (Varanasi: Motilal Banarsidass, 1983), p. 362: idānīṃ dīyata iti dāyaḥ. Rocher attempts to derive dāya through Pāṇini 3.1.138–40, but this is incorrect. 3.1.138–40 generates the nominal form 'dāya' from the verbal root √dā (via a 'dhāñ' suffix), but with an agentive meaning (i.e. 'giver'). 3.3.16–19, teach the ghañ suffix (in the sense of an action for a specific set of verbal roots) in the sense of any non-agentive verbal noun. See *Kāśīkā: Pāṇinīyāṣṭādhyāyīsūtravṛttiḥ*, ed. Anjaneya Sharma (Hyderabad: Saṃskṛtapariṣat, Usmāniyā Viśvavidyālayaḥ, 1969), pp. 256–7: padarujaviśaspṛśo **ghañ** (3.3.16); akartari ca kārake sajñāyām (3.3.19).

[87] *Dāyabhāga*, ed. H. Chatterjee, pp. 28–9: mukhyarthānupapattibījaṃ darśayati na tv [mṛtādīnāṃ tatra tyāgo 'sti] ity. tyāgaḥ svatvanivṛttyupahitaṃ na mamedam itīcchā.

ownership is not the delimiter (of the secondary usage of the verbal root √dā as 'to die')—is refuted.[88]

The crux of the debate was the logical coherence of Jīmūtavāhana's definition. Neither Śrīnātha, Acyuta nor Rāmabhadra questioned the validity of the *Dāyabhāga's* derivation of dāya because to do so would have undermined the text's broader project—defining dāya so as to exclude janmasvatva. The commentators focused on buttressing a constrained definition using the techniques of formal logic. To the extent that they disagreed, their disagreements were about the best way to render Jīmūtavāhana's arguments in accordance with Navya-Nyāya principles. In the course of time the philosophical rigour of *Dāyabhāga* commentaries grew more voluminous and the various definitions of the state of being the meaning of the verbal root √dā became increasingly precise. By the time of Śrīkṛṣṇatarkālaṅkāra, the derivation of dāya as an object noun was a monument to Navya-Nyāya definitional complexity:

> And thus, there is a secondary meaning, in the form of the state of being an action amenable to the production of ownership for a new owner and the destruction of the ownership of the previous owner, in common with such things as the pravrajyā, death of the father and the like, on the part of the verbal root '√dā', whose primary meaning is relinquishing, in the form of the state of relinquishing, whose fruit is the production of ownership for a new owner and the destruction of the ownership of the prior owner. Consequently, the meaning is that it is not inappropriate (to derive dāya this way), because the state of being an object, in the form of having that double result, in the form of the production of ownership for a new owner and the destruction of the ownership of the prior owner, which is produced by an action similar in form to death and the like, immediately after the death and the like of a relative, (on the part of the relative's assets) is unbroken.[89]

Rocher's emphasis on the absence of Navya-Nyāya in the *Dāyabhāga*—so as to warn against Navya-Nyāya being viewed, anachronistically, as the *cause* of earlier Dharmaśāstric theories of uparamasvatva—is particularly apt when we consider the vigorous support that the idea of uparamasvatva received from Dhāreśvara

[88] Ibid., p. 30: gauṇīvṛttiviṣayatāvacchedakam api tyāgānyatve sati svatvanivṛttipūrvakāparasvatvahetubhūtavyāpāratvam eveti nānanugamaḥ na vā dhanasya karmatvānupapattiḥ. etena maraṇāder dadātyarthatve tatra dādhātor gauṇatā, tatra svatvasyānavacchedakatayā na dhanasya karmatvaṃ dhātvarthatāvacchedakaphalabhāgitvasyaiva karmatvād iti dhātvarthajanyaphalabhāgitvamātreṇa pratyayasyāpi gauṇatety **ācāryacūḍāmaṇimatam** pratyuktam.

[89] Ibid., p. 30; Śrīkṛṣṇa on Dbh 2.4–5: tathā ca pūrvasvāmisvatvanivṛttiparasvāmisvatvotpattiphalakatyāgatvena rūpeṇa tyāgaśaktasya dādhātoḥ pūrvasvāmisvatvanivṛttiparasvāmisvatvotpattyanukūlavyāpāratvena pitrādimaraṇapravrajyādisādhāraṇena rūpeṇa lakṣaṇā. sambandhinidhanādyanantaram maraṇādirūpatādṛśavyāpārajanyaṃ yat pūrvasvāmisvatvanivṛttiparasvāmisvatvotpattirūpam phaladvayaṃ tacchālitvarūpaṃ karmatvam akṣatam eveti nānupapattir iti bhāvaḥ.

and the Saṃgrahakāra without any connection to Navya-Nyāya reasoning. Colebrooke, however, was right to view the *Dāyabhāga* as invariably concomitant with the practice of Navya-Nyāya philosophy in Navadvīpa's ṭols. Although later authors such as Rāmabhadra II (likely eighteenth or nineteenth century) rejected Rāmabhadra I's interpretation of inheritance as 'Śrīnātha's child's childish babble' and boasted about 'breaking [the opinion of] the 'unbreakable' (Acyuta)', these late authors retained the argumentative structure inaugurated by Śrīnātha—namely, using Navya-Nyāya techniques to defend Jīmūtavāhana's derivation of dāya from √dā.[90] This brief survey of the *Dāyabhāga* commentator's increasingly Nyāya-inflected definitions of dāya attests to that intimate connection as an essential feature of a Gauḍa school of inheritance that was centered in Bengal.

Svatva as Padārtha: Navya-Nyāya Theories of Ownership in *Dāyabhāga* Commentaries

Śrīnātha, Rāmabhadra, and Acyuta used their commentaries on the *Dāyabhāga* to enter into a contentious debate between Maithila and Gauḍa Navya-Nāyaiyikas about the philosophy of ownership. Their entry-point occurs in the first chapter of the *Dāyabhāga*, where Jīmūtavāhana introduces an opponent who argues that 'sons already have ownership in that (family estate) during their father's lifetime'.[91] For the opponent, sons must have ownership in paternal assets because: (1) acquisition is an activity (requiring) an acquirer; (2) an acquirer is someone who has the state of being an owner that depends on an act of acquisition; and 3) it is appropriate to say that birth is indeed an act of acquisition, i.e. an activity of a son (that makes him an owner).[92] Consequently, says the opponent, 'it has been stated, "sometimes birth alone (is a cause of ownership) as in the case of paternal assets"'.[93] Jīmūtavāhana's pūrvapakṣin, clearly a proponent of ownership-by-birth, whom Acyuta, Raghunandana and Śrīkṛṣṇa identify with Vijñāneśvara, prompted many scholars to argue that Jīmūtavāhana had criticized Vijñāneśvara's *Mitākṣarā*.[94] It is equally likely that Jīmūtavāhana had read the *Mitākṣarā* or that Jīmūtavāhana, as Rocher suggests, 'criticizes views that existed long before' he wrote the *Dāyabhāga*.[95]

[90] Ibid., p. 31; Rāmabhadra II on Dbh 2.4–5: iti **cuḍāmaṇibālakoktam** bālakoktam eva ... etena ... **acyutamataṃ** cyutam eva.

[91] Rocher, *Dāyabhāga*, 251: jīvaty eva pitari putrāṇāṃ tatra svatvam.

[92] Ibid.: nanv arjayitṛvyāpāro 'rjanam. arjanādhīnasvāmibhāvaś cārjayitā. tena putravyāpāro janmaivārjanaṃ yuktam.

[93] Ibid.: ata evoktaṃ kvacij janmaiva yathā pitrye dhane. Jīmūtavāhana's definition of svatva in terms of yatheṣṭaviniyogārhatā suggests that he may have been familiar with the *Ṛjuvimalāpañcikā*.

[94] Rocher, *Dāyabhāga*, pp. 21–4.

[95] Ibid., 24.

In either case, Jīmūtavāhana's commentators employ the theory of ownership-by-birth to discuss the nature of ownership in a way that recapitulates, and intervenes in internal Navya-Nyāya debates about ownership. When these commentators reject ownership-by-birth (and, explicitly, the *Mitākṣarā*) they rely on Navya-Nyāya theories of ownership as determined and as regulated by Dharmaśāstra. These commentators, however, defend theories of ownership that mirror those of Bengali Navya-Naiyāyikas and that contrast with those of Maithila Naiyāyikas.

Gauḍa Navya-Nyāya Theories of Ownership

Raghunātha Śiromaṇi returned to Bengal to found the 'University of Navadvīpa' in 1514 after his 'triumph' against Pakṣadhara Miśra in Mithilā.[96] He brought with him a philosophical tradition—Navya-Nyāya—which, in addition to a vast technical vocabulary, developed several sophisticated theories concerning the nature of ownership. Mithilā's most prominent logicians shared a theory of ownership as a quality (guṇa) of an asset, rather than as a distinct conceptual category (padārtha). Vardhamāna Upādhyāya (fourteenth century), the son of Gaṅgeśa Upādhyāya (the author of the *Tattvacintāmaṇi* and 'founder' of Navya-Nyāya), gives the first Navya-Nyāya treatment of ownership in his *Nyāyalīlāvatīprakāśa.*[97] In a discussion of various Nyāya-Vaiśeṣika conceptual categories, 'he weighs the suggestion that *svatva* could... be an additional *padārtha*'.[98] Vardhamāna rejects a definition of ownership as usability as desired for which, Kroll relates:

> the theory goes, let an asset's capacity to be used as desired be a characteristic property of svatva as a separate padārtha, and let it be produced by receiving gifts and other means of acquisition, [let it] inhere in an asset, and [let it] be conditioned by the asset's owner. And let it be destroyed by sale and other forms of alienation.[99]

The obvious problem with this definition is that one would have to accept ownership on the part of a thief because thieves use assets as desired after they have stolen it.[100] Vardhamāna rejects another possibility: that ownership is internal (i.e. bodily or mentally located) whose external asset is its describer

[96] Kroll, 'A Logical Approach to Law', pp. 101–2. [97] Ibid., p. 45. [98] Ibid., p. 46.

[99] Ibid., p. 50, fn 18; *Nyāyalīlāvatīprakāśa*: pratigrahādijanyo dharmaviśeṣaḥ kalpyate. sa ca dhanagataḥ svāminirūpyas tasya ca vikrayādinā nāśa iti matam. Kroll comments, in the same footnote, that 'Vardhamāna does not use Pārthasārathi's definition of *svatva* as *yatheṣṭaviniyojyatva* explicitly, but he implies as much by his subsequent refutation of the suggestion noted in this passage.'

[100] Ibid., p. 51, fn 19: tan na, cauryyānantaraṃ yatheṣṭaviniyogāt tatrāpi svatvakalpanāpatteḥ.

(nirūpaka).[101] Vardhamāna argues that Dharmaśāstra, rather than extra-śāstric usage, must be the epistemic warrant for ownership.[102] According to Kroll:

> Vardhamāna concludes, svatva must be defined as yatheṣṭaviniyogayogyatva (fitness for use as desired), which means that an asset acquired must be an object of those means of acquisition not opposed by law (here, dharmaśāstra), and is a form of certainty that it would be impossible to use an asset as desired if it were acquired by means that contrast with those means unopposed by law. Although the means of acquisition leading to svatva—such as purchase and receiving gifts—are actions, and are thus inconstant, being an object of those means is undeniably enduring, just as being of [sic] content of knowledge endures, though the event of knowledge itself ceases to exist. It follows, then, that one need not establish another padārtha to embrace the concept of svatva.[103]

Vācaspatimiśra II, whose Dharmaśāstra works mention Gauḍa legal opinions, but whose comments on inheritance in the *Vivādacintāmaṇi* mention neither Jīmūtavāhana nor the theory of uparamasvatva, examines ownership from a Navya-Nyāya perspective in the *Nyāyatattvāloka*. Like Vardhamāna, Vācaspatimiśra rejects the theory of ownership as a separate conceptual category. Rather, he argues:

> svatva is fitness for use as desired (yatheṣṭaviniyogayogyatva)... [that] has the form of an opposition to the prior absence of purchase or some similar valid means of acquisition, which motivates use of an asset in a manner unopposed by law. A thing's identity as 'sva', is its being the site of the destruction of the prior absence of a valid means of acquisition such as purchase, which enables the use of the legitimately acquired asset in a manner not contradictory to śāstra.[104]

Another Maithila Navya-Nāyaiyika, Bhagīratha Ṭhakkura, who trained under Pakṣadhara Miśra with Raghunātha Śiromaṇi, gives, in his *Nyāyalīlāvatīprakāśavivṛti,* the most sophisticated pre-Navadvīpa Navya-Nyāya theory of

[101] Ibid., pp. 47–8: svatvam avāhyam eva vāhyaṃ tu dhanaṃ tasya nirūpakamātram. This is the basis for Rāmabhadra I's theory of svatva. For describers, see Ingalls, *Navya-Nyāya Logic*, pp. 40–7.

[102] Kroll, 'A Logical Approach to Law', p. 52, fn 22: śabda eva hi svatve mānaṃ. tathā hi yā kriyā krayapratigrahādiḥ svatvahetutvena dharmaśāstreṇsa bodhyate tata eva tadupātte dhane svatvam utpadyate.

[103] Ibid., p. 53, fn 24: yadvyatirekeṇsa yatheṣṭaviniyogāsambhavaniścayaḥ śāstrāviruddhatadupāyaviṣayatvarūpaṃ yatheṣṭaviniyogayogyatvaṃ svatvam. tadupāyānāṃ krayapratigrahādīnāṃ kriyātvenāsthiratve 'pi tadviṣayatvaṃ sthiram eva. jñānanivṛttāv iva tadviṣayatvam. ata eva na tadvat padārthāntaratvam.

[104] Ibid., p. 63, fn 41; *Nyāyatattvāloka*: śāstr[ā]viruddhaviniyogaprayojakībhūtakrayādiprāgabhāvavirodhitvarūpaṃ yatheṣṭaviniyogayogyatvaṃ svatvam. śāstrāviruddho yo viniyogaḥ sāgamasya tatprayojako yaḥ krayādiprāgabhāvasya dhvaṃsaḥ tadvattvaṃ vastunaḥ svatvam. The translation of the second sentence is not Ethan Kroll's, but rather Lawrence McCrea's. I am very grateful for his assistance in clarifying this particularly opaque passage.

ownership.[105] Like Vardhamāna and Vācaspatimiśra II, Bhagīratha rejects a theory of ownership as a separate padārtha and defines ownership in terms of lawful (Dharmaśāstric) acts of acquisition.[106] Bhagīratha notes that:

> the conclusion of purchase and other legitimate acquisitive acts is really to be identified with svatva, and the identification of purchase, etc., as means to use, which are unopposed by law, is what endows svatva with uniformity.... Moreover... purchase and other legitimate acquisitive acts have as their qualifier an association with a potentially perpetual relational absence, the counterpositive of which is those means that are opposed by law, and is co-temporal with purchase or other legitimate means of acquisition.[107]

The three theories of ownership explored by the Maithila Navya-Nāyaiyikas are: (1) a conceptual category, characterized by usability as desired; (2) the state of being the object of a lawful act of acquisition (defined and conditioned by various attendant phenomena); and 3) an internal (bodily or ātman-residing) quality described (nirūpita) by an external asset.

Raghunātha Śiromaṇi's philosophical œuvre overturned the established conclusions of Maithila Navya-Nāyaiyikas and inaugurated a Gauḍa school of Nyāya in Navadvīpa in tandem with Śrīnāthācāryacūḍāmani's similar efforts in Dharmaśāstra. Raghunātha's brazen, sophisticated attack on his Maithila forebears made his work a touchstone—for supporters and detractors—for the subsequent history of Navya-Nyāya in Bengal, Mithilā, and India.[108] The confluence of jurisprudence and philosophy in Navadvīpa lends credibility to Vidyabhushana's claim that Raghunātha founded his 'chair' of Navya-Nyāya in 1514 at the same ṭol that Raghunandana founded a 'chair' in Dharmaśāstra.[109] Even if Raghunandana and Raghunātha studied under different teachers, the overlap between Raghunātha's theories of ownership and Acyutacakravartin's comments on the *Dāyabhāga* implies the existence of mutual influence between Gauḍa Navya-Nyāya and Gauḍa Dharmaśāstra in sixteenth-century Navadvīpa.

In the *Padārthatattvanirūpaṇa,* Raghunātha advocates a theory of ownership as a conceptual category due to the incoherence of alternative accounts. His bases his argument on three succeeding premises: (1) that ownership as usability as desired would over-extend to assets acquired through theft and violent force; (2) that legal, (i.e., Dharmaśāstric) passages listing valid means of acquisition or prohibiting theft require a pre-legal understanding of ownership (to prevent circularity); and 3) that traditional Nyāya conceptual categories such as quality and substance cannot

[105] Ibid., p. 77. [106] Ibid., p. 84.

[107] Ibid., p. 91, fn 89; *Nyāyalīlāvatīprakāśavivṛti*: vastutaḥ krayādidhvaṃsa eva svatvaṃ krayādīnāṃ ca śāstrāviruddhaviniyogopāyatvam evānugamakaṃ[.] krayādisamānakālīnavirodhyupāyapratiyogikayāvadanādisaṃsargābhāvasāhityaṃ ca viśeṣaṇsam.

[108] See Ganeri, *The Lost Age of Reason*, pp. 45–51. [109] See note 69.

accommodate ownership.[110] In the *Nyāyalīlāvatīprakāśadīdhiti*, Raghunātha explores the implications of his theory of ownership as a conceptual category in relation to earlier, Maithila Nāyaiyikas.[111] Many of the specifics that Raghunātha gives about svatva (how it is created, destroyed and how it operates in the case of inheritance) draw on the Dharmaśāstric tradition that developed around the *Dāyabhāga*, but for now, the important take-away is that Raghunātha advocates a theory of ownership as a distinct conceptual category because Maithila definitions of ownership—variations on ownership as the object of a lawful means of acquisition—are either circular or defective. Additionally, Raghunātha, like Vācaspatimiśra and Bhagīratha, relies on Dharmaśāstra as the epistemic warrant for the creation and destruction of ownership.

Theories of Ownership in the *Dāyabhāga* and *Dāyabhāga* Commentaries

In the *Dāyabhāga*, Jīmūtavāhana characterizes ownership as a śāstrically determined eligibility for use as desired (yatheṣṭaviniyogārhatva)—but one that differs from the 'eligibility' of Mīmāṃsā formulations. Dutta characterizes Jīmūtavāhana's 'svatva ... [as] closer to a strong degree of ownership over property where ownership includes a right of control over property along with transfer at pleasure'.[112] When discussing restrictions on the gift or sale of immovable assets (by a father or by undivided co-owners), Jīmūtavāhana notes that 'in this case (dāya) as well, like in the case of other [types of] assets, there is no difference in the definition of ownership, i.e., eligibility for use as desired (yatheṣṭaviniyogārhatva)'.[113] Elsewhere, Jīmūtavāhana argues that to posit that heirs, on the death of their relative, acquire ownership over the entire estate—and then replace that ownership with various new ownerships over specific assets—'would be innapropriate because of the absence of the result (of ownership), i.e., use as desired' would not occur in the first instance.[114]

In two places in the *Dāyabhāga*, Jīmūtavāhana implies that ownership arises from śāstric means. First, when Jīmūtavāhana rejects the suggestion that sons become owners by birth alone (which the commentators ascribe to Vijñāneśvara), he argues that: 'there is no authority for the statement 'ownership by birth alone'

[110] Kroll, 'A Logical Approach to Law', pp. 102–3, fn 117; *Padārthatattvanirūpaṇa*: evaṃ svatvam api padārthāntaram. yatheṣṭaviniyogayogyatvaṃ tad iti cet ko 'sau viniyogaḥ. bhakṣaṇādikam iti cet. na, parakīye 'py annādau tatsambhavāt. śāstraniṣiddhaṃ tatheti cet kiṃ tac chāstram. parasvaṃ nādadītetyādikam iti cet svatvāpratītau kathaṃ tatpravṛttiḥ. tasmāt svatvam atiriktam eva.

[111] Ibid., pp. 106–19.

[112] Manomohini Dutta, 'Inheritance, Property and Women in the *Dāyabhāga*' (PhD Dissertation, Universtiy of Texas at Austin, 2016), pp. 106–7.

[113] Rocher, *Dāyabhāga*, p. 263: yatheṣṭaviniyogārhatvalakṣaṇasya svatvasya dravyāntara ivātrāpy aviśeṣāc.

[114] Ibid., p. 250: yatheṣṭaviniyogaphalābhāvenānupayogāc.

because one does not find birth (listed) as a means of acquiring (ownership) in the smṛti'.[115] Second, when Jīmūtavāhana rejects the suggestion that ownership can accrue only to the agent of an act of acquisition, he states that 'there is nothing inconsistent with the (idea of) ownership (arising) for one person by the actions of another, because this (phenomenon) is derived from the śāstra'.[116] Jīmūtavāhana's argument that no legal treatise lists birth as a form of acquisition evokes the formulation of ownership (as an opponent) in the *Mitākṣarā* as discernible-from-the-śāstra alone.[117]

When discussing Jīmūtavāhana's opponent (that sons become owners by birth) the *Dāyabhāga* commentators explain this opponent's views in accordance with Navya-Nyāya theories of ownership (often drawn from Raghunātha and his Maithila predecessors) and they use a śāstric theory of ownership to reject ownership-by-birth as an extra-śāstric phenomenon. On DBh 1.12–14, Śrīnātha gives the formulation 'by birth alone' the infamous South Asian 'side-eye' (kaṭākṣa) but he explores the implications of this view.[118] Śrīnātha, arguing for the pūrvapakṣin, states that 'one should not say that because of the absence of birth (after the termination of the act of birth), if birth is a cause of ownership then (a son) will not have ownership after he is born'.[119] For, says Śrīnātha, 'there is no obstacle with regard to ownership, even in (assets) that will come about (after birth) because ownership has been described by the śāstra as usability as desired, whose form is discernible from the śāstra, even at the time of the birth of a son, insomuch as it is delimited by the state of being an asset of the father'.[120] Śrīnātha eventually rejects the purported śāstric statement of ownership-by-birth as inauthentic, but his defense of ownership-by-birth (insomuch as a son's ownership is known from the śāstra and is delimited by the state of being a father's asset) relies on Navya-Nyāya.[121] Śrīnātha's comments formed the basis for other *Dāyabhāga* commentators' rumination on the philsophical nature of ownership, but they do not appear to refer to Vardhamāna, Vācaspatimiśra or Raghunātha's specific arguments.

Acyuta uses the problem of ownership-by-birth (and Śrīnātha's theory of delimitation by the state of being a father's asset) as a vehicle to attack Maithila theories of ownership. In his defense of ownership-by-birth, Acyuta defends Raghunātha Śiromaṇi's theory of ownership as a conceptual category against Bhagīratha Ṭhakkura's (and Vardhamāna Upādhyāya's) theory of ownership as the state of being the object of a lawful means of acquisition. Like Raghuṇātha,

[115] Ibid., 252: janmaiva svatvam iti pramāṇābhāvāc ca arjanarūpatayā janmanaḥ smṛtāv anadhigamāt.

[116] Ibid.: anyavyāpāreṇānyasya svatvam aviruddham śāstramūlatvād asya.

[117] *Mitākṣarā* 2.114, p. 281: tatra śāstraikasamadhigamyam iti tāvad uktam.

[118] *Dāyabhāga*, ed. Bhārata Candraśiromaṇi, p. 20; *Dāyabhāgaṭippaṇī*: janmata eva svatvam iti yat kaṭākṣam.

[119] Ibid., p. 21: na ca janmanaḥ svatvahetutve paścājjātasya pitṛdhane kathaṃ svatvaṃ tadānīṃ janmābhāvād iti vācyam.

[120] Ibid.: svatvasya yatheṣṭaviniyojyatvena śāstragamyatvarūpatayā putrajanmakāla eva pitṛdhanatvāvacchedenaiva śāstreṇa tathātvāvadhānāt utpatsyamāne 'pi svatve bādhakābhāvād.

[121] For the rejection of janmasvatva, see ibid., p. 25: at[h]āha janmanaiveti, ato 'tra pramāṇāhāvāt...

Acyuta advocates his theory of ownership as a conceptual category by rejecting any definition of ownership in terms of lawful acquisition. Acyuta introduces the metaphysical problems with ownership-by-inheritance first:

> In the statement 'by birth alone', 'birth' means the posterior absence of a momentary relation, not merely a momentary relation. Consequently, there is the unwanted consequence that there will be an absence of ownership on the part of a son in an asset of a father that will be (acquired after birth) because there is an absence of 'birth' in the form of a momentary relation afterward.[122]

Acyuta's point is that it is difficult to postulate birth as a cause of ownership because birth is a momentary event. If a father acquires an asset after a son is born, that son would have no ownership in the asset then acquired. Acyuta offers a more thorough explanation of Śrīnātha's view,

> As for the opinion of Ācāryacūḍāmaṇi—that there is no obstacle to (a son's) ownership with regard to an asset of a father that will be (acquired after birth) because we know from the śāstra that the asset (of the father) is usable by him (the son) insomuch as it is delimited by the state of being an asset of the father, because ownership is knowable (from the śāstra) as usability as desired—no. It is inappropriate to say that birth itself is (a form of) acquisition, with regard to ownership (which would occur) even before birth, because we know from śāstra that a father's assets would be usable by the son even when a son is not yet born.[123]

Acyuta's rejoinder to Śrīnātha recapitulates the Navya-Nyāya argument that defining ownership in terms of usability as desired is over-extensive insomuch as virtually all assets, regardless of circumstances, can be used as desired.[124] Acyuta, however, is not content to define ownership as Vardhamāna, Vācaspatimiśra and Bhagīratha do—in terms of being the object of a valid means of acquisition. Like Raghunātha, Acyuta argues that such definitions are circular because they define ownership using śāstric passages that themselves depend on an understanding of ownership.[125] Unlike Raghunātha, Acyuta engages in a lengthy rejection of

[122] Ibid., p. 22; *Kumudacandrikā*: janmaiveti janmātra ādyakṣaṇasambandhadhvaṃso nādyakṣaṇasambandhamātram abhihitam ato bhāvipitṛdravye putrasya tadānīm ādyakṣaṇasambandharūpajanmābhāvāt svatvābhāvaprasaṅgaḥ.

[123] Ibid.: yat tu svatvasya yatheṣṭaviniyojyatvena gamyarūpatayā putrajanmakāle eva pitṛdravyatvāvacchedenaiva dravyam asya yatheṣṭaviniyojyam iti śāstreṇa bodhanāt utpatsyamānapitṛdravye svatve bādhakābhāva ity **ācāryacūḍāmaṇimataṃ** tan na[.] putrānutpattidaśāyām api pitṛdravyam putreṇa viniyojyam iti śāstreṇa bodhanāt janma[naḥ] prāg api svatve janmaivārjanam ity anupapatteḥ.

[124] See Vardhamāna's comments about food in Kroll, 'A Logical Approach to Law', pp. 51–2.

[125] Ibid., p. 22: kim ca 'svāmī rikthakrayasamvibhāgaparigrahādhigameṣv' ityādi **gautamavacanamūlabhūtaśrutāv** anvayabodhe sati yatheṣṭaviniyojyatvena śāstragamyatvajñāne śaktigrahāt svapadāt tu tadupasthitiḥ tasyāṃ ca sthitau tadanvayabodha ity anyonyāśrayāt. For Raghunātha's views, see note 110.

Bhagīratha's theory that ownership is qualified by a perpetual relational absence (saṃsargābhāva).[126] Acyuta writes that:

> As for (the idea) of some—let ownership be the opposite of that of which there is no use as desired: namely; (1) the state of possessing a relational absence by virtue of such things as being the subject of a means (of acquisition) opposed to that which is not opposed by śāstra (and); (2) that occurs at the same time as the state of being the subject of a means (of acquisition) that is not contradicted by the śāstra—that is not correct.[127]

Acyuta's objection is twofold. First, 'because farming is contradictory to the śāstra insomuch as it is prohibited for Brāhmaṇas in times of non-calamity, (ownership of such a sort) would not apply to assets obtained through that (method, generally speaking)'.[128] Second:

> if one were to say that the state of being contradictory to the śāstra is delimited by a delimiter, namely the state of being a means (of acquisition), then, because even theft is not contradictory to the śāstra insomuch as the injunction 'hungry for three days he should take/steal money from a non-Brāhmaṇa' (Yāj. 3.43.1) is delimited by a delimiter, namely the state of being a means (of acquisition) having the form of theft, (ownership of such a sort) would apply only to assets acquired through that (theft).[129]

Therefore, says Acyuta, 'the wise accept that ownership is a distinct padārtha, ownership-ness (svatvatva) is a particular indivisible imposed property (akhaṇḍopādhi) and the delimiter of (ownership's) definition-ness is knowability from śāstra as usability as desired'.[130] When Acyuta turns to 'that passage of Gautama written in the *Mitākṣarā*, namely, 'the teachers say that one becomes an owner of assets right from birth" he argues (in a fashion followed closely by Raghunandana) that *if* it is authentic, then it refers to either: (1) sons who are *in utero* when their father dies; or (2) sons, as opposed to other relatives, who obtain their father's assets because they have ownership in their progenitor's estate, by virtue of their relationship (to their father), produced merely by birth, when his

[126] See note 107.

[127] Ibid., p. 22: yat tu tadvyatirekeṇa yasya yatheṣṭaviniyogābhāvaḥ śāstrāvirodhitadupāyaviṣayakatvakālīnaṃ śāstrāviruddhayāvattadvirodhyupāyaviṣayatvādinā saṃsargābhāvavattvaṃ svatvam iti ke cit tad asat.

[128] Ibid., p. 22: anāpadi kṛṣer brāhmaṇasya niṣiddhatvena śāstravirodhitvāt tadutpannadravye 'vyāpteḥ.

[129] Ibid., p. 22: upāyatāvacchedakāvacchedena śāstravirodhitvavivakṣaṇe bubhukṣitastry ahaṃ dhānyam abrāhmaṇād dhared iti cauryasyāpi vihitatvena cauryarūpopāyatāvacchedakāvacchedena śāstrāvirodhitvāt tadupāttadravyamātre 'tivyāpteḥ

[130] Ibid., p. 22: tasmāt svatvam padārthāntaraṃ svatvatva akhaṇḍopādhiviśeṣaḥ yatheṣṭaviniyojyatvena śāstragamyatvam iti lakṣyatāvacchedakam eveti manīṣibhir bhāvyam. For akhaṇḍopādhis, see Ingalls, *Navya-Nyāya Logic*, 41–2. Śrīkṛṣṇa follows Acyuta and svatva as padārtha became the standard narrative for later *Dāyabhāga* commentators.

ownership is destroyed.[131] The statement, 'sometimes, birth alone (as in paternal assets)', that, says Acyuta, 'is from a different text', is 'an extra-śāstric authority'.[132] Acyuta implies that this ostensibly śāstric passage that undergirds the theory of ownership-by-birth is extra-śāstric. Consequently, one should reject ownership-by-birth because ownership—as defined by Acyuta—is discernible from the śāstra alone and not from extra-śāstric sources.

Acyuta's defense and rejection of ownership-by-birth reveals the close interconnection between *Dāyabhāga* commentators and Gauḍa Navya-Nāyaiyikas. Acyuta's comments do more than reject ownership-by-birth on the basis of its lack of śāstric support—they attempt to enter into Navya-Nyāya debates about the nature of ownership and defeat Maithila Nāyaiyikas such as Bhagīratha.

Like Acyuta, Rāmabhadra uses Jīmūtavāhana's pūrvapakṣa in DBh 1.12–14, which he calls 'the censured opinion of a confused person' to offer his own definition of ownership.[133] Rather than defend Raghunātha, Rāmabhadra takes an inchoate idea from Vardhamāna—that ownership is internal and that it is described by external assets—and tests this theory of ownership against the *Dāyabhāga*'s model of inheritance. Rāmabhadra defends his father, Śrīnātha, from Acyuta's criticisms and notes that the over-extension of ownership even before the birth of a son 'would apply even to the position that ownership is a distinct conceptual category'.[134] In truth, says Rāmabhadra, 'svatva is the describer of svāmya, which arises immediately after birth'.[135] In his comments on DBh 8–9, Rāmabhadra describes how this distinction between svāmya and svatva (ownership and property) can explain the sequence of a prior owner's death, ownership through inheritance, and usability after partition:

> in truth, svatva is not a distinct conceptual category located in an asset. Rather, svāmya is located in the soul and an asset is merely its describer. As for describer-ness, it is a particular peculiar-relation as in the case of the absence of knowledge and the like.[136] Thus, after a father dies, all (of the sons) acquire svāmitva in the slaves and the like (the assets of the estate), but in the course of

[131] Ibid., p. 26: utpattyaivārthaṃ svāmitvāl labhetetyācāryā iti **mitākṣarālikhitagotamavacanam** mūlam yasmin garbhasthe pitrādir mṛtas tatparam evety āśayaḥ vastutas tv ayam evārthaḥ pitṛsvatvoparame 'ṅgajatvasya śukrajatvasya śutrūjatvahetubhūtenotpattimātrasambandhenānyasambandhādhikena janakadhane putrāṇāṃ svāmitvāt taddhanam putro labhate nānyaḥ sambandhī ity ācāryā manyate iti. Compare with Raghunandana's *Dāyabhāgavyākhyāna* on *Dāyabhāga* 1.19–21: utpattyaivārthaṃ svāmitvāl labhetetyācāryā iti **mitākṣarālikhitagotamavacanasyāprāmāṇikatvāt**[.] pramāṇatve cāha janmanibandhanatvād iti; and Raghunandana's *Dāyatattva*, 1: yat tu **mitākṣarāyām** utpattyaivārthaṃ svāmitvāl labheta ityācāryāḥ iti **gotamavacanaṃ.** tad api pitṛsvatvoparame 'ṅgajatvahetutvenottpatimātrasambandhenānyasambandhādhikena janakadhane putrāṇāṃ svāmitvād dhanaṃ putro labheta nānyasambandhīty ācāryā manyante.

[132] Ibid., p. 26: kvacid iti **granthāntare**, janmaiveti laukikaprāmāṇikaṃ vākyam ity arthaḥ.

[133] Ibid, p. 21; *Dāyabhāgavivṛti*: pitrādīti etena janmaiva svatvahetuḥ iti mataṃ **calato** dūṣitam.

[134] Ibid.: padārthāntaraṃ svatvam iti pakṣe tv ayam api doṣo bodhya iti **sampradāyaḥ**.

[135] Ibid.: vastutaḥ svāmyanirūpakatvaṃ svatvam svāmyotpattir eva janmānantaram.

[136] *Dāyabhāga*, ed. H. Chatterjee, p. 74: vastuto dhananiṣṭhaṃ na svatvaṃ nāma padārthāntaraṃ kintv ātmaniṣṭhaṃ svāmyaṃ dhanaṃ tannirūpakamātraṃ, nirūpakatvaṃ tu jñānābhāvādīnām iva svarūpasambandhaviśeṣaḥ. For the particular peculiar-relation, see Ingalls, *Navya-Nyāya Logic*, pp. 40–1.

time, that (asset) will either be, or not be, a describer of this or that (person's) svāmitva. This is just like how the absence of a pot may or may not have a relation with the ground depending on whether the pot is removed or not.[137] According to Naiyāyika reasoning, svatva is merely a describer of svāmitva and there is the popular belief that it is contradictory for two people to have svatva (in the same asset) at the same time. So, having accepted that (svatva) is svāmitva-describer-ness, (we say) svāmitva arises immediately after the death of the father, etc., even with reference to (that in which) an obstruction, etc. will arise (during partition). But with regard to the production (of the obstruction) in an object of property, the state of being a describer is inferred as 'this is his'.[138]

Rāmabhadra's theory of svāmitva as described by svatva may be taken from an earlier (now lost) Nyāya work, but it seems equally likely that, like Acyuta, Rāmabhadra had read Vardhāmana, Bhagīratha, Vācaspatimiśra and Raghunātha Śiromaṇi's works on svatva and decided to articulate his own understanding of ownership—one that would not limit a father's alienation of assets in which he, unlike his sons, holds ownership. Like Acyuta and Śrīnātha, Rāmabhadra uses the theory of janmasvatva as an entry point into a discussion of svatva/svāmitva and he uses that discussion to advance a theory of ownership that was rejected by Maithila Nāyaiyikas.

Śrīnātha, Acyuta and Rāmabhadra (as well as Śrīkṛṣṇa and Raghunandana) attest to a nexus between Navya-Nyāya and Dharmaśāstra that was the hallmark of the *Dāyabhāga*-centered school of inheritance that emerged in Navadvīpa. Jīmūtavāhana did not ground his text in Navya-Nyāya reasoning, it is imprudent to ignore the contemporaneous development of a *Dāyabhāga* commentarial tradition and the emergence of Navadvīpa as a centre of Nyāya *and* Dharmaśāstra. Raghunātha's founding of Navya-Nyāya in Navadvīpa inflected the Dharmaśāstric hermeneutics of his colleagues: Śrīnātha, Acyuta, Rāmabhadra, Raghunandana and every subsequent commentator on the *Dāyabhāga* employ Navya-Nyāya terminology and Navya-Nyāya theories of ownership to demonstrate the logically impossibility of a theory of ownership-by-birth. The commentators also intervene in philosophical debates concerning the nature of ownership. In short, Bengali efforts to develop a regionally specific cluster of Dharmaśāstric texts and arguments coincide—conceptually and chronologically—with Bengali efforts to develop a scale of Nyāya texts with regard to ownership.

Table 2.2 illustrates the Gauḍa scale of theories of ownership. As in Table 2.1, the chart is organized in chronologically descending order. Horizontal rows relate an author's name, principal text(s) and theory of ownership.

[137] *Dāyabhāga*, ed. H. Chatterjee, p. 74: tathā ca pitṛmaraṇāt sarveṣāṃ svāmitvaṃ dāsyādau jāyate kālabhede tu tasya tattatsvāmitvasya nirūpakatvam anirūpakatvañ ca ghaṭābhāvasyeva ghaṭāpasāraṇānapasāraṇayor bhūtalasambandhitvāsambandhitve.

[138] Ibid.: **naiyāyikanaye** svāmitvanirūpakam eva svatvam, ekadobhayasvatvavirodhapravādaś ca. svāmitvanirūpakatvam ādāya ata evotpatsyamānanibandhādāv api pitrādimaraṇānupadam eva svāmitvaṃ jāyate. dravyotpattau tu nirūpakatvaṃ tasyedam iti dhyeyam.

Table 2.2 The Gauḍa Scale of Navya-Nyāya Texts

Author's Name, Location and Date	Treatise Relevant to Svatva	Theory of Svatva
Rāmabhadra I (Navadvīpa, 1510–70)	Dāyabhāgavivṛti	svāmyam ātmaniṣṭhaṃ. dhananiṣṭhaṃ tannirūpakatvaṃ svatvam.
Acyutacakravartin (Navadvīpa, 1510–70)	Dāyabhāgasiddhāntakumudacandrikā	svatvam padārthāntaraṃ. yatheṣṭaviniyojyatvena śāstragamyatvam. svatvatva akhaṇḍopādhiviśeṣaḥ.
Śrīnāthācāryacūḍāmaṇi (Navadvīpa, 1475–1525)	Dāyabhāgaṭippaṇī	svatvaṃ yatheṣṭaviniyojyatvena śāstragamyatvarūpam.
Raghunāthaśiromaṇi (Navadvīpa, 1460–1540)	Padārthatattvanirūpaṇa	svatvam api padārthāntaram. tac ca pratigrahopādānakrayapitrādimaraṇair janyate dānādibhiś ca nāśyate.
	1514: Emergence of Navadvīpa (Raghunātha Śiromaṇi Founds 'Chair in Nyāya)	
Bhagīratha Ṭhakkura (Mithilā, 15th–16th centuries)	Nyāyalīlāvatīprakāśavivṛti	krayādidhvaṃsaḥ svatvaṃ krayādisamānakālīnavirodhyupāyapratiyogikayā-vadanādisaṃsargābhāvasāhityaṃ
Vācaspatimiśra II (Mithilā, 1425–80)	Nyāyatattvāloka	Śāstr[ā]viruddhaviniyogaprayojakībhūtakrayādiprā-gabhāvavirodhitvarūpaṃ yatheṣṭaviniyogayogyatvaṃ svatvam.
Vardhamāna Upādhyāya (Mithilā, 14th century)	Nyāyalīlāvatīprakāśa	śāstrāviruddhatadupāyaviṣayatvarūpaṃ yatheṣṭaviniyogayo-gyatvaṃ svatvam.

The *Dāyabhāga*-Commentators' Influence on Navya-Nyāya

This section addresses the influence of Śrīnātha, Rāmabhadra, Acyuta, and Raghunandana on the works of fellow Navadvīpa Naiyāyikas that treat the topic of ownership, arguing that the roughly contemporaneous shift of Navya-Nyāya discussions of ownership from Mithilā to Bengal and emergence of a Nyāya-inflected commentarial tradition of the *Dāyabhāga* (and its embedding in a Gauḍa scale of Dharmaśāstra texts) produced a shift in the way in which Naiyāyikas approached ownership as a topic of philosophical enquiry. The *Dāyabhāga*'s theory of death as a cause of ownership became a ubiquitous feature of the theories of ownership of Raghunātha Śiromaṇi, Rāmabhadra Sārvabhauma (Bengal, late sixteenth to early seventeenth century), Jayarāma Nyāyapañcānana (Bengal/Benares, seventeenth century) and Gadādhara Bhaṭṭācārya's (mid-seventeenth century). Moreover, Jīmūtavāhana, the *Dāyabhāga* and *Dāyabhāga*-commentarial arguments appear in the writings of these logicians: Acyuta's explanation of birth as a coefficient cause of ownership and Raghunandana's principle of *factum valet* are incorporated into the Gauḍa Navya-scale of Navya-Nyāya texts and are carried to Vārāṇasī through networks of Naiyāyikas in the seventeenth century.

Raghunātha, Rāmabhadra Sārvabhauma, Jayarāma and Gadādhara Bhaṭṭācārya imply that the concept of ownership is dependent on Dharmaśāstra. These Naiyāyikas explicitly state that death and the like is the cause of ownership on the part of relatives, employ examples from the *Dāyabhāga* and, to the extent that they posit ownership as metaphysically independent of Dharmaśāstra, they rely on the Dharmaśāstra (and its accepted means of acquiring ownership) as the source of valid knowledge about ownership. Consequently, it would be difficult, logically speaking, to accept Raghunātha's theory of ownership as a padārtha brought into existence through śāstrically recognized means of acquisition and to retain Vijñāneśvara and Śālikanātha's legal theory of ownership-by-birth as an extra-śāstrically recognized means of acquisition.

Uparamasvatva in Post-Raghunātha Navya-Nyāya

Raghunātha's *Padārthatattvanirūpaṇa* marks a sea-change in the Navya-Nyāya approach to ownership as studied in Navadvīpa: uparamasvatva becomes a śāstric means of acquiring ownership. The metaphysics of inheritance appears, tangentially, as a minor concern in pre-Raghunātha (and pre-*Dāyabhāga*) Navya-Nyāya literature. For example, in the *Nyāyalīlāvatīprakāśavivṛti*, Bhagīratha assuages fears that a dead father's ownership would continue to reside in his assets and notes that:

> his very death, which would motivate use on the part of his sons and other relatives, would block the continuation of his svatva.[139]

Vācaspatimiśra II advocates a similar position in the *Nyāyatattvāloka*—that the death of a father, interposed on the continuum of his former means of acquisition does not motivate śāstric use—but these two comments are the extent of pre-Raghunātha discussions on the proprietary effects of a father's death. Furthermore, Bhagīratha and Vācaspatimiśra II's descriptions mention sons' use rather than their ownership of their fathers' assets.[140] This matches the Maithila juridical model of inheritance where the existence of ownership is not a necessary and sufficient condition for the unrestricted use of an asset.

Kroll comments that Raghunātha, in postulating ownership as a conceptual category, 'appears to make the tacit concession that people know where and when *svatva* exists through legal texts, and that their cognition of *svatva* is shaped by the legal world in which they live'.[141] Raghunātha argues that 'ownership is created by acceptance, finding, purchase and the death of a father and the like and it is destroyed through gift and the like'.[142] Raghunātha's implicit reasoning is subtle: to the extent that ownership is limited to those means of acquisition mentioned in the śāstras (i.e. the sūtras of Gautama or the smṛti of Manu) inheritance (ṛktha, dāya, etc.) must be understood as the death of one's relative. This is precisely Jīmūtavāhana's opinion (as interpreted by Acyuta and Raghunandana). In the *Nyāyalīlāvatīprakāśadīdhiti,* Raghunātha gives an account of the moving parts of this theory of inheritance: '[a] the death of a father, or [b] the destruction of his *svatva* produced by his death, occurring in either [b] the things that were his or [a] that are the substratum of that *svatva* that was destroyed with him, produces his sons' *svatva*'.[143] Raghunātha does not cite the *Dāyabhāga* nor does he name Jīmūtavāhana explicitly, but his comments imply an awareness of and enthusiasm for the theory of uparamasvatva that Jīmūtavāhana's commentators were in the process of making a hallmark of Gauḍa Navya-Nyāya.

Rāmabhadra Sārvabhauma, another Navadvīpan Navya-Naiyāyika, rejects Raghunātha's theory of ownership as a conceptual category (in favour of a syncopated pair of qualified absences), but he retains the theory of ownership as

[139] Kroll, 'A Logical Approach to Law', p. 92, fn 91; *Nyāyalīlāvatīprakāśavivṛti*: maraṇasyaiva putrādiviniyogaprayojakasya vyavadhāyakatvād.

[140] Ibid., pp. 64–5, fn 44; *Nyāyatattvāloka*: krayāder maraṇavyavadhāpitasya śāstrīyaviniyoga-prayojakatvābhāvād vikrītavad asvatvāt.

[141] Ibid., p. 103, fn 118, *Nyāyalīlāvatīprakāśadīdhiti*: pramāṇaṃ ca tatra parasvaṃ nādadītetyādikaṃ śāstram eva.

[142] Ibid.: tac ca pratigrahopādānakrayapitrādimaraṇair janyate dānādibhiś ca nāśyate.

[143] Ibid., p. 116, fn 140: (A) pitrādimaraṇaṃ (B) tajjanyasvatvavināśo vā (A) svanāśyasvatvāśraye (B) svāśraye vā putrādeḥ svatvajanakam. Kroll appears to miss the chiastic structure of this sentence.

śāstrically determined and of death as a śāstric means of acquisition.[144] In the *Padārthatattvavivecanaprakāśa*, Rāmabhadra writes that:

> because death consists of the ultimate conclusion, death itself, in some cases, when qualified by the prior absence of sale and the like on the part of the heirs, or the conclusion of the instant that constitutes the substratum of death, so qualified, can be said to constitute svatva.[145]

Jayarāma and Gadādhara, two later Bengal-trained logicians, give similar views about uparamasvatva.[146] Raghunātha and his later interlocutors would disagree with various opinions of Jīmūtavāhana about the details of uparamasvatva (alienability of undivided shares, the nature of post-parental and pre-partition ownership), but they all defend the broad thesis of the *Dāyabhāga*: ownership is limited to the śāstra and sons acquire ownership in a paternal estate only after the biological or legal death of the previous owner.

Two Theories from the *Dāyabhāga* in Navya-Nyāya Literature

Jayarāma and Gadādhara defend two related positions from the *Dāyabhāga* (and its attendant commentaries): (1) birth as a coefficient cause of ownership; and (2) the principle of *factum valet* (by which a father can dispose of immovable assets without his sons' consent). The appearance of these positions in post-Raghunātha Navya-Nyāya discussions of ownership suggests that the *Dāyabhāga* and its commentaries influenced and were influenced by contemporaneous Navya-Nyāya theories of ownership.

The Mitākṣarā, In-Utero

In the *Dāyabhāga*, Jīmūtavāhana argues that, '"sometimes birth alone", describes (inheritance) indirectly: because the father's death is the cause of (the sons') ownership and the relationship between father and son is based on birth'.[147] Recall that Śrīnātha, Acyuta, and Raghunandana reject this quote as inauthentic.[148] Acyuta makes an argument that appears to be unique in Dharmaśāstra: 'to the extent that the statement of Gautama written in the *Mitākṣarā* is authentic, it pertains to a son who is *in-utero* when his father dies'.[149]

[144] For Rāmabhadra's biography, see ibid., p. 123.

[145] Ibid., p. 128, fn 162; *Padārthatattvavivecanaprakāśa*: tatra maraṇasya ca dhvaṃsātmakatayā vikrayādiprāgabhāvaviśiṣṭaṃ tad eva kvacit svatvaṃ tadadhikaraṇakṣaṇadhvaṃso vā.

[146] Ibid., pp. 152 and 205–6.

[147] Rocher, *Dāyabhāga*, p. 252: kvacij janmaiveti ca janmanibandhanatvāt pitāputrasambandhasya pitṛmaraṇasya ca svatvakāraṇatvāt paraṃparayā varṇanam.

[148] See notes 121, 131, and 132.

[149] See note 131.

Acyuta, however, rejects this interpretation by arguing—like Raghunandana—that birth might be a coefficient cause of a son's ownership insomuch as it allows a son—and no other relative—to inherit after the death of his father.[150]

Gadādhara, however, clearly read Acyuta's commentary. In an elaborate discussion of inheritance, he argues that:

> Gautama is quoted in the Mitākṣarā as saying, 'One obtains ownership of wealth by birth'. That dictum of Gautama, logicians (prāmāṇika-s) are alleged to have argued, applies to specific instances, such as where a son is still in the womb when his father dies, and means that such a son can acquire wealth—e.g., paternal assets—through birth alone.[151]

Kroll notes that Gadādhara refers to Vijñāneśvara, the *Mitākṣarā*, and the *Dāyabhāga* in other places in the *Vādavāridhi*, but he does not realize that Gadādhara's interpretation of the *Mitākṣarā* is taken from *Dāyabhāga*—as mediated by Acyuta. Gadādhara defends Jīmūtavāhana's theory of uparamasvatva, so it comes as no surprise that he would have been influenced by *Dāyabhāga* commentators and that he would label Acyuta a logician (pramāṇika).

Factum Valet, Validated

An infamous statement occurs in the *Dāyabhāga*'s discussion of a partition initiated by a father (2.20–34). Several smṛti verses appear to prohibit a father from alienating ancestral, immovable assets without the consent of his agnatic relations. For Maithila jurists, these prohibitions are sufficient to limit a father's power of alienation. For jurists who follow the *Mitākṣarā*, however, the co-extensive ownership of sons and fathers precludes a father's alienation of ancestral assets. Jīmūtavāhana, in contrast, argues that prohibitions on a father's alienation of ancestral assets indicate the accrual of moral blemish (adharma), but not the incompletion of the sale, etc.[152] Jīmūtavāhana elaborates later that 'there is no incompletion of gift, etc., because a fact cannot be made otherwise, even by a hundred (śāstric) statements'.[153] In effect, Jīmūtavāhana's argument is limited to a defense of the logical implications of uparamasvatva: if fathers alone are owners of assets (self-acquired or ancestral) during their legal lifetime, then it follows, logically, that the transactions that they make with their property must be legally effective (even if they are inequitable). This theory is often compared to the Roman Law maxim, '*quod fieri non debuit factum valet*' (what ought not to have

[150] See note 131.

[151] Kroll, 'A Logical Approach to Law', p. 229, fn 81: ata evotpat(t)yaivārtha()svāmitva(ṃ) labhata iti **mitākṣarāyāṃ gotamaḥ** yasmin garbhasthe pitā mṛtas tasyaiva tadviṣayatvāt ata eva ca kvacij janmaivārjanaṃ tathā pi(trya)dhanam iti pravadanti **prāmāṇikāḥ**.

[152] Rocher, *Dāyabhāga*, p. 263: adharmabhāgitājñāpanārthaṃ na tu vikrayādyaniṣpattyartham.

[153] Ibid., p. 264: na tu dānādyaniṣpattiḥ vacanaśatenāpi vastuno 'nyathākaraṇāśakteḥ.

been done is valid when done).[154] In colonial Anglo-Hindu law, *factum valet*, as applied to inequitable uses of property, became a hallmark of the 'Bengal School'.[155] One reason for this is that the principle became a favourite topic for *Dāyabhāga* commentators and Navya-Naiyāyikas.

In his *Dāyabhāgavyākhyāna*, Raghunandana addresses the obvious objection to the principle of *factum valet*: if ownership is discernible from the śāstra alone, how could an alienation of ancestral assets—in defiance of śāstric restriction—be legally effective? Raghunandana writes that '"by even a hundred statements" means that when a Brāhmaṇa is killed, the absence of killing is enjoined by a specific śāstric statement, namely, "do not kill a Brāhmaṇa", but not that it (the killing) is not able to be done. Rather, it informs us of sin.'[156] An opponent points out, plausibly, that 'killing is an extra-śāstric act, so it cannot be prevented (by the śāstra), but because ownership is discernible from the śāstra alone, how can (a sale, etc.) be accomplished when (that sale, etc.) is prohibited?'[157] Raghunandana, like Jīmūtavāhana, appears to defend the validity of a father's sale or gift of ancestral, immovable assets based on a definition of ownership as usability as desired.[158]

In the following century, the principle of *factum valet* become a major point of contention between the followers of the *Mitākṣarā* (Kamalākarabhaṭṭa, Śaṅkarabhaṭṭa, etc.) and Navya-Naiyāyikas, so it comes as no surprise that one of the defining features of post-Raghunātha Navya-Nyāya treatments of ownership is an endorsement of the theory. Pre-Raghunātha Navya-Naiyāyikas argued that because śāstra is the source of knowledge about ownership, śāstric prohibitions concerning a father's alienation of ancestral immovable assets without the consent of his sons would prevent said alienations from having legal effect. Vardhamāna, for example, argues that:

> Although there may be ownership (in an asset), a prohibition on the use (of that asset) as desired (is based on) the Veda. For this reason, Vyāsa (author of an eponymous smṛti) recalls a restriction (based on the Veda) against such things as (a father's) gifting, selling or mortgaging (of immovable assets) without the consent of (his) sons.[159]

[154] Ludo Rocher, 'Jīmūtavāhana's *Dāyabhāga* and the Maxim *Factum Valet*', in *Studies in Hindu Law and Dharmaśāstra*, ed. Donald Davis (New York: Anthem Press, 2014), pp. 305–13, 309.

[155] Ibid., p. 309.

[156] *Dāyabhāga*, ed., Bhāratacandra Śiromaṇi, p. 67; *Dāyabhāgavyākhyāna* on Dbh 2.29–31: vacanaśatenāpīti, brāhmaṇaṃ na hanyād iti viśeṣavacanena brāhmaṇe hate hananābhāvo dhriyate na vā tat kartuṃ na śakyate. kim tarhi? pratyavāyeṇa jñāpyata iti.

[157] Ibid.: nanu vadhasya laukikatvāt tadaniṣpattir aśakyā svatvasya vedaikavedyatvāt kathaṃ niṣedhe tatsiddhir.

[158] Ibid.: vyavahāramātrāsiddhau svatvasyāsiddhiḥ syāt viniyogārhatvābhāvāt. Raghunandana notes (p. 67) that this logic applies to a partition made by a father: pitṛkṛtam iva.

[159] My translation. For the text of the *Nyāyalīlāvatīprakāśa*, see Kroll, 'A Logical Approach to Law', pp. 52–3, fn 23: ata eva svatve saty api yatheṣṭaviniyoganiṣedho 'pi śābda eva . . . ity anena sutānām asammatau dānavikrayādiniṣedhaḥ smaryyate. Kroll's translation of this passage is not quite accurate.

Jayarāma, however, uses Jīmūtavāhana's reasoning to defend the validity of a father's gift of immovable, ancestral assets. In the *Svatvanirūpaṇa*, Jayarāma argues that: 'according to the author of the *Dāyabhāga* (with respect to a father's gift, etc. of all of his property) gift and the like occurs (is legally valid)'.[160] Jayarāma also uses the *Dāyabhāga* to frame the question of sales of hereditary property by undivided heirs. He writes:

> in truth, in Jīmūtavāhana's opinion, because the casting of lots in the form of small metal balls manifests svatva for heirs, even when [the estate] has not yet actually been divided, a person has svatva only in his particular portion, and not in those of his brothers . . . and, as a consequence, can give, sell, or otherwise alienate only his particular portion of the ancestral [estate].[161]

Jayarāma quotes neither Raghunandana nor Acyuta, but his comments give credence to Acyuta's interpretation of DBh 2.27–32 as a rejoinder to Caṇḍeśvara, and so on's opinions that fathers and undivided heirs may not alienate the entire estate or their portion of the estate, respectively.[162] If Acyuta and Raghunandana's commentaries represent the moment when the *Dāyabhāga* was read as a Dharmaśāstra/Nyāya response to a Maithila Dharmaśāstra/Nyāya cluster of opinions, then it is unsurprising that Jayarāma, trained in Navadvīpa by Rāmabhadra Sārvabhauma, would use Jīmūtavāhana's opinions to reject a Maithila perspective on the legal validity of properties in which one might have (śāstrically established) legal ownership that is constrained by a pious, śāstric restriction.

Conclusion: Schools of Dharmaśāstra in Late Navya-Nyāya

In the *Vādavāridhi*, Gadādhara Bhaṭṭācārya frames a debate concerning the specific proprietary rights of sons after the death of their father in terms of Maithila and Gauḍa perspectives:

> Scholars from Mithilā . . . are the proponents of a single, collective svatva being first produced. According to them, after the death of a father or other relative, in each and every asset a single svatva, dependent on all the heirs, is first produced. Then, by partition, that collective svatva is destroyed, and other svatva-s, occurring exclusively in accordance with the heirs' shares, are produced . . .

[160] My translation. See ibid., p. 146, fn 16: **dāyabhāgakṛtas** . . . jāyata eva tatra dānādi(.)

[161] Ibid., fn 17: vastuto **dāyabhāgakṛnmate** guḍikāpātādeḥ svatvavyañjakatvād avibhakte [']pi svāṃśe svasyaiva svatvaṃ na tu bhrātraṃtarasya svāṃśasyaiva dānavikrayādikaṃ(.)

[162] *Dāyabhāga*, ed. H. Chatterjee, p. 67; *Kumudacandrikā* on Dbh 2.27–32 iti **caṇḍeśvarādyanumoditam** apakartum āha na ceti.

Jīmūtavāhana, however, claims that... each heir acquires svatva in the very portion that is determined to be his ultimately through the casting of lots, or some other means.[163]

Kroll argues that, although Gadādhara mentions and rejects the *Mitākṣarā*'s theory of ownership-by-birth, the 'conflict is not between the so-called *Dāyabhāga* and *Mitākṣarā* schools of thought... [but between either] divergent views on *dharmaśāstra* among Mithilā-based and Bengali writers... [or more probably between] divergent views of *naiyāyika*-s belonging to the Mithilā-based and Bengali schools of *nyāya*.'[164]

Let us return to Colebrooke's characterization of Jīmūtavāhana as 'the founder' of the Bengal school of inheritance as the 'author of the doctrine which it has adopted'.[165] This chapter focused less on the mysterious origins of Jīmūtavāhana and the *Dāyabhāga* than on the circumstances of its *adoption* by Bengali śāstrins in the ṭols of Navadvīpa. The *Dāyabhāga* became a quintessentially Bengali text at the same time that Bengali Paṇḍitas began to assert a distinct 'Gauḍa' school of thought in Dharmaśāstra. The development of a Gauḍa school of Dharmaśāstra coincides with the emergence of Navadvīpa as a centre of Navya-Nyāya and as a rival to Mithilā.

A natural consequence of these dual developments is a connection between the jurisprudence of *Dāyabhāga* commentators such as Acyutacakravartin and Raghunandana Bhaṭṭācārya and the theories of ownership of Navya-Naiyāyikas such as Raghunāthaśiromaṇi, Rāmabhadra Sārvabhauma and Jayarāma. The most notable feature of *Dāyabhāga* commentarial literature is the elaborate use of Navya-Nyāya terminology in support of Jīmūtavāhana's sometimes counter-intuitive interpretations of smṛti—for example, the derivation of dāya from √dā—and the articulation of various Navya-Nyāya-derived concepts of ownership (as a padārtha, or svāminirūpakatva).

Of course, to say that Bengali Dharmaśāstrins and Navya-Naiyāyikas shared a cluster of concepts and opinions on the issues of ownership and inheritance is not the same as proving the existence of a 'Bengal School' of Dharmaśāstra. Unlike the medieval *Mitākṣarā* 'school'—in which a discernible Dharmaśāstra/Mīmāṃsā nexus developed in the wake of Vijñāneśvara—the *Dāyabhāga* school was tied to specific educational institutions and specific disciple/son/student/rival modes of transmission. Moreover, the regional specificity of interest in the *Dāyabhāga*

[163] Kroll, 'A Logical Approach to Law', pp. 240–9, fn 95 and fn 107; *Vādavāridhi*:

sāmudāyikasvatvavādino **maithilāḥ** pitrādimaraṇottaraṃ sarveṣv eva pitrādidhaneṣu sarvvabhāginirūpitam ekaṃ svatvaṃ prathamato jāyate paścād vibhāgena tatsāmudāyika-svatvaṃ vināśya yathāñśamātravṛttisvatvāntarāny utpādyante... **dāyabhāgakṛtas** tu maraṇādijanyapitrādisvatvanāśāt sarvveṣv eva taddhaneṣu na sarvvabhāgināṃ svatvotpattiḥ kin tu guṭikāpātādinā vastugatyā yasya yo 'ñśo nirṇīto bhaviṣyati tatraivāñśe tasya svatvam utpādyate(.)

[164] Ibid., pp. 272–3.

[165] H. T. Colebrooke, *Two Treatises*, p. v.

was linked to the efforts of Navadvīpa logicians and Dharmaśāstrins to fashion a comprehensive, internally consistent, 'Gauḍa' body of legal and philosophical literature—one that, at least in the case of the Durgotsava, was probably tethered to the distinctive cultural practices of the people of Bengal. This body of literature—a scale of texts—served as a rejoinder to the works of Vācaspati II and other famous Mathila authors and reinforced Navadvīpan Paṇḍitas' efforts to establish the reputation of their emerging academic institutions.

The *Mitākṣarā* and its theory of ownership-by-birth occupied an important place in the early literature of the Bengal school as an intellectual whipping boy. Śrīnātha and Rāmabhadra were keen to reject ownership-by-birth and Raghunandana and Acyuta quote the *Mitākṣarā* by name before rejecting its arguments. Bengali Dharmaśāstrins, probably influenced by the Navya-Nyāya theory of ownership as epistemically dependent on śāstra, rejected ownership-by-birth and went to great lengths to defend uparamasvatva in their technical philosophical idiom, but their polemic appears to have been directed more at Mithilā than at Vijñāneśvara. The founding of the Bengal school had Mithilā as its target, and the *Mitākṣarā* was 'collateral damage'. When Jayarāma, Gadādhara, and other Navadvīpa-trained Navya-Naiyāyikas brought the arguments and texts of the Gauḍa school to Benares, however, they drew the ire of the city's powerful Mahārāṣṭrian Mīmāṃsakas.

3

The Bhāṭṭa School of Benares

Vārāṇasī, 1657

Seventy-seven Brāhmaṇas from Vārāṇasī's illustrious families gathered in the southern pavilion of the Kāśīviśveśvara temple. The scholars, speaking as joint representatives of India's five southern (Drāvida) and eastern (Gauḍa) lineages, issued a letter of judgment (nirṇayapatra) declaring the Devarsis, a marginalized clan of Mahārāṣṭrian Brāhmaṇas, to be fully fledged Brāhmaṇas.[1] This adjudicative assembly (Brāhmaṇasabhā) evokes an image of a resplendent, if ephemeral, moment when the holiest temple in India's most sacred city hosted a pan-Indian community of Paṇḍitas, whose piety and orthodoxy was matched only by their learning and authority. By 1669, the Kāśīviśveśvara temple lay in ruins, many scholars had ventured to other cities, and Vārāṇasī's golden age of Sanskrit learning faded.[2]

The 1657 letter of judgment's pretences of a unified body of southern and eastern Paṇḍitas belie the contentious, competitive scholarly milieu of early modern Vārānasī: a 'university town' in which families of scholars endeavoured to embody orthodox religiosity and to win patronage by debating the intricacies of Sanskrit jurisprudence, scriptural hermeneutics, and other śāstric disciplines with their rivals. It was, as evocatively described by Madhav Deshpande, a 'cheek to jowl' environment, in which claims of solidarity were checked by regional and disciplinary divisions.[3]

This chapter examines a Dharmaśāstric debate that divided two of the most famous Paṇḍitas from the 1657 Vārāṇasī assembly—Gāgābhaṭṭa (1600–1685) and Jayarāma Nyāyapañcānana (active seventeenth century)—across lines of regional identity and intellectual pedigree: the problems of inheritance and ownership. Until the early seventeenth century, followers of the *Mitākṣarā* and *Dāyabhāga* schools of thought were not in much conflict; largely because the *Dāyabhāga* and

[1] Rosalind O'Hanlon, 'Letters Home: Banaras Pandits and the Maratha Regions in Early Modern India', *Modern Asian Studies* 44.2 (2010): 201–40, 229–34.

[2] For the destruction of the Kāśīviśveśvara temple, see Richard Eaton, 'Temple Desecration and Indo-Muslim States', *Journal of Islamic Studies* 11:3 (2000): 283–319. For the decline of Vārāṇasī's Paṇḍita community, see Rosalind O'Hanlon, 'Speaking from Śiva's Temple: Banaras Scholar Households and the Brahman "Ecumene" of Mughal India', *South Asian History and Culture* 2.2 (2011): 253–77, 267.

[3] Madhav Deshpande, '"Disagreement without Disrespect": Transitions in a Lineage from Bhaṭṭoji to Nāgeśa', *South Asian History and Culture* 6.1 (2015): 32–49, 33.

Ownership and Inheritance in Sanskrit Jurisprudence. Christopher T. Fleming, Oxford University Press (2020).

DOI: 10.1093/oso/9780198852377.003.0004

Navya-Nyāya were virtually unknown outside of eastern India. By the early sixteenth century, however, the migration of Bengali scholars to Vārāṇasī introduced Paṇḍitas from northern and southern India to a new, sophisticated jurisprudence that contradicted and competed with the tenets of the *Mitākṣarā* school. A vigorous, acrimonious debate gave birth to two distinct, schools of Hindu law that were associated strongly with scholars from different regions of India—and the competing philosophical traditions of Mīmāṃsā and Navya-Nyāya.

This chapter examines the reception of *Dāyabhāga* jurisprudence and Navya-Nyāya theories of ownership in the Dharmaśāstra and Mīmāṃsā writings of the Bhaṭṭa family of Mahārāṣṭrian Deśastha Brāhmaṇas who led the southern community of Paṇḍitas in Vārāṇasī between the sixteenth and seventeenth centuries. Contemporary scholarship acknowledges the Bhaṭṭas' wide influence on Dharmaśāstra, Mīmāṃsā Vedānta, Vyākaraṇa, and Bhakti in sixteenth- and seventeenth-century Vārāṇasī.[4] The Bhaṭṭas are known most for their Mīmāṃsā writings' heavy use of Navya-Nyāya terminology and for their participation in many of the Brāhmaṇa assemblies that met in Vārāṇasī.[5] These two factors are intertwined: the Bhaṭṭas' legacy as the acme of southern Brāhmaṇism can be attributed—in no small part—to their defence of traditional Dharmaśāstra from a rival Bengali school of law. They accomplished this in three ways. First, the Bhaṭṭas crafted a comprehensive scale of Dharmaśāstra texts that rejected the opinions of prominent eastern and Bengali Dharmaśāstrins such as Vācaspatimiśra II (actually a Maithila author), Śūlapāṇi, Raghunandana Bhāṭṭācārya, and Śrīnāthācāryacūḍāmaṇi (on subjects as diverse as festivals and meat-eating) and that contrasted the views of these Bengalis with those of southerners. Second, with regard to inheritance, the Bhaṭṭas defended the *Mitākṣarā* school's theory of ownership-by-birth and its legal implications from

[4] For a general overview of the Bhaṭṭas and their works, see Sheldon Pollock, 'New Intellectuals in Seventeenth-Century India', *The Indian Economic and Social History Review* 38.1 (2001): 1–31. For Dharmaśāstra, see Ananya Vajpeyi, '*Śūdradharma* and the Legal Treatments of Caste', in *Hinduism and Law: An Introduction*, ed. Timothy Lubin, Donald Davis, and Jayanth Krishnan (Cambridge: Cambridge University Press, 2010), pp. 154–66; Rosalind O'Hanlon, Gergely Hidas, and Csaba Kiss, 'Discourses of Caste over the Longue Durée: Gopīnātha and Social Classification in India, ca. 1400–1900', *South Asian History and Culture* 6:1 (2015): 102–29; Madhav M. Deshpande, 'Kṣatriyas in the Kali Age? Gāgābhaṭṭa & His Opponents', *Indo-Iranian Journal* 53 (2010): 95–120; and Theodore Benke, 'The Śūdrācāraśiromaṇsi of Kṛṣṇsa Śeṣa: A 16th-Century Manual of Dharma for Śūdras' (PhD Dissertation, University of Pennsylvania, 2010). For Vedānta, see Christopher Minkowski, 'Advaita Vedānta in Early Modern History', in *Religious Cultures in Early Modern India: New Perspectives*, ed. Rosalind O'Hanlon and David Washbrook. Special volume of *South Asian History and Culture* 2.2 (2011): 205–31.

[5] For the Bhaṭṭas' Mīmāṃsā, see Lawrence McCrea, 'Playing with the System: Fragmentation and Individualization in Late Pre-Colonial Mīmāṃsā', *Journal of Indian Philosophy*, 36 (2008): 575–85; Lawrence McCrea, 'Novelty of Style and Novelty of Substance in Seventeenth-Century Mīmāṃsā', *Journal of Indian Philosophy* 30.5 (2002): 481–94; and Bogdan Diaconescu, 'On the New Ways of the Late Vedic Hermeneutics: Mīmāṃsā and Navya-Nyāya', *Asiatische Studien: Zeitschrift der Schweizerischen Asiengesellschaft* 66 (2012): 261–307. For their role as southern Brāhmaṇas, see O'Hanlon, 'Speaking from Śiva's Temple': 261–2.

the objections of Bengali Dharmaśāstrins. Finally, the Bhaṭṭas, in their Mīmāṃsā writings, adopted Navya-Nyāya techniques to advocate a theory of ownership as an extra-śāstrically created causal capacity (śakti) in contrast to Bengali theories of ownership as a śāstrically determined conceptual category (padārtha) or as a qualified absence (viśiṣṭābhāva). Crucially, the Bhaṭṭas' philosophical arguments concerning the metaphysics of ownership were linked to their jurisprudential arguments concerning the theory of patrilineal coparcenary trusts. Both of these positions, in turn, were implicated in the broader attempt by the Bhaṭṭas to frame their śāstric writings as a facet of their identity as exemplary southern Brāhmaṇas.

The chapter demonstrates: (a) that the Vārāṇāsī Bhaṭṭas' Dharmaśāstra writings mark the juncture at which the *Mitākṣarā* became identified with scholars from a specific geographical region of India (albeit in a schematized fashion); (b) that the Bhaṭṭas' defence of the *Mitākṣarā* against the *Dāyabhāga* was part of a broader encounter with Bengali Navya-Nyāya and Dharmaśāstra; and c) that the Bhaṭṭas' efforts to fashion themselves as authoritative arbiters of caste-status and ritual conduct in early modern Mahārāṣṭra contributed to their Dharmaśāstra texts' popularity in the Marāṭhā state.[6]

Although the *Mitākṣarā*, and its Mīmāṃsā-inflected theory of ownership-by-birth, served as the central text in an influential school of Dharmaśāstric thought from the medieval period, the challenge of the *Dāyabhāga*, and its Navya-Nyāya-inflected theory of ownership, precipitated a southern/eastern Dharmaśāstric schism that gave rise to Colebrooke's theory of schools of Hindu law—one in which intellectual discipline *and* geographical location played a prominent role. Colebrooke noted the 'considerable weight' of 'eminent writers' such as 'Camalācara [*sic*] at Benares' and 'the *Mayūc'ha* [*sic*] [of Nīlakaṇṭhabhaṭṭa] among the *Marahāttas*' and characterized these authors' defence of the *Mitākṣarā* as a school of thought opposed to the *Dāyabhāga*.[7] He also noted that the difference in legal opinion between the *Mitākṣarā* school and the *Dāyabhāga* school could be attributed to the relative prevalence of Mīmāṃsā and Navya-Nyāya in southern and in eastern India respectively.[8] The question remains, however: to what extent might the broad intellectual outline offered by Colebrooke have more concrete links with the regional cultures and histories that coalesced in India in the early modern period?

Answering this question involves tracing the Dharmaśāstra and Mīmāṃsā works of the Vārāṇasī-based Bhaṭṭas over four generations: Nārāyaṇabhaṭṭa

[6] For Colebrooke's formulation of schools of law, see Ludo Rocher, 'Schools of Hindu Law', in *Studies in Hindu Law and Dharmaśāstra*, ed. Donald Davis (New York: Anthem Press, 2014), pp. 119–41.

[7] H. T. Colebrooke, *Two Treatises on the Hindu Law of Inheritance* (Calcutta: Hindoostanee Press, 1810), p. iv.

[8] Sir Thomas Strange, *Elements of Hindu Law: Referable to British Judicature in India*, vol. 1 (London: Payne and Foss, 1825), p. 314.

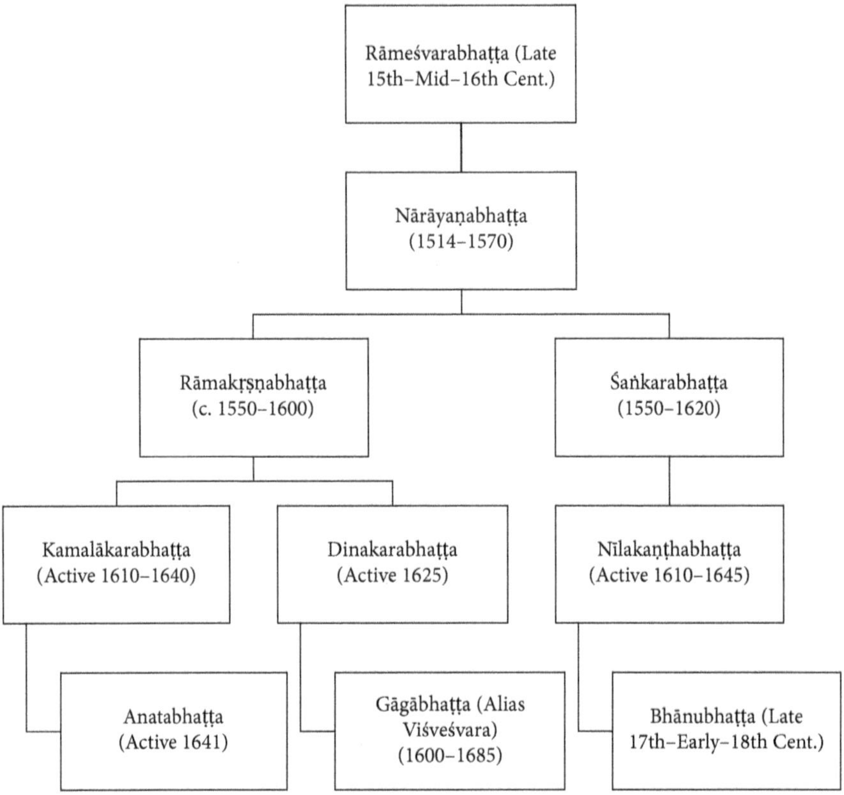

Figure 3.1 Bhaṭṭa Patrilineal Family Tree

(1513–1570), Śaṅkarabhaṭṭa (1550–1620), Rāmakṛṣṇabhaṭṭa (1550–1600), Kamalākarabhaṭṭa (active 1610–40), Nīlakaṇṭhabhaṭṭa (active 1610–45), Gāgābhaṭṭa (1600–1685) and Bhānubhaṭṭa (sixteenth and seventeenth centuries).[9] Figure 3.1 shows the family tree of the Bhaṭṭas.[10] The chapter is divided into three sections, each of which explores a facet of the Bhaṭṭas' identity as paradigmatic southern Brāhmaṇa Mīmāṃsakas and their rivalry with Bengali Navya-Naiyāyikas. The first section examines the Paṇḍitas of the Kāśīviśveśvara temple and their role as

[9] For Bhaṭṭas Nārāyaṇa, Kamalākara, and Nīlakaṇṭha, see P. V. Kāṇe, *A History of Dharmaśāstra*, vol. 1, part 2, 2nd edn (Poona: Bhandarkar Oriental Research Institute, 1975), pp. 903–7, 925–37, and 937–41 respectively. For the family in general, see James Benson, 'Śaṃkarabhaṭṭa's Family Chronicle: The *Gādhivaṃśavarṇana*', in *The Pandit: Traditional Scholarship in India*, ed. Axel Michaels (Delhi: Manohar Publishers, 2001), pp. 105–18 and Haraprasad Shastri, 'Dakshini Pandits at Benares', *Indian Antiquary* 41 (1912): 7–13.

[10] For a complete Bhaṭṭa family tree, see Śaṅkarabhaṭṭa, *Dharma-Dwaita-Nirṇaya: or Dharmic Alternatives Solved*, ed. J. R. Gharpure (Bombay: Office of the Collection of Hindu Law Texts, 1943), p. 3.

arbiters of caste in India's pan-Indian 'Brāhman ecumene'.[11] The Bhaṭṭas, in traveling to royal courts for śāstric debates, in leading Brāhmaṇasabhās at the Kāśīviśveśvara temple and in raising the caste status of Śivājī at the Marāṭhā court, positioned themselves and their Dharmaśāstric writings as the authoritative custodians of pious, southern conduct (śiṣṭācāra).

The second section explores the Bhaṭṭas as an extended 'scholar household' and attends to the 'scholarly habitus' revealed in their textual corpus.[12] Examining their works' colophons, overlap of topics and parallel passages, mutual references, attacks on Bengalis, and argumentative consistencies reveals a sociological model of knowledge, in which the Bhaṭṭas' individual intellectual contributions are delimited by a larger family unit, with its broad consistency in Mīmāṃsā methodology, in Dharmaśāstric jurisprudence and in anti-Bengali polemic.

The third section takes up the topics of ownership and inheritance, in relation to the challenge presented by the *Dāyabhāga* school and Navya-Nyāya philosophy. Exploring the intricacies of several Bhaṭṭas' Mīmāṃsā and Dharmaśāstra works that discuss ownership and inheritance, with a focus on Kamalākarabhaṭṭa's *Vivādatāṇḍava* and *Mīmāṃsākutūhala*, it argues that Kamalākara's philosophical arguments against a Navya-Nyāya theory of ownership in the *Mīmāṃsākutūhala* dovetail with his arguments against Jīmūtavāhana, Raghunandana and Śūlapāṇi's Bengali model of inheritance in the *Vivādatāṇḍava*. Examination of the works of Kamalākara's father, Rāmakṛṣṇabhaṭṭa, and his nephew, Gāgābhaṭṭa, illuminates a shared theory of ownership—argued against a Bengali-Navya-Nyāya theory of ownership—underlying their models of inheritance. Kamalākara's contribution to ownership is thus suggestive of a moment in Indian intellectual history in which the well-known Mīmāṃsā-Dharmaśāstra nexus was complicated by a rival Nyāya-Dharmaśāstra nexus.

The Bhaṭṭas, a Social History

The ascent of the Bhaṭṭa family from relative obscurity to the pinnacle of Vārāṇasī's Brāhmaṇa immigrant community and to the royal court of Shivājī Bhonsle (1674–80) was the result of increasing prominence in three areas of activity between 1500 and 1700 CE: (a) courtly śāstric disputations, particularly in the house of Rājā Ṭoḍar Mal in Delhi (≅1560–80); (b) the Brāhmaṇasabhās that assembled in the Kāśīviśveśvara temple (≅1580s–1669); and (c) direct involvement in the Marāṭhā polity in such matters as the coronation of Śivājī and the adjudication of caste-rights (1674). Furthermore, the Bhaṭṭas became *the*

[11] For the Brāhmaṇa Ecumene, see O'Hanlon, 'Speaking from Śiva's Temple': 254.

[12] Christopher Minkowski, Rosalind O'Hanlon, and Anand Venkatkrishnan, 'Social History in the Study of Indian Intellectual Cultures?', *South Asian History and Culture* 6.1 (2015): 1–9, 3.

superlatively orthodox Brāhmaṇas of Mahārāṣṭra through their long-term participation (as 'southerners') in a pan-Indian encounter between Brāhmaṇas who adhered to a 'five southern' (pañca Drāviḍa) and 'five eastern' (pañca Gauḍa) classificatory scheme.[13]

Early Modernity and the Brāhmaṇa Ecumene

The Bhaṭṭa family's rise to prominence in combined an increasing attachment to royal patronage from Delhi and from Mahārāṣṭra with concomitant efforts to promote the family's 'brand' of southern Brāhmaṇism against a rival, eastern (Bengali) brand. One of the central questions of 'Sanskrit Knowledge Systems on the Eve of Colonialism', an ongoing project of contemporary scholars of Indian intellectual and social history, is the extent to which pre-colonial India experienced a modernity analogous to that of the West.[14] For many, the distinguishing feature of early modernity in South Asia is a 'connectedness' between various areas of the subcontinent and the networks of royal patronage and śāstric knowledge production that accompanied it.[15] O'Hanlon, drawing from the work of Christopher Bayly, argues that Mughal India's Brāhmaṇa 'ecumene' was characterized by intense, pan-Indian competition for the patronage of royal courts.[16] Patronage took many forms, including rewards for victory in public disputations, commissioning Sanskrit treatises, founding Maṭhas (pedagogical foundations), or granting the income from lands.[17] Vārāṇasī was ideally situated to benefit from this early modern pan-Indian connectivity:

> The consolidation from the early sixteenth century of successor states to the Bahmani and Vijayanagar kingdoms meant a proliferation of large and smaller courtly centres in southern and central India with patronage to offer. In the north, the decade of the 1570s saw the consolidation of Akbar's state and the emergence of an expansive new Mughal cultural strategy, drawing in the

[13] For this scheme, see Madhava Deshpande, 'Panca Gauda Panca Dravida: Contested Borders of a Traditional Classification', in *Anantaṃ Śāstram: Indological and Linguistic Studies in Honour of Bertil Tikkanen*, ed. Klaus Karttunen (Helsinki: Finnish Oriental Society, 2010), pp. 29–58.

[14] For a general account of early modernity, see John Richards, 'Early Modern India and World History', *Journal of World History* 8.2 (1997): 198–203. For contrasting perspectives on the issue, see Sheldon Pollock, 'Pretextures of Time', *History and Theory* 46.3 (October 2007): 336–83; Sheldon Pollock, *The Ends of Man at the End of Premodernity* (Amsterdam: Netherlands Academy of Arts and Sciences, 2005); Parimal Patil, 'The Historical Rhythms of the Nyāya-Vaiśeṣika Knowledge-System', in *Periodization and Historiography of Indian Philosophy*, ed. Eli Franco (Vienna: Sammlung de Nobili, Institut für Südasien-, Tibet- und Buddhismuskunde der Universität Wien, 2009), pp. 91–126; and Dipesh Chakrabarty, 'The Muddle of Modernity', *American Historical Review* 116.3 (2011): 663–75.

[15] See O'Hanlon, 'Letters Home': 201. Cf. Sanjay Subrahmanyam, 'Connected Histories: Notes Towards a Reconfiguration of Early Modern Eurasia', *Modern Asian Studies* 31.3 (1997): 735–62.

[16] O'Hanlon 'Speaking from Śiva's Temple': 254.

[17] Ibid.: 254–7.

ambitious and talented from different regional and religious traditions and promoting exchange between them. Set between these northern and southern networks, Banaras seems to have attracted a new wave of intellectual specialists in the sixteenth and seventeenth centuries.[18]

The 'critical mass' of Sanskrit scholars who came to Vārāṇasī and royal courts in search of patronage resulted in an incredible heterogeneity: Brāhmaṇas from all over India, with diverging philosophical methodologies, ritual practices, religious commitments and vernacular languages, who had interacted more limitedly in the past, found themselves, suddenly and acutely, in contact and competition.[19] This heterogeneity had two effects that influenced the Bhaṭṭas' work decisively. First, 'this competitive landscape... impelled many into radical re-assessments of their own intellectual traditions', led to a 'greater systematization of schools of thought' and contributed to a 'broadening of arenas for argument and the creation of new disciplinary protocols for scholars to use within them'.[20] Second, 'at the center of this process lay a novel system of classification': the Pañca Gauḍa/Pañca Drāviḍa scheme.[21] O'Hanlon notes that:

> Until the early centuries of the second millennium, Brahman families across the subcontinent identified themselves by their sakha, or branch of Vedic learning, and their gotra, or exogamous patriliny. The new classification drew on the strengthening of regional identities, which in some cases was clearly associated with particular vernacular languages. It placed all of India's Brahmans within one of ten great groupings, the five or panca gauda in northern India and the five or panca dravida in the south.[22]

Deshpande has explored the pre-history of this classificatory scheme, but for the Bhaṭṭas and other Paṇḍita families, it proved 'useful in offering a "portable" Brahman identity in an age when Brahmans increasingly traveled in search of patronage'.[23] In the mid-seventeenth century, the 'Brahman assemblies in Banaras', dominated by the Bhaṭṭas, 'invoked the classification as a means of offering authoritative judgments in disputes about identity and ritual entitlement brought to them from Brahmans in... [other] regions'.[24] Furthermore, the Bhaṭṭas built concrete links between their Dharmaśāstric texts and the cultural practices of Mahārāṣṭrians. Consequently, the Bhaṭṭas transformed the significance of their 'southern' appellation from a *descriptive* account of their region of *origin* into a *prescriptive* account of their region of *jurisdiction*.

[18] O'Hanlon. 'Letters Home': 202. [19] O'Hanlon, 'Speaking from Śiva's Temple': 261.
[20] Minkowski, O'Hanlon, and Venkatkrishnan, 'Social History': 6.
[21] Rosalind O'Hanlon, 'Contested Conjunctures: Brahman Communities and "Early Modernity" in India', *American Historical Review* 118.3 (2013): 765–87, 777.
[22] Ibid.: 777. [23] Ibid.: 778. [24] Ibid.

Enter the Bhaṭṭas

Unlike many Paṇḍita families, who 'were, as is well known, frequently averse to situating themselves in historical time and social space', we know a substantial amount about the Bhaṭṭas, thanks to a combination of copious manuscript colophons, family chronicles, letters of judgment, Marāṭhā history and a substantial body of secondary scholarship from the nineteenth and twentieth centuries.[25] In the early sixteenth century the Bhaṭṭas were merely one of many families of itinerant scholars traveling India in search of patronage.[26] According to the *Gādhivaṃśavarṇana*, a chronicle of the Bhaṭṭa family written by Śaṅkarabhaṭṭa (Nārāyaṇabhaṭṭa's son), Rāmeśvara, the family's patriarch, left his college (Maṭha) in Paithan, Mahārāṣṭra, and travelled India (including a visit to Vijayanagar) in order to teach grammar and Vedānta before settling in Vārāṇasī in the early sixteenth century.[27] There, Rāmeśvara gathered a coterie of students, many of whom would obtain fame later as Vedāntins, logicians and Mīmāṃsakas (including Mādhava Sarasvatī and Maheśa Ṭhakkura).[28]

The Bhaṭṭas' rise began with the birth of Nārāyaṇabhaṭṭa in 1514 while Rāmeśvara was *en route* to Vārāṇasī.[29] Nārāyaṇabhaṭṭa established the family's reputation by participating in inter-regional Brāhmaṇa disputes at various centres of power in the Mughal realm; and 2) he convinced a local Muslim ruler (never named) to rebuild the Kāśīviśveśvara Temple (destroyed during the previous century) that would later host Vārāṇasī's assemblies. We know relatively little about the latter event, but the *Gādhivaṃśavarṇana* details Nārāyaṇabhaṭṭa's skill and fame in defeating 'eastern' (Gauḍa) Paṇḍitas in debates at royal courts in Orissa and in Delhi.[30] In both cases, prominent individuals had hired Brāhmaṇas from across India to debate and to compile Dharmaśāstra digests. Nārāyaṇabhaṭṭa, at least as Śaṅkara tells it, triumphed in these debates. In Orissa, the Gajapati King Pratāparudra, the lord of Utkala, invited various Paṇḍitas to debate Dharmaśāstric law.[31] Śaṅkarabhaṭṭa's description of the debate attests to the competition between southern and eastern Paṇḍitas: 'having debated with the

[25] Minkowski, O'Hanlon, and Venkatkrishnan, 'Social History': 2.

[26] O'Hanlon, 'Letters Home': 217–20.

[27] Benson, 'Śaṅkarabhaṭṭa's Chronicle'.

[28] Ibid., p. 112.

[29] Ibid., p. 111.

[30] References to the well-known legend of Nārāyaṇabhaṭṭa tend to be modern. See for example the prastāvika (introduction) to the printed edition of the *Prayogaratna*. Nārāyaṇabhaṭṭa, *Prayogaratna* (Bombay: Nirṇayasāgara Press, 1915). For an early modern reference, see Divākarbhaṭṭa's *Dānahārāvalī* in *Indian Office Sanskrit Manuscripts Part II*, p. 547: **śrīrāmeśvarasūrisūnur** abhavan **nārāyaṇākhyo** mahān / yenākari avimukte suvidhinā viśveśvarasthāpanā //. Cf. Benson, 'Śaṅkarabhaṭṭa's Chronicle', fn 19.

[31] Benson, 'Śaṅkarabhaṭṭa's Chronicle', p. 112; O'Hanlon, 'Letters Home': 219–20. Cf. Chandrika Panigrahi 'Muktimandap Sabha of Brahmans, Puri', in *Data on Caste in Orissa*, ed. Nirmal Bose (Calcutta: Anthropological Survey of India, 1960), pp. 179–92. For Pratāparudra's history, see Kāṇe, *History of Dharmaśāstra*, vol. 1, part 2, pp. 869–79.

easterners for a continuous month, he led the noble southern school to victory'.[32] Unfortunately, Śaṅkarabhaṭṭa gives no information concerning Nārāyaṇabhaṭṭa's opponents in Orissa.

Śaṅkarabhaṭṭa writes that soon afterwards, Nārāyaṇabhaṭṭa was invited to Toḍaramala's abode, the Mughal Emperor Akbar's finance minister, where he triumphed, once again, in a Dharmaśāstric debate against his eastern rivals.[33] This time, Śaṅkarabhaṭṭa states that these rival Paṇḍitas hailed from Mithilā and Bengal and that they were headed by Vidyānivāsa Bhaṭṭācārya.[34] Bhaṭṭācārya, a nephew of Vāsudeva Sarvabhauma (a founder of Navadvīpan Navya-Nyāya), was a prominent Bengali logician who enjoyed financial support from the Amer Rajputs and from the Mughal court.[35] This debate concerned the eating of meat in the Kaliyuga, a practice endorsed ubiquitously and rejected vociferously by eastern logicians and southern Mīmāṃsakas respectively.[36] Nārāyaṇabhaṭṭa devoted an entire treatise, the *Kaliśrāddhemāṃsadānavicāra*, to defeating wicked (Bengali) Brāhmaṇas 'whose tongues are eager for the taste of meat'.[37]

Furthermore, Nārāyaṇabhaṭṭa was involved, 'probably during the 1580s, in the rebuilding of Banaras's great temple to Siva'.[38] Nārāyaṇabhaṭṭa's pilgrimage guide, the *Tristhalīsetu*, contains a compilation 'a selection and arrangement of passages from the *Kāśīkāṇḍa*', a fourteenth-century digest praising Vārāṇasī, that functioned, likely, as something of a spiritual blueprint for the reconstructed Kāśīviśveśvara temple. O'Hanlon argues that Nārāyaṇabhaṭṭa's:

> arrangement of passages from the Kāśīkhaṇḍa... seems deliberately to emphasise the theme of 'southern'-ness. The Mukti mandapam, associated with

[32] Benson, 'Śaṅkarabhaṭṭa's Chronicle', p. 112: **prācyair** vivādam aniśaṃ pravidhāya māsaṃ **śrīdākṣiṇātyamatam** ūrjitataṃ nināya.

[33] For Rāja Toḍarmal, see Kāṇe, *History of Dharmaśāstra*, vol. 1, part 2, pp. 907–14. Toḍarmal commissioned a Dharmaśāstra digest, the *Ṭoḍarānanda*, to which Nārāyaṇabhaṭṭa likely contributed. For the Vyavahāra section (that does not, unfortunately, cover dāya) see *Vyavahārasaukhya*, ed. Ludo Rocher (Florence: Società Editrice Fiorentina, 2016).

[34] Benson, 'Śaṅkarabhaṭṭa's Chronicle', p. 113, fn 12: **dillīśvarākhilamahākaraṇādhikāriśrīṭoḍarasya** samitau ca jigāya sarvān / **vidyānivāsamukhamaithilagauḍavindūn** śrāddhe kalau palaniṣedhavivāda eṣaḥ //

[35] For Vidyānivāsa, see Jonardon Ganeri, *The Lost Age of Reason: Philosophy in Early Modern India 1450–1700* (Oxford: Oxford University Press, 2011), pp. 75–9.

[36] Vidyānivāsa's son, Viśvanātha Nyāyapañcānana (who signed a letter of judgment in Vārāṇasī in 1657) wrote the *Māṃsatattvaviveka*, a defence of eating meat in Śrāddhas: *Māṃsatattvaviveka*, ed. Gopīnātha Kavirāja (Benares: Vidyāvilāsa Press, 1927), p. 29: iti **mahāmahopādhyāyaśrīvidyānivāsabhaṭṭācāryātmajaviśvanāthaśarmakṛtaḥ**. For Bengali Naiyāyikas and Dharmaśāstrins' longstanding defence of eating meat in Śrāddhas, see Laugākṣi Bhāskara's *Tarkakaumudī*, cited in Samuel Wright, 'History in the Abstract: "Brahman-ness" and the Discipline of Nyāya in Seventeenth-Century Vārāṇasī', *Journal of Indian Philosophy* 44.5 (2016): 1041–69.

[37] Benson, 'Śaṅkarabhaṭṭa's Chronicle', p. 113: māṃsarasaloluparasana. Cf. *A Descriptive Catalogue of Sanskrit Manuscripts in the Library of the Calcutta Sanskrit College*, vol. II, no. 462, p. 417. Bhānubhaṭṭa has a similar rejection of meat eating in his *Dvaitanirṇayasiddhāntasaṃgraha*, ed. Gopināth Kavirāja (Benares: Sarasvatī Bhāvana no. 75., 1937), pp. 117–19: tasmād yajñātirikte śrāddhāv api kalau māṃsaṃ na bhoktavyaṃ yajamānenāpi na deyam iti dik.

[38] O'Hanlon, 'Letters Home': 219.

the kinds of study that Brahmans in particular undertake, is the 'southern' mandapam, dakṣinamaṇḍape, just as many of the Brahmans who now deliberated there were themselves 'southerners'.[39]

Intriguingly, Nārāyaṇabhaṭṭa's *Tristhalīsetu* takes a polemical tone towards easterners, particularly Vācaspatimiśra II (although not in a discussion of the Kāśīviśveśvara temple).[40] The most prominent instances in which Nārāyaṇabhaṭṭa sought to elevate the fortunes of southern Brāhmaṇas—Dharmaśāstric debates and the Kāśīviśveśvara temple—were linked to textual polemics against eastern rivals.

Speaking from Śiva's Temple

Between 1583 and 1669, the Kāśīviśveśvara temple, reconstructed through Nārāyaṇabhaṭṭa's intervention, became the meeting-place for a series of Brāhmaṇa assemblies that issued letters of judgment regarding caste-oriented disputes in Mahārāṣṭra. The Bhaṭṭa family and their Dharmaśāstra texts played a prominent role in these assemblies. The letters of judgment are remarkable in that they attest to the Bhaṭṭas' and other Vārāṇasī-based Brāhmaṇas' interest in serving as authorities in pan-Indian disputes. The letters also reveal that southern Mīmāṃsakas and eastern Navya-Naiyāyikas in Vārāṇasī portrayed themselves as a unified body for the purposes of lending authority to their judgments, even if they also sparred amongst themselves. The Vārāṇasī Brāhmaṇasabhās provided a vehicle through which the Bhaṭṭas and their texts came to exercise considerable influence in Mahārāṣṭra; and that this influence was predicated on the strategic deployment of the five southern and five eastern classificatory scheme. O'Hanlon writes that:

> Drawing on older universalizing geographies of Brahman identity in this new Mughal context, they addressed their letters of judgment to Brahman communities across the 'gauḍa' and 'drāviḍa' regions of northern and southern India and appealed explicitly to a 'we' of the pious and discerning, the 'good people' of the Brahman śiṣṭa.[41]

[39] Ibid.: 219. The *Tristhalīsetu*'s description of the Muktimaṇḍapa of the Kāśīviśveśvara Temple (Pune: Anandāśrama Press, 1915) mentions the southern pavilion twice (in sixteen verses), and emphasizes the recitation of Dharmaśāstra in that pavilion.

[40] See *The Bridge to the Three Holy Cities: The Sāmānya-praghaṭṭaka of Nārāyaṇabhaṭṭa's Tristhalīsetu*, critically ed. and transl. Richard Salomon (Delhi: Motilal Banarsidass, 1985), p. xviii. Nārāyaṇabhaṭṭa's *Tristhalīsetu* repeatedly labels the views of Vācaspatimiśra II's *Tirthacintāmaṇi* as eastern 'prācya' and rejects them at length. Salomon concludes that 'it seems therefore that there was a rather strong rivalry between NB and his followers in Benares on the one hand, and Vācaspati and his colleagues (including Gaṇeśvara Miśra) in Mithila on the other'.

[41] O'Hanlon, 'Speaking from Śiva's Temple': 255.

The Bhaṭṭas and their texts' authoritativeness exists in a productively tautological relationship. The Bhaṭṭas claim to embody southern Brāhmaṇical piety because of the authority of their textual production. Conversely, the Bhaṭṭas' texts claim authority through their authors' status as exemplary (śiṣṭa) southern Brāhmaṇas. Both aspects of their Brāhmaṇa piety—the textual and the habitual—support the Bhaṭṭas' role as arbiters of caste at the Kāśīviśveśvara assemblies.[42] Minkowski and O'Hanlon note that:

> At one level, the contemporary discussion of these matters was set within long-established parameters of Hindu judicial discourse. Here, both ācāra or inherited and customary practice, and śāstric textual models determined the dharma of a person or group. The two determinants were understood to be mutually constitutive: the ācāra of good people was in conformity with their dharma as set out in the śāstras, while the śāstras affirmed that ācāra defined in this way was a prime source for knowing a person's dharma.[43]

The first letter of judgment, issued in 1583, uses the southern/eastern classificatory scheme and includes Bengali Navya-Naiyāyikas.[44] Two Devarukhes (a sub-class of Brāhmaṇas often looked down on by their peers) from the Koñkana region of Mahārāṣṭra sought confirmation of fully fledged, 'six karman' status from 'Banaras's whole assembly of Brahmans'.[45] The list of signatories to the letter of judgment does not include any of the Bhaṭṭas, possibly because the claimants were seeking redress from the abuses of Anantabhaṭṭa (no relation), one of Rāmeśvarabhaṭṭa''s students.[46] However, the list divides the signatories according to northern and southern divisions of Brāhmaṇas: 'Sesa Krsnabhatta pandit, head of the Maharastras, Gopibhatta, head of the Gurjaras, Vidyanivasa, head of the Gaudas, Raghupati Upadhyaya, head of the Tailabhaktas' and so on.[47] Śeṣakṛṣṇa, the head of the Mahārāṣṭrians was a famous grammarian and Dharmaśāstrin (with connections to the Bhaṭṭa family) and Vidyānivāsa Bhaṭṭācārya was Nārāyaṇabhaṭṭa's principal Bengali rival from the disputation in Delhi.[48]

By 1630, the Bhaṭṭas and their Dharmaśāstric texts appear for the first time in letters of judgment. The Bhaṭṭas' participation coincides with the use of the

[42] For the 'productive tautology' between the śiṣṭācāra of Dharmaśāstrins and the Dharmaśāstric authority of śiṣṭācārins, see Donald Davis, 'Dharma in Practice: Ācāra and Authority in Medieval Dharmaśāstra', *Journal of Indian Philosophy* 32 (2004): 813–30, 818–19.

[43] Christopher Minkowski and Rosalind O'Hanlon, 'What Makes People Who They Are? Pandit Networks and the Problem of Livelihoods in Early Modern Western India', *Indian Economic Social History Review* 45 (2008): 381–416, 385.

[44] O'Hanlon, 'Letters Home': 220.

[45] Ibid.: 221: samasta kāśīkara brāhmana. For a succinct account of the karmans, see Wright, 'History in the Abstract': 1044.

[46] O'Hanlon, 'Letters Home': 222. The *Gādhivaṃśavarṇana* lists an Anantabhaṭṭa as one of Rāmeśvara's students (in the 1530s).

[47] Ibid.: 221.

[48] For Śeṣakṛṣṇa, see Benke, 'The Śūdrācāraśiromaṇi of Kṛṣṇsa Śeṣa'.

southern/eastern classification as a way to label abnormal Brāhmaṇa practices *in Mahārāṣṭra.* In 1630, Sarasvatī Brāhmaṇas living in Bombay (though originally from the Koṅkana in Mahārāṣṭra), who had attracted the ire of the local Brāhmaṇas, appealed to Vārāṇasī's assembly for confirmation of their six-karman status.[49] The letter of judgment cites Kamalākarabhaṭṭa as an authority and declares that the Sarasvatīs 'are part of the gauda category of Brahmins, and to be honoured within their own caste'.[50] In 1631 the whole of Vārāṇasī's Drāviḍa community gathered to issue a letter of judgment on behalf of a Sarasvatī Brāhmaṇa who wished to head an important pedagogical foundation (Maṭha) in Mahārāṣṭra. It opens:

> In the city of Visvesvara, the whole community of the excellent Pancadravidas, that is to say, Dravidas, Andras, Karnatakas, Maharastras and Gurjaras, these who live in the seven cities, send greetings to the Pancadravidas and Pancagaudas who live in the region of the Sahyadri mountains of the Daksina Desa.

The letter concludes that the Sarasvatīs belong to the 'eastern' (Gauḍa) category of Brāhmaṇas and that, consequently, their deplorable practices such as eating fish are not impediments to Brāhmaṇa-hood.[51] The letter is signed by Kamalākarabhaṭṭa, his brother Lakṣmaṇa, and several members of the Śeṣa and Dharmādhikara families—prominent Vārāṇasī Mahārāṣṭrians.[52] While the letter, written by and directed to southern Brāhmaṇas, supports the Sarasvatīs' claims to Brāhmaṇa-hood, it does so with a pejorative connotation: to the extent that the Sarasvatīs—warts and all—are Brāhmaṇas, they are *easterners.* This subtle distinction suggests that as the embodiment of southern Brāhmaṇism, the Bhaṭṭas could establish the boundaries of southernism, even as they determined who was a Brāhmaṇa in a more general sense.

A letter of judgment from 1657, the last before the destruction of the Kāśīviśveśvara temple in 1669, reinforces the Brāhmaṇasabhās' trend toward a southern/Bhaṭṭa influence. In the letter, 'all the families and castes of Maharastra, Karnataka, the Konkan, the Tailanga region, and of the Dravida and other places' agree that the Devarukhes (the maltreated Brāhmaṇas from the 1583 letter) are unimpeachable Brāhmaṇas.[53] The letter's signatories include Gāgābhaṭṭa and Nīlakaṇṭhabhaṭṭa and three Bengali logicians: Jayarāma Nyāyapañcānana, Govinda Śarmin (Vidyānivāsa Bhaṭṭācārya's son) and Raghudeva Nyāyālaṃkāra.[54] The Bengali Navya-Naiyāyikas' participation in the assembly suggests

[49] O'Hanlon, 'Letters Home': 224–5. [50] Ibid.: 224. [51] Ibid.: 225–6.

[52] Ibid.: 227. [53] Ibid.: 229–30. Cf. Minkowski and O'Hanlon, 'What Makes People': 404–9.

[54] O'Hanlon, 'Letters Home': 230–3. Ganeri, *The Lost Age of Reason*, p. 78. For Raghudeva and his *Padārthakhaṇḍanavyākhyā*, see Ethan Kroll 'A Logical Approach to Law' (PhD Dissertation, University of Chicago, 2010), pp. 129–30.

that Bengali Navya-Naiyāyikas and their works were well-known to the Bhaṭṭas (whose own writings demonstrate a familiarity with Navya-Nyāya).

The cooperation between the Bhaṭṭas and Bengalis at these assemblies belies deep-seated divisions between them on matters of Dharmaśāstra, Mīmāṃsā and Navya-Nyāya.[55] Anantadeva, a signatory to the 1657 letter of judgment and a prominent Mahārāṣṭrian Dharmaśāstrin, provides an evocative description of this conflict in his satirical play, the *Kṛṣṇabhakticandrikānāṭaka*. Take, for example, this memorable passage concerning 'upstart' logicians (tārkikas):

> They study the new logic (navyaṃ nyāyam), attend academic conferences puffed with conceit, boldly criticize even the revered elders (śiṣṭān), and take their seats at the head of the table. If anyone starts to speak of scripture, they give each other meaningful glances, roll their eyes sarcastically, and abuse that person to no end.[56]

While the Kāśīviśveśvara temple offered a venue for the Bhaṭṭas to define themselves as exemplary southern Brāhmaṇas, it was also a contentious place where the Bhaṭṭas' position as paradigmatic Paṇḍitas might be called into question by Bengalis like Vidyānivāsa or Jayarāma with their Navya-Nyāya techniques.

Back to the Motherland—The Bhaṭṭas in the Court of Śivājī

In 1669 Aurangzeb ordered the destruction of the Kāśīviśveśvara temple for reasons that, although not entirely clear, appear to involve the Bhaṭṭas.[57] Dārā Shukoh, Aurangzeb's brother and rival to the Mughal throne (who was executed for apostasy in 1659), had patronized some of Vārāṇasī's leading Paṇḍitas, some of whom, including Jayarāma Nyāyapañcānana, had strong connections to the Kāśīviśveśvara temple and the Brāhmaṇasabhās.[58] Furthermore, the Mahārāṣṭrian faction of the Kāśīviśveśvara temple became increasingly close to Śivājī after he 'staged his first direct assault on the Mughal imperial forces 1657'.[59] As Śivājī's rebellion began to carve out a self-consciously Sanskritized state, Śivājī found himself burdened with the 'kingly function of keeping the orders of local castes in

[55] For cooperation between Bengali logicians and Mahārāṣṭrian Navya-Naiyāyikas, see Wright, 'History in the Abstract'.

[56] Anand Venkatkrishnan, 'Ritual, Reflection, and Religion: the Devas of Banaras', *South Asian History and Culture* 6.1 (2015): 147–71, 153: navyaṃ nyāyam adhītya saṃsadam upāgatya smayāveśataḥ śiṣṭān apy avamatya dhṛṣṭamatayaḥ prauḍhāsaneṣv āsate | śāstraṃ vakti yadaiva kaścana tadā te 'nyonyam udvīkṣitair bhrūkṣepair hasitais tathopahasitair enaṃ tiraskurvate.

[57] O'Hanlon, 'Speaking from Śiva's Temple': 267.

[58] Ganeri, *The Lost Age of Reason*, pp. 14–21. For connection between the Mughal court and Vārāṇasī, see Audrey Truschke, *Culture of Encounters: Sanskrit at the Mughal Court* (New York: Columbia University Press, 2016), pp. 27–63.

[59] O'Hanlon, 'Letters Home': 234.

their place'.[60] The Bhaṭṭas, having successfully branded their family and their scholarly work as paradigms of southern Brāhmaṇism (vis-a-vis a pañca Gauḍa pañca Drāviḍa scheme) at the Kāśīviśveśvara temple, were well positioned to integrate themselves into the Marāṭhā state that 'assimilated Sivaji and his war for independence to the level of an all-India struggle between *dharma* and the *mleccha* armies of the Mughals . . . [and that] invoked . . . the principle of a singular and universal *dharma*'.[61]

In 1664 Gāgābhaṭṭa led a delegation of Paṇḍitas from Vārāṇasī to Rājapura in the Koñkana area of Mahārāṣṭra at Śivājī's request.[62] The letter of judgment that Gāgābhaṭṭa and his colleagues issued (in support of the Sarasvatī Brāhmaṇas whose fortunes appear not to have improved after the 1630 and 1631 rulings in Vārāṇasī) is remarkable because it contains an elaborate praise poem (praśasti) to Śivājī that emphasizes that the Paṇḍitas have come to Mahārāṣṭra on Śivājī's behalf.[63] As in the 1630 and 1657 Vārāṇasī assemblies, the Paṇḍitas at Rājapura based their judgment on a series of Dharmaśāstra texts weighted heavily in favour of the Bhaṭṭas. Dharmaśāstra texts include:

> Smṛtikaustubha, the great digest of dharmastra compiled by Ananta Deva; the Dinakaroddyota, a compendious work on dharma begun by Gaga Bhatta's father Dinakara and completed by Gaga himself; the Bhagavantabhaskara.[64]

By 1664, the Bhaṭṭas became agents of the Hindu king of Mahārāṣṭra and took an interest in a caste whose status was of tremendous concern to Śivājī: scribes (Kāyasthas).[65] Kāyasthas, with their valuable writing skills and relatively high ritual status, benefited tremendously from the vast expansion of paper-based bureaucracy in early modern India, particularly in Mahārāṣṭra.[66] However, the Cāndrasenīya Kāyastha Prabhus, influential Mahārāṣṭrian scribes, attracted the envy of their local Brāhmaṇa counterparts who 'had hitherto commanded more exclusive possession of scribal skills' and lucrative positions in the Marāṭhā bureaucracy.[67] The debate between the Mahārāṣṭrian Brāhmaṇas and the Kāyasthas took the form of a caste dispute: whether or not the Kāyasthas were Śūdras (low caste) or Kṣatriyas (higher caste).

In the 1670's Balajī Avajī, Śivājī's personal secretary, appealed to Gāgābhaṭṭa to defend the Kāyasthas' status as Kṣatriyas—worthy of ritual entitlements and unworthy of maltreatment from the Mahārāṣṭrian Brāhmaṇas.[68] Drawing on his uncle Kamalākarabhaṭṭa's Dharmaśāstra treatise on Śūdras, the *Śūdrakamalākara,*

[60] Ibid.: 235. [61] O'Hanlon, 'Contested Conjunctures': 780.

[62] Minkowski and O'Hanlon, 'What Makes People': 393–4. [63] Ibid.: 394. [64] Ibid.: 395.

[65] Rosalind O'Hanlon, 'The Social Worth of Scribes: Brahmins, Kayasthas and the Social Order in Early Modern India', *Indian Economic Social History Review* 47.4 (2010): 563–95, 566.

[66] Ibid.: 577–8. [67] Ibid.: 566. [68] Ibid.: 585.

Gāgābhaṭṭa crafted the 'Light on the Dharma of Kāyasthas' (*Kāyasthadharma-pradīpa*).[69] The *Kāyasthadharmadīpa* praises Śivājī as:

> an ocean of compassion, destroyer of yavanas, saviour of Brahmins from Aurangzeb, who struck fear into the hearts of the kings of Golconda, Bijapur and Delhi. [Whose] father, Sahaji, had emerged as the new embodiment of Kṣatriya dharma and Kṣatriya families, afflicted by the terror of Parasurama, have found shelter beneath Sivaji's royal umbrella.[70]

Gāgābhaṭṭa argues that there *are* Kṣatriyas in the current age (Kaliyuga), albeit in 'seed' form and that the Kāyasthas are indeed Kṣatriyas.[71] Intruigingly, Gāgābhaṭṭa, like Kamalākara before him, bases his argument on a Paraśurāma myth cycle found in the *Sahyādrikhaṇḍa* of the *Skandapurāṇa*.[72] The Bhaṭṭas' use of *Sahyādrikhaṇḍa*, the Purāṇa of place (sthalapurāṇa) for 'the Sahyadri mountain range and the Konkan region', reflects a wider feature in the writings of Vārāṇasī-based southern Brāhmaṇas: a strong association with the histories, cultures, and linneages of the regions of India *from* which they hailed and *for* which they claimed religio-legal jurisdiction.[73]

The epitome of the Bhaṭṭas' connection with Mahārāṣṭra and the Marāṭhā polity is Gāgābhaṭṭa and Anantabhaṭṭa's consecration of Śivājī as a Chakravartin in 1674 (soon after Aurangzeb's destruction of the Kāśīviśveśvara temple in 1669). For Gāgābhaṭṭa and other Vārāṇasī-based Mahārāṣṭrian Brāhmaṇas:

> with their already established traditions of dependence on a Sanskritic religious culture, and the prestigious meeting place of their Banaras peers now reduced to ruins, Sivaji's rebellion against Mughal power offered something very different: the chance to assert the values of Brahman religious orthodoxy as fundamental to the new Maratha state.[74]

For Gāgābhaṭṭa, the consecration of Śivājī represented an ideal opportunity to: (1) prove that Śivājī was a Kṣatriya, rather than a Śūdra (thereby upholding traditional Brāhmaṇic Varṇāśramadharma); and (2) compile an authoritative Dharmaśāstric manual for the Vedic consecration of Cakravartins.[75] Gāgābhaṭṭa accomplished these tasks by appealing, again, to his uncle's Dharmaśāstric œuvre,

[69] Ibid. [70] Ibid.: 586.

[71] For the particulars of this argument, see Deshpande, 'Kṣatriyas'.

[72] O'Hanlon, 'Social Worth of Scribes': 571–2.

[73] Kamalākarabhaṭṭa's *Nirṇayasindhu*, for example, endeavours to classify and defend the validity of various ritual practices that appear to be distinctly Mahārāṣṭrian. See my analysis in the following sections of this chapter. For the relationship between the Devas, another Mahārāṣṭrian Paṇḍita family that flourished in Vārāṇasī in the seventeenth century, see Venkatkrishnan, 'Ritual, Reflection'.

[74] O'Hanlon, 'Contested Conjunctures': 779–80.

[75] O'Hanlon, 'Social Worth of Scribes': 585; Deshpande, 'Kṣatriyas': 96–102.

particularly the *Śūdrakamalākara* and the *Rājyābhiṣekaprayoga* (a manual on royal consecration).[76]

In the following century, the Marāṭhā empire developed a legal system that enshrined many of the Bhaṭṭas' Dharmaśāstra texts as authoritative treatises on matters of caste and ritual entitlements.[77] The Peshwas, Brāhmaṇa prime ministers of the Marāṭhā empire, who 'inherited the task of mediating conflicts between Maharashtra's Brahman communities and of pressing and persuading all of them to adhere to common norms of conduct appropriate to the śiṣṭa', relied on Bhaṭṭa Dharmaśāstra texts, particularly Kamalākarabhaṭṭa's *Nirṇayasindhu* and *Śūdrakamalākara*, in their administration of western India (even when arguing against some of the Bhaṭṭas' more 'progressive' views on caste).[78]

Early modernity in Mughal India—an expansion of paper-based bureaucracies, increasingly interconnected networks of trade and communication, and a proliferation of opportunities for lucrative patronage—provided an opportunity for the Bhaṭṭa family of Vārāṇasī to craft an identity as exemplary *southern* Brāhmaṇas in contrast to eastern rivals—at least in part by drawing on certain regionally distinctive texts and practices. The Bhaṭṭas ensured that their Dharmaśāstric texts were studied in Mahārāṣṭra.[79]

A Family Affair—Knowledge Production in the Scholar Family

The Bhaṭṭa family was an extended scholar household. A 'scholar household' refers to the phenomenon of extended, agnatic Brāhmaṇa families living—and migrating—together in the same dwelling, while pursuing domestic, ritual, scholarly, and economic activities jointly.[80] One distinguishing feature of the Bhaṭṭas' śāstric œuvre is continuity: of topics, methodology, opinion and polemic. Kamalākarabhaṭṭa and Gāgābhaṭṭa, for example, write treatises on a shared series of topics in Mīmāṃsā and in Dharmaśāstra. They use a similar style of identification—tracing their pedigree to Nārāyaṇabhaṭṭa—in their texts' colophons. They quote one another's work (often positively, though sometimes critically), defend a series of opinions that are broadly similar, and utilize a remarkably consistent Mīmāṃsā technique. The Bhaṭṭas also carry on a polemic against Bengali and Maithila Dharmaśāstrins and Navya-Naiyāyikas such as Vācaspatimiśra II, Śūlapāṇi, and Raghunandana Bhaṭṭācārya. In this sense, the Bhaṭṭa family's collective śāstric corpus might be conceived, meaningfully, as a

[76] Ibid.: 98–9. [77] See O'Hanlon, 'Speaking from Śiva's Temple': 268.

[78] Ibid.; O'Hanlon and Minkowski, 'What Makes People?': 411; Deshpande, 'Kṣatriyas': 109.

[79] Evidenced in no small part by the prominence of the Bhaṭṭas' texts amongst the Paṇḍitas hired by the agents of the British East India Company in the eighteenth century.

[80] The best description of a Brāhmaṇa 'scholar household' is in O'Hanlon, 'Speaking from Śiva's Temple': 257–61.

series of works that together form a composite whole: a Bhāṭṭa scale of texts. Intriguingly, the Bhaṭṭas' family-centred mode of textual production parallels forms of land tenure that were popular amongst Brāhmaṇa families in early modern western India—wherein the brotherhood of the extended family shared property.[81]

Minkowski and O'Hanlon link the habitus of scholar households such as those of the Bhaṭṭas with the competitive marketplace of ideas of early modern India:

> Banaras became home to an unusually large and diverse collection of scholar households... For such families, it was above all the scholar household that shaped the education and frequently the career opportunities of Sanskrit intellectuals. It offered a way to maximize family intellectual and pedagogical resources and to accumulate the libraries necessary for high-level intellectual work.... [It] forged the two kinds of affiliation that mattered most in Sanskrit intellectual culture: that between fathers and the sons they educated, and that between teachers and their students, often brought into the scholar household to study alongside the family's own sons.[82]

The Bhaṭṭas' proclivity for defending the arguments of other family members, combined with a Navya-Nyāya-inflected Mīmāṃsā methodology and with a multi-generational polemic against Gauḍa Paṇḍitas, meant that Jīmūtavāhana's theory of uparamasvatva (ownership-by-cessation) and Raghunāthaśiromaṇi's theory of ownership as a conceptual category were viciously and systematically rejected in the Bhaṭṭas' Dharmaśāstra and Mīmāṃsā writings. Furthermore, the Gauḍa attack on the *Mitākṣarā*'s model of ownership-by-birth would have called into question the organizing juridical principle behind the Bhaṭṭa family's scholar household as a property-sharing institution.

The Textual Structure of the Bhāṭṭa School: Topics and Colophons

Successive generations of the Bhaṭṭa family commented on the works of their forebears, rewrote earlier treatises, completed partially finished compendia or wrote texts for the benefit of their children.[83] We find a remarkable continuity

[81] Ibid. [82] Minkowski, O'Hanlon, and Venkatkrishnan, 'Social History': 3.

[83] To note a few instances, Gāgābhaṭṭa completed his father Dinakarabhaṭṭa's uncompleted Dharmaśāstra digest, the *Dinakaryoddyota*. Nīlakaṇṭha's discussion of divyas in the *Vyavahāramayūkha* borrows heavily from a similar discussion in Nārāyaṇabhaṭṭa's *Divyānuṣṭhānapaddhati*. Gāgābhaṭṭa copied much of Kamalākara's *Rājyābhiṣekaprayoga* when compiling the *Rājyābhiṣekapaddhati*, the handbook for royal consecration he used when crowning Śivājī Bhonsle in 1674.

of Dharmaśāstra topics—Śrāddha, Tīrtha, Vyavahāra, Ācāra—that each member of the Bhaṭṭa family wrote on in turn. The Bhaṭṭas' voluminous Dharmaśāstric production was matched by an equally large number of Bhāṭṭa and Prābhākara-Mīmāṃsā treatises.[84] McCrea notes that Vārāṇasī-based Dharmaśāstrins, particularly the Bhaṭṭa family, 'wrote on Mīmāṃsā as well and this growing professional convergence between the two fields is perhaps related to the shift toward more overtly critical methods in the Dharmaśāstra literature of the period'.[85]

Colophons from manuscripts of the Bhaṭṭas' works reveals the tight connections between individual family members. As the family's fame grew, its members attached greater significance to their pedigree and they use their colophons to emphasize the relationship between the Mīmāṃsā acumen of their ancestors and the authority of their Dharmaśāstric opinions. For example, Nārāyaṇabhaṭṭa identifies himself in his colophons as 'clever Nārāyaṇa, son of Rāmeśvara', or as 'Nārāyaṇabhaṭṭa, son of the learned, noble Rāmeśvara.'[86] Nārāyaṇabhaṭṭa's sons Rāmakṛṣṇabhaṭṭa and Śaṅkarabhaṭṭa give lengthy and more colourful accounts of themselves that centre on Nārāyaṇabhaṭṭa and Mīmāṃsā. Rāmakṛṣṇabhaṭṭa calls himself 'Rāmakṛṣṇabhaṭṭa, son of noble Nārāyaṇa, the blessed, learned, noble crown jewel and the son of the blessed Rāmeśvara, whose feet are accustomed to praise'.[87] At the end of his *Dharmadvaitanirṇaya*, Śaṅkarabhaṭṭa describes himself baroquely as:

> Śaṅkarabhaṭṭa, son of the blessed Nārāyaṇabhaṭṭa, sovereign of the empire of non-dual (Vedānta) and Mīmāṃsā, chief of those who have crossed to the farthest shore of Vyākaraṇa, Mīmāṃsā, and Nyāya.[88]

The colophons emphasize the continuity of a patrilineal line and use Nārāyaṇabhaṭṭa as a touchstone for future Bhaṭṭas' acumen in śāstra. Kamalākarabhaṭṭa, who describes himself as the son of Rāmakṛṣṇa and the grandson of Nārāyaṇa, emphasizes the skill of his ancestors in Mīmāṃsā.[89]

[84] For a list of these Mīmāṃsā texts, see Diaconescu, 'On the New Ways'.

[85] Lawrence McCrea, 'Hindu Jurisprudence and Scriptural Hermeneutics', in *Hinduism and Law: An Introduction*, ed. Timothy Lubin, Donald Davis, and Jayanth Krishnan (Cambridge: Cambridge University Press, 2010), pp. 123–36, 134.

[86] *Descriptive Catalogue of the Government Collections of Manuscripts Deposited at the Deccan College, Poona*, ed. N. D. Banhatti (Bombay: The Government of Bombay, 1916), p. 76, no. 79 (140/1886–92), *Ārāmotsargapaddhati*, fol. 9a: **bhaṭṭarāmeśvarasuto bhaṭṭanārāyaṇaḥ** sudhīḥ. Ibid., p. 169, no. 207 (218/1879–80), *Antyeṣṭipaddhati*, fol. 50b: iti **śrībhaṭṭarāmeśvarasūrisūnunārāyaṇabhaṭṭena.**

[87] Ibid., p. 416, no. 479 (362/1891–5), *Jīvatpitṛkakartavyasaṃcaya*, fol. 40a: iti **śrīmadvindu-vandyapādaśrīrāmeśvarabhaṭṭasūnuśrīmadvidvanmukuṭamāṇikyaśrīnārāyaṇasūnurāmakṛṣṇabhaṭṭa**

[88] *Dharma-Dwaita-Nirṇaya*, p. 147: **śrīmadpadavākyapramāṇapārāvāravārīṇadhurīṇamīmāṃ-sādvaitasāmrājyadhuraṃdharaśrībhaṭṭanārāyaṇātmajabhaṭṭaśaṅkara**. I am grateful for Lawrence McCrea's kind assistance in deciphering the compound 'padavākya[pra]māṇa'.

[89] See for example, Kamalākarabhaṭṭa's *Rājyābhiṣekaprayoga*, *Descriptive Catalogue, Deccan College*, pp. 10–11, no. 1113 (295/1887–91), fol. 15b: iti **śrīmīmāṃsakarāmakṛṣṇabhaṭṭātmaja-mahāmahopādhyāyakamalākarabhaṭṭa**; Bori 324. Also see ibid, p. 342, no. 376 (586/1882–3), *Gotrapravaranirṇaya*, fol. 35a: iti **śrīmadrāmeśvarabhaṭṭasūrisununārāyaṇabhaṭṭātmajamimāṃś-**[*sic*]**akaśrīrāmakṛṣṇabhaṭṭasutadinakarabhaṭṭānujaśrīkamalākarabhaṭṭa**

Kamalākara praises his father Rāmakṛṣṇa as the 'helmsman on the vast ocean of Bhaṭṭa Mīmāṃsā, also the divulger of secrets in all of the other śāstras'.[90] The colophons connect the Bhaṭṭas' biological and pedagogical lineages. For example, Nārāyaṇabhaṭṭa notes that he learns the smṛtis and śāstras at the feet of his father and one of Nīlakaṇṭhabhaṭṭa's favourite ways of identifying himself is as the son of a distinguished Mīmāṃsaka.[91]

By the fourth generation of Vārāṇasī Bhaṭṭas—Gāgā, Ananta and Bhānu—the colophons read like elaborate genealogies. Take, for example, Gāgābhaṭṭa's remarks at the end of the *Vyavahārakāṇḍa* (a text begun by his father):

> so ends the *Vyavahārakāṇḍa* in the *Dinakaroddyota*, completed by Viśveśvabhaṭṭa, alias Gāgābhaṭṭa, son of Dinakarabhaṭṭa, son of the blessed Rāmakṛṣṇabhaṭṭa, son of the venerable, blessed, learned Nārāyaṇabhaṭṭa, whose pair of lotus feet are colored red by the rubies in the crowns (of kings).[92]

Kamalākara's son Anantabhaṭṭa gives a similar, effusive account of his ancestry in the *Rāmakalpadrūma*.[93] The remarkable continuity of topics in the Vārāṇasī Bhaṭṭa corpus (especially in Dharmaśāstra and Mīmāṃsā) was matched by a continuity of self-identification in these texts' colophons.

Bhāṭṭa Intertextuality: Citations and Arguments

The intertextuality of multiple Bhaṭṭa Dharmaśāstra and Mīmāṃsā writings suggests that the Bhaṭṭa corpus might be viewed as a single, integrated meta-text. Reading, for example, Nīlakaṇṭhabhaṭṭa's *Vyavahāramayūkha* requires one to meander into his father Śaṅkarabhaṭṭa's *Dharmadvaitanirṇaya*, his grandfather

[90] Kāṇe, *History of Dharmaśāstra*, vol. 1, part 2, p. 925: yo bhaṭṭatantragahanārṇavakarṇadhāraḥ śāstrāntareṣu nikhileṣv api marmabhettā. yo 'tra śramaḥ kila kṛtaḥ **kamalākareṇa** prīto 'munāstu sukṛtī **budharāmakṛṣṇa**. This occurs at the end of the second pariccheda of the *Nirṇayasindhu*.

[91] Nārāyaṇabhaṭṭa takes pride in having acquired his remarkable training in Mīmāṃsā and Dharmaśāstra at the feet of his father. See *The Bridge to the Three Holy Cities*, p. 2: śāstreṣv adhītī pitur eva yaḥ śrutīḥ smṛtīḥ samālocya ca deśarītīḥ / **nārāyaṇas** tattanayo 'vimukte tīrthatrayīsetum asau vidhatte. For Nīlakaṇṭhabhaṭṭa and consistent identification of Śaṅkara as a Mīmāṃsaka, see H. P. Shastri, *A Descriptive Catalogue of Sanskrit Manuscripts in the Government Collection Under the Care of Asiatic Society of Bengal*, vol. 3 (Calcutta: Asiatic Society of Bengal, 1917), p. 149, Ms no 5725/2046, *Samayamayūkha* colophon: **śrījagadgurubhaṭṭanārāyaṇasūrisūnupaṇḍitaśiroratna-mīmāṃsakaśaṅkarabhaṭṭātmajabhaṭṭanīlakaṇṭh**[a]; and ibid., p. 150, Ms. no 4460/2047, *Nītimayūkha*, Opening verses: virodhimārgadvayadarśanārthaṃ dvedhā babhūvātra paraḥ pumān yaḥ / **śrīśaṅkaro bhaṭṭa** ihekakṛtyo mīmāṃsakādvaitam urīcakāra.

[92] *Descriptive Catalogue, Deccan College*, p. 61, no. 614 (502/1883–4) *Vyavahārakāṇḍa*, fol. 105a: iti **śrīmadvidvanmukuṭamāṇikyamarīcipimjarītapadadvandvāravindaśrīmannārāyaṇabhaṭṭasūrisūnu-śrīmadrāmakṛṣṇātmajadinakarabhaṭṭasūnugāgābhaṭṭaparanāmakaviśveśvarabhaṭṭapūrṇite** dinakaroddyote vyavahārakāṇḍaṃ samāptam.

[93] Ibid., pp. 13–14, no. 1117 (236/1884–7), *Rāmakalpadrūma*, fol. 78a: **śrīmatpadavākyapramāṇapārāvarapārīṇaśrīmannārāyaṇabhaṭṭasūrisūnuśrīrāmakṛṣṇabhaṭṭasutaśrīmajjagadgurukamalākarabhaṭṭātmajānantabhaṭṭa.**

Nārāyaṇabhaṭṭa's *Divyānuṣṭhānapaddhati*, and his cousin Kamalākarabhaṭṭa's *Nirṇayasindhu*. The Bhaṭṭas signal their familial intertextuality in various ways: by identifying a certain argument as 'the Bhāṭṭa opinion', by noting that 'this is my father's opinion', by citing parallel passages verbatim, by pointing the reader to another family member's text 'for more information on this topic' or by invoking a Mīmāṃsā theory elaborated in another text. The Bhaṭṭas do not always agree with one another, but this pattern of intertextuality sets the boundaries of a discernible school of thought that proved hostile to certain Bengali ideas.

In the *Nirṇayasindhu*, Kamalākarabhaṭṭa uses many of these patterns of citation. One way he identifies the siddhāntin (conclusion) to a Dharmic dilemma (often drawn in contrast to a 'Gauḍa' opinion) is to add 'iti bhaṭṭa' to an opinion.[94] In other places, he states that 'as for what the Gauḍas have said, this was soiled by my grandfather's feet in the *Prayāgavidhi* (in his *Tristhalīsetu*)'.[95] Discussing the atyantakarman, Kamalākara writes that 'to know about such things as the giving of a cow for the purpose of crossing the Vaitariṇī, see the *Antyeṣṭapaddhati* composed by (Nārāyaṇa)bhaṭṭa'.[96] Kamalākara occasionally argues against Nārāyaṇabhaṭṭa (on relatively small matters).[97] He cites his cousin Nīlakaṇṭha's views from the *Vyavahāramayūkha* (that fathers have no ownership in their sons) in a discussion of adopted sons (dattakaputra).[98] Kamalākarabhaṭṭa's reasoning, which was endorsed later by Gāgābhaṭṭa in the *Bhāṭṭacintāmaṇi*, is based on a close reading of the *Mīmāṃsāsūtras*. He writes that:

> As for the discussion of the Viśvajit (sacrifice in which one gives away all of one's 'own') in the sixth (chapter of the *Mīmāṃsāsūtras*), there is a doubt concerning the gift (of a son) as a son because sons and the like are referred to, using the word 'own', in the sense of relative. It is not possible to give (a son) in the sense of progeny, but it is possible to give (a son) in the sense of servant. Therefore, (a father) certainly has ownership, i.e. eligibility for use as desired (in his son), and someone who says otherwise is a fool indeed.[99]

[94] See his comments on impurity on the eleventh day after the death of a Brahman (ekādaśa). *Nirṇayasindhu*, ed. N. R. Ācārya (Mumbai: Nirṇayasāgara, 1949), p. 418: iti **bhaṭṭāḥ**.

[95] Ibid., p. 391: yat tu **gauḍāḥ**... ity āhuḥ, taddūṣaṇam **pitāmahacaraṇaiḥ prayāgavidhau**.

[96] Ibid., p. 402: daśadānavaitariṇīdhenūtkrāntidhenudānādi **bhaṭṭakṛtāntyeṣṭipaddhatau** jñeyam.

[97] See Kāṇe, *History of Dharmaśāstra*, vol. 1, part 2, p. 935.

[98] For the debate, see ibid., pp. 932–3; *Vyavahāramayūkha*, ed. P. V. Kāṇe (Delhi: Amar Press, 2009), p. 58: nanu svīyagavādijananeneva svabhāryāyām utpattyā kanyāputrādāv api svatvaṃ syāt. iṣṭāpattau **viśvajiti** sarvasvaṃ dadātīti vihite sarvasvadāne kanyāputrādidānāpattyā kanyāputrādi na deyam iti **ṣāṣṭhasiddhāntavirodha** iti cen na. Nīlakaṇṭha bases his reasoning on Pārthasārathimiśra's *Tantraratna*: ata eva putrādīnāṃ dānaṃ gauṇam iti **tantraratne miśrāḥ**.

[99] *Nirṇayasindhu*, p. 185: yat tu viśvajidadhikaraṇaṃ **ṣaṣṭhe**, tatra putrādīnāṃ jñātitvena svaśabdavācyatvāt putratvena dānam āśaṅkya nirākṛtaṃ; janyapuṃstvasya dānenāniṣpatteḥ. dāsatvena dānam bhavaty eva. tasmād yatheṣṭaviniyogārhatvaṃ svatvam bhavaty eva. putre svatvābhāvaṃ vadan... mūrkha eva. See chapter 1 for a discussion of the Viśvajit sacrifice, Mīmāṃsā, and ownership. In brief, one of Śabara's pūrvapakṣins argues that it may be reprehensible to give away one's relatives as slave, but one could do so nevertheless. The siddhāntin accepts that the

Kamalākara's comments reveal the fine distinctions that Mīmāṃsā reasoning can bring to Dharmaśāstric debates, and Gāgābhaṭṭa adopted them in his *Bhāṭṭacintāmaṇi* (whose theory of ownership was indebted to Kamalākara). The Bhaṭṭas' Mīmāṃsā grew increasingly inflected by Navya-Nyāya, so that Gāgābhaṭṭa's *Bhāṭṭacintāmaṇi* employs Navya-Nyāya terminology and quotes the opinions of the logicians (Navya-Nāyaiyikas) with as much regularity as he quotes his father's *Bhāṭṭadinakara* (a commentary on Pārthasārathimiśra's *Śāstradīpikā*).[100]

The Bhaṭṭas' texts carry a consistent polemic levelled against easterners. From Nārāyaṇabhaṭṭa to Gāgā and Bhānubhaṭṭa, the views of the Bhaṭṭas are contrasted with rivals including Vācaspatimiśra (and Miśrāḥ more generally), Śūlapāṇi, Raghunanda Bhaṭṭācārya and a string of Navadvīpan and Maithila Navya-Naiyāyikas (especially Raghunātha Śiromaṇi). The Bhaṭṭas were among the first non-Bengali Paṇḍitas to encounter the Gauḍa school of Navadvīpan Dharmaśāstra and Navya-Nyāya. The Bhaṭṭas' dealt with the Gauḍa school by rejecting it in a way that emphasized the Bhaṭṭas' superior status as exemplary southern Brāhmaṇas. During his debate with Vidyānivāsa in the house of Ṭoḍar Mal, Nārāyaṇabhaṭṭa argued that eating meat in Śrāddhas was prohibited—contrary to the Bengali love of meat—a polemic that his treatise on meat eating, the *Kaliśrāddhemāṃsadānavicāra*, examined at length.[101] Śaṅkarabhaṭṭa and Bhānubhaṭṭa adopt a similarly polemical tone in their discussion (and rejection) of meat eating during śrāddhas in their *Dharmadvaitanirṇaya* and *Dvaitanirṇayasiddhāntasaṅgraha* respectively.[102]

Kamalākara draws a strong contrast between his own intellectual tradition and those of the 'Gauḍas' and 'Maithilas' when he discusses marriage (vivāha) and kinship (sāpiṇḍya) in the third section (pariccheda) of the *Nirṇayasindhu*. Kamālakara quotes *Mānavadharmaśāstra* 3.5—that a man should marry a woman who is not a sapiṇḍa of his mother—and argues, quoting the *Ṛjumitākṣarā* (on Yāj. 1.52) almost verbatim, that:

sin of the action is sufficient to obviate the application of injunction—to give away everything—with regard to one's relatives.

[100] *Bhāṭṭacintāmaṇi: Tarkapāda*, ed. Śukla, Sūryanārāyaṇa (Benares: Chowkhamba Sanskrit Series Office, 1933). For his father, see pp. 54, 63–4, 72, and 103. For Naiyāyikas, see pp. 23, 35, 71, and 80 (among many others).

[101] See note 37.

[102] Derrett argues that Śaṅkarabhaṭṭa and Bhāṇubhaṭṭa's discussion of Dattāpradānika (non-delivery of a gift) in the *Dharmadvaitanirṇaya* and *Dharmadvaitanirṇayasaṃgraha* rejects the theory of *factum valet* developed by Jīmūtavāhana and his Gauḍa followers (in Dharmaśāstra and Navya-Nyāya). See J. D. Derrett, 'Prohibition and Nullity: Indian Struggles with a Jurisprudential Lacuna', *Bulletin of the School of Oriental and African Studies* 20.1 (1957): 203–15. This is a plausible assertion, because it dovetails with the rejection of meat eating. Kamalākara and Nīlakaṇṭha reject the principle of *factum valet* in their discussions of vibhāga initiated by a father, so this may be another facet of the Bhāṭṭa school of jurisprudence's opposition to the Gauḍa school.

> 'Not a sapiṇḍa' (means) devoid of sāpiṇḍya (kinship). And that (kinship) arises through (their) being connected by particles of one body. For the particles of the body of the father or of the mother of one person are sown, either immediately or by descent, in sons, grandsons, etc., in the form of semen, blood, etc. Although that (kinship) does not arise mutually for wives with their husband and for the wives of brothers, nevertheless, there is certainly a connection by particles of one body (for these women) in terms of being the receptacle (for children born of the father)... For, according to the *Madanaratna(pradīpa)*, Pārijāta, and Vijñāneśvara, etc., the particles of the body of the father of one (person) are deposited in them (mothers) by means of sons. Such is the case even for Gauḍas and Maithilas, etc., such as Vācaspatimiśra (the second), the *Śuddhiviveka*, and Śūlapāṇi.[103]

Recall that Vijñāneśvara's definition of kinship (sāpiṇḍya) as a blood relation formed a faultline in the formation of Gauḍa/Maithila schools of jurisprudence in eastern India.[104] Here, Kamalākara draws a sharp contrast between Vijñāneśvara (and his followers) on the one hand and Maithila and Gauḍa authors on the other—even as he acknowledges that all three camps agree, ostensibly, on the role that producing offspring plays in forging kinship relations between non-biologically-related spouses. Kamalākara does not, however, reveal to the reader that the *Mitākṣarā* and Maithila Dharmaśāstrins share a theory of kinship as consanguinity (and a juridical model of inheritance) jointly opposed to that of Gauḍa Dharmaśāstrins.

Elsewhere in the *Nirṇayasindhu*, Kamalākara uses the term Gauḍa, consistently, to identify positions with which he disagrees and that he contrasts with southern, or Bhāṭṭa opinions as conclusions.[105] Sarkar, in charting the proselytization of Durgāpūjā in the Gauḍa school of Dharmaśāstra, reveals that Kamalākarabhaṭṭa is the first Southern Dharmaśāstrin to refer to the Durgāpūjā literature of Raghunandana, Śūlapāṇi and Śrīnāthācāryacūḍāmaṇi.[106] Sarkar notes that Kamalākara brackets the foreignness of these texts by referring to them as

[103] *Nirṇayasindhu* (1985 Nirṇayasāgara edition), p. 203: asapiṇḍā ca yā mātur asagotrā ca yā pituḥ / sā praśāstā dvijānāṃ dārakarmaṇi maithune //3.5// asapiṇḍāṃ sāpiṇḍyarahitām. tac caikaśarīrāvayavānvayena bhavati. ekasya hi pitur mātur vā śarīrasyāvayavāḥ putrapautrādiṣu sākṣāt paraṃparayā vā śukraśoṇitādirūpeṇānusyūtāḥ. yady api patnyāḥ patyā saha bhrātṛpatnīnāṃ ca parasparaṃ naitat saṃbhavati, tathāpi ādhāratvenaikaśarīrāvayavānvayo 'sty eva...ekasya hi pitṛśarīrasyāvayavāḥ putradvārā tāsv āhitā iti **madanaratnapārijātavijñāneśvarādayaḥ. vācaspatiśuddhivivekaśūlapāṇyādigauḍamaithilādayo** 'py evam.

[104] See 'Inheritance and Ownership in Maithila Dharmaśāstra and Navya-Nyāya' in Chapter 2.

[105] See for example, *Nirṇayasindhu*, p. 417: yac ca **gauḍagranthe**... iti **mūrkhoktiḥ** parāstā vacanād āśaucamadhya iva tatrāpy avirodhāt; 418: **śūlapāṇiḥ smārtagauḍaś** ca parāstaḥ; 423: **gauḍas** tu... iti **śūlapāṇiḥ**... tan **maurkhyakṛtam**.

[106] Bihani Sarkar, 'The Rite of Durgā in Medieval Bengal: An Introductory Study of Raghunandana's *Durgāpūjātattva* with Text and Translation of the Principal Rites', *Journal of the Royal Asiatic Society* 22.2 (2012): 325–90, 333–5.

'Gauḍa', and Deshpande adds that Kamalākara contrasts these Gauḍa texts with southern rituals.[107] Taken in conjunction with other Bhāṭṭa polemics, Kamalākara's quibbling reveals that his family's encounter with the Gauḍa school of Dharmaśāstra was one of resistance and rejection. The appearance of Śrīnāthācāryacūḍāmaṇi, the first commentator on Jīmūtavāhana's *Dāyabhāga* and a Navya-Naiyāyika of Navadvīpa, as an opponent in Kamalākara's *Nirṇayasindhu* suggests that the hostile response to Jīmūtavāhana and Raghunātha seen in the Bhaṭṭas' works of inheritance and ownership was part of a broader anti-Bengali trend in the Bhāṭṭa school of thought.

Ownership and Inheritance in the Bhāṭṭa Corpus

Three generations of Bhaṭṭas—Rāmakṛṣṇa, Kamalākara, and Gāgā—defend the *Mitākṣarā* against what they perceive as attacks from Bengali Dharmaśāstrins and Navya-Naiyāyikas. In the *Vibhāgatattvavicāra*, Rāmakṛṣṇabhaṭṭa reveals that the Bhaṭṭas follow the *Mitākṣarā*'s theories of ownership-by-birth and unobstructed inheritance.[108] Rāmakṛṣṇabhaṭṭa defends ownership-by-birth from opponents whom he characterizes as deficient in their knowledge of Mīmāṃsā. Rāmakṛṣṇa's son, Kamalākarabhaṭṭa, discusses ownership and inheritance in two of his most famous works—the *Vivādatāṇḍava* and the *Mīmāṃsākutūhala* - where he attacks Jīmūtavāhana and other easterns at length.[109] In the *Vivādatāṇḍava*, Kamalākara argues for a theory of svatva as an extra-śāstrically produced fitness for use as desired (yatheṣṭhaviniyogayogyatva) in order to defend the 'southern' view of inheritance developed in the *Mitākṣarā* against the eastern views of Jīmūtavāhana's *Dāyabhāga*. There, he refers to various theories of ownership that he explores in the *Mīmāṃsākutūhala*. Kamalākara engages in a complicated treatment of these theories of ownership in the idiom of Navya-Nyāya in the *Mīmāṃsākutūhala*, where he rejects two Navadvīpan

[107] Ibid.: 333. *Nirṇayasindhu*, **kṛtyatattvārṇavodāhṛtavacanāt**... iti **tithitattve**... iti **gauḍāḥ. dākṣiṇātyās** tu. Cf. Deshpande, 'Pañca Gauḍa'; for other references to Śrīnāthācāryacūḍāmaṇi, see pp. 129 and 189. Nīlakaṇṭhabhaṭṭa describes himself rather modestly in the colophon of his *Nītimayūkha* as 'the (crown) jewel of the learned (bhaṭṭa) lineage, the garland of the Southern (tradition)'. See Julius Eggeling, *Catalogue of the Sanskrit Manuscripts in the Library of the India Office, Vol. 1* (London, 1887), pp. 428, #1444: vibudhakulamaṇir **dākṣiṇātyāvataṃso bhaṭṭaḥ śrīnīlakaṇṭhaḥ**...

[108] *Vibhāgatattvavicāra*. Asiatic Society Library Manuscript #1064. I would like to thank Bihani Sarkar for helping me to acquire a copy of this manuscript.

[109] Kamalākarabhaṭṭa, *Mīmāṃsākutūhala*, ed. Paṭṭābhirāma Śāstrī (Varanasi: Sarasvatībhavanagranthamālā No. 123, Sampurnanand Sanskrit University, 1987);
'Vivādatāṇḍava: Dāyabhāga Portion', in ed. Herambha Chatterjee, *Our Heritage* 7.2 (1959): 1–23; 8.2 (1960): 25–37; 11.1 (1963): 39–50; 13.1 (1965): 51–8; *Vivādatāṇḍava*, ed. & trans. (Gujarati) M. N. Dvivedī. (Baroda: Lakṣmīvilāsa Press, 1901).

Navya-Naiyāyikas' definitions of ownership on the basis, in part, of their incongruity with the theory of ownership-by-birth developed in the *Vivādatāṇḍava*.

Finally, Gāgābhaṭṭa, in the *Vyavahārakāṇḍa* and the *Dānakāṇḍa* of his Dharmaśāstra compendium, the *Dinakaroddyota*, delineates his theories of ownership and inheritance.[110] Gāgābhaṭṭa quotes Kamalākara's arguments at length in both texts and his arguments rely on the theory of ownership developed by Kamalākara. His doing so suggests that Kamalākara's scale of texts was not a one-off. Rather, it was adopted and extended by subsequent members of the Bhaṭṭa family so that the *Dāyabhāga/Mitākṣarā* debate became a hallmark of Vārāṇaseya and Mahārāṣṭrian Dharmaśāstra. The Bhaṭṭas are thus the first Dharmaśāstrins to attack a *Dāyabhāga* school of thought and to characterize that school of thought as antithetical to southern Brāhmaṇism and Mīmāṃsā philosophy. When taken in conjunction with the Bhaṭṭa family's efforts to portray themselves as southern rivals to eastern Paṇḍitas in Vārāṇasī, Kamalākara's arguments about ownership and inheritance—arguments that combine a Mīmāṃsā/Navya-Nyāya debate about metaphysics and a *Mitākṣarā/Dāyabhāga* debate about ownership-by-birth—are suggestive of a moment in Indian intellectual history in which the well-known Mīmāṃsā-Dharmaśāstra nexus was rivalled by a competing Navya-Nyāya-Dharmaśāstra nexus.

The *Mitākṣarā* as a Bhāṭṭa text: Rāmakṛṣṇabhaṭṭa's *Vibhāgatattvavicāra*

The *Vibhāgatattvavicāra* is the earliest known existing Dharmaśāstra work from the Bhaṭṭa family that discusses inheritance. In this text, Rāmakṛṣṇabhaṭṭa argues, vociferously, in defence of Vijñāneśvara. Rāmakṛṣṇabhaṭṭa was a Dharmaśāstrin and Mīmāṃsaka who died young, probably sometime in the mid-sixteenth century.[111] Rāmakṛṣṇa's period of literary activity is just at the cusp of reception of the *Dāyabhāga* in Vārāṇasī. In the *Dāyatattvavicāra* he makes three arguments that reveal the extent of the Bhaṭṭas' adherence to the *Mitākṣarā*'s theory of ownership-by-birth and to the *Mīmāṃsānayaviveka*'s theory of ownership as extra-śāstric: (1) he attacks the opponents of Vijñāneśvara (Jīmūtavāhana or Raghunandana?) as ignorant of Mīmāṃsā; (2) he argues that women and adopted sons acquire ownership by 'birth' (in the metaphorical sense of the word); and (3) he defends women's right to unobstructed inheritance (apratibandhadāya) by dissociating inheritance rights from sacrificial entitlements (a characteristically

[110] *Dānadinakaroddyota*, Bhandarkar Oriental Research Institute Ms. No 617 (82/1895–8); *Vyavahāradinakaroddyota*, BORI Ms. No 613 (37/1866–8).

[111] See Diaconescu, 'On the New Ways': 285; and Kāṇe, *History of Dharmaśāstra*, vol. 1, part 2, p. 925 The *New Catalogus Catalogorum* does not list any Mīmāṃsā texts authored by Rāmakṛṣṇa.

Mīmāṃsā-inflected argument). Although this does not prove that Rāmakṛṣṇa targets the *Dāyabhāga* school explicitly, it demonstrates the importance of the *Mitākṣarā* to the Bhaṭṭas.

Rāmakṛṣṇa opens the *Vibhāgatattvavicāra* with an accusation:

> The authoritative statements pertaining to the division of inheritance have been determined by Vijñāneśvara and others learned in the essence of Mīmāṃsā logic. However, some fools, (Jīmūtavāhana and the like?) ignorant of the essence of such logic, hold false opinions in reference to their (the authoritative statements') performance. Because of this they make logically fallacious indictments (of Vijñāneśvara's opinions).[112]

Rāmakṛṣṇa immediately makes explicit the connection between the *Mitākṣarā*—and its theory of unobstructed inheritance—and Mīmāṃsā reasoning.[113] Unfortunately, Rāmakṛṣṇa's polemic does not extend beyond his opening salvo, so it is difficult to ascertain the identity of his opponents. The remaining twenty-six folia are devoted to a relatively calm explanation of Rāmakṛṣṇa's theory of inheritance. Rāmakṛṣṇa does not seem keen to replicate his opponents' theories as opponents. He does, however, foreground ownership-by-birth as an essential feature of his system of inheritance. In a discussion of women's inheritance rights, Rāmakṛṣṇa notes that 'this division involving women certainly pertains to direct inheritance (the coparcenary trust)'.[114] Rāmakṛṣṇa argues that a man's wives—like his sons—may take a share of the estate when it is divided (before or after their husband's death). Rāmakṛṣṇa's reasoning involves an expansion of 'birth' as an extra-śāstrically recognized means of acquiring ownership. He writes that:

> Being a wife, like being a son is a cause of (acquiring) ownership. There is the convention that sons have ownership-by-birth. But one should not err and (postulate) an inequality (between sons and) a wife based on (a wife's) lack of birth from their husband. Because there would be the unwanted consequence that adopted sons and the like would not have ownership because they lack birth (from their adopted father). But if one were to think that adopted sons' ownership (arises) immediately after the death of their adopted father—just like in the

[112] *Vibhāgatattvavicāra*, fol. 1b: vibhāgaviṣaye **mīmāṃsānyāyatattvābhijñavijñāneśvarādibhir** nirṇīte 'pi vākyārthe nyāyatattvānabhijñā mūḍhā dūṣaṇābhāsodbhāvena tadanuṣṭhāne vipratipadyante. tannirāsāya nyāyānurodhena **vijñāneśvarādyabhimato** vākyārtha ujjvalīkriyate. tatra vibhāgo d(v)ividhaḥ apratibandhasapratibandhadāyaviṣayatvena.

[113] For Rāmakṛṣṇa's division of dāya, see ibid., fol. 1b: tatra prathamaḥ putrādīnām pitrādidhanaviṣayaḥ janmanā svatvāt tasya. dvitīyo duhitrādīnām pitrādidhanaviṣayaḥ. tasya pitrādimaraṇānantaram svatvāt. Cf Chapter 1, fn 16: *Mitākṣarā* on *Yājñāvalkyasmṛti* 2.114: sa ca dvividhaḥ apratibandhaḥ sapratibandhaś ca. tatra putrāṇām pautrāṇām ca putratvena pautratvena ca pitṛdhanam pitāmahadhanam ca svam bhavatīty apratibandho dāyaḥ. pitṛvyabhrātrādīnām tu putrābhāve svāmyabhāve ca svam bhavatīti sapratibandho dāyaḥ.

[114] Ibid., fol. 17b: ayaṃ ca strīvibhāgo 'pratibandhadāyaviṣaya eva.

> cause of the obstructed inheritance of daughters and the like—there would then be the problem of svatva arising from partition with reference to partition (made by) the adopted son and the like while the father is alive. Therefore, because of the prohibition of ownership (arising) from partition, because ownership is stated (to arise) by birth, it is understood that the word 'birth' has the metaphorical meaning of all the causes of ownership. And that (cause of ownership) is birth in the case of a natural son, adoption in the case of an adopted son and also marriage for a wife. Therefore, as with sons, it is proved that a wife's inheritance is unobstructed.[115]

Ownership-by-birth allows Rāmakṛṣṇa to approach a thorny issue of inheritance—concerning wives as heirs—by expanding the semantic range of the term 'birth'. Rāmakṛṣṇa's theory relies on an implicit argument: marriage's inclusion as a cause of ownership is based, at least partly, on birth's recognition as an extra-śāstric means of acquiring ownership.

Rāmakṛṣṇa makes his reliance on Mīmāṃsā theories of ownership as an extra-śāstric matter explicit in a defence of the *Mitākṣarā*. He writes that:

> As for those who expectorate filth onto the *Mitākṣarā* and say that assets are for the purpose of the sacrifice and that the purpose of the sacrifice is for assets and pleasure, they do not understand the lesson of Mīmāṃsā. In the fourth chapter (of the *Mīmāṃsāsūtras*) the acquisition of assets is proved to be puruṣārtha and not kratvartha.[116]

Jīmūtavāhana, Raghunandana, and other Bengali Dharmaśāstrins do not argue that the acquisition of assets serves the purposes of the sacrifice, but Rāmakṛṣṇabhaṭṭa's harsh comments attest to the vehemence with which the Bhaṭṭas adhered to the Mīmāṃsā and Dharmaśāstric implications of Vijñāneśvara's *Mitākṣarā*. We saw in Chapter 1 that the fourth adhyāya of the *Mīmāṃsāsūtras* (and commentary thereon) is the location where Mīmāṃsakas defend theories of ownership as extra-śāstric and of birth (and marriage) as a cause of ownership.[117] Taken together with his expansion of ownership-by-birth and his opening polemic, Rāmakṛṣṇabhaṭṭa's appeal to the theory of acquisition as puruṣārtha speaks to the existence of a Mīmāṃsā/Dharmaśāstra nexus at the heart

[115] Ibid., fol. 18a: putratvasyeva bhāryātvasyāpi svatvahetutvāt. na ca janmanā putrāṇām svatvam iti vyavahārād bhāryāyāś ca bhartṛto janmābhāvād vaiṣamyam iti bhramitavyam. dattakādiputrāṇām api janmābhāvenāsvatvaprasaṅgāt. yadi tu sapratibandhadāya iva duhitrādīnām pitṛmaraṇānantaram eva dattakādīnām svatvam iti manyeta tato jīvati pitari dattakādivibhāge vibhāgāt svatvāpattiḥ. tasmād vibhāgāt svatvaniṣeddhu[?] janmanā svatvasyoktatvād janmapadasya sakalasvatvahetūpalakṣanārthatvam avagamyate. sa caurase putre janma dattakādiṣu tūpādānādi evam bhāryāyā api pariṇayanam… tena putravadbhāryāyā apy apratibandha eva dāya iti siddham.

[116] Ibid., fol. 13b: yat tu kaś cin **mitākṣarādūṣaṇavyasatī** dravyasya yajñārthatvam yajñārthasyāpi cārthakāmārthatvam āhā, etam mīmāṃsādhy[ā]ya[ṃ] na vidhur… tatra hi **caturthe** dravyārjanasya kratvarthatvanirāsena puruṣārthatvaṃ sādhitam.

[117] See 'Onwership in Śabara's *Bhāṣya*' in Chapter 1.

of the Bhaṭṭa family's model of inheritance. The *Vibhāgatattvavicāra* may be the earliest extant rejoinder to the *Dāyabhāga*. If not, Kamalākarabhaṭṭa's *Vivādatāṇḍava* (a text modelled on the *Vibhāgatattvavicāra*), is the earliest rejoinder to the *Dāyabhāga*.

Kamalākarabhaṭṭa: The Founder of the Bhāṭṭa School of Inheritance

Kamalākara wrote treatises on, among other things, Mīmāṃsā, Dharmaśāstra, Vedānta, and Alaṅkāraśāstra, many of which have attracted significant attention from colonial and contemporary scholars.[118] Kamalākarabhaṭṭa may have been influenced by his father Rāmakṛṣṇabhaṭṭa's defence of the *Mitākṣarā*, but he is certainly the founder of a Bhāṭṭa school of inheritance—opposed to the *Dāyabhāga* school of inheritance. This is because he crafted a scale of Dharmaśāstra and Mīmāṃsā texts that acknowledged and rejected the Dharmaśāstra and Navya-Nyāya theories of ownership and inheritance that were promulgated by eastern Paṇḍitas from Navadvīpa and Vārāṇasī. We saw earlier that Kamalākarabhaṭṭa's *Nirṇayasindhu*—likely the first treatise outside of Bengal to acknowledge the writings of Śrīnāthācāryacūḍāmaṇi—takes a hostile attitude to 'Gauḍa' opinions, so the anti-Bengali thrust of his opinions regarding ownership and inheritance dovetail with his broader project of promoting the Bhāṭṭa brand of southern Brāhmaṇism against a rival eastern brand of Brāhmaṇism.

Table 3.1 outlines Kamalākarabhaṭṭa's scale of texts. The table charts the various texts that are arranged hierarchically. The table is arranged horizontally to display the nexus between legal and philosophical treatises: i.e. the *Vivādatāṇḍava* and the *Mīmāṃsākutūhala* share a common theory of ownership. Columns one and three list the treatises whose opinion Kamalākara supports (typically ownership-by-birth and ownership as an extra-śāstric phenomenon) while columns two and four list the linked Dharmaśāstra and Navya-Nyāya (or Mīmāṃsā) texts that are rejected. The chart is arranged vertically to display the chronological levels of Kamalākara's scale of texts—with higher texts coming later than lower texts. The texts in each vertical column are linked, so that Kamalākara's *Vivādatāṇḍava* amounts to a defence of the *Mitākṣarā* against the *Dāyabhāga*.

A Scale of Smṛtis: Svatva in the Vivādatāṇḍava

The *Vivādatāṇḍava*, Kamalākara's treatise on legal procedure, discusses topics such as the qualification of judges, forms of plaint, and the eighteen titles of law

[118] See note 9.

Table 3.1 Kamalākarabhaṭṭa's Scale of Dharmaśāstra Texts (1640)

I	II	III	IV
Dharmaśāstra Texts	Opponent's Dharmaśāstra Texts	**Mīmāṃsā Texts**	Opponent's Philosophical Texts
Vivādatāṇḍava (Kamalākara)		*Mīmāṃsākutūhala* (Kamalākara)	
	Dāyabhāga/ Dāyabhāgaṭippaṇī (Jīmūtavāhana/ Śrīnāthācārya)		*Padārthatattvanirūpaṇa* (Raghunāthaśiromaṇi)
	University of Navadvīpa Founded 1514		
Madanaratnapradīpa (Madanasiṃharāja)		*Mīmāṃsānayaviveka* (Bhavanātha)	
	Dhāreśvara/ *Smṛtisaṅgraha* (Pūrvapakṣins in *Madanaratnapradīpa*)		*Mīmāṃsātantraratna* (Pārthasārathimiśra)
Mitākṣarā (Vijñāneśvara)		*Ṛjuvimalāpañcikā* (Śālikanātha)	
	Manubhāṣya (Medhātithi)		*Śābarabhāṣya* (Śabara)
Smṛtis/Dharmasūtras			***Mīmāṃsāsūtras***

(vivādapadas), which include the division of inheritance, sale without ownership, failure to pay wages and so on.[119] The *Vivādatāṇḍava* appears to be a later work in Kamalākara's corpus because he closes the text by boasting of having written more than twenty works on topics including Bhāṭṭa and Prābhākara-Mīmāṃsā, Vedānta, grammar, and the *Nirṇayasindhu*.[120] Kamalākara's discussion of ownership occurs in the first few pages of the *Dāyaprakaraṇa*, the section of the *Vivādatāṇḍava* devoted to determining the law of inheritance.[121]

Kamalākara's discussion of ownership and inheritance in the *Vivādatāṇḍava* is remarkably similar to the discussion of ownership and inheritance in the *Madanaratnapradīpa* (fifteenth century CE).[122] Both authors argue for a theory of ownership as an extra-śāstrically produced quality of an asset, namely fitness for use as desired (yatheṣṭhavinyogayogyatva). Both authors rely on the

[119] For the history and importance of the eighteen vivādapadas see P. V. Kāṇe, *A History of Dharmaśāstra*, vol. 3, 2nd edn (Poona: Bhandarkar Oriental Research Institute, 1973), pp. 248–8.

[120] Dvivedī, *Vivādatāṇḍava*, p. 731.

[121] Chatterjee, 'Vivādatāṇḍava', pp. 1–9 and Dvivedī, *Vivādatāṇḍava*, pp. 277–91.

[122] For the dates and historical context of the *Madanaratna* see Kāṇe, *History of Dharmaśāstra*, vol. 1, part 2, pp. 804–9.

Mīmāṃsānayaviveka (eleventh century) account of ownership's metaphysics to defend an extra-śāstric theory of ownership. Moreover, both authors combine these two arguments to defend a theory of a son's ownership in a family trust by birth.

Kamalākara's innovations in the *Vivādatāṇḍava* are twofold. First, Kamalākara employs the *Madanaratnapradīpa*'s arguments—originally levelled against Dhāreśvara and Saṃgrahakāra—to attack Jīmūtavāhana and his commentators (Raghunandana and Śūlapāṇi) and to defend the Bhaṭṭa family's southern views of inheritance developed in the *Mitākṣarā* against the eastern views of the *Dāyabhāga*. Kamalākara places Vijñāneśvara and Madanasiṃha in opposition to Jīmūtavāhana and Raghunandana. Second, Kamalākara lists three possibilities for ownership's ontological status: a causal capacity (śakti), a conceptual category, or the state of being the object of a legal transaction (vyavahāraviṣayatā). This signals an awareness of Navadvīpan, Navya-Nyāya debates concerning ownership that developed in tandem with the *Dāyabhāga* commentarial tradition and which advocated a theory of uparamasvatva and of ownership as a śāstric phenomenon. Kamalākara's preference for ownership as a causal capacity (śakti)—as opposed to a conceptual category (padārtha)—is connected to his defence of ownership as an extra-śāstric phenomenon, his theory of ownership as usability as desired, and his broader polemic against the *Dāyabhāga* school of thought.

Kamalākara's treatment of inheritance in the *Vivādatāṇḍava* undermines Jīmūtavāhana systematically: he defends a definition of inheritance amenable to the *Mitākṣarā*'s theory of ownership-by-birth; he bifurcates inheritance into obstructed and unobstructed categories; he discusses the extra-śāstric nature of ownership; and he uses this discussion to reject Jīmūtavāhana's theory of uparamasvatva. Kamalākara concludes that, 'therefore, there is [on the part of sons] extra-śāstric ownership existent prior to partition which is divided into [individual] shares at the time of partition'.[123]

Kamalākara offers three definitions of inheritance which implicitly contradict the *Dāyabhāga*'s definition, defended by Raghunandana and others, that inheritance 'is used in a secondary sense to refer to assets in which there is ownership (for another), contingent on a connection with the previous owner, when that (previous owner's) ownership expires'.[124] Kamalākara's definitions of inheritance do not entail the lapse of a prior owner's proprietary right as a precondition for the acquisition of a proprietary right on the part of a new owner. First (following *Nāradasmṛti* 13.1) Kamalākara defines the division of inheritance, as 'when sons

[123] Chatterjee, 'Vivādatāṇḍava', p. 9: tena vibhāgapūrvaṃ sad eva laukikaṃ svatvaṃ vibhāgād aṃśeṣu paricchidyate.

[124] *Dāyabhāga*, p. 250: See I. S. Pawate, *Dāya-Vibhāga: or, the Individualization of Communal Property and the Communalization of Individual Property in the Mitakshara Law*, 2nd edn (Dharwar: Karnatak University, 1975), p. 23 for Bālambhaṭṭa's insistence in the *Bālambhaṭṭī* that the *Mitākṣarā* definition of dāya undermines the view of the easterners (prācya).

undertake the division of paternal assets'.[125] Kamalākara expands this definition and argues that 'paternal' refers to 'parents' (i.e. mother and father), that this entails a relation which is a cause of ownership, and that 'sons' refers to 'grandsons, brothers and sons and the like'.[126] Kamalākara's second definition, taken from the *Nighaṇṭu*, states that 'the sages declare inheritance to be paternal possessions eligible for division' and clarifies the definition's meaning as 'inheritance is an asset, eligible for division, which becomes someone else's property because they have a connection to the owner'.[127] Kamalākara identifies the *Madanaratna* and also the *Smṛtisaṃgraha* as his source for his third definition of inheritance and states: 'an asset which comes from the father and an asset which comes from the mother is called inheritance'.[128] Following Vijñāneśvara almost verbatim, Kamalākara states that inheritance is of two kinds: obstructed and unobstructed.[129]

Next, Kamalākara defends the scriptural and moral legitimacy of this definition of inheritance by following the *Madanaratnapradīpa*'s assertion that birth is a śāstric and an extra-śāstric method of acquisition. Kamalākara accomplishes this by situating his two-fold division of inheritance within smṛti and by postulating ownership as something extra-śāstric. Kamalākara argues that according to the 'Gautama' birth is a canonical means of acquisition.[130] He locates unobstructed inheritance in the canonical sūtras of Gautama and argues that unobstructed and unobstructed inheritance correlate to Gautama's ṛktha (inheritance) and saṃvibhāga (partition), respectively.[131]

Kamalākara, following the *Madanaratnapradīpa*, hedges his bets when he argues that Gautama's restrictions on acquisition are actually anuvādas, statements of something that has already been stated.[132] He undermines the legal force of these śāstric restrictions even as he attempts to locate birth within them. Furthermore, he deploys two arguments, culled from the *Mīmāṃsānayaviveka*

125 Chatterjee, 'Vivādatāṇḍava', p. 1: vibhāgo (a)rthasya paitrasya putrair yatra prakalpyate / dāyabhāga iti proktaṃ vyavahārapadam budhaiḥ.

126 Ibid.: pitror idaṃ paitraṃ. idaṃ svatvanimittasaṃbandhiparaṃ. putrapadaṃ pautrabhrātṛputrādiparaṃ. Compare with *Mitākṣarā*, 280: tatra dāyaśabdena yad dhanaṃ svāmisaṃbandhād eva nimittād anyasya svaṃ bhavati.

127 *Vivādatāṇḍava*, p. 1: dāyo vibhāgārhadravyaṃ, anyadīyaṃ dravyaṃ svāmisaṃbandhigāmīty arthaḥ. Cf. *Vyavahāramayūkha*, p. 59.

128 Ibid., p. 1: pitṛdvārāgataṃ dravyaṃ mātṛdvārāgataṃ ca yat / kathitaṃ dāyaśabdena tadvibhāgo (a)dhunocyate. See *Madanaratnapradīpa: Vyavahāravivekoddyota*, ed. P. V. Kāṇe (Bikaner: Anup Sanskrit Library, Ganga Oriental Series no. 6, 1948), p. 321 (who also cites the *Smṛtisaṃgraha*).

129 *Vivādatāṇḍava*, p. 1.

130 Ibid., p. 2: utpattyaivārthasvāmitvaṃ labhate ity ācāryā iti **gautamokteś** ca. For the emergence of this apocryphal sūtra in the Prābhākara school of Mīmāṃsā and in the *Mitākṣarā* school of Dharmaśāstra, see Chapter 1, this volume. See Chapter 2 for the Navadvīpan response.

131 *Vivādatāṇḍava*, p. 2: apratibandho dāya ṛktham tena janmnaiva svatvam. sapratibandho dāyaḥ saṃvibhāgaḥ. Ṛktha is an estate which passes to the family members of a deceased person. Saṃvibhāga is the process by which individuals divide a communal property into individual portions either while the former owner/s is/are alive or when they have died.

132 Ibid., p. 4: **gautamoktis** tu lokasiddhānām evānuvādaḥ. See Pawate, *Dāyavibhāga*, pp. 207–11.

(that appear in the *Madanaratnapradīpa*). Kamalākara paraphrases the *Madanaratnapradīpa*'s comments on the *Nayaviveka*, stating that '(in Dharmaśāstra), as in Vyākaraṇa(śāstra), only something known in the (extra-śāstric) world is (identified as) proper; and it is said in the *Mahābhāṣya* that 'śāstra explains words that exist'.[133] Furthermore, Kamalākara argues, based on the *Nayaviveka* and *Madanaratna*, that ownership is not an asset's usability as desired, but an asset's fitness for use as desired.[134]

Kamalākara uses the argument that Gautama's list of methods of acquisition is based on real-world usage to refute an objection which Jīmūtavāhana makes against ownership-by-birth: that smṛtis nowhere list birth as a means of acquisition.[135] Kamalākara calls Jīmūtavāhana a fool because he ignores the sūtras of Gautama (based on extra-śāstric practice) delineating birth as a cause of ownership and because he rejects the two-fold division of inheritance.[136] There is an implicit idea undergirding Kamalākara's refutation of Jīmūtavāhana on this point: Gautama's list of the means of acquisition is based on an extra-śāstric practice which recognizes birth and two kinds of inheritance (ṛktha/apratibandha and saṃvibhāga/sapratibandha). The definition of ownership as fitness for use as desired also appears to be an important, if implicit, rejoinder to Jīmūtavāhana's assertion that sons lack use as desired in their living father's estate.[137]

Kamalākara does not directly respond to this argument, but a conception of ownership as fitness for use as desired supports a theory of inheritance in which a son and father may have ownership in an asset but have limited rights of alienation.[138] The force of the argument is thus: Jīmūtavāhana and his followers want ownership to be produced only from śāstric sources. For them, birth and unobstructed inheritance are not sources of ownership in canonical smṛtis. Even if one were to say that sons had some right to their father's assets, Devala and others prohibit sons from using those assets as they desire. Kamalākara uses the

[133] *Vivādatāṇḍava*, p. 4: yathā **vyākaraṇe** lokasiddham eva sādhu, uktañ ca **mahābhāṣye** sadanvākhyānāc chāstrasyeti. Cf. *Madanaratnapradīpa*, 324–5, and *Mīmāṃsānayaviveka*, vol. 3, ed. S Subrahmanya Shastri (New Delhi: Rashtriya Sanskrit Sansthan, 2004), p. 47.

[134] Ibid., 5: yac ca yatheṣṭaviniyogayogyatvam iti **nayaviveka madanaratne** ca, na hi suvarṇatvādinā krayahetutvaṃ kiṃ tu svatvenaiva. Cf *Madanaratnapradīpa*, 325.

[135] *Vivādatāṇḍava*, pp. 6–7: yat tu **jīmūtavāhanādayaḥ** pūrvasvāmini mṛte parasya svaṃ dāyaḥ. tac ca svatvaṃ svāmināśād vibhāgād votpadyate na tu putrāder janmanā svatvaṃ tasya svatvahetuṣv apāṭhāt yatheṣṭaviniyogābhāvenānupayogāc ca.

[136] Ibid., p. 7: te sarvatra sapratibandhasyaiva dāyasya sattvāt rikthasaṃvibhāgayor bhedābhāvāt **gautamavirodhāt** pūrvoktayuktivirodhān mūrkhā eva.

[137] Jīmūtavāhana does not make this argument in the *Dāyabhāga*. He rejects the argument that sons have svatva but not svātantrya: *Dāyabhāga* 1.16. He seems to adopt yatheṣṭaviniyoga as the characteristic of svatva in *Dāyabhāga* 1.8. See *Jīmūtavāhana's Dāyabhāga: The Hindu Law of Inheritance in Bengal*, ed. and trans. Ludo Rocher (Oxford: Oxford University Press, 2002), p. 55.

[138] See, for example, Kamalākara's take on Devala 1563: 'After their father's death his sons may partition his assets; for they do not own it as long as he is alive and competent.' Kamalākara interprets this verse as preventing a son from spending his father's self-acquired assets on things such as gambling. *Vivādatāṇḍava*, p. 3: iti tat pitrarjite svātantryaniṣedhārthaṃ, na paitāmahe pūrvatāpi kṛtādiniṣedhārtham eva na tu dharmavyaye iti vakṣyāmaḥ.

Nayaviveka to argue that śāstric texts are based on local usage and they can therefore be understood to accommodate his understanding of unobstructed inheritance. His theory of ownership as the *fitness* for use as desired allows him to say that sons have ownership even if that does not entail a substantive right to *use* their property.

The issue of ownership-by-birth provides a framework for Kamalākara's subsequent defence of positions on inheritance that are opposed to Jīmūtavāhana (such as a son's right to force a father to partition). As Kamalākara develops his extended theory of inheritance after his section on the nature of ownership and its sources, he repeatedly attacks Jīmūtavāhana and his followers. In a discussion of the rights of primary and secondary mothers (those without sons), Kamalākara singles out 'Jīmūtavāhana, Śūlapāṇi, Smārtagauḍa (Raghunandana) and the like' for censure.[139] The same list of authors, with the addition of the *Vivādacintāmaṇi*, appears a few pages later as an opponent.[140] Kamalākara uses Vijñāneśvara as an authority in rejecting Jīmūtavāhana's claim that a father is always entitled to an extra share of ancestral assets during a division.[141] In a discussion of a verse attributed to Bṛhaspati establishing an equality of shares between fathers and sons, Kamalākara argues that Jīmūtavāhana's interpretation is the result of 'his being blinded by hatred of the *Mitākṣarā*'.[142]

Kamalākara makes a brief reference to the Navya-Nyāya philosophy of ownership in the *Vivādatāṇḍava*. He notes, immediately after defining obstructed inheritance as ownership which arises only in the absence of the son of an object's former owner, that Raghunātha Śiromaṇabhaṭṭācārya defines ownership as a separate conceptual category.[143] Kamalākara also states 'others say that ownership is the fact that something may be the subject of a legal transaction or a particular causal capacity'.[144] Kamalākara mentions a similar list of possibilities in the *Dānakamalākara*:

> and some say that ownership is (an asset's) fitness for being the subject of a cognition: 'this is mine'. Śiromaṇibhaṭṭācārya (says that ownership) is merely another conceptual category while others, such as Devala, (say that ownership is) a particular causal capacity.[145]

[139] *Vivādatāṇḍava*, p. 14: ūrdhvaṃ tu saputrāṇām evāṃśo nāputrāṇām iti **jīmūtavāhanaśūlapāṇismārtgauḍādayaḥ prācyāḥ**. 'The easterners such as Jīmūtavāhana, Śūlapāṇi and Smārtagauḍa (Raghunandana) hold that only "mothers" with sons and not "mothers" without sons are entitled to a share of the inheritance.'

[140] *Vivādatāṇḍava*, 1901 edn, pp. 305, 307.

[141] Ibid., p. 313.

[142] Ibid., p. 318. tan **mitākṣarāpradveṣajāndhyakṛtaṃ**.

[143] *Vivādatāṇḍava*, p. 3. tatra svatvaṃ padārthāntaram iti **śiromaṇibhaṭṭācāryāḥ**.

[144] *Vivādatāṇḍava*, p. 3. svam iti vyavahāraviṣayatvaṃ śaktiviṣayatvaṃ vā. The 1901 edition seems to have a more persuasive reading: 'śaktiviśeṣa', p. 279.

[145] *Dānakamalākara*, Bhandarkar Oriental Research Institute Ms. No 575 (103/Visrama (1)) fol. 2a: svatvam ca svam iti buddhiviṣayatvayogyatetyeke. padārthāntaram eveti **śiromaṇibhaṭṭācāryāḥ** śaktiviśeṣa ityanye **devalo** 'pi.

These statements signal an awareness of an extensive series of debates, about ownership that were carried out by Bengali Navya-Naiyāyikas in Navadvīpa and in Vārāṇasī. The earliest *Dāyabhāga* commentators—Śrīnāthācāryacūḍāmaṇi and Acyutacakravartin—lived and worked alongside Raghunātha Śiromaṇi. Given the convergence between Navya-Nyāya discussions of ownership, *Dāyabhāga* commentarial literature and the emergence of a Gauḍa school of Dharmaśāstra (rivaling the Bhaṭṭas' southern school of thought), Kamalākarabhaṭṭa's reference to Raghunāthaśiromaṇi in a polemic against Jīmūtavāhana is hardly coincidental.

The Metaphysics of Ownership: Svatvaśakti in the Mīmāṃsākutūhala

Kamalākara's *Mīmāṃsākutūhala*, an investigation of the principal metaphysics of Mīmāṃsā, engages with several novel discussions in early modern śāstric debate. Examples include the relationship between Bhakti and Mīmāṃsā and the denotative capacity of vernacular languages.[146] Another novel topic addressed in a relatively short section of this text is ownership. Kamalākara quotes from the works of Raghunātha Śiromaṇi and Rāmabhadra Sarvabhauma, two prominent Naiyāyikas from Navadvīpa whose treatises on ownership combine a defence of uparamasvatva with a view of ownership's causes as determined by śāstra.[147] Kamalākara rejects these logicians' theories and argues for a metaphysics of ownership which coincides with the conclusions of the inheritance section of his *Vivādatāṇḍava*. For Kamalākara, ownership is a causal capacity, neither a conceptual category nor a qualified absence. The *Mīmāṃsākutūhala* reveals that Navya-Nyāya debates concerning ownership were enough of a challenge to the *Mitākṣarā's* theory of inheritance that they warranted a sustained analysis in a Nyāya-inflected Mīṃāṃsā idiom.

In the *Mīmāṃsākutūhala*, Kamalākara weighs Raghunātha Śiromaṇi's arguments from the *Padārthatattvanirūpaṇa*—that ownership is a conceptual category which is cognized as a connection between an individual and an object, namely, 'this is his'.[148] Fitness for use as desired cannot be a valid definition of ownership because someone else's food might be *fit* to eat and food is, generally, fit to eat before *and* after sale and purchase.[149] Raghunātha argues that the use of Dharmaśāstric injunctions such as 'don't take someone else's things' to support the definition of ownership as fitness for use as desired are circular because they

[146] For Kamalākara's rejection of Kauṇḍa Bhaṭṭa, a 'New Grammarian's' attempt to posit bhāṣābhidhānaśakti, and Kamalākara's defence of Bhakti, see Pollock, 'New Intellectuals': 3–31. For an analysis of Kamalākara's defence of the 'jñānakarmasamuccaya', see Anand Venkatkrishnan, 'Mīmāṃsā, Vedānta, and the Bhakti Movement' (PhD Dissertation, Columbia University, 2015), p. 176.

[147] For Raghunātha and Rāmabhadra, see Kroll, 'A Logical Approach to Law', pp. 98–100, 123–4.

[148] *Mīmāṃsākutūhala*, p. 28: tathā hi—caitrasyedaṃ dhanam iti dhanavṛttiś caitrasambandhaḥ pratīyate.

[149] Ibid.: na ca yatheṣṭaviniyogayogyatvaṃ tat, viniyogo hi na bhakṣaṇādikaṃ, parakīye tatsambhavāt... kiñca yogyatvaṃ nāma na dhanasvarūpaṃ, tasya krayavikrayādeḥ prāg ūrdhvañ ca sattvāt.

rely on an understanding of ownership themselves.[150] Rather, ownership must be a conceptual category of its own which is created by acts such as purchase and a father's death and destroyed through acts such as sale.[151] All of this follows Raghunātha's *Padārthatattvanirūpaṇa* almost verbatim.[152] Kamalākara, parroting Raghunātha, asks 'how then can a son have ownership in his father's assets while his father is alive?'[153] Raghunātha asks how, if one only acquires ownership on the death or relinquishment of its previous owner, there could there be a division of preexisting property.[154]

Kamalākara answers both objections by appealing to the *Mitākṣarā*: he states that sons have a proprietary right in their father's assets because those assets are unobstructed inheritance and because Vijñāneśvara and others argue that ownership is extra-śāstric.[155] Kamalākara's arguments are intriguing because his objection to a theory of ownership as a conceptual category is predicated on his commitments in Dharmaśāstra. Kamalākara is unwilling at this stage in the argument to accept a definition of ownership which relies on Dharmaśāstra to determine its causes (śāstraikasamadhigamya), because that contradicts Vijñāneśvara's formulation of ownership as an extra-śāstric phenomenon. Kamalākara's argument is not particularly convincing without taking into account his defence of Vijñāneśvara in the *Vivādatāṇḍava*.

Kamalākara weighs Rāmabhadra Sārvabhauma's arguments from a commentary on the *Padārthatattvanirūpaṇa*, the *Padārthatattvavivecanaprakāśa*. Rāmabhadra argues that ownership is best understood through the conceptual category of absence (abhāva). He defines ownership as 'the completion of acts such as purchase which produce ownership, qualified by the prior absence of acts such as sale which destroy ownership, or the prior absence of acts such as sale and donation which destroy ownership qualified by the completion of acts such as purchase which create ownership.'[156] Rāmabhadra assumes, like Raghunātha,

[150] Ibid.: na ca śāstrāniṣiddhaṃ bhakṣaṇādikaṃ viniyogaḥ. parasvaṃ nādadīta ityādiśāstrasya hi svatvāpratītau kathaṃ pravṛttiḥ? tataś ca parasparāśrayaḥ.

[151] Ibid., p. 29: tac ca pratigrahakrayapitrādimaraṇair janyate. dānavikrayādyaiś ca nāśyate.

[152] Kroll, 'A Logical Approach to Law', pp. 98–9 and 103: evaṃ svatvam api padārthāntaram. yatheṣṭaviniyogayogyatvaṃ tad iti cet ko 'sau viniyogaḥ. bhakṣaṇādikam iti cet. na, parakīye 'py annādau tatsambhavāt. śāstraniṣiddhaṃ tatheti cet kiṃ tac chāstram. parasvaṃ nādadītetyādikam iti cet svatvāpratītau kathaṃ tatpravṛttiḥ. tasmāt svatvam atiriktam eva. pramāṇaṃ ca tatra parasvaṃ nādadītetyādikaṃ śāstram eva. tac ca pratigrahopādānakrayapitrādimaraṇair janyate dānādibhiś ca nāśyate. kāraṇānām ekaśaktima[t]tvāt kāryāṇāṃ vaijātyād cā kāryakāraṇabhāvanirvāhaḥ iti dik.

[153] *Mīmāṃsākutūhala*, p. 29: kathaṃ tarhi pitṛjīvane taddhane putrasya svatvam?

[154] Ibid.: kathaṃ tarhi svasya sato vibhāgaḥ?

[155] Ibid.: tasyāpratibandhadāyatvāt … laukikaṃ hi svatvam iti **vijñāneśvarādayaḥ**.

[156] Ibid.: paramate svatvasya yāni nāśakāni vikrayādīni teṣāṃ prāgabhāvaviśiṣṭāḥ svatvotpādakāḥ krayapratigrahādidhvaṃsāḥ taddhvaṃsaviśiṣṭā vā vikrayadānaprāgabhāvāḥ svattvaṃ. Cf. *Padārthatattvavivecanaprakāśa*, p. 84, cited in Kroll, 'A Logical Approach to Law', p. 128: tathāpi yathoktaviniyogārhatvāder apāstatayā kim idaṃ svatvam iti cet[.] kvacid vikrayaprāgabhāvaviśiṣṭakrayā[di]vināśḥ kvacic ca dānādiprāgabhāvaviśiṣṭaḥ[] pratigrahādidhvaṃsa eva[.] tathā pratigrahādeḥ pūrvaṃ na tathā pratyayaḥ pratigrahādidhvaṃsavirahāt dānādyanantaraṃ ca na svatvavyavahāras tatprāgabhāvavirahāt[.] tatra maraṇasya ca dhvaṃsātmakatayā vikrayādiprāgabhāvaviśiṣṭaṃ tad eva kvacit svatvaṃ tadadhikaraṇakṣaṇadhvaṃso vā.

that a single capacity can produce and destroy various instances of ownership, but dispenses with ownership as a conceptual category by postulating svatvatva (property-ness) as an indivisible imposed property (akhaṇḍopādhi).[157] Rāmabhadra's argument is that because we conventionally describe the completion of purchase as creating ownership and the completion of sale as destroying ownership, one would need to postulate a super-padārtha, svatvatva, if svatva was a padārtha. It is simply easier in his opinion to postulate a single ownership and different absences.[158] Rāmabhadra's position is not entirely clear, but it appears that he argues for a theory of svatvatva (as well as svatvanāśatva) as akhaṇḍopādhis and ownership as inhering in various forms of absence generated by actions which share a single causal capacity to produce ownership.

Kamalākara's objections are threefold. First, following his criticism of Raghunātha, he argues that a theory of ownership as a completed action qualified by a prior absence would not be able to account for a son's proprietary right in his father's estate.[159] Neither Raghunātha nor Rāmabhadra, Bengalis from Navadvīpa, support a son's right by birth and Kamalākara immediately rejects a theory which prohibits a son's right by birth.[160]

Next, Kamalākara argues that Rāmabhadra's definition of ownership 'suffers from a lack of generality (ananugamagrasta) because there is no way to distinguish [between a dhvaṃsa qualified by a prāgabhāva or a prāgabhāva qualified by dhvaṃsa] (vinigamanāvirahāt)'.[161] For Kamalākara, it is unduly complicated to postulate ownership as accomplished through the inherence of different absences in an asset because it is far simpler to postulate ownership as inhering in an asset. Kamalākara argues that '[such a definition] is throttled by its [svatva's] accomplishment [sādhana] through the inherence [samavāya] of different absences [bhinnābhāva] in a material locus [adhikaraṇa]'. After all, 'it is simpler to postulate a distinct ownership than to postulate ownership on the part of manifold completions [dhvaṃsas]'.[162] Kamalākara ends his critique with a brusque 'fine,

[157] *Mīmāṃsākutūhala*, p. 29: nāśe jāter abhāve (a)py akhaṇḍopādhayaḥ kāryatāvacchedakāḥ, nānāvaijātyāpekṣayaikaśakter eva laghutvāt. Cf. Kroll, 'A Logical Approach to Law', p. 127.

[158] *Mīmāṃsākutūhala*, p. 29: ādyam ādāya svattvotpattiḥ, dvitīyam ādāya naṣṭam iti ca vyavahāraḥ, bhinne svatve svatvatvam api bhinnam upeyam, tadvaraṃ kḷpteṣu dhvaṃseṣu svatvam eva kalpitam iti. Cf. Kroll, 'A Logical Approach to Law', p. 129: 'It is unclear whether Rāmabhadra is talking about postulating *svatvatva* or is actually considering a *padārtha* of *svatvatva*. What is written above reflects this study's belief that Rāmabhadra likes the imposed properties *svatvatva* and *svatvanāśatva*, and may still believe in Raghunātha's *śakti* theory.'

[159] *Mīmāṃsākutūhala*, p. 29: tad etat pitryapitāmahadhane putrasya svatve (a)vyāptam. Kamalākara offers no warrant for this assertion.

[160] Kroll, 'A Logical Approach to Law', p. 128: Rāmabhadra argues that 'because death consists of the ultimate conclusion, death itself, in some cases, when qualified by the prior absence of sale and the like on the part of the heirs, or the conclusion of the instant that constitutes the substratum of death, so qualified, can be said to constitute *svatva*'.

[161] *Mīmāṃsākutūhala*, p. 29. Generality, anugama, and its opposite, ananugama, are difficult to translate. For a brief overview, see C. Goekoop, *The Logic of Invariable Concomitance in the Tattvacintāmaṇi: Gaṅgeśa's Anumitinirūpaṇa and Vyāptivāda* (Dordrecht: D. Reidel, 1967), p. 131.

[162] *Mīmāṃsākutūhala*, p. 29: nānādhvaṃsānāṃ svatvakalpanāpekṣayā bhinnasvatvasyaiva laghutvād adhikaraṇabhinnābhāvasamavāyasādhanena galahastitañ ca.

whatever' (astu yathā tathā).[163] Rather, he says, it is extremely clear that ownership is placed inside the conceptual category of śakti, for how else could one account for such things as the creation of the ownership of one person upon the abandonment of the ownership of another person?[164] Kamalākara favours a theory of svatva as a causal capacity. His cousin, Nīlakaṇṭha, also argues that ownership 'is a kind of causal capacity arising from purchase, acceptance (of a gift) and the like... [and] that purchase and the like are the causes of ownership is understood from extra-śāstric usage alone and not from śāstra'.[165]

Kamalākara's philosophical approach to ownership attempts to bring his understanding of inheritance into alignment with the metaphysics of Mīmāṃsā. He is not content merely to apply Mīmāṃsā rules of interpretation to ambiguities and controversies in Dharmaśāstra. Instead, he wants to advance a definition of ownership which could be applied consistently across disciplines without compromising its coherence. For Kamalākara it is important that ownership as a causal capacity be both logically efficient and legally accommodating. Kamalākara's rejection of ownership as a conceptual category for reasons of logical coherence is buttressed by its inability to account for sons' coexistent ownership in a family estate. This is not surprising given that Kamalākara's opponents such as Raghunātha and Rāmabhadra employed their logical studies of svatva to reject the *Mitākṣarā*'s system of inheritance in favour of Jīmūtavāhana's.

Kamalākara's engagement with Navya-Nyāya in the *Mīmāṃsākutūhala* thus represents a necessary adjunct to his defence of (and Vijñāneśvara's) extra-śāstric theory of ownership in the *Vivādatāṇḍava*. Kamalākara's encounter with Raghunātha and Rāmabhadra may also help us to understand the importance of his polemic against Jīmūtavāhana within the context of Benares' competitive intellectual milieu. Śrīnāthācāryacūḍāmaṇi, Raghunātha Śiromaṇi and Raghunandana were contemporaries in Navadvīpa and their approaches to ownership and inheritance display a consistency of thought. We saw earlier that Kamalākara quoted and rejected a Gauḍa school of Dharmaśāstra—and Śrīnāthācārya in particular—at length in his *Nirṇayasindhu* and that the Bhaṭṭa family generally took a hostile attitude toward Gauḍa Dharmaśāstrins and Navya-Naiyāyikas.[166]

This debate occurred *across disciplines*—Kamalākara's Mīmāṃsā and Dharmaśāstra writing are inexorably linked. The Mīmāṃsā/Dharmaśāstra nexus that formed the core of the medieval *Mitākṣarā* school was rivalled in the

[163] Ibid., p. 26.

[164] Ibid.: tathāpy atikṣālyamānaṃ svatvaṃ śaktikukṣinikṣiptam eva, katham anyathā svatvatyāgaparasvattvādikaṃ sambhaved iti. Kamalākara also discusses śakti in ibid., pp. 12–14.

[165] *Vyavahāramayūkha*, p. 59: tac ca [svatvaṃ] krayapratigrahādijanyaḥ śaktiviśeṣaḥ. tatkāraṇatā tu krayādīnāṃ lokavyavahārād eva gamyate na śāstrāt.

[166] See notes 95 and 100–7.

seventeenth century by the rise of a competing Navya-Nyāya/Dharmaśāstra nexus in Bengal. Kamalākara's limited adoption of the Navya-Nyāya idiom in his *Mīmaṃsākutūhala* would have demonstrated that he too could argue within and against a difficult and prestigious discursive register. If Rāmabhadra's *Padārthatattvavivecanaprakāśa* presented the latest and greatest discussion of svatva, then we might understand why Kamalākara was keen to summarize and reject it. Similarly, if Jīmūtavāhana and Raghunandana's comments on inheritance presented a hitherto unaddressed polemic against the *Mitākṣarā* in Dharmaśāstra, it would make sense that Kamalākara and his father would devote their energies to responding to them.

Ownership and Inheritance According to Gāgābhaṭṭa

If Kamalākarabhaṭṭa was the principal champion of the Bhaṭṭas' southern brand, Gāgābhaṭṭa, alias Viśveśvarabhaṭṭa, was its chief salesperson. Gāgābhaṭṭa, a polymath like his uncle Kamalākarabhaṭṭa, wrote on virtually every subject in Dharmaśāstra and Mīmāṃsā.[167] Unlike Kamalākara, Gāgābhaṭṭa took a direct interest in politics. He travelled to Mahārāṣṭra on at least two occasions, one of which was to perform Śivājī's coronation in 1674.[168] Gāgābhaṭṭa's sojourns were integral to the Marāṭha state's adoption of Bhāṭṭa Dharmaśāstra as the śāstric root of its legal system. Like other members of the family, Gāgābhaṭṭa quotes his forebears extensively—often without identifying his sources. Gāgābhaṭṭa had a particular preference for Kamalākarabhaṭṭa's works.[169] Gāgābhaṭṭa adopts two of Kamalākarabhaṭṭa's signature arguments: a polemic against the *Dāyabhāga*'s theory of uparamasvatva; and a discussion of ownership that rejects Navya-Nyāya theories of ownership as regulated by the śāstra.

Examination of three of Gāgābhaṭṭa's works—the *Vyavahāra* and *Dānakāṇḍas* of the *Dinakaroddyota* and the sixth adhyāya of *Bhāṭṭacintāmaṇi*—illuminates two facets of the Bhaṭṭas' school of thought.[170] First, Gāgābhaṭṭa's Dharmaśāstric arguments follow Kamalākarabhaṭṭa's comments in the *Vivādatāṇḍava* and in the *Mīmāṃsākutūhala* and attest to the Bhaṭṭas' nexus between Navya-Nyāya-inflected Mīmāṃsā and southern Dharmaśāstra. Second, Gāgābhaṭṭa's arguments suggest that a hostility to a Gauḍa school of inheritance was an enduring feature of the Bhaṭṭas' Dharmaśāstra corpus—and not a one-off from Kamalākarabhaṭṭa.

[167] Gāgā completed his father's *Dinakaroddyota*—a comprehensive Dharmaśāstra digest divided into subject-specific kāṇḍas. He wrote commentaries on the *Mīmāṃsāsūtras* (*Bhāṭṭacintāmaṇi* and *Kusumāñjali*) and he wrote a verse summary of portions of the *Mīmāṃsāsūtras* after the *Tarkapāda*.

[168] See 'Back to the Motherland—The Bhaṭṭas in the Court of Śivājī', above.

[169] For example, he draws on the *Dānakamalākara*, the *Śūdrakamalākara*, and the *Rājyābhiṣekhapaddhati*.

[170] *Bhāṭṭacintāmaṇi*, Bhandarkar Oriental Research Institute Ms. No 627/1887–91.

Inheritance in the Vyavahārakāṇḍa of the Dinakaroddyota

In the *Vyavahārakāṇḍa* of the *Dinakaroddyota* Gāgabhaṭṭa defines the division of inheritance as 'the division into separate (shares) of that (paternal) estate'.[171] Furthermore, 'this definition extends to a partition (made by) sons, because sons, grandsons and the like have that (ownership before partition) in as much as ownership is produced in the assets of the father and the like by birth alone.'[172] Gāgā gives two warrants for this assertion, which he attributes to the author of the *Mitākṣarā*: extra-śāstric convention and the occurrence of restrictions on a father and grandfather's independent ownership when they have grandsons (and sons).[173]

According to others, Gāgā relates, 'division is the making of separate (shares, which) gives birth to the production of ownership'.[174] For them, this is 'because that (ownership on the part of sons) arises from division alone in as much as a son does not have ownership in the assets of (his) father, etc., before partition'.[175] For these opponents—almost certainly defenders of the *Dāyabhāga*—śāstra is the source of knowledge about ownership's causes. They argue that one does not hear of birth as a cause of ownership in smṛti passages from Gautama (which list various causes of ownership).[176]

Gāgābhaṭṭa's opponent pins his argument on a śloka attributed to Yājñavalkya that states that 'a father is not the master of all immovable assets', which while intuitively a statement that supports ownership-by-birth, is read by Jīmūtavāhana and his followers as the inverse.[177] Gāgā's opponent parrots Jīmūtavāhana when they state that 'one should certainly not ask "if partition produces fitness for use as desired (i.e., ownership), how could that (ownership) arise for a single son (after the death of his father) in so much as there is no partition (by that son)"'.[178] In

[171] *Vyavahārakāṇḍa*, fol. 89a: atha vibhāgākhyaṃ vivādapadaṃ nirūpyate. tallakṣaṇam uktaṃ **nāredena**. vibhāgo 'rthasya paitrasya putrair yatra prakalpyate/ dāyabhāga iti proktam tadvivādapadaṃ budhaiḥ. tasya svasya pṛtak[k]araṇavibhāgaḥ.

[172] Ibid.: na ca putrasya pitur dravye svatvābhāvāt putravibhāge avyāptiḥ. putrapautrādīnām utpatyaiva pitrādidravye svatvotpatyā tatsattvāt. This is a reference to the apocryphal sūtra of Gautama.

[173] Ibid.: loke tathaiva vyavahārāt. evaṃ ca sthāvarasyaiva sarvasya na pitāmaha iti pautrasatve 'pi svatve pitṛpitāmahayo svātantryaniṣedha upapadyata iti **mitākṣarākāraḥ.**

[174] Ibid.: anye tu svatvotpatijanapṛthakkaraṇaṃ vibhāgaḥ. This of course is the position taken by the Gauḍa school.

[175] Ibid.: pit[r]ā[d]idravye putrasya vibhāgāt pūrve svatvābhāvena vibhāgād eva tadutpatteḥ.

[176] Ibid.: svāmīrikthakrayasaṃvibhāgaparigrahādhigameṣv ityādismṛtiṣu svatvajanakatvenāśravaṇāt. The connection between śāstra and ownership is implied.

[177] Ibid.: ata eva maṇimuktāpravālānāṃ sarvasyaiva pitā prabhur iti putrasatve pituḥ svātantryānuvāda upapadyate. Cf *Dāyabhāga*, 2.22–4: māṇimuktāpravālānāṃ sarvasyaiva pitā prabhur / sthāvarasya tu sarvasya na pitā na pitāmahaḥ // A quintessential feature of the *Dāyabhāga* school is to read against the straight-forward spirit of the verse—that fathers and grandfathers may dispense with *all* of their movable assets, but not *all* of their immovable assets—and argue that the repetition of 'all' (sarvasya) in the second line iterates a father and grandfather's absolute independence with regard to their property. Nīlakaṇṭha and Kamalākara read this verse as restricting a father's powers of alienation over *all* kinds of assets severely.

[178] Ibid., fol. 89b: na caivaṃ vibhāgasya yatheṣṭaviniyogayogyatājanakatayā ekaputrasya vibhāgābhāvena kathaṃ tadutpattir iti vācyam. Cf *Dāyabhāga* 2.12.2.

truth, says the opponent, 'in that case, the death of the father alone produces that (ownership for the son)'.[179] Having summarized Jīmūtavāhana's arguments, Gāgābhaṭṭa instructs the reader to consider the examination of ownership and the like in his *Dānakāṇḍa*.[180]

Ownership in the Dānakāṇḍa and in the Bhāṭṭacintāmaṇi

Gāgābhaṭṭa opens the *Dānakāṇḍa* with a definition of gifting as an activity amenable to the production of the ownership of another (preceded by) the cessation of the svatva (of the previous owner).[181] Before Gāgābhaṭṭa turns to the definition of ownership, he reproduces an argument from Kamalākarabhaṭṭa's *Dānakamalākara* to the effect that Raghunandana Bhaṭṭācārya's assertion in the *Śuddhitattva*—that ownership of an unaccepted gift returns to the giver—is mistaken.[182] Gāgābhaṭṭa opens his discussion concerning ownership itself by turning to the problem of the Viśvajit sacrifice from the sixth adhyāya of the *Mīmāṃsāsūtras*. Gāgābhaṭṭa introduces an opponent who argues that:

> with regard to the gift of a son or a daughter, that is giving in the secondary sense because: 1) it is impossible to destroy that (sva relationship to the son or to the daughter) inasmuch as that svatva (personal relationship) is not distinct from the state of being a son or a daughter. After all, the śiṣṭas wouldn't use the word 'mine' with reference to a gift of that (child of theirs).[183]

Gāgābhaṭṭa responds by claiming that birth (utpatti) is cause of ownership for (or with reference to) sons and daughters and that the gift of a son or daughter is a gift in the primary sense because giving destroys that—proprietary—ownership.[184] Gāgābhaṭṭa appeals, implicitly, to extra-śāstric convention when he adds that 'the recognition "the given daughter is not my sva" is experienced (by everyone) from the wives (of lowly) shepherds to the wives of Paṇḍitas'.[185] Gāgā's terse analysis appears to posit a theory of janmasvatva on the part of a father in his children and on the part of children in their father's assets.

[179] Ibid.: pitādimaraṇasyaiva tatra tadutpadam. Cf *Dāyabhāga* 1.3.

[180] Ibid.: svatvādinirūpaṇam **matkṛtadānakāṇḍe** tu saṃdhyeyām.

[181] *Dānakāṇḍa*, fol. 1b: dānatvaṃ tu svatvadhvaṃsaparasvatvotpatyanukūlavyāpāratvam.

[182] Ibid., fol. 2b: yat tu tatra dātuḥ svatva[m] punarutpadyata iti **smārttabhattācācāryāḥ**. tan na. Cf. *Dānakamalākara*, fol. 2a: yat tu **śuddhitattve** saṃpradānāgrahe tyāgāmaṣṭam [this is a bit unclear] api dātu svatvam punar utpadyate. iti **smārtta**. tan na.

[183] *Dānakāṇḍa*, fols 3a–b: kanyāputradāne tu putratvakanyātvātiriktasvatvābhāvena tannāśāsaṃbhavāt. pratigrahītur yatheṣṭaviniyogyatvarūpasvatvotpādāsaṃbhavāt ca na mukhyadānatvam. ata eva taddānena mameti śabdaprayogaṃ nācaraṇti śiṣṭā ity āhu.

[184] Ibid., fol. 3b: evam putrakanyayor api utpatter eva svatvajanakatāstu. tasya dānena nāśān mukhyam eva dānatvam.

[185] Ibid.: ata eva dattā kanyā na mama svam iti pratītir āgopālāṅganam ā[ｃ]āpaṇḍitam ānubhāvikī. See Monier Monier-Williams, *A Sanskrit–English Dictionary* 2nd Ed. (Oxford: Clarendon Press, 1899), p. 126 for a similar usage of ā+(caste) to denote a range of castes.

Gāgābhaṭṭa, citing Kamalākarabhaṭṭa's *Dānakamalākara*, notes that 'ownership is the state of being the object of the cognition "mine", fitness for use as desired or, according to (Raghunātha) Śiromaṇi, a distinct conceptual category'.[186] In his discussion of the Viśvajit sacrifice in the sixth adhyāya of the *Bhāṭṭacintāmaṇi*, Gāgā repeats his tripartite definition of ownership.[187] Gāgā, however, does not include ownership in his list of conceptual categories in his *Bhāṭṭacintāmaṇi*, so his reference to Raghunātha is not likely one of acceptance.[188] Gāgābhaṭṭa employs Navya-Nyāya terminology (especially delimiter—avacchedaka) to distinguish between proprietary and familial relationships (although as we have seen, birth may establish a proprietary *and* a familial relationship). In what appears to be an echo of Kamalākarabhaṭṭa and Nīlakaṇṭhabhaṭṭa's theory of ownership as a causal capacity, Gāgābhaṭṭa frames the difference between a familial and a proprietary relation in terms of śakyatā—capacity.[189]

Returning to the *Dānakāṇḍa*, Gāgābhaṭṭa appears, at first blush, to support Raghunātha's opinion that ownership's causes are limited to those causes mentioned in Dharmaśāstra explicitly.[190] Gāgā, like Kamalākara and Madanasiṃha, argues that unobstructed and obstructed inheritance are mentioned by Gautama explicitly.[191] Gāgā, however, does not seem content to defend ownership-by-birth by appealing to its instantiation in smṛti alone. Rather, he turns to an extra-śāstric theory of ownership, by appealing to Mīmāṃsā again. He states that 'if theft, etc., are also means of producing ownership, then (the only difference is that) inheritance, etc., are dharmic'.[192] An opponent scoffs at the proposition that theft and the like—prohibited by the śāstra—might be a means of acquiring ownership, but Gāgābhaṭṭa responds that there is no contradiction between being a means of acquiring ownership and being prohibited by the śāstra.[193] This is a startling admission and Gāgābhaṭṭa justifies it by paraphrasing the Prābhākara-Mīmāṃsā

[186] *Dānakāṇḍa*, fol 3b: svatvaṃ ca svam iti buddhiviṣayatvaṃ. yatheṣṭaviniyogyatvaṃ vā padārthāntaram iti **śiromaṇi**.

[187] *Bhāṭṭacintāmaṇi*, fols 22b–23a: svatvaṃ ca svam iti buddhiviṣayatvayatheṣṭaviniyojyatvaṃ vā padārthāntaram ity anye.

[188] The fourth adhyāya of the *Bhāṭṭacintāmaṇi*—in which Gāgābhaṭṭa almost certainly gives his preferred definition of ownership—is not available to me at present. However, the Tarkapāda of the *Bhāṭṭacintāmaṇi* lists seven padārthas, so it seems likely that he rejected Raghunātha's theory of svatva as padārtha. *Bhāṭṭacintāmaṇi*, p. 17: evaṃ ca dravyaguṇakarmasāmānyasamavāyaśaktyabhāvāḥ sapta padārthāḥ.

[189] *Bhāṭṭacintāmaṇi*, fol 23a: svaśabdasya vācyatāvacchedakadhatatvādinānā[?]. tena nānārtho 'pi śakyatāvacchedakabhedāt. The manuscript of the *Bhāṭṭacintāmaṇi* that is available to me appears to be corrupt in many places. As I understand this passage, differences in śakytā are what delimit the different meaning of the word sva—when used in reference to one's children and family. I hope to examine the fourth adhyāya of the Bhāṭṭacintāmaṇi at a later date.

[190] *Dānakāṇḍa*, fol. 3b: tasyotpādakāni svāmī rikthakrayasaṃvibhāgaparigrahādhigameṣv iti **gautamenoktāni**.

[191] Ibid.: sapratibandho dāyo ri[kth]am yathā mātāmahadhane dauhitrasya tatputrapratibandhāt. apratibandho dāyaḥ saṃvibhāgaḥ. yathā pitṛdhane putrasya.

[192] Ibid.: yady api cauryādayo 'pi svatvotpattyupāyāḥ santi. tathāpi rikthādīnāṃ dharmyatvaṃ.

[193] Ibid.: nanu cauryādīnāṃ niṣiddhatayā kathaṃ svatvopāya iti cen na. niṣiddhatvasvatvopāyatvayor avirodhāt.

school's understanding of the restrictions on acquiring ownership from the fourth adhyāya of the *Mīmāṃsāsūtras*. Gāgā concludes that these (restrictions regarding ownership) are puruṣārtha, so a man sins if he gives or sacrifices, etc., with assets acquired by means prohibited (by the śāstra), but the gift, etc. is (legally) valid.[194]

Gāgābhaṭṭa's reasoning about ownership and its causes in the *Dānakāṇḍa* supports his defence of the *Mitākṣarā*. He attempts to locate unobstructed and obstructed inheritance in the *Gautamadharmasūtras* explicitly. He makes two implicit arguments that are far more persuasive. First, he argues that ownership-by-birth is rooted in everyday experience. Second, he argues that śāstric restrictions concerning acquisition do not have the force of law. It is improbable that Gāgābhaṭṭa endorsed a view of theft as a cause of ownership (something Kamalākara and virtually every advocate of an extra-śāstric theory of ownership reject vociferously). Rather, Gāgābhaṭṭa appears to argue that Dharmaśāstra does not determine what is or is not a legally valid means of acquiring ownership. That, as Kamalākara and Madanasiṃha argue, is best left to the extra-śāstric world. Taken together, Gāgābhaṭṭa's defence of the *Mitākṣarā* in the *Vyavahārakāṇḍa*—from the attacks of an opponent very much in Jīmūtavāhana's mould—and his rejection of Raghunātha's theory of ownership—as determined by the śāstra—in the *Dānakāṇḍa* are linked. They form, like Kamalākarabhaṭṭa's arguments in the *Vivādatāṇḍava* and *Mīmāṃsākutūhala*, a comprehensive, Bhāṭṭa rejoinder to a Gauḍa school of thought. That Bhāṭṭa rejoinder continues the Mīmāṃsā/Dharmaśāstra nexus formed by the medieval *Mitākṣarā* school of thought but responds to new, Bengali opponents.

Conclusion

If Śrīnāthācārya founded a Gauḍa school of thought by combining theories of uparamasvatva (from Jīmūtavāhana's *Dāyabhāga*), śāstrically determined svatva (from Raghunāthaśiromaṇi's *Padārthatattvanirūpaṇa*) and miscellaneous religious festivals (from Śūlapāṇi, among others), the Bhaṭṭa family seem to have developed a rival, Bhāṭṭa school of thought that covered śrāddha, inheritance, ownership, and virtually every conceivable topic in Dharmaśāstra. Furthermore, at least portions of this comprehensive school of Dharmaśāstra involved texts and practices that were localized to the region of Mahārāṣṭra (the *Sahyādrikhaṇḍa*, and the the Durgotsava mentioned by Kamalākarabhaṭṭa in the *Nirṇayasindhu*, for example). Ownership and inheritance formed one crucial facet of this

[194] Ibid., fol. 4a: ata eva teṣā[m] puruṣārthatām... tena niṣiddhopāyārjitena dānayāgādyanuṣṭhāne puruṣasya pratyavāyo na dānādivaiguṇyam. See chapter 1 for the nature of puruṣārtha and kratvārtha and its relationship to the *Mitākṣarā* school of thought.

much larger formation of a southern (Dākṣinātya), Bhāṭṭa school of Sanskrit jurisprudence.

Kamalākarabhaṭṭa in particular defended the *Mitākṣarā*—of which his father was a keen advocate—by arguing against the *Dāyabhāga* and against the *Padārthatattvanirūpaṇa*. He was followed by Gāgābhaṭṭa, and possibly by Nīlakaṇṭhabhaṭṭa. Kamalākara's selection of Rāmabhadra and Jīmūtavāhana for particular censure represents a continuation of the Bhaṭṭa family's debates against Bengali logicians and Dharmaśāstrins who competed with them for prestige in the city of Vārāṇasī—and who endorsed a series of opinions that ran contrary to several core positions of the Bhaṭṭas. The *Dāyabhāga* rose to prominence in the sixteenth century when Śrīnāthācārya began to teach the text in his ṭol in Navadvīpa to pupils including Raghunandana.[195] Raghunandana held the 'chair' in smṛti at the same ṭol as Raghunātha Śiromaṇi.[196] We know little about Rāmabhadra Sārvabhauma, but he was 'reported to have headed a famous *ṭol*, presumably somewhere in Navadvīpa, and to have instructed the great scholars Mathurānātha Tarkavāgīśa, Jayarāma Nyāyapañcānana, and Jagadīśa Tarkālaṃkāra'.[197] Jayarāma Nyāyapañcānana and Raghudeva Bhaṭṭācārya, a scholar of logic who wrote on ownership, were Gauḍa signatories of the 1657 Banaras letter of judgment also signed by Nīlakaṇṭha and Gāgābhaṭṭa.[198] These Bengali authors typically rejected ownership-by-birth in their work on ownership and some, like Raghudeva, also wrote works on Dharmaśāstra.[199]

If the 1657 letter of judgment is authentic it implies an uninterrupted, if indirect, chain of transmission from early *Dāyabhāga* commentaries to Kamalākara's social milieu. Śrīnāthācārya taught the *Dāyabhāga* to Raghunandana, who worked in the same academy as Raghunātha. Rāmabhadra commented on Raghunātha's work, perhaps at the same ṭol in Bengal where Raghunandana taught the *Dāyabhāga*. Rāmabhadra wrote on ownership and taught Jayarāma Nyāyapañcānana and Raghudeva, who also wrote on ownership and Dharmaśāstra and lived in Vārāṇasī alongside the Bhaṭṭas. Śaṅkarabhaṭṭa attributed enormous importance to Nārāyaṇabhaṭṭa's defeat of the leading Pandits of eastern India in Orissa and Delhi and ownership and inheritance would have been exceptionally potent places for Kamalākara to continue Nārāyaṇabhaṭṭa's legacy.[200]

The Bhaṭṭas' defence of the *Mitākṣarā* in the seventeenth century represents the first time that the *Mitākṣarā* was read *against* Jīmūtavāhana's *Dāyabhāga* and against a Bengali school of Dharmaśāstra more generally. The medieval *Mitākṣarā* school followed contemporary developments in Prābhākara-Mīmāṃsā texts, but its opponents were essentially the same as those in the *Mitākṣarā*. Concomitantly,

[195] Rocher, 'Schools of Hindu Law', p. 125.
[196] Kroll, 'A Logical Approach to Law', pp. 101–2.
[197] Ibid., p. 123.
[198] Ibid., p. 139.
[199] For Raghudeva, see Kroll, 'A Logical Approach to Law', p. 130.
[200] O'Hanlon, 'Letters Home': 217–18. Also see Shastri, 'Dakshini Pandits at Benares': 9–10.

the Bhaṭṭas localized the *Mitākṣarā* as the root text of Vārāṇasī, of southern, Mahārāṣṭrian Brāhmaṇas, and of Mīmāṃsakas—in both the identitarian sense that they began to describe it as a southern text and in the jurisdictional sense that they wove it into a broader body of jurisprudence that they actively applied to Brāhmaṇa communities in Mahārāṣṭra. In the eighteenth century, H.T. Colebrooke encountered a thriving, largely Mahārāṣṭrian school of thought in Vārāṇasī that continued to defend the *Mitākṣarā* against more recent Bengali logicians' critiques and that appealed to the Bhaṭṭas' texts as authoritative works on inheritance and ownership.

4

Anglo-Indian Schools of Hindu Law

In 1810, Henry Thomas Colebrooke (1765–1837), a judge of the Superior Civil Court of Bengal and Professor of Sanskrit and Law at Fort William College in Calcutta completed, *Two Treatises on the Hindu Law of Inheritance: Jimutavahana and Vijnaneshwara*. In his preface, Colebrooke argues that Jīmūtavāhana's *Dāyabhāga* (twelfth to fifteenth centuries) and Vijñāneśvara's *Mitākṣarā* (eleventh to twelfth centuries) are:

> the two standard authorities of the Hindu law of inheritance in the school of Benares and Bengal respectively; and considerable advantage must be derived to the study of this branch of law, from access to those authentic works, in which the entire doctrine of each school . . . is supported, may be seen at one view . . . by exhibiting in an exact translation the text of the author with selected glosses of his commentators or from, the works of other writers of the same school.[1]

Over the course of the nineteenth century, colonial Indologists and their native collaborators added to Colebrooke's legal schematic by recovering and translating the commentaries and works associated with the Bengali, Maithila, Vārāṇaseya, Mahārāṣṭrian, and Dravidian schools of inheritance.[2] The orientalists' philological endeavors coincided with the expansion and consolidation of the colonial Dīwānī 'Adālats court system that attempted to codify and to regulate the personal property of its Hindu (and Muslim) subjects—ostensibly in an effort to promote a liberal political economy.[3]

Colebrooke's formulation of schools of Hindu law has been subjected to withering critiques in recent scholarship.[4] Historians and anthropologists such

[1] H. T. Colebrooke, *Two Treatises on the Hindu Law of Inheritance* (Calcutta: Hindoostanee Press, 1810), p. iii. For a biography of Henry Colebrooke, see Rosane Rocher and Ludo Rocher, *The Making of Western Indology: Henry Thomas Colebrooke and the East India Company* (London: Routledge, 2012).

[2] After the publication of *Two Treatises* in 1810, Colebrooke arranged the printing of the *Mitākṣarā*, the *Mānavadharmaśāstra* (with Kullūkabhaṭṭa's commentary), the *Dāyabhāga* (with Śrīkṛṣṇa's commentary), and *Vīramitrodaya* (1812–15). Henry Borradaile (attached to the Bombay Court) published an edition and translation of the *Vyavahāramayūkha* in 1827.

[3] See, among others, David Washbrook, 'Law, State and Agrarian Society in Colonial India', *Modern Asian Studies* 15.3 (1981): 649–721. For the later implications of religious personal law for religion, gender, and the state in India, see Eleanor Newbigin, *The Hindu Family and the Emergence of Modern India: Law, Citizenship and Community* (Cambridge: Cambridge University Press, 2013).

[4] Bernard Cohn, *Colonialism and Its Forms of Knowledge: The British in India* (Princeton, NJ: Princeton University Press, 1996); Neeladri Bhattacharya, 'Remaking Custom: The Discourse and

Ownership and Inheritance in Sanskrit Jurisprudence. Christopher T. Fleming, Oxford University Press (2020).

DOI: 10.1093/oso/9780198852377.003.0005

as Bernard Cohn and Christi Merrill, contend that distinctly European conceptualizations of religion, law, and sacred texts lay at the heart of the British construction of Hinduism and Hindu law as stable categories that could be recovered from careful textual study.[5] Sanskritists, including Ludo Rocher and Donald Davis, accept the proposition that Dharmaśāstra constitutes neither positive law nor a record of Hindu custom, but they add a further criticism of Anglo-Hindu law: that a close reading of Dharmaśāstra cannot support Colebrooke's formulation of schools of Hindu law.[6] Davis characterizes Colebrooke's theory of schools of Hindu law as 'a phony, artificial creation', while Rocher argues for an intriguing theory of Dharmaśāstric 'school[s] of thought'.[7] Rocher accepts Colebrooke's selection of the *Dāyabhāga* as the representative Bengali Dharmaśāstric text on inheritance as warranted—provided that one accepts its purely academic status.[8] Rocher notes, however, that 'the choice of the *Mitākṣarā* puzzles me... [because] I personally think that the lawbook for "the others" [the Paṇḍitas of Mithilā and, subsequently, Vārāṇasī] did not matter too much'.[9] Rocher admits that 'there is no doubt that...there is *some* underlying regional unity...[in Dharmaśāstric texts because] when it comes to such basic principles as the role of the joint family manager, it makes sense to speak of "the" Maithilas and of "the"...Gauḍas...but, as far as anything beyond the general principles is concerned, pure individual sophistry prevails'.[10]

This chapter brings clarity to the issue of schools of Hindu law by tracing the construction of schools of Anglo-Hindu law between 1772 and 1825—Hastings' Judicial Plan to Strange's *Elements of Hindu Law*. The chapter examines three Sanskrit legal digests that were compiled at the behest of the British East India Company and whose English translations were utilized by British jurists in

Practice of Colonial Codification', in *Tradition, Dissent and Ideology: Essay in Honour of Romila Thapar*, ed. R. Champakalakshmi and S. Gopal (New Delhi: Oxford University Press, 1996), pp. 20–51; Nandini Bhattacarya-Panda, *Appropriation and Invention of Tradition: The East India Company and Hindu Law in Bengal* (New Delhi: Oxford, 2008). Also see Raymond Schwab, *The Oriental Renaissance: Europe's Rediscovery of India and the East, 1680–1880* (New York: Columbia University Press, 1984), and P. J. Marshall, *The British Discovery of Hinduism in the Eighteenth Century* (Cambridge: Cambridge University Press, 1970).

[5] Christi Merrill, 'The Afterlives of Panditry: Rethinking Fidelity in Sacred Texts with Multiple Origins', in *Decentering Translation Studies*, ed. Judy Wakabayashi and Rita Kothari (Amsterdam: John Benjamin, 2009), pp. 75–94. For 'Hinduism' as a discursive object, see Ronald Inden, *Imagining India* (Oxford: Blackwell, 1990).

[6] Ludo Rocher, 'Schools of Hindu Law', in *Studies in Hindu Law and Dharmaśāstra*, ed. Donald Davis (London: Anthem, 2014), pp. 119–28; Ludo Rocher, 'Changing Patterns of Diversification in Hindu Law', in *Studies in Hindu Law and Dharmaśāstra*, ed. Donald Davis (London: Anthem, 2014), pp. 129–44; Donald Davis, *The Spirit of Hindu Law* (Cambridge: Cambridge University Press, 2010), pp. 89–107. Also see Rocher and Rocher, *The Making of Western Indology*, pp. 112–16. Davis' assertion that Colebrooke 'made up' these schools in 1825 is incorrect. The preface to *Two Treatises* (1810) makes a claim for the existence of schools of Hindu law fifteen year earlier.

[7] Rocher, 'Schools of Hindu Law', p. 127.

[8] Ibid., p. 125.

[9] Rocher, 'Changing Patterns', p. 138.

[10] Ibid., p. 137.

colonial courts: the *Vivādārṇavasetu* (translated in 1776 as *A Code of Gentoo Laws*), the *Vivādabhaṅgārṇava* (translated in 1795–6 as *A Digest of Hindu Law on Contracts and Successions*), and the *Vyavahārabālambhaṭṭī* (which served as an impetus for Colebrooke's *Two Treatises*). These Dharmaśāstra digests recapitulate the eastern and southern scales of Dharmaśāstra texts that developed originally in Mithilā, Navadvīpa and Vārāṇasī between the fifteenth and seventeenth centuries.

The *Vivādārṇavasetu* and the *Vivādabhaṅgārṇava*, compiled by teams of Bengali logicians, synthesize and defend the *Dāyabhāga*'s Bengali (Gauḍa) theories of ownership-by-the-cessation-of-the-ownership-of-the-previous-owner (upa ramasvatva), ownership as discernible-from-the-śāstra-alone (śāstraikasamadhigamyatva), and a Sanskrit version of *quod fieri non debuit factum valet* (what ought not to have been done is valid when done) against the opinions of Maithila rivals (often utilizing the formal techniques of Navya-Nyāya philosophy).[11] On the other hand, the *Vyavahārabālambhaṭṭī*—compiled by a Mahārāṣṭrian Mīmāṃsaka—synthesizes and defends the *Mitākṣarā*'s southern (Dākṣinātya) theories of ownership-by-birth (janmasvatva) and of ownership as extra-śāstric (laukika) against the *Dāyabhāga* and logicians identified as Bengali (Prācya, Gauḍa, etc.). Colebrooke's collaboration with Bālambhaṭṭa marks an important and unacknowledged juncture in the history of Anglo-Hindu jurisprudence: when the Gauḍa/Maithila debates found in the *Vivādārṇavasetu* and the *Vivādabhaṅgārṇava* were recalibrated as a debate between Gauḍa/Southern Paṇḍitas concerning the *Dāyabhāga* and the *Mitākṣarā*.

Conceiving of Dharmaśāstra as positive law and positing the existence of regionally specific schools of Dharmaśāstric jurisprudential philosophy constitute two independent propositions. Rejecting the first proposition and accepting the second proposition makes it possible to defend Colebrooke's formulation of schools of law—particularly his formulation of Dharmaśāstric theories of ownership and inheritance as rooted in the *Dāyabhāga* and *Mitākṣarā*—as a logical and appropriate understanding of the state of Dharmaśāstra that he encountered directly in the Dharmaśāstra digests compiled for the British and through his collaboration with Bengali, Maithila and Mahārāṣṭrian Paṇḍitas. Colebrooke's hypothesis that Navya-Nyāya and Mīmāṃsā theories of ownership lie at the heart of the division of *Dāyabhāga* and *Mitākṣarā* schools of Sanskrit jurisprudence is supported by the *Vivādārṇavasetu*, the *Vivādabhaṅgārṇava*, and the *Vyavahārabālambhaṭṭī*'s discussions of ownership and inheritance.

The practical impetus for British jurists' elevation of these various schools of *jurisprudence* to the status of positive *law*, universally applicable to Hindus within

[11] Jīmūtavāhana argues that certain transactions involving property must be legally effective even if they are inequitable. For the history of this doctrine, see J. Duncan Derrett, 'Factum Valet: The Adventures of a Maxim', in *Essays in Classical and Modern Hindu Law: Anglo-Hindu Law*, ed. J. Duncan Derrett (Leiden: Brill, 1977), pp. 1–24.

certain jurisdictions, however, lay largely in the expansion of the colonial states' Dīwānī 'Adālat system of judicature to the territories of Bengal (1772/1781/1793), Bihar (1772/1781/1793), Benares (1795), Bombay (1799/1827), and Madras (1802). In Bihar, Bengal, and Benares, colonial legal jurisdictions overlapped with pre-colonial patterns of jurisprudential thought. In Bombay and Madras, however, Sanskrit colonial jurisdictional boundaries were imposed on Sanskrit jurisprudential texts.[12] See Table 4.1, which outlines the positions and histories of the schools of Anglo-Hindu law.

Two consequences of the formulation of schools of Hindu law taking its cue from jurisdictional boundaries were the unwarranted distinction between Vārāṇaseya and Mahārāṣṭrian schools of Dharmaśāstra—the Bhaṭṭa family's writings being central to both—and the controversial, unwarranted fabrication of a Drāviḍa school of law (complete with three sub-schools—Andhra, Karnataka, and 'Dravida-Proper'). These errors notwithstanding, the Dharmaśāstra compendia of the eighteenth century and the earlier intellectual history of ownership and inheritance support a threefold model of schools of Sanskrit jurisprudence (Gauḍa, Maithila, and Dākṣinātya/Vārāṇaseya).

Furthermore, this chapter argues against the common claim that the Paṇḍitas who assisted European orientalists were patients, rather than intellectual agents, whose texts ought to be viewed primarily in terms of the British construction of essentialized indigenous categories.[13] In a rejoinder to the Saidian wave crashing on Indology in the 1990's, Rosalind O'Hanlon and David Washbrook argue that:

> In fact, there is much to suggest that some at least of what we now call 'colonial knowledge' about India emerged from the late eighteenth century as the jointly authored product of officials of the East India Company and of their chosen and interested Indian informants...to overlook their participation in projects of colonial knowledge not only ignores a considerable body of evidence; it also deprives us of important insights into continuities from the pre-colonial period, and hence into reasons why the 'essentialised knowledges' of early colonialism appeared to find such ready recognition among some at least of their Indian audiences.[14]

[12] For an historical account of colonial juridicature in India, see M. P. Jain, *Outlines of Indian Legal and Constitutional History*, 6th edn (New Delhi: Wadhwa and Company Nagpur, 2006), pp. 52–206. The multiple dates for Bengal and Bihar account for the major transformation of the 'Adālat, which culminated in the Judicial Scheme of 1793 and the Permanent Settlement. It was this 1793, 'Cornwallis' form of the 'Adālat system which was replicated in the Benares, Bombay, and Madras territories.

[13] For a representative example, regarding caste, see Nicholas Dirks, *Castes of Mind: Colonialism and the Making of Modern India* (Princeton, NJ: Princeton University Press, 2001).

[14] Rosalind O'Hanlon and David Washbrook, 'Histories in Transition: Approach to the Study of Colonialism and Culture in India', *History Workshop* 32 (1991): 110–27, 115.

Table 4.1 Schools of Sanskrit Jurisprudence Regarding Ownership and Inheritance

Name of School	Date	Location	Key Authors	Theory of Ownership (Causes and Incidents)	Philosophical Basis of Ownership	Theory of Sapiṇḍa-ship	Ownership by Birth?	Factum Valet?	Rival School?	Legitimate Colonial Codification?
Mitākṣarā	12th–16th centuries	Kalyāṇa (Southern India), not geographically specific	Vijāneśvara, Devaṇṇabhaṭṭa, Madanasiṃha	Custom (ācāra)	Mīmāṃsā	Consanguinity	Yes	No	None. Smṛtisaṃgrahakāra/ Dhāreśvara	Yes (As General School Opposed to Gauḍas)
Maithila	14th–18th centuries	Mithilā, I.E. Darbhanga and other Cities (Later, 'Where Maithili is Spoken')	Caṇḍeśvara, Vācaspatimiśra II, Misarumiśra, Maheśa Ṭhakkura	Dharmaśāstra (Causes and Incidents)	Navya-Nyāya	Consanguinity	Silent on issue generally	No	None. Cultural rivalry with Gauḍas. Apparent Discomfort with Mīmāṃsā Theories of Ownership	Yes. *Vivādārṇavasetu, Vivādasārārṇava,* and *Vivādabhaṅgārṇava*
Gauḍa	15th–18th centuries	Navadvīpa/ Other Ṭols of Bengal (Later, 'Where Bengali is Spoken')	Jīmūtavāhana, Śrīnāthācāryacūḍāmaṇi, Raghunandana	Dharmaśāstra (Causes but not Incidents)	Navya-Nyāya	Spiritual Benefit	No	Yes	Mithilā (and, sometimes, *Mitākṣarā*)	Yes. *Vivādārṇavasetu* and *Vivādabhaṅgārṇava*
Bhāṭṭa/ Dākṣinātya/ Drāviḍa/ Vārāṇaseya (Followers of *Mitākṣarā*)	16th–19th centuries	Vārāṇasī/Pune (Applicable in Bengal Presidency excepting other Schools)	Kamalākarabhaṭṭa, Nīlakaṇṭhabhaṭṭa, Mitramiśra	Custom (ācāra)	Mīmāṃsā	Consanguinity	Yes	No	Gauḍas and Maithilas (The latter only Occasionally)	Yes. *Vyavahārabālambhaṭṭī*

Mitākṣarā Sub-Schools of Hindu Law generated by colonial jurisdictions of Bombay and Madras Presidencies and by ethno-linguistic divisions within those jurisdictions										
Bombay	19th century	Pune/Bombay ('Where Marāṭhī is Spoken')	Nīlakaṇṭhabhaṭṭa, Kamalākarabhaṭṭa	Custom (ācāra)	Mīmāṃsā	Consanguinity	Yes	No	Gauḍas and Maithilas (The latter only Occasionally)	No. Bombay Presidency Marāṭhā Language
Dravida Proper	19th century	Portion of Madras Presidency 'Where Tamil is Spoken.'	Devaṇṇabhaṭṭa, Madhavācārya, Pratāparudra	Custom (ācāra)	Mīmāṃsā	Consanguinity	Yes	No	None	No. Madras Presidency and Tamil Language
Karnataka	19th century	Portion of Madras Presidency 'Where Kannada is Spoken'	Devaṇṇabhaṭṭa, Madhavācārya, Pratāparudra	Custom (ācāra)	Mīmāṃsā	Consanguinity	Yes	No	None	No. Madras Presidency and Kannada Language
Andhra	19th century	Portion of Madras Presidency 'Where Telegu is Spoken'	Devaṇṇabhaṭṭa, Madhavācārya, Pratāparudra	Custom (ācāra)	Mīmāṃsā	Consanguinity	Yes	No	None	No. Madras Presidency and Telegu Language

I heed Rosane Rocher's call for 'historians of Orientalist scholarship to recover in as rich texture as possible the bicultural nature of its production and rise'.[15] Each section of this chapter examines a colonial-era Dharmaśāstra digest from three angles: 1) the objectives of the East India Company officials in commissioning the digest; 2) the backgrounds of, and the relationships between, the Paṇḍitas who compiled the digest and the orientalists who translated the digest; and 3) the degree to which the theories of ownership and inheritance articulated in the Sanskrit digests and English translations give an authentic portrait of traditional Sanskrit Dharmaśāstra at the time and support the historical existence of the conception of regional schools of Dharmaśāstric thought.

The first section examines the *Vivādārṇavasetu*, 'A Bridge Over the Ocean of Litigation', compiled at the behest of Governor Warren Hastings in 1773 by a team of eleven Bengali Paṇḍitas from the court of Rāja Kṛṣṇacandra of Navadvīpa, Bengal (1728–1782). The section attends to the ways in which Hastings' Judicial Plan of 1772 sought to validate Company rule by recovering indigenous, Hindu theories of ownership and inheritance from Dharmaśāstric sources and enforcing them through the newly established Ṣadr Dīwānī 'Adālat (Superior Civil Court). The *Vivādārṇavasetu* articulates a theory of ownership and inheritance very much in conformity with the Gauḍa followers of the *Dāyabhāga* and very much contrasted with the opposing views of Maithila Dharmaśāstrins and the *Mitākṣarā*. Indeed, the compilers of the *Vivādārṇavasetu*, who were primarily Bengali logicians trained in Navadvīpa, advance a cluster of opinions that are characteristic of the scale of Dharmaśāstra texts reconstructed in the second chapter of this monograph: ownership arising for sons on the death of their father, ownership in joint assets held severally, and ownership as a virtually unrestrained right to alienate as desired (even in contravention of śāstric restrictions).

The second section examines the *Vivādabhaṅgārṇava*, 'An Ocean of Resolutions to Litigation', compiled by Jagannātha Tarkapañcānana, Rādhākānta Tarkavāgīśa and a team of Paṇḍitas between 1788 and 1794 under the supervision of William Jones. The section also examines the *Vivādasārāṇava*, a digest of Maithila Dharmaśāstra compiled for Jones alongside the *Vivādabhaṅgārṇava*. The dramatic expansion of European Sanskrit studies via the Asiatic Society (founded by Jones in 1784) dovetailed with a desire of British jurists (including Jones) to develop/uncover distinct systems of personal law for

[15] For such efforts, see J. Duncan Derrett, 'The British as Patrons of the Śāstra', in *Religion, Law and the State in India*, ed. J Duncan Derrett (London: Faber & Faber, 1968), pp. 225–73. Rosane Rocher, 'Weaving Knowledge: Sir William Jones and Indian Pandits', in *Objects of Enquiry: The Life, Contributions, and Influences of Sir William Jones, 1746–1794*, ed. Garland Cannon and Kevin Brine (New York: New York University Press, 1995), pp. 51–79; Rosane Rocher, 'The Career of Rādhākānta Tarkavāgīśa, an Eighteenth-Century Pandit in British Employ', *Journal of the American Oriental Society* 109.4 (1989): 627–33. For a similar project in nineteenth-century Bengal, see Brian Hatcher, 'Sanskrit and the Morning After: The Metaphorics and Theory of Intellectual Change', *Indian Economic and Social History Review* 44.3 (2007): 333–61.

the Hindu inhabitants of the provinces of Bengal and Bihar. The *Vivādabhaṅgārṇava* displays a clear emphasis on the Bengal school, against the *Mitākṣarā* and against Mithilā based authors, while the *Vivādasārārṇava* introduces the *Mitākṣarā*'s categories of obstructed inheritance (sapratibandhadāya) and unobstructed inheritance (apratibandhadāya) to the traditional Maithila scale of Dharmaśāstra texts.

The *Vivādabhaṅgārṇava* combines the juridical opinions of the Dharmaśāstrins who follow the *Dāyabhāga* with a series of Navya-Nyāya philosophical arguments culled from late *Dāyabhāga* commentators (such as Śrīkṛṣṇa Tarkālaṅkāra) and logicians (such as Gadādhara Bhaṭṭācārya). The personal histories of Jones' Paṇḍita collaborators, Jagannātha, Rādhākānta, and Sarvoru Trivedi, suggest that a theory of regionally specific schools of Dharmaśāstra (particularly with regard to ownership and inheritance) was as much a reflection of the state of Dharmaśāstra amongst the indigenous informants who compiled the *Vivādabhaṅgārṇava* and *Vivādasārārṇava* as it was a product of territorial and jurisdiction concerns amongst colonial bureaucrats.

The third section explores Colebrooke's formulation of *Mitākṣarā* and *Dāyabhāga* schools of Hindu law against the backdrop of his Sanskrit studies and judicial service in the province of Benares. The time period of focus is the critical juncture of Colebrooke's tenure as a judge and magistrate at Mirzapur, in the newly annexed province of Benares (1795–1801).[16] During this time, Colebrooke completed his translation of the *Vivādabhaṅgārṇava* and set about compiling a Dharmaśāstra digest of his own design.[17] Colebrooke's interaction with Bālambhaṭṭa and collaboration with the Paṇḍitas of Vārāṇasī led to his encounter with (or greater expertise in) a series of southern, Vārāṇasī-based, and Mahārāṣṭrian Dharmaśāstra treatises (including the *Vīramitrodaya* and Kamalākarabhaṭṭa's *Vivādatāṇḍava*) that articulate a distinctly southern, Mīmāṃsā-inflected view of ownership and inheritance that identifies and rejects, explicitly, the *Dāyabhāga* as an eastern, Bengali treatise. Colebrooke's deep immersion in traditional, contemporary Sanskrit learning in the late eighteenth century, *combined with* the practical necessity of crafting a new school of law for the Ṣadr Dīwānī 'Adālat to adjudicate disputes amongst Hindus in the Benares province, led him to identify a *Dāyabhāga/Navya-Nyāya/Bengal* and *Mitākṣarā/Mīmāṃsā/Vārāṇasī* divide as the core basis of regional schools of law. Colebrooke's description of these schools of Hindu law in his (1810) *Two Treatises* (a translation of the *Mitākṣarā* and the *Dāyabhāga* on inheritance),

[16] For the appointment, and its connection to Colebrooke's translation of the *Vivādabhaṅgārṇava*, see Rocher and Rocher, *The Making of Western Indology*, pp. 35–6. For the Company's gradual exertion of direct control over the Rājas of Vārāṇasī between 1788 and 1795, see Bernard Cohn, 'The Initial British Impact on India: A Case Study of the Benares Region', *The Journal of Asian Studies* 19.4 (1960): 418–31.

[17] Ibid.: 46.

reflects an awareness of authentic Gauḍa and Maithila jurisprudence between 1785 and 1801 and Vārāṇaseya (heavily Mahārāṣṭrian and Mīmāṃsā-influenced) paṇḍitic culture between 1795 and 1801. See the timeline in Figure 4.1 for details. Divided into three sections, it charts the expansion of Company rule, the

Figure 4.1 Timeline of Anglo-Hindu Law (1757–1864)

A. Expansion of Company Rule in India

1757—Battle of Plassey
1765—East India Company acquires the Dīwānī of Bengal, Bihar, and Orissa
1772—Warren Hastings assumes the Governorship of EIC, introduces Judicial Plan
1772—Ṣadr Dīwānī 'Adālat (Superior Civil Court) established in Bengal, Bihar and Orissa
1774—Supreme Court of Judicature at Fort William established
1781—Ṣadr Dīwānī 'Adālat accorded recognition as a Court of Record on par with the Supreme Court in Calcutta, introduction of 'Justice, Equity, and Good Conscience'
1786—Cornwallis appointed Governor General
1793—Permanent Settlement, Ṣadr Dīwānī 'Adālat reorganized according to 'Cornwallis System'
1795—Government of Bengal and Bihar (including 'Adālat System) extended to Benares
1799—'Adālat System expanded to territories subject to Bombay Government (Concomitant creation of a 'Mahratta School of Law')
1802—'Adālat System expanded to territories subject to Madras Government
(Concomitant creation of a Dravida School of Law in Madras)
1827—'Adālat System in Bombay Presidency reorganized
1862—After Indian High Courts Act of 1861, Supreme Courts and 'Adālats merged

B. The Development of Western Indology

1776—Halhed's *Code of Gentoo Laws* published in London
1783—William Jones Arrives in Calcutta as a Puisne Judge of the Supreme Court, Henry Colebrooke arrives as a Writer for the EIC
1784—Jones founds the Asiatic Society in Calcutta
1788—Jones' plan for a *Digest of Hindu Law* accepted by Cornwallis
1791—Benares Sanskrit College founded by Resident Jonathan Duncan
1794—Jones Translates *Manusmṛti*, Dies in Calcutta
1795—Colebrooke tasked with translating the *Vivādabhaṅgārṇava.* Appointed Judge and Magistrate of Mirzapur
1797—Colebrooke visits Benares and hires Bālambhaṭṭa Pāyaguṇḍe. Proposes a new digest (which would include the opinions of the Benares School)
1797-8—Colebrooke's *Digest of Hindu Laws* published
1800—College of Fort William (for Oriental Laws and Languages) founded
1801—Colebrooke appointed Puisne Judge of Superior Court and Professor of Sanskrit at the College of Fort William
1810—Colebrooke's *Two Treatises* published
1811-15—*Mānavadharmaśāstra, Dāyabhāga, Mitākṣarā*, and *Vīramitrodaya* published by Bāburāma's Sanskrit Press in Calcutta.
1827—Henry Borradaile publishes translation of *Vyavahāramayūkha*

C. Paṇḍitas in the Company's Employ

1773—Bāṇeśvara Vidyālaṅkāra and ten Bengali paṇḍits hired to compile the *Vivādārṇavasetu*
1783—Rādhākānta Tarkavāgīśa composes the *Purāṇārthaprakāśa* for Warren Hastings
1785—Rāmalocana Vaidya of Navadvīpa Hired as Jones' first Paṇḍita
1787—Rādhākānta Tarkavāgīśa of Navadvīpa meets William Jones
1788-94—Jagannātha Tarkapañcānana, *et al.*, compiles the *Vivādabhaṅgārṇava*
1789—Sarvoru Trivedi Compiles the *Vivādasārāṇava* for William Jones
1794—Rādhākānta and Sarvoru Trivedi Appointed to the Ṣadr Dīwānī 'Adālat
1797—Bālambhaṭṭa Pāyaguṇḍe crafts a commentary and digest for Colebrooke
1803—Rādhākānta dies. Jagannātha Tarkapañcānana's grandson, Ghanaśyāma, appointed as a Paṇḍita to the Supreme Court in Calcutta in his place
1864—Paṇḍit Assistants to the High Courts dismissed

development of Western Indology, and the state of Dharmaśāstra in the late eighteenth century.

First Steps (1765–87)

In 1765, Robert Clive obtained the Dīwānī (the formal right to collect revenue) with regard to the provinces comprising the Subah of Bengal, Bihar, and Orissa, from the Mughal Emperor Shah Alam II (r. 1759–1806) for the British East India Company.[18] Along with the right to collect revenue from these provinces, Company officials found themselves responsible for maintaining the pre-colonial, Mughal legal system. This legal system governing native Indians was of a distinctly Islamic character, but it expressly recognized the right of Hindus to 'settle disputes... according to their own laws and customs'.[19]

After seven years of chaotic, turbulent rule, the Government, at the behest of Governor Warren Hastings, adopted 'A Plan for the Administration for Justice in Bengal' and established an integrated hierarchy of civil courts (Dīwānī 'Adālats), culminating in the Ṣadr Dīwānī 'Adālat, to which Hindus and Muslims could appeal.[20] The key innovation in Hastings' 'Judicial Plan' was that 'in all suits regarding inheritance, marriage, caste, and other religious usages, or institutions, the laws of the Koran with respect to Mahometans and those of the *Shaster* with respect to the Gentoos shall be invariably adhered to'.[21] British administrators lacked any knowledge of Sanskrit. Consequently, Paṇḍita 'law officers' were hired and tasked with consulting the Dharmaśāstras and rendering letters of judgment (Vyavasthās) that gave an established conclusion on Hindu law relevant to a given case.[22] The judges of the Ṣadr Dīwānī 'Adālat (including Warren Hastings) found

[18] Derrett, 'The British as Patrons', p. 229. See Jain, *Outlines of Indian Legal and Constitutional History*, p. 53, fn 1 for the observation that the 'Orissa' in Company's domain 'referred to the modern district of Midnapur in the State of West Bengal. What is now modern Orissa was not acquired by the Company until 1803'.

[19] Derrett, 'The British as Patrons', p. 229. For an overview of the Company's earlier legal responsibilities see G. C. Rankin, 'Civil Law in British India before the Codes', *Law Quarterly Review* 58.4 (1942): 467–82.

[20] Rosane Rocher, 'The Creation of Anglo-Hindu Law', in *Hinduism and Law: An Introduction*, ed. Timothy Lubin, Donald Davis, and Jayanth K. Krishnan (Cambridge: Cambridge University Press, 2010), pp. 79–88, 78–9; Atul Chandra Patra, *The Administration of Justice under the East India Company in Bengal, Bihar and Orissa* (New Delhi: Asia Publishing House, 1962); M. P. Jain, *Outlines of Indian Legal History* (Bombay: Tripathi, 1966). Islamic criminal law was administered through Ṣadr Faujdari Adālats.

[21] George Forrest, *Selections from the Letters, Dispatches and Other State Papers Preserved in the Foreign Department of the government of India, 1772–1785, Vol 2* (Calcutta, Government Press, 1890), p. 290, cited in Derrett, 'The British as Patrons', p. 232, fn 2. Cf. Rosane Rocher, 'The Creation of Anglo-Hindu Law', p. 79.

[22] Derrett, 'The British as Patrons', p. 234. A collection of Vyavasthās from Vārāṇasī appear in *Sanskrit Documents: Being Sanskrit Letters and Other Documents Preserved in the Oriental Collection at the National Archives of India*, ed. Surendranath Sen and Umesha Mishra (Allahabad: Ganganatha Jha Research Institute, 1951).

the apparent malleability these letters of judgment deeply troubling and in 1773 the Company commissioned the compilation of a 'Code of Gentoo Laws'.[23]

The resulting Dharmaśāstra digest, the *Vivādārṇavasetu*, articulates a theory of ownership and inheritance distinctly in line with the school of thought that developed through commentaries on Jīmūtavāhana's *Dāyabhāga* in Navadvīpa, and other Navya-Nyāya establishments in Bengal, in the fifteenth century. The *Vivādārṇavasetu*'s compilers, many of whom trained in Navya-Nyāya and Dharmaśāstra in Navadvīpa and Mithilā, contrasted the theories of the *Dāyabhāga* school with the opinions of the Maithila school in the resulting legal digest. At this stage, the regionally-specific identities of Maithila and Gauḍa Paṇḍitas, and their contrasting scales of Dharmaśāstra treatises matched, hand in glove, the Company's territorial divisions of Bihar and Bengal respectively.

Warren Hastings' Judicial Plan of 1772, A Rule of Property in Bengal

Hastings' Judicial Plan of 1772 inaugurated the errant belief that Dharmaśāstra could be digested, permanently, as a body of positive law, rather than as an evolving jurisprudential tradition. In pre-colonial times, Paṇḍitas were often called upon to render opinions on various legal disputes, to adjudicate caste, to assign ritual penances, and to perform consecrations, but they were neither lawyers nor judges.[24] The core of the misunderstanding lay in the Company's officials' assumption of the relatively stable divisions between ecclesiastical and secular jurisdictions in Britain, where matters of inheritance, adoptions, marriage and the other 'religious' issues were resolved by biblical interpretation.[25] Christi Merrill argues that 'Hastings made the straightforward assumption that there were sacred texts in India that would offer a source for interpretation comparable to ecclesiastical authorities in British law.'[26] If a British distinction between secular and ecclesiastic jurisdictions set the stage for the creation of Hindu law, the emerging orientalist project, which 'saw ancient texts as the source of authentic knowledge about immemorial custom and tradition', ensured that, with regard to Hindus, Dharmaśāstra would serve as its script, and Paṇḍitas—soon to be framed

[23] Rosane Rocher, *Orientalism, Poetry, and the Millennium: The Checkered Life of Nathaniel Brassey Halhed, 1751–1830* (Delhi: Motilal Banarsidass, 1983), pp. 48–9.

[24] Ludo Rocher, 'Law Books in an Oral Culture: the Indian Dharmaśāstra', in *Studies in Hindu Law and Dharmaśāstra*, ed. Donald Davis (London: Anthem, 2014), pp. 103–17; Derrett, 'The British as Patrons', pp. 229–31. Derrett makes the odd assertion that '*dharmaśāstra* supplied actual rules of law in a wide variety of contexts'.

[25] Merrill, 'The Afterlives of Panditry', p. 79. Also see Rachel Sturman, 'Property and Attachments: Defining Autonomy and the Claims of Family in Nineteenth-Century Western India', *Comparative Studies in Society and History* 47.3 (2005): 611–37.

[26] Merrill, 'The Afterlives of Panditry', p. 79.

as 'jurists' and as 'lawgivers'—would be its actors.[27] Indeed, it seems that one of Hastings' primary motivations in commissioning the *Vivādārṇavasetu* was to stave off British Home interference in the legal affairs of the Company by proving that Hindus possessed legal codes of their own (and thus did not require the introduction of British civil law).[28]

In 1773, Hastings wrote to Lord Chief Justice Mansfield to inform him that the *Vivādārṇavasetu* would serve as:

> proof that the inhabitants of this land are not in the savage state in which they have been unfairly represented…and as a specimen of the principles which constitute the rights of property among them.[29]

Of course, the broader setting for these efforts to codify and to promote the property rights of the Company's subjects included the strategy by which the Company first came to power in Bengal—though cultivating alliances with Bengali Zamindars as well as Hindu, Jain, and other commercial families who viewed the Company as a safeguard against the confiscatory inclinations of Siraj ud-Daulah's Nizamat.[30] The subject of property (and related topics such as inheritance and contracts) probably came from Hastings' direct intervention, but the *Vivādārṇavasetu*'s compilers drew on a vast, and intellectually robust jurisprudence of ownership and inheritance that was most certainly not a British invention.

Gauḍas and Maithilas in the *Vivādārṇavasetu*

In 1773, Warren Hastings arranged for the compilation of a digest of Hindu laws. Rāja Rājavallabha, the Diwan of Khalsa, secured the services of eleven Paṇḍitas—

[27] Bhattacharya, 'Remaking Custom', p. 22.

[28] Rocher, *Orientalism, Poetry, and the Millennium*, pp. 52–3. Bernard Cohn, 'Law and the Colonial State in India', in *History and Power in the Study of Law: New Directions in Legal Anthropology*, ed. June Starr and Jane F. Collier (Ithaca, NY: Cornell University Press, 1989), pp. 131–52; Bhattacarya-Panda, *Appropriation and Invention*, pp. 36–88. As Cohn notes, Hastings was keen to disprove the prevailing assumption in London that India was a lawless despotism by demonstrating that India had an 'ancient constitution' embodied, 'from remotest antiquity' in Dharmaśāstric texts.

[29] Rocher, *Orientalism, Poetry and the Millennium*, p. 54.

[30] For the standard view, in which Jagat Seth and other commercial elites allied with the Company against the Nawab, see P. J. Marshall, 'The Crisis of Empire, 1740–65', in *Bengal: The British Bridgehead: Eastern India 1740–1828*, ed. P. J. Marshall (Cambridge: Cambridge University Press, 1988), pp. 70–92. For a nuanced perspective on property relations in the Nizamat, see T. Mukherjee, 'The Co-ordinating State and the Economy: The Nizamat in Eighteenth-Century Bengal', *Modern Asian Studies* 43.2 (2009): 389–436. For an analysis of relations between the Company and Bengali merchant families, Sushil Chaudhury, 'Merchants, Companies and Rulers: Bengal in the Eighteenth Century', *Journal of the Economic and Social History of the Orient* 31.1 (1988): 74–109.

some of whom held a connection with the court of Rāja Kṛṣṇacandra Roy of Navadvīpa, while others, including a Bhaṭṭa, were patronized by Rājavallabha.[31] Several of the Paṇḍitas were accomplished logicians and/or Dharmaśāstrins: Bāṇeśvara lectured in Navya-Nyāya in Navadvīpa, Rāmagopāla taught Navya-Nyāya at Rāja Kṛṣṇacandra's court and authored a Dharmaśāstra treatise on purification (the *Śuddhinirṇaya*) and Kṛṣṇacandra Sārvabhauma composed a comprehensive Dharmaśāstra digest, the *Navyadharmapradīpa*, which he dedicated to Rāja Kṛṣṇacandra.[32] The Paṇḍitas labored on their treatise at Fort William in Calcutta between 1773 and 1775. The result, the *Vivādārṇavasetu*, was promptly translated (paraphrased) into Persian so that Nathaniel Halhed, one of Hastings' protégés, could render the text into English.[33] In 1776, the Company published Halhed's translation in London, to much fanfare as *A Code of Gentoo Laws: Or, Ordinations of the Pundits, from a Persian Translation, Made from the Original, Written in the Shanscrit Language*.[34] The *Code* satisfied metropolitan demands for proof that Hindus possessed written laws and inaugurated European interest in Sanskrit language and literature, but it failed to settle Hindu law decisively or to make much of an impact on the practice of Hindu law in India.[35]

Due to the use of a Persian intermediary, the *Code* deviates substantially its Sanskrit original (usually in simplifying complicated śāstric passages).[36] Rosane Rocher, however, rightly admires the fidelity of Colebrooke's personal Sanskrit copy of the *Vivādārṇavasetu* to contemporaneous Dharmaśāstra digests.[37] Indeed, J. H. Nelson, a vocal critic of Colebrooke's formulation of 'schools of Hindu law', argued that, despite the *Code*'s many flaws, the Sanskrit *Vivādārṇavasetu* gives an accurate portrait of Dharmaśāstra 'before opinions had been expressed upon these matters by Englishmen; before any . . . treatise . . . had been declared to be the "paramount authority", and before the existence of "schools of law"'.[38] In fact, the *Vivādārṇavasetu*'s use of regional appellations for Gauḍa and Maithila

[31] Rocher, *Orientalism, Poetry and the Millennium*, p. 49. The Paṇḍitas were: (1) Bāṇeśvara Vidyālaṅkāra, (2) Kṛṣṇajīvana Nyāyālaṅkāra, (3) Rāmagopāla Nyāyālaṅkāra, (4) Vīreśvara Tarkapañcānana, (5) Kṛparāma Tarkasiddhānta, (6) Kṛṣṇakeśava Tarkālaṅkāra, (7) Kṛṣṇacandra Sārvabhauma, (8) Sītārāma Bhaṭṭa, (9) Kālīśaṅkara Vidyāvāgīśā, (10) Gaurīkānta Tarkasiddhānta, and (11) Śyāmasundara Nyāyasiddhānta. Sītārāma Bhaṭṭa may have been a Mahārāṣṭrian, which would suggest that Jones might have had some familiarity with the *Mitākṣarā* from the start.

[32] Ibid. [33] Ibid.

[34] Nathaniel Halhed, *A Code of Gentoo Laws: Or, Ordinations of the Pundits, from a Persian Translation, Made from the Original, Written in the Shanscrit Language* (London: Printed for the East India Company, 1776).

[35] Rocher, *Orientalism, Poetry and the Millennium*, pp. 54–62. Admirers included Jeremy Bentham, while James Mill was its chief detractor. Derrett, 'The British as Patrons', p. 241, notes that 'the Board at Murshidabad relied on the *Code* in 1779, Sir William Jones relies upon it in a judgment from 1788, and we find it relied upon as late as 1791'.

[36] Rocher, *Orientalism, Poetry and the Millennium*, p. 62. [37] Ibid., p. 51.

[38] J. H. Nelson, *Prospectus of the Scientific Study of the Hindu Law* (London: Kegan Paul & Co., 1881), p. 14. Cf. Rocher, *Orientalism, Poetry and the Millennium*, pp. 63–4.

opinions led Ludo Rocher to defend the 'existence of schools of Hindu law' on ownership and inheritance (inasmuch as these schools are academic in nature).[39]

The *Vivādārṇavasetu* draws on the principal treatises of the Bengal school, articulates a relatively concise summary of the *Dāyabhāga* and contrasts those views with the followers of Mithilā. It contains little Mīmāṃsā, scant Navya-Nyāya, and has almost nothing to say about the philosophical nature of ownership—issues that are ubiquitous in the early modern Sanskrit jurisprudence of inheritance. The *Vivādārṇavasetu* reads like a pared-down introductory treatise.

In the opening verses of the *Vivādārṇasetu*, the treatise's compilers list the texts and authors that they consulted:

> Caṇḍeśvara, Dhāreśvara, Viśvarūpa, the author of the *Mitākṣarā* (Vijñāneśvara) and Halāyudha. Also, Śrīkṛṣṇa, Vācaspati(miśra), the author of the *Dharmaratna* (Jīmūtavāhana), Śrīkara, Śūlapāṇī, Govinda, Lakṣmīdhara, the author of the [*Dharma*]*tattva* (Raghunandana), Ācāryacūḍāmaṇi and (Kullūka)bhaṭṭa. Having consulted these author's statements carefully, we compose a treatise called the *Breakwater of the Ocean of Litigation.*[40]

Halhed's Paṇḍitas drew on a wide variety of sources, but the bulk of the later, more sophisticated texts belong to Bengalis such as Śūlapāṇi, Jīmūtavāhana and Raghunandana, and to Navadvīpan commentators such as Ācāryacūḍāmaṇi and Śrīkṛṣṇa (whose arguments the compilers deploy against Caṇḍeśvara and Vācaspatimiśra II).[41] This list, however jumbled and bearing the resemblance of a Dharmaśāstric grab-bag, indexes the texts that the *Vivādārṇavasetu* attempts to organize into a coherent whole. The Gauḍa school is represented by Śrīkṛṣṇa Tarkālaṅkāra, Śrīnāthācāryacūḍāmaṇi, Raghunandana, Jīmūtavāhana, and Śūlapāṇi, while the Maithila authors Vācaspatimiśra II and Caṇḍeśvara appear alongside Vijñāneśvara and a bevy of earlier digest writers. The compilers often privilege the opinions of Bengalis—particularly Śrīkṛṣṇa.

Halhed's translation elides many of the śāstric intricacies of the original Sanskrit digest, particularly the *Vivādārṇavasetu*'s preference for the theories of uparamasvatva and *factum valet* that Jīmūtavāhana develops in the *Dāyabhāga*. The first notable feature of the *Vivādārṇavasetu*'s adherence to a Gauḍa school of jurisprudence is its extensive citation of the *Dāyabhāga* concerning the definition

[39] Rocher, 'Schools of Hindu Law', pp. 120–1.

[40] *Vivādārṇavasetu*, India Office Library Ms. No 1506/3145a, fol. 1b: **caṇdeśadhāreśvaraviśvarūpā mitākṣarākārahalāyudhau** ca **śrīkṛṣṇavācaspatidharmaratnakṛtas** tathā **śrīkaraśūlapāṇī** / **govinda-lakṣmīdharatattvakārā ācāryacūḍāmaṇinā** ca **bhaṭṭaḥ**. vākyāni caiṣāṃ suvimṛśya kūrmo granthaṃ **vivādārṇavabhañjanākhyam**. A note on emendations: all bracketed material in the footnotes in this chapter reflect additions—rather than subtractions—to the extant manuscripts. There are very few defective passages in the various manuscripts in Colebrooke's collection

[41] Halhed, *A Code of Gentoo Laws*, vol. 1, pp. 27–8.

of inheritance (dāya) and partition (vibhāga). The *Vivādārṇavasetu's* chapter on inheritance opens with a quote from the *Nāradasmṛti.*[42] The compilers gloss this verse by turning to the *Dāyabhāga.* They write that: 'In the above verse, the "paternal estate", that has come from the father, is something in which ownership (for the sons, etc.) arises, contingent on the death or loss of caste of the father, etc.'[43] The compilers reproduce Jīmūtavāhana's derivation of the word inheritance from the verbal root √dā, to give. They write that:

> The word 'inheritance' is derived in the passive sense as 'something given, 'and this is a secondary use of the verbal root 'to give' because of the similarity in the result (between the primary and secondary verbal usage), namely, the production of ownership for another person preceded by the destruction of the ownership (of the previous owner) who has died, gone forth, etc. Thus, the word 'inheritance' is used in a technical sense to refer to that asset in which there is ownership, contingent on a relationship with a prior owner, when the ownership of the prior owner ceases.[44]

Jīmūtavāhana's derivation of the word dāya from √dā constitutes one of the major unifying features of the school of jurisprudence that developed in Navadvīpa. This passage signals that the *Vivādārṇavasetu,* from its outset, will follow the *Dāyabhāga*'s theory of uparamasvatva. The compilers argue, implicitly, for the quintessentially Gauḍa principle of *factum valet* in a passage that appeals to Jīmūtavāhana's theory of ownership as a 'hard' right to use an asset as desired and that rejects the *Mitākṣarā*'s theory of ownership-by-birth.[45] The *Vivādārṇavasetu* introduces the problem of a father's rights to alienate self-acquired and ancestral assets in a discussion of a division of property performed during the lifetime and at the discretion of a father (pitṛkṛtavibhāga).[46] The *Vivādārṇavasetu* notes that a statement from the *Viṣṇusmṛti* permits a father to divide his self-acquired assets as he wishes, but not ancestral assets because a son and a father have equal ownership with respect to them.[47]

[42] *Vivādārṇavsetu,* fol. 28b: vibhāgo 'rthasya pitryasya putrair yatra prakalpyate, dāyabhāga iti proktaṃ vyavahārapadam budhaiḥ. Cf. Ludo Rocher, *Jīmūtavāhana's Dāyabhāga: The Hindu Law of Inheritance in Bengal* (Oxford: Oxford University Press, 2002), 249.

[43] *Vivādārṇavasetu,* fol. 28b: pitṛta āgatam pitryam pitṛmaraṇapātityādyadhīnajātasvatvakam iti yāvat. Cf. Rocher, *Dāyabhāga,* 249: pitṛta āgatam pitryaṃ. tac ca pitṛmaraṇopajātasvatvam ucyate.

[44] *Vivādārṇavasetu,* fol. 28b: dīyata iti vyutpat[t]yā dāyaśabdo[.] dadātiprayogaś ca gauṇaḥ mṛtapravrajitādisvatvanivṛttipūrvakaparasvatvotpattirūpaphalasāmyāt[.] tataś ca pūrvasvāminaḥ svatvoparame pūrvasvāmisambandhādhīnaṃ yatra dravye svatvaṃ tatra nirūḍhadāyaśabdaḥ. Cf. Rocher, *Dāyabhāga,* 250.

[45] For the importance of the principle of *factum valet* in Anglo-Hindu law, see Ludo Rocher, 'Jīmūtavāhana's *Dāyabhāga* and the Maxim *Factum Valet*', in *Studies in Hindu Law and Dharmaśāstra,* ed. Donald Davis (New York: Anthem Press, 2014), pp. 305–13.

[46] *Vivādārṇavasetu,* fol. 39a: atha pitṛkṛtavibhāgo nirūpyate.

[47] Ibid., fol. 39a: pitā cet putrān vibhajet tasya svecchā svayamupātte 'rthe[.] paitāmahe tu pitāputrayos tulyaṃ svāmyam iti **viśṇuvacanāt.** asyārthaḥ. pituḥ svārjite 'rthe yāvad eva gṛhītum

Like Jīmūtavāhana, the *Vivādārṇavasetu*'s compilers circumvent śāstric restrictions on a father's right to alienate ancestral assets by appealing to a definition of ownership as an eligibility for use as desired (yatheṣṭaviniyogārha[tā])[48] and by quoting an apocryphal verse from the *Yājñavalkyasmṛti*: 'the father is master of exactly all gems, pearls, and corals; neither the father nor the grandfather is the master of all of the immovable assets'.[49] Jīmūtavāhana and the *Vivādārṇavasetu* argue that the repetition of the word 'all' implies that a father may sell or give *some*, or *most* of the immovable ancestral assets provided that he makes provisions for the maintenance of his family.[50] Jīmūtavāhana hangs his argument for *factum valet*—where a father's gift or sale of ancestral assets is in contravention of śāstric requirements—on the peg of ownership as an eligibility for use as desired. If a father has dominion (prabhutva) over ancestral, immovable assets by virtue of Yājñavalkya's verse on gems, pearls and corals, then his transactions—even those made in contravention of śāstric restrictions—must be legally valid.[51] The *Vivādārṇavasetu* never goes quite so far, but it certainly follows and quotes Jīmūtavāhana in its rather wide interpretation of a father's rights of ownership.

The *Vivādārṇavasetu* argues against ownership-by-birth and for a father's extensive, nearly unencumbered rights of ownership, but it also juxtaposes those views with the views of 'the Miśras', the Maithilas. For example, the *Vivādārṇavasetu* distinguishes between 'Śrīkṛṣṇatarkālaṅkāra, Smārttabhaṭṭācārya and Jīmūtavāhana' and 'the Miśras' on the topic of a childless wife's right to inherit the divided or undivided immovable assets of her deceased husband.[52] The *Vivādārṇavasetu* compares Śrīkṛṣṇa and Jīmūtavāhana with the Miśras, or

i[c]chat[y] ardhabhāgadvayaṃ trayaṃ vā tatsarvaṃ tac ca śāstrānumataṃ na tu paitāmaham. Cf. *Dāyabhāga*, p. 261.

[48] Ibid., fol. 39a: prabhuḥ svecchayā yatheṣṭaviniyogārhaḥ. Cf. *Dāyabhāga*, 263: yatheṣṭaviniyogārhatvalakṣaṇasya svatvasya dravyāntara ivātrāpy aviśeṣāt.

[49] *Vivādārṇavasetu*, fol. 40a: maṇimuktāpravālānāṃ sarvasyaiva pitā prabhuḥ / sthāvarasya samastasya [sarvasya in the *Mitākṣarā*] na pitā na pitāmahaḥ iti **yājñavalkyīyāc** ca. Cf. *Dāyabhāga*, pp. 73 and 262.

[50] *Vivādārṇavasetu*, fol. 40a: atra maṇimuktāpravālānām ity upādāya punaḥ sarvasyety upādānaṃ sarveṣām bhūmyāditritayabhinnasuvarṇādidravyāṇāṃ dānādiṣu pituḥ svācchandyārthaṃ—tatrāpi sarvasyety upādānāt sarvasya kuṭumbavartanahetor dānādiniṣedhaḥ[.] kuṭumbavarttanāvirodheyasthāvarāder na dānādiniṣedha iti **dāyabhāga.** Cf. *Dāyabhāga*, pp. 262–3: maṇimuktādyupādāya punaḥ sarvasyety upādānāt sarveṣām bhūmyādivyatiriktānāṃ dānādiṣu pituḥ prabhutvaṃ na sthāvaranibandhadravyāṇām. tatrāpi sarvasyety upādānāt sarvasya kuṭumbavartanahetor dānādiniṣedhaḥ kuṭumbasyāvaśyam bharaṇīyatvāt.

[51] *Dāyabhāga*, pp. 263–4. See Chapter 2, of this monograph, for Jīmūtavāhana's argument.

[52] *Vivādārṇavasetu*, fol. 29a: eṣām abhāve vibhaktāvibhaktāsthāvarādidhane patnī adhikāriṇīti **śrīkṛṣṇatarkālaṅkārasmārttabhaṭṭācāryajīmūtavāhanaprabhṛtayaḥ** prāhuḥ. vibhaktadhane patnī adhikāriṇī. avibhaktadhane bhrātrādayaḥ krameṇādhikāriṇaḥ patnī tu grāsāchādanabhāginīti **miśrāḥ**. Without going into extraordinary detail, this difference of opinion turns on a point of law: whether united brothers (after the death of their father) own joint assets severally or communally. The Bengalis, who hold that the property is owned severally, allow for a childless wife to act as her husband's heir.

with Caṇḍeśvara (another Maithila), regularly.[53] Many of these specific instances of drawing sharp distinctions between Bengalis—Jīmūtavāhana, et al.—and Maithilas—Vācaspatimiśra and the like—do not appear in Halhed's translation. There is no mention of the *Mitākṣarā*'s theory of ownership-by-birth, nor is there any mention of Navya-Nyāya and Mīmāṃsā theories of ownership. Indeed, there is virtually no discussion of ownership as a category. However, the basic contours of the Gauḍa school of jurisprudence are unmistakable: uparamasvatva and its manifold implications in constructing a comprehensive law of inheritance.

The *Vivādārṇavasetu*'s arguments correlate with the social and intellectual backgrounds of its largely Bengali and Maithila compilers—the pedigree of Sītārāma Bhaṭṭa notwithstanding. The text is regrettably thin on detailed digression—a fact much lamented by Jones and Colebrooke—and this probably accounted for its limited utility to the Paṇḍitas and judges of the Ṣadr Dīwānī 'Adālat. Even the bare-bones arguments of the *Vivādārṇavasetu* demonstrate, however, that its compilers crafted a simple, if clear, scale of Dharmaśāstra texts on inheritance, in which, following Raghunandana and Śrīkṛṣṇa's commentaries, the *Dāyabhāga* is read, anachronistically, as a rejoinder to Vācaspatimiśra and Caṇḍeśvara. Jones and Colebrooke, however, followed the interwoven threads of ownership, inheritance and schools of jurisprudence outlined first in the *Vivādārṇavasetu* to a logical conclusion in the following decades.

The Search for Certainty (1787–94)

In 1783, William Jones (1746–1794) arrived in Calcutta to take up a position as a puisne judge of the Supreme Court of Judicature at Fort William.[54] Jones' initial interest in Sanskrit sprang from a desire to achieve an independent knowledge of Hindu law.[55] In 1788, Jones acquired funding from Governor Cornwallis to assemble a team of pandits, hired as representatives of the schools of Mithilā and Bengal, and nominally under the leadership of Jagannātha Tarkapañcānana of Triveṇī, to compile a digest of Hindu laws on contract and succession.[56] Two Sanskrit digests emerged from the project: the *Vivādasārārṇava* (never translated, but intended to represent the opinions of the Paṇḍitas of Mithilā), and the *Vivādabhaṅgārṇava* (translated as a *Digest of Hindu Law* in 1801, and intended to represent the opinions of the Paṇḍitas of Bengal). Unlike the *Vivādārṇavasetu*

[53] See, for example fol. 33b: iti **vivādaratnākarakāradhṛtamanuvacanāc** ca . . . . apatyānām putrāṇāṃ tadaṃśinī putrasya samāṃśinī . . . iti **caṇḍeśvaraḥ**. **jīmūtavāhanena** tu . . . For further examples, see Rocher, 'Schools of Hindu Law', pp. 120–1.

[54] For Jones' life and works, in relation to law and Sanskrit, see Rocher, 'Weaving Knowledge'. For a general biography of Jones, see Garland Cannon, *The Life and Mind of Oriental Jones: Sir William Jones, the Father of Modern Linguistics* (Cambridge: Cambridge University Press, 1990).

[55] Rocher, 'Weaving Knowledge', p. 54. [56] Ibid., pp. 61–2.

and the *Vivādasārārṇava*, the *Vivādabhaṅgārṇava* is a vast work that fills three back-buckling volumes. The *Vivādabhaṅgārṇava* offers intricate, Navya-Nyāya-inflected discussions of a smaller number of titles of law (vivādapadas) than the *Vivādārṇavasetu*—reflecting the more limited focus on 'contracts and succession' that Jones set for the project from the outset.[57]

The *Vivādabhaṅgārṇava* articulates a distinctly Bengali theory of ownership and inheritance that combines Navya-Nyāya philosophical reasoning with *Dāyabhāga* legal principles. The *Vivādabhaṅgārṇava* combines the *Dāyabhāga* principles of uparamasvatva (ownership-by-the-cessation-of-the-ownership-of-the-previous-owner) and *factum valet* with the Navya-Nyāya theory of ownership as produced by the modes of acquisition mentioned explicitly by the śāstra and with the principle that the ownership of one person is an obstructor (bādhaka) to the coordinate ownership of others. The digest combines these principles into a sophisticated, comprehensive model of contract and succession, and contrasts the arguments of late commentators on the *Dāyabhāga* (Śrīkṛṣṇa Tarkālaṅkāra and Candraśekhara Vācaspati Bhaṭṭācārya) with the opinions of Maithila Paṇḍitas and the author of the *Mitākṣarā*.

During the Court's fall vacation of 1785, Jones travelled to Navadvīpa, having heard Reverend Donald McKinnon's (a chaplain for the East India Company's army) description of 'Nuddea University' at the Asiatic Society earlier in the year.[58] Jones arrived just as the Paṇḍitas of Navadvīpa left 'to celebrate the yearly Durgāpūjā rituals for princely patrons'. Consequently, he learned his first bits of Sanskrit from Rāmalocana, whom Jones describes as 'a man of the medical cast[e]', and who taught grammar to various pupils in Navadvīpa.[59] Rāmalocana's tuition—they read the *Hitopadeśa*, 'the aphorisms of Cāṇakya', and the *Bhaṭṭikāvya* (all secular works)—seems to have equipped Jones with enough proficiency in Sanskrit for him to read a Sanskrit copy of the *Mānavadharmaśāstra* by comparing it with a Persian translation.[60] In the summer of 1786 Jones used his knowledge of the *Mānavadharmaśāstra* to overrule the opinion of one of the Supreme Court's Paṇḍitas.[61]

There is an irony in Jones' inchoate knowledge of a single smṛti overriding the interpretive proficiencies of a trained Paṇḍita on the assumption of the *Mānavadharmaśāstra*'s superior authenticity. Rocher notes that 'Jones'

[57] For the vivādapadas, see Davis, *The Spirit of Hindu Law*, pp. 77–81. Jones mentions this limited focus in a letter to Governor Cornwallis, dated 19 March 1788. See *The Letters of William Jones*, vol. 2, ed. Garland Cannon (Oxford: Oxford University Press, 1970), p. 796.

[58] Rocher, 'Weaving Knowledge', 56.

[59] Ibid., p. 56. For the great importance that Durgāpūjā played in the formation of a Bengal school of Dharmaśāstra, see Chapter 2. See *The Letters of William Jones*, vol. 2, p. 682. I would like to thank Rosane Rocher for pointing out that the reason Jones met Rāmalocana—rather than a Brāhmaṇa—in Navadvīpa was because he had not been invited to officiate at the Durgāpūjā along with his Brāhmaṇa colleagues.

[60] Ibid., 57. [61] Ibid., 57.

knowledge of Sanskrit and of an antiquarian text was being used to decide on the merits of the court pandits' opinions and thereby in effect to subvert their authority as contemporary sources of Hindu law.'[62] At this point, Jones' relationship with Dharmaśāstra highlights what Arindam Chakrabarti characterizes as 'a profound asymmetry of epistemic prestige'.[63] Jones' limited encounter with the traditional Sanskrit learning of Navadvīpa appears to have left one very important imprint on his understanding of Dharmaśāstra: the importance of Jīmūtavāhana's *Dāyabhāga*. In a letter, dated 24 October 1786, he floated the idea of a new digest of Hindu laws, in which he wished to see included '*Jimut Bahun*, the best book on Inheritance'.[64]

Jones' dreams of a new digest and of proficiency in the Sanskrit language came dramatically closer to fulfillment when financial hardship drove Rādhākānta Tarkavāgīśa to seek employment as Jones' tutor in early 1787. Rādhākānta, born in the early eighteenth century, trained under the renowned Naiyāyika Jagannātha Tarkapañcānana of Triveṇī, Bengal.[65] He and Jagannātha were members of the court of Mahārāja Navakṛṣṇa of Sobha Bazar (1733–1797), a close associate of the British during the formative years of Company Rule.[66] Before encountering Jones, Rādhākānta had received patronage (in the form of tax-free land grants) from Navakṛṣṇa and from Warren Hastings.[67] Rādhākānta came to the attention of the Company's agents when he was hired by Warren Hastings (through Navakṛṣṇa, presumably) to compose the *Purāṇārthaprakāśa*, a paurāṇic (ancient tales) digest that Hastings hoped could give the Company's officials a better understanding of Indian history.[68] Rādhākānta became John Shore's (a future Governor of Bengal) personal Paṇḍita sometime in 1783.[69] Previously, Rādhākānta had declined a position as a Paṇḍita to the Supreme Court. By 1787, however, Rādhākānta grew heavily indebted by, as Jones put it, 'following the duty of Brahmans . . . to teach the youths of their sect . . . [and] to relieve those who are poor', and he sought financial stability in Jones' patronage.[70]

With Rādhākānta's tuition, Jones boasts of his membership in 'the celebrated University of *Brahmans* at *Navadwipa*, or *Nuddea*' and his stream of articles in the journals of the Asiatic Society—'On the Chronology of the Hindus' (January, 1788), 'Inscriptions on the Staff of Fīrūz Shah' (March, 1788) and 'On The Indian

[62] Ibid., 57.

[63] Arindam Chakrabarti, 'Introduction', *Philosophy East and West*, 51.4, (2001): 449–51, p. 449.

[64] Rocher, *Jīmūtavāhana's Dāyabhāga*, p. 20, fn 53. Cf. *The Letters of William Jones*, 722.

[65] Rocher, 'The Career of Rādhākānta': 627.

[66] For the biography of Navakṛṣṇa, see Ranji Sen, 'The Emergence of a Service Elite in Bengal in the Half of the Eighteenth Century: A New Dimension of Collaboration', *Proceedings of the Indian History Congress* 36 (1975): 511–22; and N. N. Ghose, *Memoirs of Maharaja Nubkissen Bahadur* (Calcutta: Edinburgh Press, 1901).

[67] Rocher, 'The Career of Rādhākānta': 627–8.

[68] Ibid.: 628. Rocher notes that the Persian translation of this text was entrusted to Halhed, who never translated it into English. See I.O. Or Ms 1124 for this Persian translation.

[69] Rocher, 'The Career of Rādhākānta': 628.

[70] Ibid.: 629.

Game of Chess' (1789)—attest to Rādhākānta's influence.[71] Rādhākānta appears to have been the one who encouraged Jones' groundbreaking translation of Kālidāsa's *Abhijñāśakuntala* (1789).[72]

William Jones, Rādhākānta Tarkavāgīśa, and Jagannātha Tarkapañcānana

In 1785, Jones acquired a Persian translation of the *Mānavadharmaśāstra*, so that he could determine the trustworthiness of the Court's Paṇḍitas against 'the oldest book on the Hindu laws'.[73] In October of 1786, Jones, who had visited Navadvīpa the previous year, floated the idea of a new digest of Hindu laws, in which he wished to see included '*Jimut Bahun*, the best book on Inheritance'.[74] In early 1787, Rādhākānta Tarkavāgīśa, an erstwhile pupil of the renowned Naiyāyika Jagannātha Tarkapañcānana of Triveṇī, Bengal became Jones' tutor.[75] Rādhākānta and Jagannātha were members of the court of Mahārāja Navakṛṣṇa of Sobha Bazar (1733–1797), a close associate of the British during the formative years of Company Rule.[76] Jones and Rādhākānta read a Sanskrit copy of the *Vivādārṇavasetu* together, and with Rādhākānta's assistance, Jones deployed a passage from the *Vivādārṇavasetu* in a case concerning a brother's right to alienate his share of undivided assets during the lifetime of his mother.[77]

In March of 1788, Jones wrote to Governor Cornwallis to propose a new digest, 'after the model of Justinian's inestimable Pandects, compiled by the most learned of the native lawyers'.[78] Jones proposed hiring two Paṇḍitas: Rādhākānta, as a representative of Bengal, and Sarvoru Trivedi, for Mithilā. Jones justified these Paṇḍitas' appointment, because Rādhākānta was 'highly revered by the Hindus in Bengal' and Sarvoru, of Mithilā, was 'universally esteemed in that province'.[79] Jones' letter to Cornwallis suggests that for Jones, there was an essential connection between the division of the paṇḍitic cultures of Navadvīpa and Mithilā into competing schools of jurisprudence, and the division of the Hindu law of

[71] Ibid.: 629–30. [72] Ibid.: 629.

[73] Rocher, 'Weaving Knowledge', p. 54. Cf. *The Letters of William Jones*, vol. 2, p. 664.

[74] Rocher, *Jīmūtavāhana's Dāyabhāga*, p. 20, fn 53. Cf. *The Letters of William Jones*, 722.

[75] Rocher, 'The Career of Rādhākānta': 627.

[76] For the biography of Navakṛṣṇa, see Ranji Sen, 'The Emergence of a Service Elite in Bengal in the Half of the Eighteenth Century: A New Dimension of Collaboration', *Proceedings of the Indian History Congress* 36 (1975): 511–22; and N. N. Ghose, *Memoirs of Maharaja Nubkissen Bahadur* (Calcutta: Edinburgh Press, 1901).

[77] The case was *Kistnochurn Mullick* v. *Ramnarain Mullick*, reported in T. A. Row, *Indian Decisions (Old Series)*, vol. 1: *Supreme Court Reports, Bengal* (Madras: Law Printing House, 1911), pp. 178–9. Cf. *The Letters of William Jones*, 797.

[78] *The Letters of William Jones*, pp. 794–800. Cf. Rocher, 'Weaving Knowledge', p. 62.

[79] Ibid., p. 798. Cf. Rocher, 'Weaving Knowledge', p. 62.

inheritance into separate jurisdictions for the provinces of Bengal and Bihar. Sarvoru Trivedi broke off from the main project almost immediately and completed an exclusively Maithila treatise, the *Vivādasārārṇava*, in 1789.[80]

Sarvoru Trivedi's model of inheritance follows the works of Caṇḍeśvara, Vācaspatimiśra II, Misarumiśra, and Maheśa Ṭhakkura more or less verbatim. He notes that in the case of a partition made during the lifetime of their father, sons do not have the right to force a partition of those assets over which a father has independent control.[81] Trivedi argues that such restrictions (on a son's right to demand partition during the lifetime of his father) apply only to assets acquired by a father without the assistance of the assets of another (presumably a grandfather or son). After all, 'according to the *Viṣṇusmṛti*, should a father partition with his sons, he may do as he pleases with his self-acquired assets'.[82] Recall, from Chapter 2, that Maithila Dharmaśāstrins argue, either explicitly or implicitly, that Dharmaśāstric injunctions prohibit fathers and grandfathers from alienating ancestral assets without the consent of their sons and grandsons (a distinctive feature of Gauḍa jurisprudence). Maithila authors do this without resorting to the Mīmāṃsā-derived theories of ownership as an extra-śāstric phenomenon which form the core of the *Mitākṣarā* school of jurisprudence (and that were antithetical to Maithila and Gauḍa Navya-Nyāya theories of ownership as a patently Dharmaśāstric phenomenon).

Although Trivedi does not invoke Vijñāneśvara's theory of kinship (sāpiṇḍya) as a blood relation, as his Maithila forebears do, he employs Vijñāneśvara's twofold model of 'unobstructed inheritance (apratibandhadāya)' and 'obstructed inheritance (sapratibandhadāya)'.[83] This accounts, perhaps, for the persistent impression amongst colonial-era jurists that the Maithila school of jurisprudence could be framed as a *Mitākṣarā* sub-school. Trivedi does not, however, link this definition of inheritance with a notion of ownership-by-birth—the Maithila school neither endorses nor rejects this theory. The *Vivādasārārṇava* displays none of the *Vivādārṇavasetu* or *Vivādabhaṅgārṇava*'s fiery polemic and

[80] Ibid.

[81] *Vivādasārārṇava*, India Office Library Ms. No 1505/3145b, 60b: jīvatpitṛkaḥ pitrananumato na tatsvatantradhane vibhāgādhikārī.

[82] *Vivādasārārṇava*, fol. 60b: idaṃ ca anyadhanānupaśliṣṭasvārjitaviṣayaṃ. pitā cet putrān vibhajeta tasya sve[c]chā svayamupātte (')rthe iti **viṣṇu[ḥ]smṛteḥ**.

[83] *Vivādasārārṇava*, fol. 59a: ataḥ dāyabhāgo nirūpyate. tatra dāyo nāma yad dhanaṃ svāmisambandhahetunānyadīyam api svaṃ bhavati tad ucyate. sa ca dvividhaḥ apratibandhaḥ sapratibandhaś ca. tatra putrāṇām pautrāṇāṃ ca pitṛpitāmahadhanam putratvapautratvamātrasāpekṣam eva svam bhavatīty apratibandho dāya[ḥ]. pitṛvyabhrātrādīnāṃ tu putrasvāminor abhāve bhrātṛjādidhanaṃ svaṃ bhavatīti putrasvāmisadbhāvaḥ pratibandha iti teṣāṃ sapratibandhadāyaḥ. vibhāgo nāma dravyasamudāyaviṣayānām anekasvāmyānāṃ tadekadeśeṣu vyavasthāpanam. yad āha **naradaḥ** vibhāgo 'rthasya paitrasya tanayair yatra kalpyate / dāyabhāga iti proktaṃ vyavahārapadaṃ budhaiḥ iti. paitrasyeti svasvatvanimittasambandhopalakṣaṇam.

this may explain the relative obscurity of the treatise in the development of colonial schools of Hindu law.

As Jones' endeavour picked up steam—and fractured along regional lines—Rādhākānta arranged for six additional Bengali Paṇḍitas to join the team compiling the *Vivādabhaṅgārṇava*: his teacher, Jagannātha Tarkapañcāna, Jagannātha's son, Rāmanidhi, Jagannātha's grandson, Ghanaśyāma, and also Guruprasāda, Rāmamohana, and Gaṅgādhara.[84] Jaganātha Tarkapañcānana was born in Triveṇī in 1695 to Rudradeva, a prominent scholar from a long line of logicians.[85] As a boy, Jagannātha mastered Navya-Nyāya in the ṭols of his uncles, Bhāvadeva Nyāyālaṅkāra, and Raghudeva Vācaspati, and when Jagannātha's father died in 1718, he opened his own ṭol.[86] Like Rādhākānta, Jagannātha was patronized by Rāja Navakṛṣṇa. In the early nineteenth century, William Ward noted that:

> Jagunnath'hu Turku Punchannu, a few years ago, presided at a large school in Trivenēē. He was acquainted in some measure with the vedu, and is said to have studied the vedantu, the sankhyu, the patunjulu, the nyayu, the smritee, the tuntru, the kavyu, the pooranu, and other shastrus. He was supposed to be the most learned as well as the oldest man in Bengal, being 109 years old at the time of his death.[87]

Jagannātha's grandfather, Candraśekhara Vācaspati Bhaṭṭācārya, who flourished in the seventeenth century, wrote two Dharmaśāstric treatises whose ideas appear frequently in the *Vivādabhaṅgārṇava*: the *Dvaitanirṇaya* (composed in 1640) and the *Smṛtisārasaṃgraha*.[88]

The Paṇḍitas completed the bulk of the *Vivādabhaṅgārṇava* by 1792 and were dismissed (with the exception of Rādhākānta who stayed on to assist Jones).[89] After finishing his work on the *Vivādabhaṅgārṇava*, Jagannātha returned to Triveni, where he 'went on teaching younger pandits at his home' and received a pension of 300 rupees a month which he secured from the British authorities with Jones' assistance.[90]

[84] Rocher, 'Weaving Knowledge', p. 62.

[85] Samita Sinha, *Pandits in a Changing Environment: Centres of Sanskrit Learning in Nineteenth-Century Bengal* (Calcutta: Sarat Book House: 1993), pp. 221–2. Also see Brajendranath Banerji, *Dawn of New India* (Calcutta: M. C. Sarkar, 1927), pp. 84–91.

[86] Sinha, *Pandits in a Changing Environment*, p. 222.

[87] William Ward, *A View of the History, Literature, and Mythology of the Hindoos*, vol. 2 (London: Kingsbury, Parbury, and Allen, 1822), p. 496.

[88] See the *New Catalogus Catalogorum: An Alphabetical Register of Sanskrit and Allied Works and Authors*, vol. 6, ed. K. Raja (Madras: University of Madras, 1971), p. 370.

[89] Rocher, 'The Career of Rādhākānta': 631.

[90] Rocher, 'Weaving Knowledge', p. 70. Cf. Banerji, *Dawn of New India*, p. 90. See Rocher, 'The Career of Rādhākānta': 631, fn 43, for the prominent role that several of the *Vivādabhaṅgārṇva's* Paṇḍitas played in Anglo-Hindu courts in the nineteenth century.

The *Vivādabhaṅgārṇava*, an Ocean of Navya-Nyāya Jurisprudence

The *Vivādabhaṅgārṇava*, the Sanskrit treatise compiled by Jagannātha's team of Bengali Paṇḍitas, displays a clear preference for the opinions of the Bengal school, against the *Mitākṣarā* and against Maithila authors. It adds to the *Vivādārṇavasetu* by combining the juridical opinions of the Dharmaśāstrins who follow the *Dāyabhāga* with a series of Navya-Nyāya philosophical arguments culled from late *Dāyabhāga* commentators (such as Śrīkṛṣṇa Tarkālaṅkāra) and logicians (such as Gadādhara Bhaṭṭācārya). The compilers of the *Vivādabhaṅgārṇava* show a clear interest in the philosophical nature of ownership and the implications of philosophical considerations on thorny jurisprudential questions, particularly with regard to inheritance.

A consistent theory of ownership as a śāstrically determined eligibility for use as desired, that exists for only one individual at any given time, runs throughout the *Vivādabhaṅgārṇava*. Three juridical questions attest to the existence of this robust, distinctly Gauḍa theory in the *Vivādabhaṅgārṇava*: (1) the definition of dāya (inheritance) and division (vibhāga); (2) the possibility of ownership-by-birth; and (3) the legal validity of a father and of undivided sons' alienation of immovable assets in contravention of śāstric regulations (*factum valet*). In each instance, the compilers of the *Vivādabhaṅgārnava* defend Jīmūtavāhana's *Dāyabhāga* from the attacks of the 'Miśras' and/or 'the author of the *Mitākṣarā*' by appealing to the commentary of Śrīkṛṣṇa Tarkālaṅkāra and Navya-Nyāya treatises on ownership. The cumulative weight of these arguments suggests that the *Vivādabhaṅgārnava* articulates an identifiably Bengali, Navya-Nyāya-inflected scale of Dharmaśāstra texts that contrasts with a rival, Maithila scale of Dharmaśāstra texts primarily, and with the *Mitākṣarā*, secondarily.

The *Vivādabhaṅgārnava*'s section on inheritance uses Śrīkṛṣṇatarkālaṅkāra's commentary on the *Dāyabhāga* to defend Jīmūtavāhana's theory of uparamasvatva from the attacks of Raghunandana, the *Mitākṣarā*, and Vācaspatimiśra. It does this by invoking Navya-Nyāya theories of ownership as a 'blocker' (bādhaka) to the ownership of another. The section opens by quoting a verse from the *Nāradasmṛti*: 'the wise call that title of law (vivādapada), under which a division of paternal assets is initiated by (a man's) sons, the division of inheritance'.[91] The compilers, citing Jīmūtavāhana nearly verbatim, interpret 'paternal' assets as assets in which ownership arises from the death of the father.[92] The *Vivādabhaṅgārṇava* questions whether this title of law refers to the *assets* in

[91] *Vivādabhaṅgārṇava*, Bodleian Library Ms. No. 720, fol. 1b: atha dāyabhāgaḥ. tatra **nāradaḥ.** vibhāgo 'rthasya pitryasya putrair yatra prakalpyate / dāyabhāga iti proktaṃ tad vivādapadam budhaiḥ. Cf. *Dāyabhāga*, p. 249.

[92] Ibid., fol. 1b: pitṛta āgatam pitryaṃ tac ca pitṛmaraṇopajātasvatvam ucyate…iti uktavān iti **jīmūtavāhanaḥ.**

which ownership arises subsequent to the death of a father, or to the *ownership* (of the sons, etc.) that arises in respect of their father's assets when he dies.[93] The compilers try out various possibilities, but they conclude that the division of inheritance is:

> in fact, that distribution, participation, or ownership of the paternal estate (or wealth descending from the father in consequence of his death or the like, or, in other words, property of the deceased father) which is established or acknowledged by the sons to vest in a certain owner, as a term of law relative to ownership. Consequently, from the relation of the term, ownership itself being the title of law, the property of the estate, which belonged to a deceased owner, being vested in another by reason of consanguinity, is inheritance.[94]

The compilers' comments presuppose that after the death of their father, sons and other relatives obtain ownership in their father's assets *severally*. If inheritance constitutes the *ownership* that arises in specific assets, then division constitutes the ascertainment of that ownership. The compilers write:

> The act of ascertaining individual rights of ownership, or the ascertainment of a separate ownership, is partition, or division; for, on the death of the father, his ownership is destroyed, and the ownership of his sons, etc. arises. And, in the case of two or more sons, ownership arises only for whatever son in whatever asset that will belong to him: but, since that [ownership] is absolutely invisible, and cannot be perceived by the eyes or senses, it is ascertained by lots or the like, and argued from logical inference alone; that solely constitutes ascertainment: or the act in which it culminates, such as distribution by casting lots or the like, is signified by the term partition.[95]

The elaborate complexity of the *Vivādabhaṅgārṇava*'s language (characteristic of Navya-Nyāya-inflected jurisprudence) obscures its relatively simple meaning:

[93] Ibid., fol. 1b: artho dhanam pitryam pitṛtvasambandhāl[labdham] iti **smārtāḥ**. tathā ca sambandhādhīn[a]svatvavaddhanasya vibhāgo vibhajanaṃ yatra dhane kalpy[a]te taddhanaṃ dāyabhāganāmakam. The alternative option, that it refers to ownership, appears later.

[94] Ibid., fol. 2b: vastutas tu pitryasya pitṛta āgatasya pitṛmaraṇādinā vinaṣṭapitṛsvatvasyeti yāvat. tādṛśasya arthasya vibhāgaḥ bhajanaṃ [svāmitvaṃ yatra svāmini kalpyate jñāpyate putraiḥ] [tat]-svāmiviśiṣṭaṃ vivādapadaṃ. tathā ca viśeṣaṇatvāt svāmitvasyāpi vivādapadatvena naṣṭasvāmikadhanasya sambandhīnāṃ svāmitvam eva dāyabhāga iti. The translation of the passage is Colebrooke's. Henry Thomas Colebrooke, *A Digest* of *Hindu Law on Contracts and Successions*, vol. 2 (Calcutta: Company Press, 1801), p. 504.

[95] Ibid., fols 2b–3a: atrocyate. svatvanirṇayakavyāpāraḥ svatva[viśeṣa]nirṇayo vā vaṇṭanaṃ sa eva vibhāgaḥ. tathā hi pitari uparate tatsvatvaṃ naśyati tatputrādīnāṃ ca svatvaṃ jāyate[.] tac c[ā]nekaputrasthale yena yena putreṇa yad yad dhane sthāpsyate tatra tatraiva tasya tasya svatvaṃ jāyate kiṃ tu tasyātīndriyatvena cakṣurādīnām [a]grāhyatvād guṭikāpātādinānumānenaiva nirṇayo bhavati sa eva nirṇayaḥ [tadanta]vyāpāro vā guṭikāpātādir vibhāgapadārthaḥ. Cf. *Dāyabhāga*, 1.7–8, p. 250. The translation is adapted from Colebrooke's.

when a father dies (biologically, or legally), his relations acquire ownership in specific assets. The act of division, which one might assume *creates* ownership, or *divides* an existing ownership of various relatives, actually constitutes the act of *knowing* who already owns what asset.

This theory of individual ownership after the death of the father forms a faultline between Jīmūtavāhana and Raghunandana, the Maithilas, and Vijñāneśvara. The latter hold that sons own assets jointly after the death of their father and partition replaces their joint ownership over the entire estate with ownership over particular assets within the estate. The *Vivādabhaṅgārṇava*, following Jīmūtavāhana, explains that:

> Because the son's ownership only becomes possible after the loss of the father's ownership, (and since) even at the moment of the loss of the father's ownership there is no legally ascertainable means for knowing of the loss of the sons' collective ownership and of the arising of a different sort of ownership (for each of them), and though (we concede that) only the śāstras that provide legally ascertainable knowledge about partition are capable of providing legally ascertainable knowledge on this particular matter, it is cumbersome to suppose that one form of (filial) ownership perishes and another arises. Therefore, the ownership of each (son) is postulated in that which will become his by lot.[96]

The *Vivādabhaṅgārṇava*'s compilers state Raghunandana's contrasting view (that sons acquire coordinate ownership over the entire estate after their father's death) and note, with obvious discomfort, that such an opinion is accepted by, among others, the author of the *Mitākṣarā* and Vācaspatimiśra II.[97] The compilers' discomfort is apparent because they enclose this statement within two quotations from Śrīkṛṣṇa's commentary on the *Dāyabhāga*: (1) that co-ordinate ownership (glossed by Colebrooke as 'property') amounts to assets in which individual shares exist, but are not yet determined; and (2) that co-ordinate ownership *of the same nature* (sajātīya) in a single asset is impossible for two individuals at the same time.[98] Śrīkṛṣṇa's opinion, that coordinate ownerships are

[96] Ibid., fols 9a–b: putrasvatvasya pitṛsvatvanāśānantaram eva sambhavāt pitṛsvatvanāś[e] 'pīti vibhāgānantaram putrāṇāṃ samudāyikasvatvanāśe svatvāntarotpattau ca pramāṇābhāvam vibhāgabodhakaśāstrāṇām eva tadbodhakatve 'pi ekasvatvanāśaparasvatvotpattikalpane gauravam iti tasmāt yatra yasya guṭikāpāto bhaviṣyati tatraiva tasya svatvaṃ kalpyate. The translation is adapted from Colebrooke's.

[97] Ibid., fol. 10a: anayor matayoḥ **samudayikasvatvavādismārtamatam** eva **harināthamitākṣarākāravācaspatimiśrabhavadevādīnāṃ** sammatam.

[98] Ibid., fol. 10a–b: **śrīkṛṣṇatarkālaṅkārāḥ** sādhāraṇadhanopaṣṭambhaśabdena [iti] anirṇīta-[viśeṣa]sva[tva]dhanopaṣṭambhasyaiva bodhanāt na tatra vyavahāravirodha ity āhuḥ[.] tathā ca sati ekasmin ekadravye ekadaiva nānāsvatvas[vī]kārāt sajātīyasvatve pratisajātīyasvatvena pratibandhakatvaṃ kalpanīyam etad evoktaṃ **śrīkṛṣṇatarkālaṅkāraiḥ.** Cf. *Dāyabhāga*, ed. Heramba Chatterjee (Howrah: Howrah Saṃskṛta Sāhitya Samāja, 1978), pp. 35–6: Śrīkṛṣṇa on *Dāyabhāga* 1.5: sajātīyasvatvam prati sajātīyasvatvaṃ virodhi.

possible, provided they do not share a similar nature, feels very much like an awkward solution to a difficult philosophical problem. Ultimately, Śrīkṛṣṇa and the compilers of the *Vivādabhaṅgārṇava* reject the possibility of sons and fathers holding co-ordinate ownership and that these authors allow undivided sons (i.e., sons whose father has died, but who have not yet divided the paternal estate amongst themselves) to sell their shares severally. Śrīkṛṣṇa's solution to the Raghunandana/Jīmūtavāhana debate seems to be to postulate something of a theoretical, sub-proprietary right of ownership for undivided heirs in the entire estate that cannot prevent any heir from alienating their individual share of the estate.

The *Vivādabhaṅgārṇava* and Śrīkṛṣṇa sail uncomfortably close to the wind in their attempts to harmonize the mechanics of Raghunandana and Jīmūtavāhana's theories of uparamasvatva, but they appear to be following—if following roughly—a debate that Gadādhara Bhaṭṭācarya explores in the *Svatvarahasya*, a complex, Navya-Nyāya discussion of ownership.[99] Gadādhara weighs 'Gauḍa' and 'Maithila' opinions concerning the collective ownership of sons in their deceased father's estate.[100] Gadhādhara accepts that in some instances, such as when a father's estate consists of a single slave or a single gold coin, sons may have co-ordinate ownership, but he concludes his argument—ambiguously—with the statement that because 'there would be no opposition to the theory of the Maithila-s mentioned above (regarding a collective *svatva* for the sons upon the father's death)... it is necessary, and economical, for *svatva* generally to obstruct [the] production of another entity delimited by *svatva*'.[101]

Gadādhara's argument, articulated in a Navya-Nyāya idiom and embedded in a running debate that gives few settled conclusions, leaves much to be desired. Gadādhara frames the argument as a debate between Gauḍas—represented by Jīmūtavāhana—and Maithilas. This suggests that the *Vivādabhaṅgārṇava*'s Nyāya-laden analysis of the metaphysical mechanics of uparamasvatva emerges from a debate between Bengali and Maithla Paṇḍitas (and to a lesser extent, the

[99] For the date and authorship of the *Svatvarahasya*, see Ethan Kroll, 'A Logical Approach to Law' (PhD Dissertation, University of Chicago, 2010), pp. 198–203.

[100] Kroll, 'A Logical Approach to Law', pp. 240–51. See p. 249, fn 107, for the *Svatvarahasya*'s Navya-Nyāya laden gloss of Jīmūtavāhana's *Dāyabhāga*: vikrayādimaraṇādijanyasvatvanāśotpattikṣaṇse bhrātrantarāṇsāṃ svatvam avinaṣṭam api taddhanāvṛttitasya [kā]likāvyāpyavṛttitvāt[.] evañ ca svatvānavacchedakasamaye 'p[y] ekasya vikrayādinā kret[r]ādisvatvotpattau bādhakābhāva ity āhuḥ[.] **dāyabhāgakṛtas** tu maraṇādijanyapitrādisvatvanāśāt sarvveṣv eva taddhaneṣu na sarvvabhāgināṃ svatvotpattiḥ kin tu guṭikāpātādinā vastugatyā yasya yo 'ñśo nirṇīto bhaviṣyati tatraivāñśe tasya svatvam utpādyate[.]

[101] Ibid., p. 251. See fn 111 for *Svatvarahasya*, fols 38a–b: sāmānyataḥ svatvatvāvacchinnaṃ prati svatvatvena pratibandhakasvatvasya **prāguktamaithilamate** 'py āvaśyakatayā tanmate 'py a[pr]atīkārāt. This comment is formally structured as a warrant (hetu), rather than as an assertion. The author of the *Svatvarahasya* links a long series of these warrants (which individually constitute assertions in their own right) when formulating his description of ownership.

Mitākṣarā) regarding different opinions and theories of ownership and their legal implications.

The compilers of the *Vivādabhaṅgārṇava* weigh and reject the theory of ownership-by-birth. In doing so, they contrast Navya-Nyāya and Mīmāṃsā theories of ownership. While they conclude—in conformity with Navya-Nyāya tradition—that the causes of ownership are limited to those modes of acquisitions stated explicitly in the smṛti, they accept the canonical status of the apocryphal passages—attributed to the *Gautamadharmasūtras*—that the *Mitākṣarā* uses to justify ownership-by-birth. The compilers defeat the theory of ownership-by-birth by exploring the theory that the ownership of one person obstructs the ownership of another person in the same asset, generally. In doing so, the *Vivādabhaṅgārṇava*'s compilers extend a common conceptual thread—of ownership—from its definition of inheritance and division, to a consideration of ownership's causes, and to an analysis of ownership-by-birth.

The *Vivādabhaṅgārṇava* introduces the possibility of ownership-by-birth by exploring the philosophical nature of ownership itself. The *Vivādābhaṅgārṇava* quotes Jagannātha's grandfather, Candraśekharavācaspati:

> does ownership belong to one of the seven padārtha's, substance, etc., or is it a distinct (padārtha)? On this issue, (my) grandfather, assuming the opinion of the Mīmāṃsakas (for argument's sake) states that as far as ownership is concerned, (ownership) is a particular saṃskāra (mental impression) that operates on this or that substance. But, he says, according to the (correct) opinion of the Naiyāyikas, svāmitva (ownership from the owner's side of things) is an effect, existing in an owner, described by this or that substance, and that exists in a substance by the relation of describer-ness.[102]

The *Vivādabhaṅgārṇava* concludes that the correct definition of ownership is that of Śiromaṇibhaṭṭācārya: that ownership is a distinct conceptual category (padārtha).[103] The text considers several metaphysical details of ownership from within the Navya-Nyāya tradition, such as whether ownership abides in substances or in people, and whether ownership abides in qualities (such as blackness,

[102] *Vivādabhaṅgārṇava*, fols 3a–b: atra svatvam eva kiṃ dravyādisaptapadāntargatam atiriktaṃ vā. atra **pitāmahacaraṇāḥ** svatve tāvat tat[tad]dravyavṛttisaṃskāraviśeṣa iti **mīmāṃsakamatam** āśrityāhu[ḥ]. **naiyāyikamate** tu tattaddravyanirūpitasvāmivṛtt[y]apūrvam eva svāmitvaṃ tac ca nirūpakatāsambandhena dravyavṛttīty āhaḥ.

[103] Ibid., fol. 3b: tad eva samyak na tu yatheṣṭaviniyogārhatvaṃ yatheṣṭaviniyogārhatvena śāstra[g]amyatvaṃ vā svasvatve sati yatheṣṭaviniyogaḥ yatheṣṭaviniyogārhaṃ ca svam ity ānāśrayāt, śāstreṇāpi svasvatvāspadībhūtasyaiva yatheṣṭaviniyogo bodhita iti tathaivātmāśrayāc ca. ata evātiriktaḥ padārtha eva svatvam iti **padārthatattve śiromaṇiḥ**. tasya ca saṃskāratvakalpane pramāṇābhāvāt, guṇatvādau ca pramāṇābhāvāt saptapadārthātiriktapadārthatvam iti tasyābhiprāyaḥ tac ca suvarṇarajatagavādirūpadravyavṛttiḥ. For Raghunātha's theory of ownership, see Section 2.B.1. Cf. Karl Potter, *The Padārthatattvanirūpaṇam of Raghunātha Śiromaṇi* (Cambridge, MA: Harvard University Press, 1957).

etc.), and it concludes with a statement from Candraśekhara Vācaspati's *Dvaitanirṇaya*, that 'acquisition alone is the cause of ownership and that (acquisition) is the activity of an acquirer (that is) stated in śāstra'.[104]

The *Vivādabhaṅgārṇva* gives no further details about this Mīmāṃsā theory of ownership. The Mīmāṃsakas advocate a theory of ownership as a causal capacity (śakti) or as a fitness for use as desired (yatheṣṭhaviniyogayogyatva) that is produced by modes of acquisition recognized by extra-śāstric communal norms. Indeed, the *Mīmāṃsānayaviveka*, one of the principal Mīmāṃsā treatises for the followers of the *Mitākṣarā* school of Dharmaśāstra, weighs a theory of ownership as a mentally-cognizable Dharma (perhaps a saṃskāra?).[105] The *Vivādabhaṅgārṇava*'s distinction between Mīmāṃsā and Navya-Nyāya theories of ownership prefaces a discussion of ownership-by-birth. This signals the compilers' awareness of the broader Mīmāṃsā/*Mitākṣarā* and Navya-Nyāya/*Dāyabhāga* debates of the seventeenth and eighteenth centuries.

Candraśekhara Vācaspati makes a concession to the proponents of ownership-by-birth: in the case of inheritance, acquisition is bodily, because the birth of sons and the like is itself an act of acquisition by means of the relation of being a son, or the like. This is because of the smṛti passage 'sometimes acquisition by birth alone' and because of the statement of Gautama, 'by birth alone one obtains assets'.[106] We saw in Chapter 2 that, although Jīmūtavāhana rejected these apocryphal śāstric passages as inauthentic, his followers—in Dharmaśāstra and Navya-Nyāya—tend to accept their authenticity for argument's sake.[107] From their initial textualization as a maxim of cultural usage in Śālikanātha's *Ṛjuvimalāpañcikā* (tenth century), these statements endorsing ownership-by-birth gradually gained authenticity.[108] The *Vivādabhaṅgārṇava* accepts the authenticity of these passages without giving the game away—the compilers insist that ownership is a śāstric matter and they use these statements to launch into a discussion of ownership-by-birth. The *Vivādabhaṅgārṇava's* argument against ownership-by-birth runs as follows:

> Might a son have ownership in the [assets] of his living father? That would not be a desirable outcome because it contradicts the śāstra, because the Devalasmṛti states that sons are asvāmya while their father exists without a blemish...

[104] *Vivādabhaṅgārṇava*, fol. 4a: tatra kāraṇaṃ ki[m]. atra **pitāmahacaraṇāḥ**. arjanam eva sva-[tvahetus] tac cārjanaṃ śāstroktārjayitṛvyāpāra eva. See Chapter 2 of this monograph for the *Dāyabhāga* school's rejection of janmasvatva—a rejection predicated on the theory that ownership's causes are limited to those stated in the śāstra.

[105] See 'Bhavanātha's *Mīmāṃsānayaviveka:* Mīmāṃsā's First Metaphysics of Ownership' in Chapter 2.

[106] Ibid., fol. 4a: dāyasthale tu kvacij janmaiv[ā]rjanam iti smaraṇāt utpat[ty]aivārthaṃ labheteti **gotamavacanāc** ca putratv[ād]isambandhadv[ā]rā putrādīnām utpattir evārjanaṃ tad api ca kāyikam.

[107] See, for example, '*The Mitākṣarā In-Utero*' in Chapter 2.

[108] *Bṛhatī of Prabhākaramiśra with the Ṛjuvimalā of Śālikanātha*, vol. 4, ed. S. Subrahmanyan Shastri (Madras: University of Madras Press, 1964), p. 962, Ṛj on *Bṛhatī* on *Śābarabhāṣya* on *Mīmāṃsāsūtra* 4.1.2: arjanam ca nānārūpam kvacij janma, yathā paitṛkeṣu.

> Therefore, the conclusion is that (death, etc. on the part of the father) is the cause (of his sons' ownership) insomuch as it destroys the ownership of the father.[109]

This constitutes a fairly typical defence of uparamasvatva, but the *Vivādabhaṅgārṇava*'s next argument is more inspired. One might argue that if the destruction of a father's ownership in a given asset generates a son's ownership in that same asset by reason of filiation, then, when a father gives or sells any asset—an activity that involves, *a priori*, the destruction of his ownership—a son's ownership would arise and preclude the donee or purchaser from acquiring ownership.[110] The *Vivādabhaṅgārṇava*'s conclusion invokes the principle of ownership as an obstructor to defend uparamasvatva and to reject ownership-by-birth:

> We reply that even when some asset is not (yet) given, ownership arises for the purchaser by accepting the offer to trade and the price and for the donee by acceptance, because of the postulation that ownership blocks counter-ownership (for another person). Thus, there is no need to postulate a cause (of ownership for a son) other than the destruction of an opposing ownership (on the part of a father). If there be an opposing ownership (on the part of a donee), then the ownership of a son does not arise. Therefore, a son's lack of ownership while his father lives is what is presented as doctrine.[111]

The logic, which mirrors a similar discussion in Gadādhara's *Svatvarahasya*, appears to assume that a living father's ownership blocks the ownership of his sons.[112] This is another instance in which the *Vivādabhaṅgārṇava* and the *Svatvarahasya*'s views of ownership and inheritance converge: both authors employ a theory of ownership as an obstructor to defeat Maithila or *Mitākṣarā* theories of collective ownership and/or ownership-by-birth. Like the *Vivādabhaṅgārṇava*, the *Svatvarahasya* accepts the statement 'by birth alone' as an authentic sūtra of Gautama, but Gadādhara writes that this refers to the progeny born from the father's male and female slaves and livestock after

[109] *Vivādabhaṅgārṇava*, fol. 4b: nanu jīvataḥ pitur dhane putrasya svatvaṃ syāt[.] na ceṣṭāpattiḥ śāstravirodhāt. pitary uparate putrā vibhajeyur dhanam pituḥ / asvāmyaṃ hi bhaved eṣāṃ nirdoṣe pitari sthite. iti **devalena** [uktam] … [maraṇādeḥ] pitṛsvatvanāśatvena hetutvam iti phalitam.

[110] Ibid., fols 4b–5a: (ii.) pitṛsvatvanāśatvena hetutvam iti phalitam. brāhmaṇebhyaḥ pitrā dīyamāne dhane putrasvatvāpatter durvāratvāt. Unfortunately, the *Vivādabhaṅgārṇava* leaves much of this to be inferred by the reader.

[111] Ibid., fols 4b–5a: atrocyate. adatte 'pi dhane mūlyasaṃkalpasvīkārābhyāṃ kretuḥ svīkārāc ca prat[i]grahītuḥ svatv[ot]pattyā svatvam, pratisvatva[sya] pratibandhakatvakalpanād evaṃ ca pratisvatvanāśatvena kāraṇatvāntaraṃ na kalpanīyaṃ. yadi pratisvatve sati putrasvatvaṃ na jāyate tadā tu … pitari jīvati putrasya asvāmitvam iti pratipāditam.

[112] See Kroll, 'A Logical Approach to Law', p. 252, fn 112, for *Svatvarahasya*, fols 38b–39a: ata eva jīvati pitari taddhane 'pi putrāṇāṃ nādhikāraḥ svatvavati svatvāntarānutpattyā tadīyasvatvaṃ prati tadīyasvatvābhāvaviśiṣṭasya tadīyetarasvatvasya pratibandhakatayā ca pitṛsvatvasatve putrasvatvotpatter asambhavāt.

the father has died.[113] Generally, however, 'the scribbling of the *Mitākṣarā*, viz., "A son acquires svatva in his father's assets by his mere act of being born alone", are unacceptable, since they are contrary to reason'.[114]

The *Vivādabhaṅgārṇava*, following the *Svatvarahasya*, tackles an issue that lay at the heart of eighteenth-century Sanskrit jurisprudence in Bengal: how to accept the *Mitākṣarā*'s apocryphal statements that 'one becomes an owner by birth alone' without conceding that sons might obtain ownership (of any sort) in ancestral assets during the lifetime of their fathers. Various Dharmaśāstrins and Navya-Naiyāyikas developed novel solutions—Govinda Bhaṭṭācārya, for example, combines birth and a theory of counter-positives (pratiyogins) to articulate a causal sequence in which sons do not have ownership rights while their fathers live—but the core structure remains the same. Defending Jīmūtavāhana from the *Mitākṣarā*'s theory of ownership-by-birth (a theory connected to Mīmāṃsā theories of ownership) required Navya-Nyāya reasoning.[115] In short, the second jurisprudential question that the compilers of the *Vivādabhaṅgārṇava* tackle continues the theme of mobilizing a Gauḍa scale of Dharmaśāstra and Nyāya texts to defeat Maithila and *Mitākṣarā* rivals.

A third jurisprudential question explored by the *Vivādabhaṅgārṇava* is the legal validity of a father's or of undivided brothers' alienation of immovable assets in contravention of śāstric regulations (*factum valet*). The compilers accepted two premises: 1) that a father holds exclusive rights of ownership over ancestral assets during his lifetime; and 2) that when their father dies (legally or biologically), the brothers, if undivided, obtain ownership rights in their joint assets *severally*. A core theory of the *Mitākṣarā* school of jurisprudence is that a father's alienation of ancestral assets is legally void because his sons have ownership in those assets during his lifetime. A core theory of the Mithilā school of jurisprudence is that a single, united brother may not alienate joint assets because his brothers have co-ordinate ownership in these assets. The *Vivādabhaṅgārṇava* rejects both views and argues for the legal validity of transactions made in contravention of śāstric restrictions. The compilers defend morally suspect alienations—a principle enshrined in Jīmūtavāhana's *Dāyabhāga* and in Navya-Nyāya discourse—by appealing to philosophical debates about the nature of ownership.

The *Vivādabhaṅgārṇava* discusses the validity of śāstrically prohibited transactions in its discussion of the non-delivery of gifts (dattānapakarman).[116] The

[113] Ibid., p. 252, fn 12, for *Svatvarahasya*, fol. 39a: utpattyaivārth[a]svāmitv[aṃ] labhata iti **gotamavacanasya** kvacij janmaivārjanaṃ yathā pitṛdhan[a] iti prāmāṇikābhidhānasya ca prāguktarītyā pitṛmaraṇottarajāte paitṛkadāsadāsīgavādijanyāpatyaparamparārūpārthaviṣayakatvāt. This interpretation strains credulity.

[114] Ibid., p. 253 (for translation) and fn 113 for *Svatvarahasya*, fols. 38b–39a: janmamātreṇaiva putrasya pitṛdhane svatvam utpadyata iti **mitākṣarālikhanasya** ca yuktiviruddhatvenānupādeyatvāt.

[115] Samuel Wright, 'The Practice and Theory of Property in Seventeenth-Century Bengal', *Indian Economic and Social History Review* 54.2 (2017): 147–82, 169.

[116] This section is missing from the Bodleian Library's manuscript of the *Vivādabhaṅgārṇava*. The Sanskrit passages quoted are extracted from Colebrooke's copy of the *Vivādabhaṅgārṇava* held by the British Library. India Office Ms. No. 1534/1770.

Vivādabhaṅgārṇava introduces a verse from the *Nāradasmṛti* that states that for undivided brothers 'if they give or sell their own shares (of the paternal estate) they may do as they please with all that. They are masters of their own assets.'[117] An enduring question that appears frequently in seventeenth and eighteenth-century Dharmaśāstra and Nyāya is whether an undivided brother's alienation of his own, or of *all* of the undivided estate is legally valid. The *Vivādabhaṅgārṇava* dispenses with the erroneous notion that one brother could alienate *all* of his and his brothers' joint assets. The compilers argue that if (a parcener) gives common, communal assets without the consent of the other parceners, then that gift is invalid indeed because the desire of one (parcener) cannot destroy ownership described by 'all'.[118] However, they argue that:

> Because nothing blocks the disappearance or appearance of ownership by way of there being a desire present in the owner that is the describer of ownership in a particular gift due to a particular desire; therefore, with regard to that (individual asset), the ownership of the giver goes only to the recipient. The ownerships of the other (brothers) remain. There is, however, the accomplishment of a gift conforming to one's own share because the individual ownerships of all of the brothers arise in all of the assets (severally).[119]

The compilers hold that united brothers hold joint assets severally, but the question—which appears in the *Vivādabhaṅgārṇava*'s discussion of partition—arises: do brothers hold a fractional ownership over the entire estate collectively, or do they hold complete ownership over individual portions of the estate severally? The compilers appear to accept that different ownerships arise in different properties for different people (when a father dies).[120] The reason is that 'in the opinion of the Naiyāyikas, there is no acceptance of the existence of a quality in two places except for conjunction'.[121]

[117] *Vivādabhaṅgārṇava*, fol. 5a: svabhāgān yadi dadyus te vikrīṇīyur tathāpi vā / kuyur yatheṣṭaṃ tat sarvam iśās te svadhanasya vai (*Nāradasmṛti* 13.43).

[118] Ibid., fol. 5b: yadi tu samudāyadhanaṃ sādhāraṇaṃ dāyādāntarānumatiṃ vinā dadāti tadā tu dānāsiddhir eva sarvanirūpitasvatvānām ekecchayā nāśāsambhavāt.

[119] Ibid., fol. 5b: ek[ai]kecchād ekasya dānasya svatvanirūpakasvāminiṣṭhecchātvena svatvanāśajanakatāyā bādhakābhāvāt[.] tasmād atra dātuḥ svāmitvaṃ sampradānam evopagacchati. anyeṣāṃ svāmitvāni . . . tiṣṭhant[i] . . . svāṃśayogyadānasiddhis tu bhavaty eva sarveṣv eva dhaneṣu sarvabhrātṛnirūpitāni ekaikāni svatvāni jāyante.

[120] Ibid., fol. 6a: dhanabhedāt puruṣabhedāc ca svatvāni jāyante.

[121] Ibid., fol. 6a: **naiyāyikānām** mate tu . . . samyogādyatiriktaguṇānāṃ ubhayavṛtt[eḥ] [n]a svīkāraś. The text is a bit unclear in this section. The meaning—taken from Colebrooke's translation—is understandable and conforms with the legal conclusions at the end of the discussion of *factum valet*.

The *Vivādabhaṅgārṇava* contrasts this theory of sons holding ownership severally in their deceased father's estate with a rival theory that its compilers attribute to 'the Miśras'. The Miśras argue that if a father cannot alienate joint assets, his sons or his wife (as chattel property), because he lacks *independence* (svātantrya), then logically, undivided brothers lack independence with regard to joint assets.[122] Consequently, 'one infers (darśana) from Miśra's explanation that (an undivided) brother's gift of his own share from the undivided assets is void in the absence of consent from the other heirs'.[123] The compilers of the *Vivādabhaṅgārṇava* answer that:

> We say that the gift of the whole of the joint assets by one (of the undivided brothers) is void, but not a gift in accordance with his own share. For, the giver (of the whole of the assets) is not able to destroy the ownership of the others by his desire. This does not apply, however, to his own particular ownership, even when it pertains to joint assets, because one observes that activity, unobstructed, amongst partners in trade.[124]

The compilers argue for a model of the joint family as something akin to a British tenancy-in-common—where common property is held severally. However, the Gauḍa compilers of the *Vivādabhaṅgārṇava* add the caveat that joint families often—but not always—hold ownership in separate assets within the estate. Once again, the *Vivādabhaṅgārṇava* extends a coherent theory of ownership that it uses to undermine the arguments of its Maithila opponents.

The Gauḍas commonly argue that a father, as a sole owner of family property, may give or sell that property however he chooses, provided that he makes reasonable arrangements for the support of his family.[125] This triggers a question: if a father alienates his entire estate without making arrangements for the support of his dependents, is the alienation of his estate (made in contravention of śāstric rules enjoining the support of one's dependents) legally void? For the Gauḍas, unlike for the Maithilas or the followers of the *Mitākṣarā*, the answer is no.[126] A verse that Jīmūtavāhana and Vijñāneśvara attribute to the *Yājñavalkyasmṛti* states that:

[122] Ibid., fol. 8a: atra ca sāmānyam anekasvāmikam[.] atra sāmānyaputradāreṣu cāsvātantryād dānāsiddhir iti asvātantryañ ca sāmānyasya nyāyād iti ca **miśraḥ.**

[123] Ibid., fol. 8a: atra **miśravyākhyādarśanāt** dāyadāntarānanumatau avibhaktadhanāt svāṃśadāna[m] asiddham.

[124] Ibid., fol. 8a: ekena samudāyasya sādhāraṇasya dānam asiddhaṃ na tu svāṃśayogyasya iti brūmaḥ. tathā hi dātā svecchayā parasvāmitvam eva nāśayituṃ na prāpnoti[.] na tu sādhāraṇadhanagatam api svamātrasvāmitvaṃ, saṃbhūyavanijāṃ avyāhata tathā vyavahāradarśaṇāt.

[125] See notes 49–51.

[126] J. Duncan Derrett, 'Prohibition and Nullity: Indian Struggles with a Jurisprudential Lacuna', *Bulletin of the School of Oriental and African Studies* 20 (1957): 203–15.

the father is master of exactly all gems, pearls, and corals; neither the father nor the grandfather is the master of all of the immovable assets.[127]

The *Mitākṣarā* reads this śloka, plausibly, as proof that sons have ownership in ancestral immovable assets (and that this ownership prevents a father or grandfather from alienating said assets).[128] Jīmūtavāhana argues, say the compilers of the *Vivādabhaṅgārṇava*, that:

> With reference to the statement of Yājñavalkya, that is cited by Jīmūtavānaha, the 'non-master-ness' of the father and the grandfather is merely a statement of the absence of the necessity of performing gift and the like, in order to convey the adharma (of gift, etc.). But the meaning (of such statements) is not that gift, etc. may not occur. This is because, in this case (of immovable assets), as in other (classes) of assets, there is no difference in the ownership, characterized by an eligibility for use as desired (on the part of the father or the grandfather).[129]

The *Vivādabhaṅgārṇava* and Jīmūtavāhana ground their juridical opinion—that fathers, like sons, may alienate whatever is *their* property, even if such an alienation contradicts śāstric regulations (on not alienating the family estate or on not alienating undivided, communal property)—on a theory of ownership as a firm right to alienate as desired. Jīmūtavāhana and the *Vivādabhaṅgārṇava* argue that 'because there is no difference between different types of ownership, a fact cannot be made otherwise, even by a hundred (śāstric) statements'.[130] Śāstric statements limiting the power of fathers (with regard to ancestral assets), of undivided brothers (with regard to joint assets), of women (with regard to their 'women's property') are legion in the Dharmaśāstra and the *Vivādabhaṅgārṇava* quotes several of them. The compilers conclude that these statements do not indicate that *dependence* entails that legal transactions are invalid (for these individuals with regard to property that they own). This, say the compilers, 'is

[127] *Vivādabhaṅgārṇava*, fol. 13a: **y[ā]jñ[avalkye]** maṇimuktāpravālānāṃ sarvasyaiva pitā prabhuḥ, sthāvarasya samastasya na pitā na pitāmahaḥ. See notes 49–51, in this chapter.

[128] Rosane Rocher and Ludo Rocher, 'Ownership by Birth: The *Mitākṣarā* Stand', *Journal of Indian Philosophy* 29 (2001): 241–55, 249; *Yājñavalkyasmṛti: with the Mitākṣarā of Vijñāneśvara*, ed. R. K. Panda (Delhi: Bharatiya Kala Prakashan, 2011), 2.114, 283; yat tu 'bhartrā prītena' ity ādi **viṣṇuvacanam** sthāvarasya prītidānajñāpanam tat svopārjitasyāpi putrādyabhyanujñayaiveti vyākhyeyam. pūrvoktair **maṇimuktādivacanaiḥ** sthāvaravyatiriktasyaiva prītidānayogyatvaniścayāt. The verses involving 'gems and pearls' read: maṇimuktāpravālānām sarvasyaiva pitā prabhuḥ / sthāvarasya tu sarvasya na pitā na pitāmahaḥ // pitṛprasādād bhujyante vastrāṇy ābharaṇāni ca / sthāvaram tu na bhujyeta prasāde sati paitṛke //

[129] *Vivādabhaṅgārṇava*, fol. 13b: **jīmūtavāhanadhṛtayājñavalkyavacane** yad aprabhutvam uktam pituḥ pitāmahasya ca…tad adharmajñāpanāya dānādikarttavyatābhāvavacanamātram. na tu dānādyaniṣpattyartham iti **jīmūtavāhanenoktaṃ**…yatheṣṭaviniyogārhatvalakṣanasvatvasya dravyāntara iva atrāpy aviśeṣād. Cf. *Dāyabhāga*, pp. 262–3.

[130] Ibid., fol. 13b: vacanaśatenāpi vastuno 'nyathākaraṇāśaktiś…svāmitvāviśeṣād. Cf. *Dāyabhāga*, p. 264.

the path followed by Jīmūtavāhana and accepted by many Gauḍīyas'.[131] Indeed, 'this is the sense of the *Smṛtisāra* (of Candreśekhara Vācaspati): the gift (by the father) with reference to all his property is valid because it is made by an owner, but the giver sins because he does not follow the restrictions (of the śāstra).'[132]

The *Vivādabhaṅgārṇava* follows the *Dāyabhāga* and defends a theory of ownership that supports what the compilers identify explicitly as Gauḍa jurisprudence. That theory of ownership—existing for one individual at any given time and affording that individual a virtually unrestricted right to use his property as he pleases—receives a vigorous defence in contemporaneous Navya-Nyāya literature. Gauḍa jurisprudence and Gauḍa Navya-Nyāya philosophy share a common cluster of opinions on ownership, inheritance and sale, demonstrated by the close connections between Gadādhara's *Svatvarahasya* and Jagannātha Tarkapañcānana's *Vivādabhaṅgārṇava*.

From Two Digests to Two Treatises (1794–1825)

Henry Colebrooke arrived in Calcutta in 1783 to take up a post as a writer for the East India Company, and to reverse his family's ill fortune.[133] Henry's father, Sir George Colebrooke (1729–1809), a sometime powerful chairman of the East India Company (1767–71 and 1772–3) and member of parliament, acquired and squandered a vast fortune through his lucrative patronage and through reckless speculation.[134] Financial desperation drove George to seek careers for his sons with the Company in India. Unlike William Jones, who came to India in the same year as a fully educated adult to take a prestigious position at the Supreme Court—with a cluster of intellectual and cultural prejudices formed from years of English education—Colebrooke started at the bottom of the Company's bureaucratic pyramid.[135] During his young, formative years, Colebrooke collected Sanskrit manuscripts and studied a variety of śāstric topics—astronomy, grammar, literature and law—with traditionally trained Paṇḍitas from Mithilā and Bengal. Colebrooke's Sanskrit learning blossomed alongside his career in the Company's civil service, and by 1802, he took up positions as a judge of Superior Civil Court (the Ṣadr Dīwānī 'Adālat) and as a Professor of Sanskrit and Hindu Law at Fort William College in Calcutta.[136]

The turning point of Colebrooke's career was his appointment, after William Jones' premature death in 1794, to complete a translation of the *Vivādabhaṅgārṇava* for the benefit of the Company and Crown's courts in India. Colebrooke

[131] Ibid., fol. 15b: **jīmūtavāhanānusārīpanthāḥ** bahubhir **gauḍīyair** āsthitaḥ.

[132] Ibid., fol. 16b: sarvasve dānaṃ siddhyata eva svāmikṛtatvāt kin tu dātuḥ pratyavāyo niṣiddhācaraṇād iti **smṛtisārasyāpy** abhiprāyaḥ.

[133] Rocher and Rocher, *The Making of Western Indology*, p. 11.

[134] Ibid., pp. 1–12.

[135] Ibid., pp. 13–16.

[136] Ibid., pp. 61–2.

completed his translation, *A Digest of Hindu Law on Contracts and Successions* (Calcutta: Company Press, 1801), between 1795 and 1796.[137] For all of its faults—prolixity, a predilection for convoluted philosophical digression, idiosyncratic organization, and a lack of clear conclusions—the *Vivādabhaṅgārṇava* revolutionized the practice and theory of Anglo-Hindu law in the nineteenth century. Colebrooke's efforts to follow the *Vivādabhaṅgārṇava*'s different intellectual threads led him to pursue three related problems in the intellectual history of Sanskrit jurisprudence: 1) the regional differences in the Sanskrit jurisprudence of ownership and inheritance; 2) the philosophical bases of these regional differences; and 3) the foundational treatises of these regional schools of law. In his research, Colebrooke collaborated with Paṇḍitas from North India's three major centres of Sanskrit learning—Bengal, Mithilā and Vārāṇasī—and assembled the world's most extensive collection of Sanskrit legal manuscripts. In consultation with these Paṇḍitas and on consideration of these manuscripts, Colebrooke concluded that the Sanskrit jurisprudence of inheritance contained three regionally and methodologically specific schools: Vārāṇasī, Mithilā and Bengal. Ironically, and, in a way similar to the case of William Jones, the intellectual predilections and prejudices of Colebrooke's Paṇḍita collaborators dovetailed with territorial divisions within the Bengal Presidency.

Colebrooke's encounter with Vārāṇasī-based Paṇḍitas and with Dharmaśāstric texts that defended the *Mitākṣarā*'s Mīmāṃsā-inflected theories of ownership-by-birth compelled him to select the *Mitākṣarā* and the *Dāyabhāga* for translation and to model his theory of schools of Hindu law on Mīmāṃsā and Navya-Nyāya based interpretations of these two core treatises. Rocher and Davis' cautionary warnings notwithstanding, Colebrooke's theory that there was a *Mitākṣarā/Dāyabhāga* faultline in Dharmaśāstra constitutes a justified and reasonable understanding of the state of Dharmaśāstra commentaries in the eighteenth century. Colebrooke encountered and recreated the scales of Dharmaśāstra texts fashioned in Vārāṇasī by the Bhaṭṭas and by the logicians of Navadvīpa in the seventeenth and eighteenth centuries—even if Benares' recent annexation and the extension of the Anglo-Indian 'Adālat system provided an impetus for this project.

This section examines two of Bālambhaṭṭa's treatises that, coupled with the arguments of the *Vivādabhaṅgārṇava*, most influenced Colebrooke's interest in a Vārāṇaseya/*Mitākṣarā* school of Dharmaśāstra: the *Dharmaśāstrasaṃgraha* (compiled for Colebrooke in 1797) and the *Vyavahārabālambhaṭṭī*, a sub-commentary on the *Mitākṣarā* (possibly written before Bālambhaṭṭa's encounter with Colebrooke). These two treatises synthesize arguments from the Bhaṭṭa family and from the *Vīramitrodaya* to defend the theories of the *Mitākṣarā*

[137] Ibid., pp. 34–5.

from the opinions of the easterners (prācyāḥ). Bālambhaṭṭa's polemic against Jīmūtavāhana and other easterners recapitulates the polemic found in the writings of the Bhaṭṭa family, (examined in the third chapter of this monograph): a desire to defend an exemplary, southern Brāhmaṇa pedagogical lineage—built around expertise in Mīmāṃsā and Dharmaśāstra—from a rival, Bengali Navya-Nyāya, Dharmaśāstra nexus. The *Vyavahārabālambhaṭṭī*, in framing the *Mitākṣarā* as a rejoinder to the *Dāyabhāga*, completes the scheme of schools of law as a debate between three centres of learning—Vārāṇasī, Navadvīpa, and Mithilā—and between two principal texts—the *Mitākṣarā* and the *Dāyabhāga*.

Henry Colebrooke and the Making of Western Indology

Colebrooke's pursuit of his twin interests—advancement in the bureaucracy of the East India Company and proficiency in traditional Sanskrit knowledge systems—exemplifies the remarkable tale of the British discovery (rather than invention) of Dharmaśāstric schools of jurisprudence. Just as the largely Bengali compilers of the *Vivādārṇavasetu* inspired William Jones to craft digests of Maithila and Gauḍa law, so Jagannātha and the other compilers of the *Vivādabhaṅgārṇava* drove Colebrooke to search for the formative texts of the Vārāṇaseya school of law. That story—of a shift from a Maithila/Gauḍa debate to a *Dāyabhāga*/*Mitākṣarā* debate—took place in Mirzapur, a bustling commercial city close to Vārāṇasī, in 1796, where British lawyers and Indologists worked to integrate the new province into colonial legal and knowledge systems that were based in Bengal. There, Colebrooke, who had previously been immersed in Gauḍa and Maithila Dharmaśāstra, plunged himself in the vast ocean of Bhāṭṭa treatises and other Dharmaśāstric texts that were popular amongst the city's Paṇḍitas.

Colebrooke's study of Sanskrit began, in all probability, whilst he served as an assistant to the collector of Tirhut (Mithilā) between 1786 and 1789.[138] It was only in 1790, however, when he was appointed as registrar of Purnia, Bihar, that 'Colebrooke devoted for the first time sustained attention to Sanskrit studies'.[139] Unlike Jones, who dove headlong into Dharmaśāstra and Kāvya without a solid grasp of śāstric fundamentals, Colebrooke's first interests were grammar, astronomy, and lexicography: he read the *Bījagaṇita*, the *Siddhāntaśiromaṇi*, the *Prakriyākaumudī* and the *Amarakośa* with a local, Maithila Paṇḍita, Citrapati Jhā—who would follow Colebrooke throughout the years.[140] By 1794, Colebrooke gained considerable proficiency in śāstric Sanskrit and submitted his first paper, 'On the Duties of a Faithful Hindu Widow' to the Asiatic Society.[141] The paper, read by Sir William Jones during his final meeting of the Society, elevated

[138] Ibid., pp. 16–17. [139] Ibid., p. 21. [140] Ibid. [141] Ibid., p. 24.

Colebrooke's status as a competent Sanskritist, but it also generated a fair bit of controversy—since widow burning (satī) featured in the essay.[142] One detail that is often overlooked is that Colebrooke's sources for his essay appear to have been drawn—either directly or indirectly—from Raghunandana's *Śuddhitattva*.[143] It seems that at the earliest stage of his career, Colebrooke was immersed in a dual environment, in which he was exposed to Maithila and Gauḍa Dharmaśāstric culture.

After Jones' death in 1794, Colebrooke was appointed by Governor John Shore to translate the *Vivādabhaṅgārṇava*.[144] In 1795, when the East India Company 'extended the system of government of Bengal and Bihar to the newly annexed province of Banaras', Colebrooke received an appointment to a position as a magistrate of Mirzapur.[145] Colebrooke was pleased because this posting would afford him 'ready access to the Hindu College' and its many Paṇḍitas.[146] On arriving in Mirzapur in October of 1795, Colebrooke seems to have immediately begun a correspondence with the Paṇḍitas of the Benares Sanskrit College and to have begun assembling a collection of Sanskrit manuscripts from the city.[147] Colebrooke completed his translation of the *Vivādabhaṅgārṇava* in Mirzapur in 1796.

In the preface to his translation, in which he complains that 'Jagannātha has added a copious commentary, sometimes indeed pursuing frivolous disquisitions', Colebrooke gives an overview of the principal Dharmaśāstric texts.[148] It is here, rather than in the introduction to *Two Treatises*, that Colebrooke first formulates the theory of schools of Hindu law. He writes that the '*Dīpacalicā* by *Śūlapāṇi* ... is in deserved repute with the *Garīya* [*sic*] school', that the 'works of Raghunandana ... are highly respected by the *Gaurīya* school', and that Jīmūtavāhana's 'chapter on Inheritance is extant, with a commentary by Śrī Crīshṇa Tercālancāra ... who belongs to the *Gaurīya* school'.[149] Likewise, Colebrooke states that the '*Vivāda Retnācara* ... Chaṇḍēśwara ... the *Vivāda Chintāmeni, Vyavahāra Chintāmeni* and other works of Vāchespati Misra, are ... much respected in the *Mit'hilā* school.'[150] Colebrooke's list of texts are drawn from the *Vivādabhaṅgārṇava*, and so it comes as no surprise that he, like William Jones, would distinguish between these two principal schools using appellations found in the texts of the tradition—rather than Bengal and Bihar. Colebrooke makes a remarkable argument:

> An excellent commentary [on the *Yājñavalkyasmṛti*] intitled [*sic*] Mitācsharā, was composed by Vijnyanēśwara, a hermit, who cites other legislators in the

[142] Ibid., pp. 24–6.

[143] Ibid., p. 25. Colebrooke follows the *Śuddhitattva*'s gloss of *Ṛgveda* 10.18.7 (where an 'agre' is read as 'agneḥ').

[144] Ibid., pp. 34–5. [145] Ibid., p. 35. [146] Ibid. [147] Ibid., pp. 39–41.

[148] Henry Thomas Colebrooke, *A Digest of Hindu Law on Contracts and Successions*, vol. 1 (Calcutta: Company Press, 1801), p. xi.

[149] Ibid., pp. xvi–xxi. [150] Ibid., pp. xix–xx.

> progress of his work, and expounds their texts, as well as those of his author, thus composing a treatise which may supply the place of a regular digest: it is so used in the province of Benares, where it is preferred to other law tracts.[151]

This is the first description of the *Mitākṣarā* in English and although Colebrooke does not yet describe it as foundational to a school of law, he makes a strong association between it and the Paṇḍitas of Vārāṇasī. Colebrooke mentions the *Mitākṣarā* sparingly, but his comments, coming immediately after his initial encounter with the Sanskritic intellectual culture of Vārāṇasī, suggest a jurisprudential divide between Vārāṇasī on the one hand, and Bengal and Bihar on the other.

One reason for the *Mitākṣarā*'s popularity in Vārāṇasī is the strikingly strong concentration of Mahārāṣṭrian Paṇḍitas in the city in the late seventeenth century. William Ward, a British missionary who recorded many features of Indian life at the end of the eighteenth century, records the names of the city's leading Paṇḍitas, many of whom hail from Mahārāṣṭra.[152] We saw in Chapter 3 of this monograph that the Bhaṭṭas viewed a rigorous defence of the *Mitākṣarā*'s theory of ownership-by-birth and of the Prābhākara-Mīmāṃsā theory of ownership as an extra-śāstric phenomenon as a key facet of the Bhaṭṭa family's status as exemplary southern brāhmaṇas in the city of Vārāṇasī. Furthermore, the Bhaṭṭas defence of the *Mitākṣarā* was oriented against Bengali Dharmaśāstrins who followed the *Dāyabhāga* and against Bengali Navya-Naiyāyikas who followed Raghunātha Śiromaṇi's *Padārthatattvanirūpaṇa*. The Mahārāṣṭrian Paṇḍitas that Colebrooke encountered in Vārāṇsasī probably held views similar to those of their illustrious forebears, the Bhaṭṭas.

Jonathan Duncan (1756–1811), the British Resident of Benares from 1788 to 1795, founded the Benares Sanskrit College in 1791 (with the assistance of Governor Cornwallis) with the goal of:

> preserving and disseminating a knowledge of Hindu Law and proving a nursery of future doctors and expounders thereof, to assist the European judges in the due, regular and uniform administration of its genuine letter and spirit to the body of the people.[153]

[151] Ibid., p. xv.

[152] Ward, *History of the Hindoos*, vol. 2, pp. 490–4. For more on the preponderance of Mahārāṣṭrian Paṇḍitas in Vārāṇasī, see *Sanskrit Documents: Being Sanskrit Letters and Other Documents Preserved in the Oriental Collection at the National Archives of India*, ed. Surendranath Sen and Umesha Mishra (Allahabad: Ganganatha Jha Research Institute, 1951), p. 4, quoting James Prinsep's *Benares Illustrated in a Series of Drawings* (Calcutta: Baptist Mission Press, 1831), to the effect that 'there were no less than **11,311 Maharashtra, 1,231 Nagara and 3,000 Bengali** residents at Benares in 1829'.

[153] George Nicholls, *Sketch of the Rise and Progress of the Benares Patschalla or Sanskrit College, Now Forming the Sanskrit Department of the Sanskrit College* (written 1848) (Allahabad: Government Press, 1907), p. 1. Also see Vishnu Narain, *Jonathan Duncan and Varanasi* (Calcutta: Firma K. L. Mukhopadhyay, 1959).

The son of Kāśīnātha Upādhyāya (Duncan's Bengali Paṇḍita), served as the first rector of the college and the 'curriculum was left entirely to the teachers'.[154] It is a pity that we do not know the curriculum for the early Benares Sanskrit College. Judging from the prominence of Bengalis, however, and from the fact that only one 'Bhat' is listed amongst the first batch of professors, it seems unlikely that Colebrooke would have garnered his interest in the *Mitākṣarā* at the Sanskrit College.[155] In an 1810 memorandum, however, Colebrooke writes that in:

> the school of Benares, the prevailing one in middle India . . . the Mităcsharā of Vijnyāneśwara . . . is implicitly followed . . . so much so, that the ordinary phraseology of references for law opinions of Pandits, from the native judges of Courts established there . . . required the Pandit, to whom the reference was addressed, 'to consult the Mitācsharā', and report the exposition of the law, there found, applicable to the case propounded. A host of writers might be named, belonging to this school, who expound, illustrate, and defend the Mitācsharā's interpretation of the law. It may be sufficient to indicate, in this place, the Vīramitrodaya of Mitra Miśra, and the Vivādatāṇḍava and other works of Camalācara.[156]

The source of Colebrooke's fascination with Bhāṭṭa jurisprudence, and of his comments on the prominence of the *Mitākṣarā* in Vārāṇasī, appears to have been his relationship with a Paṇḍita outside of the Banaras Sanskrit College. In 1797, as Colebrooke settled into his role as a magistrate in Mirzapur, he spent his free time collecting manuscripts, preferably those that 'had been much used and studied' from various Paṇḍitas from the city of Vārāṇasī.[157] In the same year, Colebrooke received permission from the Company to pursue a new digest of Hindu law that 'would be much less diffuse than the digest [of Jones]'.[158] Colebrooke hired Bāla Śarman Pāyaguṇḍe, alias Bālambhaṭṭa, to compose a new digest, the *Dharmaśāstrasaṃgraha*.[159] Colebrooke met Bālambhaṭṭa earlier, when he

[154] Vasudha Dalmia, 'Sanskrit Scholars and Pandits of the Old School: The Benares Sanskrit College and the Constitution of Authority in the Late Nineteenth Century', *Journal of Indian Philosophy* 24 (1996): 321–37. Also see Michael Dodson, 'Re-presented for the Pandits: James Ballantyne, "Useful Knowledge", and Sanskrit Scholarship in Benares College during the Mid-Nineteenth Century', *Modern Asian Studies* 36.2 (2002): 257–98.

[155] Nicholls, *Sketch of the Rise*, pp. 63, 120. The College principal does list the *Mitākṣarā* as the Dharmaśāstra text studied for the academic year of 1820—well after Colebrooke published *Two Treatises*. In 1839, the College's Paṇḍitas answered questionnaires about their departments. In response to the question, 'What kinds of Law are studied by your pupils?', the Paṇḍitas answered 'the books read in the Deccan, those read in the Western Provinces and in Bengal are studied by the students of the college (here follows the names of different works)'. See *Sanskrit Documents*, nos 1, 11, 12, 14, and 19 for examples of eighteenth-century Vyavasthās in which the Paṇḍitas of Vārāṇasī cite the *Mitākṣarā* (primarily), *Madanaratnapradīpa*, *Viramitrodaya* and the *Vyavahāramayūkha*.

[156] T. E. Colebrooke, *The Life of H. T. Colebrooke* (London: Trübner & Co., 1873), p. 96.

[157] Rocher and Rocher, *The Making of Western Indology*, p. 41. Colebrooke's contacts included one Dhanapati Sūri, professor of Vedānta at the Benares Sanskrit College who composed a *Vidyāratnākara* at Colebrooke's request.

[158] Ibid., p. 43. [159] Ibid., p. 47.

procured a series of Sanskrit treatises on Pāṇinīan grammar.[160] Colebrooke took an unfavourable view of the digest. Colebrooke's copy of the *Dharmaśāstrasaṃgraha,* which breaks off abruptly in the middle of its treatment of Vyavahāra (judicial procedure), contains a note from Colebrooke which reads:

> 1st May, 1800, This is little else but the Vīramitrodaya revised...but as Mitra Miśra's work is far better than Pāyaguṇḍe is capable of producing himself, there is no reason to regret this imposition...After the experience I have had, that no Pandit is capable...to compile a digest in the form I require, I must now seriously set about compiling it myself.[161]

The *Dharmaśāstrasaṃgraha* does not contain a section on inheritance, but Colebrooke's collaboration with Bālambhaṭṭa and the Vārāṇaseya Paṇḍita establishment marks the juncture at which Colebrooke resolved to create a treatise of Dharmaśāstra, which was abandoned in favour of the *Two Treatises.*

Bālambhaṭṭa served as a conduit between Colebrooke and the Bhāṭṭa Dharmaśāstra texts of the seventeenth century that frame the Hindu law of inheritance as a southern/eastern, Mīmāṃsā/Nyāya and *Mitākṣarā/Dāyabhāga* debate. This, coupled with Colebrooke's earlier encounter with the *Mitākṣarā* during his work on the *Vivādabhaṅgārṇava* (he possessed a copy of the *Mitākṣarā* in 1795), shaped his *Two Treatises.* Bālambhaṭṭa was the son of Vaidyanātha Pāyaguṇḍa (1690–1780), and both were pupils of the famous grammarian Nāgeśabhaṭṭa (1650–1730).[162] Nāgeśabhaṭṭa Kāḷe was a close relative of the Bhaṭṭa family (the Bhaṭṭas intermarried with the Kāḷes regularly) and all three scholars wrote extensively on Dharmaśāstric topics.[163] In their writings, they often cite the opinions of Kamalākara, Nīlakaṇṭha and Gāgābhaṭṭa (although not, to my knowledge, on inheritance) and Vaidyanātha and Bālamabhaṭṭa's treatises proved influential in the contentious issue of caste identity in eighteenth-and-nineteenth-century Mahārāṣṭra.[164]

Bālambhaṭṭa wrote an influential, if idiosyncratic, commentary on the *Mitākṣarā,* the *Bālambhaṭṭī,* which Colebrooke relies on in his *Two Treatises* and which frames the *Mitākṣarā* as a Mīmāṃsā-inflected response to the

[160] Ibid.

[161] Julius Eggeling, *Catalogue of the Sanskrit Manuscripts in the Library of the India Office,* vol. 1 (London,: Printed by Order of the Secretary of State for India in Council, 1887), pp. 458–9, #1507.

[162] See Kāṇe, *A History of Dharmaśāstra,* vol. 1, part 2, 2nd edn (Poona: Bhandarkar Oriental Research Institute, 1975), pp. 965–6. For Bālambhaṭṭa to have still been active, having studied with Nāgeśa at least 56 years earlier, he would have to have been exceptionally young when he did so.

[163] For intermarriage between the Bhaṭṭas and the Kāḷes, see Kāṇe, *History of Dharmaśāstra,* vol. 1, part 2, p. 703.

[164] Ibid., p. 968. For the role of the Pāyaguṇḍes in Mahārāṣṭra, see Madhav Deshpande, 'Kṣatriyas in the Kali Age? Gāgābhaṭṭa & His Opponents', *Indo-Iranian Journal* 53 (2010): 95–100.

Dāyabhāga.[165] The *Bālambhaṭṭī*'s treatment of inheritance provides a good idea of what the section on inheritance in the *Dharmaśāstrasaṃgraha* would have looked like and how Bālambhaṭṭa would have explained the *Mitākṣarā* school of inheritance to Colebrooke. He continues the Bhaṭṭas' signature approach to the Dharmaśāstric jurisprudence of inheritance—a defence of the *Mitākṣarā* from Gauḍa opponents. This continuity of jurisprudential thought provides the missing link between Colebrooke's *Digest* and Colebrooke's *Two Treatises* because it accounts for Colebrooke's interest in the *Mitākṣarā/Dāyabhāga* debate as one based on regional identity and philosophical discipline.

Bālambhaṭṭa, the *Mitākṣarā*, and the *Vīramitrodaya*

This subsection examines the treatment of ownership and inheritance in the *Bālambhaṭṭī*'s comments on the *Mitākṣarā*'s introduction to *Yājñavalkyasmṛti* 2.114. Bālambhaṭṭa follows Kamalākara, Nīlakaṇṭha and Mitramiśra's seventeenth-century arguments—that the *Mitākṣarā* rejects the *Dāyabhāga*—and defends a southern theory of inheritance against the attacks of eastern (prācya) rivals. Bālambhaṭṭa frames three of the *Mitākṣarā*'s arguments as responses to 'the Easterners' and he quotes the *Dāyabhāga* at length (before rejecting its opinions invariably). I examine three features of Bālambhaṭṭa's texts: (1) the definition of inheritance; (2) the Mīmāṃsā theory of ownership as established extra-śāstrically; and (3) the theory of ownership-by-birth.

Bālambhaṭṭa glosses the *Mitākṣarā*'s definition of inheritance as 'assets which becomes the property of another, solely on account of (that person's) relation to the (asset's) owner'.[166] He states that:

> Thus (through this definition, Vijñāneśvara) distinguishes (relation) from merely other causes in the form of purchase, which are known about in (the extra-śāstric) world. And 'relation', namely the state of being begetter and begotten, means a relation between 'another', namely sons and the like, with the owner of the asset. Therefore, what has been said by the Easterners, that 'the word inheritance is used in a technical sense to refer to ownership, contingent on a relationship with the previous owner of that asset (which arises) when that owner dies' is rejected.[167]

[165] Bālambhaṭṭa, *Vyavahārabālambhaṭṭī*, fasc. 5, ed. Nityanand Pant Parvatiya (Benares: Chowkhambā Sanskrit Book Depot, 1912). All translations of the *Bālambhaṭṭī* are my own.

[166] *Mitākṣarā*, 280: tatra dāyaśabdena yad dhanam svāmisambandhād eva nimittād anyasya svam bhavati tad ucyate.

[167] *Bālambhaṭṭī* on *Mitākṣarā*, introduction to Yāj. 2.114: dāyaśabdārthaṃ tāvad āha tatreti. nirūpaṇīye dāyabhāge ity arthaḥ. etena lokaprasiddhakrayādirūpanimittāntaramātravyavacchedaḥ. sambandhaś ca janyajanakabhāvādir dhanasvāminā sahānyasya putrāder bodhyaḥ. etena pūrvadravyasvāmisambandhādhīnaṃ tatsvāmyuparame yatra dravye svatvaṃ tatra nirūḍho

Bālambhaṭṭa goes on to divide inheritance into two categories: unobstructed and obstructed (apratibandha and sapratibandha). Bālamabhaṭṭa offers some detail on why Vijñāneśvara's definition of inheritance rejects the opinions of the Easterners:

> Now, having stated the meaning of the word inheritance, he (Vijñāneśvara) states the meaning of the word division. The word division means the fixing, one by one, of the manifold ownership located in the sons, etc., which is described by the entire undivided assets, as pertaining to individual assets. Therefore, the statement of the Easterners, that 'division is the determination, through the casting of lots, etc., of ownership, that has certainly arisen in the land and gold (of the estate), that exists in individual places (but that) is unrealized insomuch as it is not fit for particular transactions because of the absence of a criterion for distinguishing (one ownership from another)' is rejected.[168]

Bālambhaṭṭa's strategy for explaining the comments of the *Mitākṣarā* is to place the *Mitākṣarā* in direct contrast with the *Dāyabhāga*. In Chapter 3, we saw that Kamalākara and his family tend to summarize and reject the Gauḍas' opinions generally, but Bālamabhaṭṭa is very keen to place the two primary texts (the *Mitākṣarā* and the *Dāyabhāga*) side by side.

Bālambhaṭṭa follows these comments with a lengthy digression on the Mīmāṃsā theory of ownership as extra-śāstric. He recapitulates the arguments that form the core theories of the *Mitākṣarā* school of thought that appear first in the *Mīmāṃsānayaviveka*: (1) that ownership is an extra-śāstric relation between an owner and their property; (2) which is like that between an acquirer and an object acquired; and (3) that such a relationship is like the relationship between a father and son.[169] Bālambhaṭṭa introduces and rejects—at length—the theory (propounded by Raghunāthaśiromaṇi) that ownership is a distinct conceptual category that is produced by those means of acquisition mentioned explicitly by

dāyaśabda iti **prācyoktam** apāstam. Cf. *Dāyabhāga*, 250: tataś ca pūrvasvāmisambandhādhīnaṃ tatsvāmyoparame yatra drave tatra nirūḍho dāyaśabdaḥ.

[168] Ibid., 418–19: evam dāyaśabdārtham uktvā vibhāgaśabdārtham āha—vibhāgo nāmeti. avibhaktadravyasamudāyanirūpitānām anekeṣām putrādiniṣṭhasvāmyānāṃ tadekadeśeṣu samuditadravyaikadeśeṣu tadviṣayatayā tannirūpitatayā vyavasthāpanaṃ viśeṣeṇa pratyekam avasthāpanaṃ yat tat bhāgaśabdavācyaṃ, ity arthaḥ... etenaikadeśagatasyaiva bhūhiraṇyādāv utpannasyaiva svatvasya vinigamanapramāṇābhāvena vaiśeṣikavyavahārānarhatayā avasthitasya guṭikāpātādinā svatvavyañjanaṃ vibhāga it **prācyoktam** apāstam. Cf. *Dāyabhāga*, p. 250.

[169] Ibid., 424–8: tac ca svatvaṃ janmanā putratvādikavat arjanenārjakārjyayoḥ tādṛśasvatvavat svasvāmisambandharūpaṃ laukikam eva manyante vṛddhāḥ... kriyāmūlakaḥ kartṛkarmaṇoḥ sambandho lokasiddho na mānāntarāpekṣaḥ. na caivam arjanakriyāpāye tajjanyasya tasyāpy apāyaḥ. sambandhinor āśrayayoḥ sattvāt. na hi pituḥ kriyāpāye pitṛtvam apaiti... arjanaṃ nāmārjakadharmaḥ prāguktarūpas tatprayuktaḥ svasvāmibhāvaḥ sambandhaḥ. sa ca dviniṣṭhaḥ pitṛputratvavat.

the śāstra (which would preclude ownership-by-birth).[170] Bālambhaṭṭa concludes that ownership is 'inferable from use, directly by direct perception and from extra-śāstric sources, used with reference to (property) called communal and non-communal, destroyed by partition, as it is destroyed by gift and sale, and *not* produced by partition.'[171]

Bālambhaṭṭa's final conclusion, based on his aforementioned analysis of ownership, is that:

> What has been said by the Easterners, that: (1) because if that were the case (ownership-by-birth) there would be the unwanted consequence that partition would occur even without the desire of the father; (2) because there is no authority for ownership by birth alone; and (3) because birth is not stated in smṛti as a form of acquisition, there is no ownership (for sons) while their parents are alive, but there is ownership when they die or become outcastes', is rejected.[172]

Bālambhaṭṭa's commentary on the *Mitākṣarā*'s chapter on inheritance follows this pattern of quoting and rejecting the *Dāyabhāga* wherever it and the *Mitākṣarā* differ. His Mīmāṃsā-inflected theory of ownership as extra-śāstric (indeed, radically so when one considers that he thinks of ownership as directly perceptible) establishes the fundamental point of departure from the Bengalis.[173]

Bālambhaṭṭa follows Kamalākara's and the other Bhaṭṭas' strategy of defending the *Mitākṣarā* from the *Dāyabhāga* by quoting the *Mīmāṃsānayaviveka*'s theories of ownership at length and of citing and rejecting Raghunāthaśiromaṇi's *Padārthatattvanirūpaṇa*, but his innovation is to cite the *Dāyabhāga* explicitly and to read the *Mitākṣarā* as rejecting the *Dāyabhāga*. Rather than defending the *Mitākṣarā* from Jīmūtavāhana's attacks, Bālamabhaṭṭa reads the *Mitākṣarā* as an attack on the *Dāyabhāga* and on Navya-Nyāya theories of ownership—theories that limited ownership to being the result of methods of acquisition that are recognized by the śāstra.

[170] Ibid., 428–9: śāstrāniṣiddhaṃ yatheṣṭaviniyogopāyabhūtakrayapratigrahādiviṣayatvaṃ . . . dānādināśyasya pratigrahādijanyasya padārthaviśeṣasyaiva svīkārāt. Bālambhaṭṭa's comments ramble quite a bit, and it is difficult to extract a single, coherent thread of argument from which his opponent's theory could be described. However, the idea of a distinct padārtha, generated by śāstrically recognized sources is undeniably reminiscent of the Gauḍa school of thought.

[171] Ibid., 431: evaṃ ca vibhāgājanyaṃ dānakrayanāśyavad vibhāganāśyaṃ sādhāraṇāsādhāraṇoktanimittaprayojyaṃ lokapramāṇapratyakṣagamyam bhogādyanumeyaṃ ca svatvam.

[172] Ibid., 439–40: tathā sati (uparamasvatve) pitur anicchayāpi vibhāgāpatteś ca. janmanaiva svatve mānābhāvāc ca. arjanarūpatayā janmanaḥ smṛtāv anukteḥ . . . pitroḥ satoḥ svāmitvam eva na. nidhanapātityādau tu svāmitvam iti **prācyoktam** apāstam. Cf. *Dāyabhāga*, p. 252.

[173] For another example of Bālambhaṭṭa rejecting the opinion of the Bengalis, see ibid., 444: etena kāladvayam eva pitur icchā tannidhanaṃ ca na tṛtīyo 'pīti mātur nivṛtte rajasīti pitāmahādidhanaviṣayam iti **prācyoktam** apāstam.

The Bhaṭṭa family was not the only influence on Bālambhaṭṭa's work. As Colebrooke noted in the margins of Bālambhaṭṭa's *Dharmaśāstrasaṃgraha*, Bālambhaṭṭa borrowed heavily from the seventeenth-century *Vīramitrodaya* of Mitramiśra (active 1610–40), a vast Dharmaśāstra digest commissioned by Vīrasiṃha Deva (Birsinghdeo, King of Orccha from 1605 to 1627).[174] We know surprisingly little about Mitramiśra. His grandfather hailed from Gwalior, his father, Paraśurāmapaṇḍita, trained in Vārāṇasī under a guru called Candraśekhara, and, whilst preparing the *Vīramitrodaya*, he was assisted by a Maithila paṇḍita called Sadānanda.[175] Like Kamalākarabhaṭṭa's *Vivādatāṇḍava* and like Nīlakaṇṭhabhaṭṭa's *Vyavahāramayūkha*, the *Vīramitrodaya*'s section on inheritance militates, vociferously, against the opinions of Jīmūtavāhana, Raghunandana and other Gauḍa authors.[176] In the *Vīramitrodaya*, Mitramiśra rejects Jīmūtavāhana's definition of ownership, Jīmūtavāhana's theory that only those means listed explicitly in the śāstra result in ownership, and Jīmūtavāhana's argument that partition *manifests* rights of ownership that already exist in individual assets.[177]

The *Vīramitrodaya* summarizes the state of the jurisprudential debate between Vārāṇasī-based Mīmāṃsakas and Navadvīpan Navya-Naiyāyikas in the seventeenth century. If Colebrooke, in his interactions with the Paṇḍitas of the Benares Sanskrit College, read Bālambhaṭṭa's *Bālambhaṭṭī*, Mitramiśra's *Vīramitrodaya* and Kamalākarabhaṭṭa's *Vivādatāṇḍava*, he had excellent reason to view the Dharmaśāstric jurisprudence of inheritance as a debate between southern Paṇḍitas based in Vārāṇasī and eastern Paṇḍitas based in Navadvīpa (subdivided into Maithila and Gauḍa schools). Bālambhaṭṭa reproduces the southern scale of texts that the Paṇḍitas of the Bhaṭṭa family established in the seventeenth century and Colebrooke appears to have latched onto this scale of texts when reading Bālambhaṭṭa, Mitramiśra and Kamalākarabhaṭṭa's works.

Colebrooke's encounter with Bālambhaṭṭa and the Benares Sanskrit College prompted him to pursue a new digest of Hindu laws, and towards that end he assembled an impressively comprehensive collection of Sanskrit manuscripts on the subjects of ownership and inheritance. The Colebrooke collection of manuscripts in the India Office Collection at the British Library contains copies of Mahārāṣṭrian digests (such as Kamalākara's *Vivādatāṇḍava*), and dozens of Bengali treatises, (including Gadādhara's *Svatvarahasya*).[178]

[174] See Kāṇe, *History of Dharmaśāstra*, vol. 1, part 2, pp. 941–53.

[175] Ibid., pp. 946–7. Sadānanda's exposure to Navya-Nyāya philosophy in Mithilā (and possibly Bengal) might account for the unusually detailed accounts of eastern ideas about ownership and inheritance in the *Vīramitrodaya*.

[176] *Vīramitrodaya*, ed. and trans. G. S. Śāstrī (Calcutta: Thacker, Spink & Co., 1879).

[177] Ibid., Sec 1, paragraphs 3, 43, 49, and 55.

[178] See Kroll, 'A Logical Approach to Law', pp. 198–9.

In any case, Colebrooke never completed his enhanced digest of Hindu law, but in his preface to the *Two Treatises*, he writes that:

> I long ago undertook a new compilation of the law of successions with other collections of Hindu law... its final completion and publication have been hitherto delayed by important avocations; and it has been judged mean time advisable to offer to the publick in a detached form, a complete translation of two works materially connected with that compilation.[179]

Colebrooke's translation features copious extracts from commentaries on the *Dāyabhāga* and on the *Mitākṣarā*. These extracts, generally from Śrīkṛṣṇa Tarkālaṅkāra and from Bālambhaṭṭa respectively, suggest that Colebrooke approached the *Dāyabhāga* and the *Mitākṣarā* as two principal texts whose commentators' predilection for Navya-Nyāya or for Mīmāṃsā theories of ownership led them to develop competing theories of the jurisprudence of inheritance. Colebrooke's division of the Dharmaśāstric jurisprudence of inheritance into *Dāyabhāga* and *Mitākṣarā* schools appears justified. Moreover, his identification of three competing regions: (1) Navadvīpa/Bengal with its theory of uparamasvatva and of partition as *manifesting* ownership; (2) Vārāṇasī with its theory of ownership-by-birth and joint ownership; and (3) Mithilā with its theory of uparamasvatva and joint ownership, is supported by the Dharmaśāstric texts of the seventeenth and eighteenth centuries. Furthermore, the Dharmaśāstra texts that Colebrooke knew, but also other texts with which he was not familiar, corroborate his theories.

The Limits and Limitations of Schools of Hindu Law

Colebrooke was justified in arguing for a model of regional schools of Hindu law inasmuch as the Paṇḍitas of three centres of śāstric learning in the sixteenth, seventeenth, and eighteenth centuries developed scales of Dharmaśāstric texts that they contrasted with and defended from rival scales of Dharmaśāstric texts. Ownership and inheritance—articulated in relation to the *Dāyabhāga* and the *Mitākṣarā*—formed a key topic for these debates. Mīmāṃsā and Navya-Nyāya reasoning played an important role in the development of the *Mitākṣarā* and *Dāyabhāga* schools and in distinguishing between Gauḍa and Maithila theories of ownership and inheritance. Colebrooke makes his best argument in defence of schools of law in 1825. He writes that:

> In the eastern part of India, viz. Bengal and Bahar, where the Vedas are less read, and the Mīmānsā less studied than in the south, the dialectic philosophy, or

[179] Colebrooke, *Two Treatises*, p. iii.

> Nyāya, is more consulted, and is relied on for rules of reasoning and interpretation upon questions of law, as well as upon metaphysical topics. Hence have arisen two principal sects or schools, which, construing the same text variously, deduce upon some important points of law different inferences from the same maxims of law.[180]

Warren Hastings, William Jones, and H. T. Colebrooke were gravely mistaken in their assumption that Dharmaśāstra texts reflected the cultural customs and ancient laws of all Hindus. A combination of prejudice (the positive law must be found in books) and expediency (a desire to extend company rule over Indians' property) drove orientalists and judges to transform academic Dharmaśāstra into applied, positive law.[181]

The misguided assumption that each region of India—at least those regions within the jurisdiction of 'Adālat courts—must, *a priori*, possess an authoritative Dharmaśāstric tradition that describes that region's essential culture drove the erroneous quest for specific sub-schools of the *Mitākṣarā*, for which virtually no evidence exists. One explanation for the theory of four sub-schools of Hindu law, articulated by Justice Syed Mahmud in 1887, is that Colebrooke patterned Hindu law on Islamic law (with its Shia and Sunni branches).[182] A more plausible possibility is that the subdivision of schools of Hindu law followed the expansion of the 'Cornwallis System' of 'Adālat courts in the Province of Banaras and the Presidencies of Bombay and Madras in the late eighteenth and early nineteenth centuries.[183]

Colebrooke lists the principal texts associated with each school: (1) the *Vivādacintāmaṇi*, *Vivādaratnākara* and the *Vivādacandra* in Mithilā; (2) the *Vīramitrodaya* and the *Vivādatāṇḍava* in Vārāṇasī; (3) the *Vyavahāramayūkha* in Mahārāṣṭra; (4) the *Smṛticandrikā* in 'Southern India;' and (5) the *Dāyabhāga* and the *Dāyatattva* in Bengal.[184] There is ample evidence for the existence of Maithila and Gauḍa schools of Dharmaśāstra (as seen from Chapter 2 and from the analysis of the *Vivādārṇavasetu* and the *Vivādabhaṅgārṇava*), but Colebrooke's distinction between a Vārāṇaseya (Benares) and a Mahārāṣṭrian school of law is inexplicable without taking into consideration the introduction of the 'Adālat system in the Bombay Presidency in 1799.

[180] Sir Thomas Strange, *Elements of Hindu Law: Referable to British Judicature in India, Vol. 1* (London: Payne and Foss, 1825), p. 314.

[181] See, for example Derrett, 'The British as Patrons', pp. 267–9.

[182] Syed Mahmood, *Indian Law Review: Allahabad Series* (Madras: Law Reports Office, 1887), p. 9. Cited in Rocher and Rocher, *The Making of Western Indology*, p. 112.

[183] See Rocher, 'Changing Patterns', pp. 138–9, for further evidence for this position. Rocher sees a connection between the development of 'a number of separate and different pyramids, with a High Court or Supreme Court' in Madras, Bombay, and Vārāṇasī, and the subdivision of the *Mitākṣarā* school of law into sub-schools.

[184] Colebrooke, *Two Treatises*, p. iv.

Perhaps the *Vyavahāramayūkha* enjoyed greater popularity among the Paṇḍitas of Mahārāṣṭra than among the Paṇḍitas of Vārāṇasī, but Kamalākara and Nīlakaṇṭha thought of themselves as part of a single, southern, Bhāṭṭa school of law whose authority extended from Mahārāṣṭra to Vārāṇasī (and which rejected the opinions of a Maithila and a Gauḍa school of law). The *Vīramitrodaya* may have enjoyed less popularity in Mahārāṣṭra (as its author did not enjoy the same social prestige as the Bhaṭṭas did in the country) and more popularity in Vārāṇasī (due to its more comprehensive, academic tone). The *Bālambhaṭṭī* and the *Dharmaśāstrasaṃgraha* suggest, however, that Mahārāṣṭrian and Vārāṇasī-based Paṇḍitas read Bhāṭṭa digests and the *Vīramitrodaya* as articulating a shared body of jurisprudence. Consequently, Colebrooke's endorsement of a split between Kamalākarabhaṭṭa and Nīlakaṇṭha's Dharmaśāstra texts into two separate schools of law demonstrates that, at some point, the jurisdictional boundaries of Anglo-Hindu *law* became unmoored from the intellectual boundaries of Sanskrit *jurisprudence*.

Furthermore, for all of his considerable knowledge of northern India, Colebrooke lacked a significant exposure to southern India and his assertion that the *Smṛticandrikā* (and later, the *Sarasvatīvilāsa*) constitute the principal treatises of a distinct, Drāviḍan sub-school (along with its three sub-branches) are based on considerations other than the self-representation of Dharmaśāstric authors. J. H. Nelson, district judge in Madras, wrote in 1881 that the introduction of the *Mitākṣarā* (as interpreted by the *Smṛticandrikā* and the *Sarasvatīvilāsa*) was the result of 'the absurdly great authority conceded to Colebrooke, who knew nothing about Madras'.[185] One explanation for the fierce debates between orientalists in Calcutta and Madras about the nature of the Madras school of Hindu law—between Dharmaśāstra texts and customary practice—is that the intense, Dharmaśāstric debates amongst Mīmāṃsā and Navya-Nyāya trained Paṇḍitas that flourished in northern India did not extend to Tamil Nadu, Andhra Pradesh, or Kerala.[186]

Despite his critics' concerns, Colebrooke's dual appointment to the High Court and to the College of Fort William in 1801, ensured that his theory of schools of Hindu law—equal parts accurate and flawed—set the foundation for the academic study of Hindu law in the Company's colleges.[187] A string of editions and

[185] Rocher and Rocher, *The Making of Western Indology*, p. 115. For the resistance in Madras to Colebrooke's schools of law, see A. C. Burnell, *The Law of Partition and Succession: from the MS. Sanskrit Text of Varadarāja's Vyavahāranirnaya* (Mangalore: Stolz, 1872), pp. iii–viii.

[186] For the Madras School of Orientalism, see Donald Davis, 'Law in the Mirror of Language: The Madras School of Orientalism on Hindu Law', in *The Madras School of Orientalism: Producing Knowledge in Colonial South India*, ed. Thomas Trautman (Oxford: Oxford University Press, 2009), pp. 288–309.

[187] See Derrett, 'The British as Patrons', pp. 237–8 for a list of Dharmaśāstra texts on the curriculum of the College Fort William between 1821 and 1837: *Mānavadharmaśāstra*, *Mitākṣarā*, *Dāyabhāga*, *Dāyatattva*, *Dāyakramasaṃgraha* (of Śrīkṛṣṇa), and Raghunandana's other *Tattvas*.

translations of the principal texts of the various schools of Hindu law followed in the nineteenth century, and by 1864, the courts terminated the employment of Paṇḍita assistants because the significant body of translated Dharmaśāstra and case-law obviated the need for Paṇḍita informants.[188] Although a model of regional schools of Hindu law was, to some extent, justified in Bengal, Bihar, and Benares, the expansion of the 'Adālat system to Bombay and to Madras appears to have pressured Indologists into applying this model to other regions uncritically. In 1858, after the coalescence of the model of five schools of Hindu law, William Morley rejected false analogies to Islamic law, offering an alternative and more persuasive explanation for the idiosyncratic distinctions between the Benares, Maharashtra, and Dravida (along with its Andhra, Karnataka, and Dravida Proper sub-divisions) Schools of Law:

> Looking to the west and south of India, we find that the main distinction between the Benares, Maharashtra, and Dravida schools, is, in fact, rather a preference shewn by each respectively for some particular work as their authority of Law, than any real or important difference of doctrine. It is very probable that this preference for particular treatises arose originally, not so much from their actual, or even fancied, superiority over other works, as from the ignorance of the lawyers, practically, of the existence of authorities not generally current in their respective provinces, and from the fact that such law-books were, in most cases, first promulgated in the very districts in which they are now pre-eminent.[189]

The story of early Indology and its relationship to the construction of Anglo-Indian schools of Hindu law involves an intermingling of native Dharmaśāstric appellations and colonial geography. Hastings' Judicial Plan of 1772 (and Cornwallis' Plan of 1793) required the Company's 'Adālat courts to adjudicate intra-Hindu disputes according to Dharmaśāstra. At the onset of the project, the Paṇḍitas of Bengal, Bihar, and Benares most certainly divided themselves into different jurisprudential schools—due to the unique intellectual history of ownership and inheritance traced in this monograph. As time wore on—and as the Cornwallis System expanded to other presidencies and to more territories—the congruence between pre-colonial Dharmaśāstric schools of jurisprudence and Anglo-Indian jurisdictional boundaries declined. One cannot, however, go so far as A.C. Burnell, who retorted that:

[188] Rocher, 'Weaving Knowledge', p. 71.

[189] William Morley, *The Administration of Justice in British India; Its Past History and Present State* (London: Williams and Norgate, 1858), pp. 200–2. This helps to account for the prominence of the *Vyavahāramayūkha* in Bombay. When preparing his translation of this text, Henry Borradaile, a civil servant in Bombay Presidency, notes that he worked with 'the four Shastrees, of the [presidency's] Sudur Udalut' and that one of Nilakaṇṭha's descendents, 'Huru Bhuttu Kasseekur', 'resided till very lately' in Pune.

> As all the digests proceed according to one system of interpretation, viz., the Mimamsa, the different conclusions at which the authors often arrive, are to be traced to differences in their interpretation of original texts from Smrtis, not to local usage; and the distinction of 'schools of law' is (besides being entirely strange to the books themselves) quite meaningless. The Daya-bhaga has long been studied at Nava-dvipa, and commentaries written on it there, so Colebrooke could safely write of the Bengal as opposed to the Benares school where the Mitaxara was studied and annotated, but the addition made by subsequent writers of Andhra, Dravidian, and other schools, is without foundation and useless. Except the Daya-bhaga and its commentaries, all the other treatises on law are mere recasts of the Mitaxara and the Smrti-Candrika, and written entirely without reference to local peculiarities.[190]

The Paṇḍitas of Mithilā and of Navadvīpa drew more on Navya-Nyāya than on Mīmāṃsā in their understanding of ownership and inheritance and they saw themselves as operating within distinctive schools of thought that were defined, at least in part, by the particular locality (if not the local customs) of their participants. While Vācaspatimiśra and other Maithila logicians declined to extend their philosophical theories of ownership (which were, generally, opposed to Mīmāṃsā theories of ownership) to the realm of Dharmaśāstra *overtly*, Navadvīpan Dharmaśāstrins developed a strongly interlocking corpus of philosophical and legal positions concerning ownership and inheritance. Furthermore, the Mahārāṣṭrian Paṇḍitas of early modern Vārāṇasī cast *both* Maithila and Gauḍa Paṇḍitas as 'eastern' opponents of a 'southern' Dharmaśāstra/Mīmāṃsā nexus. Burnell appears to have been justified in rejecting Andhra, Dravidian, Karnataka, and Maharashtrian schools of law, but one need not throw out the baby of Jones and Colebrooke's early work with the bathwater of Colebrooke's later work and that of his successors.

I would ask the reader to return to the map on the inside jacket of this book. It is a modified version of one that appears in Standish Grady's 1868 account of the Hindu law of inheritance.[191] Britain's colonial geography was, to quote Lauren Benton, 'politically fragmented; legally differentiated; and encased in irregular, porous, and sometimes undefined borders'.[192] The evolution of Anglo-Indian schools of Hindu law, with their unusual, often ill-defined boundaries, reflects 'the progression of British power in India... [wherein] Imperial authority had spread to the interior of India from coastal enclaves at Bombay, Madras, and

[190] A. C. Burnell, *Dāyavibhāga: The Law of Inheritance Translated from the Unpublished Sanskrit text of the Vyavahārakāṇḍa of the Mādhavīya Commentary on the Parāśarasmṛti* (Madras: Higginbotham, 1868), pp. xiv–xv.

[191] Standish Grady, *A Treatise on The Hindoo Law* (London: Wildy and Sons, 1868).

[192] Lauren Benton, *A Search for Sovereignty: Law and Geography in European Empires, 1400–1900* (New York: Cambridge University Press, 2010), p. 2.

Calcutta'.[193] The Mithilā School, philosophically robust and legally thin, sits alone in a diminutive enclave around Darbhanga, the capitol of the Khaṇḍavalā dynasty, an idiosyncratic province surrounded by Bengal.

The Bengal School flourishes around Navadvīpa in Bengal proper (and in Assam), but the other provinces of the Bengal Presidency (Orissa and Benares, for example), which do not share the Bengali language (or the predilections of its Paṇḍitas), fall within the vast remit of the Benares School and the *Mitākṣarā*. The territorial boundaries of the Bombay Presidency—and the Marāṭhī language of the erstwhile Marāṭhā Confederacy—create an otherwise inexplicable distinction between Vārāṇasī (the centre of the early modern Bhaṭṭas' influence) and Mahārāṣṭra (the ancestral homeland whose intellectual heritage the Bhaṭṭas defended so vociferously in the seventeenth century). The Madras Presidency, with its implausible, language-derived subdivisions of a postulated Dravida School, traces the furthest, limits of Colebrooke's grand notion of schools of Hindu law. Recall that Kamalākarabhaṭṭa and his family framed themselves and their works as being part of a broad, 'Drāviḍa' grouping of Brāhmaṇas (in competition with a broad, eastern grouping of Brāhmaṇas). The map brings into critical relief the heuristic value of a schools-based approach to Dharmaśāstra: it reveals the initial durability of indigenous juridical identities and their ineluctable subordination to 'the gradual formation of a single legal framework for [Britain's Indian] territory'.[194]

193 Ibid., p. 240.

194 Ibid.

Conclusion

Market Governance, (Neo)Liberalism, and the Future of Dharmaśāstra in the Twenty-First Century

By roughly 1825 (the date of the publication of Sir Thomas Strange's *Elements of Hindu Law*), the courts of the Bengal, Bombay, and Madras Presidencies enforced Colebrooke's system of schools of Hindu personal law with the assistance of native Paṇḍitas.[1] This system involved enormous variation. A Hindu family who moved from one region to another would remain under the jurisdiction of the school of law of their place of origin. Furthermore, the various schools of Hindu law were enforced differently in the Bengal, Bombay, and Madras Presidencies.[2] With the passage of the Hindu Code Bills in 1955–6, that diversity gave way to uniformity.

This conclusion charts the gradual homogenization of Hindu law, between 1825 and the present, against the backdrop of three related trends in the legal and political history of the Indian subcontinent: (1) the privileging of precedent (*stare decisis* and *communis error facit ius*) and statute over native interpretations of Hindu law (culminating in the dismissal of court Paṇḍitas in 1864 and in the Hindu Code Bills of 1955–6 respectively); (2) the development of a 'modern', liberal market economy (particularly in the latter half of the nineteenth century); and (3) the fashioning of flattened, politicized Hindu and Muslim public identities. The radical (if ostensibly progressive) *uniformity* of Hindu personal law (and of 'Hindus' more generally) supplanted the radical *particularity* of the Sanskrit jurisprudence of ownership and inheritance (and its varied notions of subjectivity) alongside a concomitant recasting of the modern state as the guarantor of individuals' rights and of a standardized, largely free market practice.

The Dharmaśāstric jurisprudence of ownership and inheritance, however, offers a productive, indigenously Indian venue for disrupting the universality of India's liberal market paradigm (and of property specifically) and for viewing 'Hindu' as a vastly more diverse legal category. The principles of the Sanskrit jurisprudence of ownership and inheritance—of collective ownership by extended

[1] For the Elphinstone Code, see William Morley, *The Administration of Justice in British India: Its Past History and Present State* (London: Williams and Norgate, 1858), pp. 102–7.

[2] J. Duncan Derrett, *Introduction to Modern Hindu Law* (Oxford: Oxford University Press, 1963), pp. 25–9.

Ownership and Inheritance in Sanskrit Jurisprudence. Christopher Fleming, Oxford University Press (2020).

DOI: 10.1093/oso/9780198852377.003.0006

networks (of families, temples, and education institutions) and of proprietary rights as circumscribed by various entitlements to ritual rites—challenge the principles of personal property, individual subjectivity, secularism, and equality before the law which lie at the heart of (neo)liberal political economy.

From Paṇḍitas to Precedents (1816–64)

Colebrooke's critics' complaints notwithstanding, 'the regional differentiation that Colebrooke had established [in his *Two Treatises* and other works] remained paramount' in the early nineteenth century.[3] Once these schools (and the juridical authority of the Bengal, Bombay, and Madras Presidencies) were established, however, colonial jurists shifted their focus from enforcing 'as faithful an application of original textual and customary sources as seemed feasible, to foregrounding [judicial] precedents'.[4] Until 1864, colonial courts continued to consult Paṇḍitas, who crafted new treatises and who compiled letters of judgment (vyavasthās), but,

> The courts used less and less the recent miscellaneous works [from Dharmaśāstrins] and relied more upon the ancient works which had been translated. The pandit as a professor of a living science was rejected for the more or less fossilized treatises which would head the pandits' lists of references.[5]

Furthermore, the accumulation of judicial judgments, recorded in, for example, Strange's *Notes of Cases in the Court of the Recorder and in the Supreme Court of Judicature at Madras* (1816) and *Elements of Hindu Law* (1825), Henry Borradaile's *Reports of Civil Causes Adjudged by the Court of the Sudur Udlut, for the Presidency of Bombay* (1825), and William Macnaghten's *Reports of Cases Determined in the Court of Sudder Dewanny Adawlut* (1827–35) and *Principles and Precedents of Hindu Law* (1828–9), along with the introduction of the common-law principles of *stare decisis* (stand by prior decisions) and *communis error facit ius* (a common error makes law), ensured that 'Anglo-Hindu law amounted to an Anglo disposition of Hindu law'.[6]

Along with *stare decisis*, the treatment of Hindu law as a fixed textual phenomenon located in *Dharmaśāstra*—rather than in custom, in Paṇḍita-jurists, or in ad hoc tribunals—ensured that innovation would come from *outside* the indigenous

[3] Rosane Rocher, 'The Creation of Anglo-Hindu Law', in *Hinduism and Law: An Introduction*, ed. Timothy Lubin, Donald Davis, and Jayanth K. Krishnan (Cambridge: Cambridge University Press, 2010), pp. 79–88, 84–5.

[4] Ibid., p. 85.

[5] See J. Duncan Derrett, *Religion, Law and the State in India* (Delhi: Oxford University Press, 1999), p. 255. For a list of late Sanskrit works, see ibid., pp. 270–3.

[6] Ibid., p. 86. See also Alan Gledhill, 'The Influence of Common Law and Equity on Hindu Law since 1800', *The International and Comparative Law Quarterly* 3.4 (1954): 576–603.

jurisprudential tradition.[7] Although early orientalists were justified in postulating the existence of a diversity of regionally-specific schools of Dharmaśāstric jurisprudence, the orientalists' forensic, text-historical approach to Dharmaśāstra's legal utility effectively capped the tradition's internal development. Once the Anglo-Indian courts shifted their search for authentic knowledge about Hindu law from the creation of new Dharmaśāstra digests (such as Jagannātha Tarkapañcānana's *Vivādabhaṅgārṇava*) to the translation and interpretation of a finite set of existing Dharmaśāstra treatises (a departure best marked by Colebrooke's 1810 translation of the *Mitākṣarā* and *Dāyabhāga*), the discipline of traditional Hindu jurisprudence—including the arsenal of interpretive techniques developed in Mīmāṃsā, Navya-Nyāya, and Vyākaraṇa—became an historical enterprise which could, at best, account for the intellectual configuration of Dharmaśāstra roughly *circa* 1800.[8]

Innovation and liberal reform to Hindu law came through legislative acts and judicial intervention. In 1834, the first Law Commission of India began its appointed task of recommending various statutory reforms to the Indian legal system.[9] Building on presidency-specific regulations (Regulation VII, 1832 of the Bengal Code, for example), the Company passed India-wide reforms including the Caste Disabilities Removal Act (1850), and the Hindu Widows' Remarriage Act (1856).[10] Judicial intervention came in the form of Justice Elijah Impey's (Chief Justice of the Supreme Court of Juridicature at Fort William and of the Ṣadr Dīwānī 'Adālat) introduction of 'justice, equity, and good conscience' via the Administration of Justice Regulation (Bengal) in 1781.[11] The criteria of justice, equity, and good conscience ensured that courts could, and would, separate enforceable 'rules of positive law' from merely pious 'religious or moral precepts'

[7] Of course, 'custom and usage' became important sources of legal knowledge—sometimes more so than the Dharmaśāstra—during and after the colonial period. See for example Neeladri Bhattacharya, 'Remaking Custom: the Discourse and Practice of Colonial Codification', in *Tradition, Dissent and Ideology: Essay in Honour of Romila Thapar*, ed. R. Champakalakshmi and S. Gopal (New Delhi: Oxford University Press, 1996), pp. 20–51; Rachel Sturman, 'Custom and Human Value in the Debates on Hindu Marriage', in *Government of Social Life in Colonial India: Liberalism, Religious Law and Women's Rights* (Cambridge: Cambridge University Press, 2012), pp. 148–95; John Mayne, *A Treatise on Hindu Law and Usage* (Madras: Higginbotham, 1878).

[8] See Chapter 4 for the *Vivādabhaṅgārṇava*. The case of Ishwar Chandra Vidyasagar's 1856 *Vidhavavivāha*, a Dharmaśāstric digest that advocated widow remarriage forms a notable exception to this statement. Ishwar Chandra Vidyasagar was a principal at the Sanskrit College in Bengal at the time. See Davis, 'Modern Legal Framework', and Brian Hatcher, *Vidyasagar: The Life and After-life of an Eminent Indian* (New Delhi: Routledge, 2014).

[9] For the Law Commission of India, see George Rankin, *Background to Indian Law* (Cambridge: Cambridge University Press, 1946), pp. 22–45.

[10] Derrett, *Religion, Law and the State*, p. 327. For the text of these Acts, see Derrett, *Introduction to Modern Hindu Law*, pp. 619–22.

[11] See, for example, Ludo Rocher, 'Hindu Law and Religion: Where to Draw the Line', in *Studies in Hindu Law and Dharmaśāstra*, ed. Donald Davis (London: Anthem, 2014), pp. 83–102, 83, 100; Ludo Rocher, 'Indian Response to Anglo-Hindu Law', in *Studies in Hindu Law and Dharmaśāstra*, ed. Donald Davis (London: Anthem, 2014), pp. 634–42 for several cases in which the equity paradigm was invoked. Also see Rocher, 'The Creation of Anglo-Hindu Law', p. 87; and Derrett, 'Justice, Equity, and Good Conscience', in *Changing Law in Developing Countries*, ed. J. Anderson (London: George Allen & Unwin, 1963), pp. 114–54. Justice, Equity, and Good Conscience was extended to the Bombay Presidency in Section 26 of the Regulation of 1827.

in an idiosyncratic, *ad hoc* fashion (although indebted to culturally-specific British notions of equity).[12] The telos of the use of justice, equity, and good conscience dovetailed with that of piecemeal statutory reform of Hindu law: both attempted to maximize the property rights—and commensurate political autonomy—of individual Hindus by freeing property from the constraints of religious restrictions.[13] In essence, the reform of Hindu law fragmented the proprietary and ritual connections of the joint Hindu family—and the commensurate legal disabilities of women—and replaced the joint family with autonomous, right-and-capital bearing individuals.

Between the Hands Invisible and Dead (1864–1956)

In 1858, the British Crown took over the direct administration of colonial India. In 1861, Parliament passed the Indian High Courts Act, amalgamating the Crown's Supreme Courts of Juridicature (in Calcutta, Bombay, and Madras) and the Company's Ṣadr Dīwānī ʿAdālats into a series of High Courts.[14] In 1864, Act XI dismissed Qazis and Paṇḍitas as court officers and transferred juridical knowledge of Dharmaśāstra and Fiqh (Islamic jurisprudence) to the High Courts.[15] At this point, '*dharmaśāstra* as a living and responsible science in matters which might come before a court of law died'.[16] In the course of time, colonial jurists framed Dharmaśāstra and Hindu personal law as an ossified, private, and *cultural* constraint on the free, public, liberal exchange of capital—a dead hand strangling its cousin, the invisible hand. As the colonial state sought to standardize commercial law, 'the foundational assumptions of liberal thought came to pervade personal law, with the capacity to hold property and equal rights to property coming to signify autonomy, equality, and full legal subjecthood'.[17] This ushered in the gradual codification, liberalization, and homogenization of Hindu personal law through statutory acts.

In *Stages of Capital*, Ritu Birla summarizes the way in which the Hindu Undivided Family (and its patterns of property-holding) became an object of colonial 'market governance:'

> In colonial India, where an ideology of free trade legitimized an economic system intended to profit Britain, law directed at the free circulation of capital referred first and foremost to the releasing of capital from the binds of tradition and customary codes. But despite these concerns, new legal measures . . . did not

[12] Rocher, 'Hindu Law and Religion', p. 83.

[13] Rachel Sturman, 'Marriage and Family in Colonial Hindu Law', in *Hinduism and Law: An Introduction*, ed. Timothy Lubin, Donald Davis, and Jayanth K. Krishnan (Cambridge: Cambridge University Press, 2010), pp. 89–104, 90.

[14] For the Indian High Courts Act, see M. P. Jain, *Outlines of Indian Legal History*, 6th edn (Bombay: Tripathi, 2006), pp. 407–29.

[15] Rocher, 'The Creation of Anglo-Hindu Law', p. 83; Derrett, *Religion, Law and the State*, p. 250.

[16] Ibid. [17] Sturman, 'Marriage and Family', p. 90.

> simply render indigenous market norms unilaterally illegal by abolishing them summarily. Even as statutes and jurisprudence established universal models for modern market practice, they regularly insisted on establishing exceptions for vernacular capitalism...kinship-based firms [especially the joint-Hindu family] were placed under the purview of the personal law that governed what were considered 'private concerns...' colonial authorities regulated vernacular capitalism exactly by coding it as a rarefied cultural formation.[18]

In Birla's estimation, Hindu (and Muslim) personal law typifies the paradoxical position wherein 'reinventing living practices as petrified mandates, the "private" domain thus emerged, not as a site of cultural protection, but rather as a space that enabled new techniques of sovereign regulation'.[19]

A series of statutory legal reforms, enacted between 1861 and 1950, highlights the way in which 'market governance produced and managed two general modes of community: state, civil society, and market, on the one hand (as *Gesellschaft*), and family, caste, and culture (as *Gemeinschaft*)'.[20] The property relations of the Hindu Undivided Family occupied an ambiguous position in late colonial market governance. The 1882 Companies Act provided a standard with which to distinguish commercial activities, such as limited liability partnerships 'that benefited the public and produced the wealth of the colony (and proto-nation)', from customary, filial systems of caste and religion 'that produced wealth for private consumption'.[21] The Hindu Undivided Family, as a profit-oriented firm that was coded as 'cultural' in colonial law:

> defied the public/private dichotomy in its very liminality as an institution that produced a public exchange of credit and goods based on marriage and kinship, and predicated marriage and kinship on the necessities of credit and trade.[22]

Although the Hindu Undivided Family was viewed as an indigenous (and defective) foil to the commercial partnerships of the 1882 Companies Act, it was subject, via the Indian Income Tax Act of 1886, to assessment based on 'analogies between the HUF/family firm, on the one hand, and the public limited liability company on the other'.[23] Coding the Hindu Undivided Family as a private partnership 'which distorted market ethics' relied on the existence of proper public companies as a standard of comparison—the invisible hand pulling a frozen cultural institution towards liberal reform.[24]

Even as British notions of the invisible hand pulled the legal model of the Hindu Undivided Family towards liberal reform, British notions of mortmain

[18] Ritu Birla, *Stages of Capital: Law, Culture, and Market Governance in Late Colonial India* (Durham, NC: Duke University Press, 2009), p. 5. Birla defines 'market governance' (pp. 22–3) as: 'the production of "the economy" as an object of governance, but also the utopic production of "the market" as an ethico-political sovereign: that is, as a model for social relations'.

[19] Ibid., p. 14. [20] Ibid., p. 27. [21] Ibid., pp. 52–3. [22] Ibid., p. 52.

[23] Ibid., p. 56. [24] For mortmain and its contentious history in England, see ibid., pp. 68–70.

(from the Latin *manus mortus*), the 'dead hand' drew certain proprietary features of the Hindu Undivided Family into the legal domain of charitable *res extra commercium* (non-circulating property held tightly in trust according to the pious intentions of a founder).[25] Generally speaking, perpetuities, restrictions on making an estate inalienable perpetually, were and are prohibited in Anglo-India law.[26] The exceptions in India were religious and charitable endowments, particularly those made to deities (devasva), in which joint family property held by a deity was managed by family members who acted in a position similar to that of a trustee.[27] Just as the Companies Act of 1882 failed to capture much of the nuance of the Hindu Undivided Family firm, the Indian Trusts Act of 1882 coded religious endowments as 'trusts' 'for future legal reference' even as it framed them as essentially deficient forms of trust.[28] In the late nineteenth century, colonial 'jurists asked whether joint family coparcenary property was *inherently* a form of perpetual holding. [and] if so, could the Hindu endowment be a legitimate alienation from joint family property'.[29] Commercial and trusts law, once codified in late colonial India, served as standards of comparison, whereby Hindu personal law, notwithstanding its perceived resistance to 'proper' public/private distinctions, could be brought gradually into alignment with a liberal market economy.

Although the standardization of Hindu personal law resulted in 'the expansion of [higher caste] patriarchal practices regarding marriage, divorce, widowhood, and the like to lower-caste communities that had never practiced them', statutory reforms, such as the Hindu Gains of Learning Act (1930), resulted in a Hindu personal law that 'increasingly came to treat... [Hindu] men as autonomous subjects of the state'.[30] In the case of women, 'as caste Hindu men were increasingly treated as autonomous property holders' the property rights of Hindu daughters and widows 'took on an asymptotic quality... approaching but never quite attaining the legal position of Hindu men'.[31]A series of acts, including the Hindu Inheritance Removal of Disabilities Act (1928), the Hindu Gains of Learning Act (1930), and the Hindu Women's Rights to Property Act (1937), sought to bring Hindu personal law into alignment with the free market, but that level of reform would not occur until after independence.[32]

Table C.1 outlines the history of the pan-Indian codification of commercial and personal law. The Hindu Undivided Family appears in the middle column, caught

[25] Ibid., p. 89. [26] Ibid., p. 90.

[27] For devasva, see Günther-Dietz Sontheimer, 'Religious Endowments in India: The Juristic Personality of Hindu Deities', in ed. Heidrun Brückner, Anne Feldhaus, and Aditya Malik. , *Essays on Religion, Literature and Law* (New Delhi: Manohar, 2004), pp. 15–68. For fiduciary relations in Anglo-Hindu jurisprudence, see Vikramaditya Khanna, 'Fiduciary Principles in Indian Law', in *The Oxford Handbook of Fiduciary* Law, ed. Evan Criddle, Paul Miller, and Rober Sitkoff (New York: Oxford University Press, 2019), pp. 623–42. For Hindu trusts, see B. L. Mukherjea, *The Hindu Law of Religious and Charitable Trusts*, 2nd edn (Calcutta: Eastern Law House, 1962).

[28] Birla, *Stages of Capital*, p. 82. [29] Ibid., p. 90.

[30] Sturman, 'Marriage and Family', p. 98. [31] Ibid., p. 100.

[32] Derrett, *Religion, Law, and the State*, p. 327. See Derrett, *Introduction to Modern Hindu Law*, pp. 617–31, for earlier acts regarding Hindu personal law.

Table C.1 The Hindu Undivided Family between the Hands Invisible and Dead (1833–1961)

<table>
<tr><td>Commercial Law and Taxation (The Invisible Hand)</td><td>Hindu Personal Law</td><td>Charity and Trusts Law (The Dead Hand)</td></tr>
<tr><td colspan="3">Privy Council Established as Court of Appeal (1833) First Indian Law Commission (1834)</td></tr>
<tr><td></td><td>Caste Disabilities Removal Act (1850)</td><td></td></tr>
<tr><td colspan="3">Second Indian Law Commission (1853)</td></tr>
<tr><td></td><td>Hindu Widows' Remarriage Act (1856)</td><td></td></tr>
<tr><td>Code of Civil Procedure (1859)
Law of Limitation (1859)
Income Tax Act (1860)</td><td>Advent of Crown Rule (1858)</td><td></td></tr>
<tr><td colspan="3">Indian High Courts Act (1861) Third Indian Law Commission (1861)</td></tr>
<tr><td>Income Tax Act (1860)</td><td>Indian Succession Act (1865)</td><td>Religious Endowments Act (1863)</td></tr>
<tr><td>Companies Act (1866)
Contract Act (1872)</td><td>Hindu Wills Act (1870)</td><td></td></tr>
<tr><td colspan="3">Fourth Indian Law Commission (1879)</td></tr>
<tr><td>Transfer of Property Act (1882)
Companies Act (1882)</td><td>Probate and Administration Act (1881)</td><td>Indian Trusts Act (1882)</td></tr>
<tr><td>Income Tax Act (1886)</td><td>Hindu Disposition of Property Act (1916)</td><td>Charitable Endowments Act (1890)</td></tr>
<tr><td></td><td>Indian Succession Act (1925)</td><td>Charitable and Religious Trusts Act (1920)</td></tr>
<tr><td></td><td>Hindu Inheritance (Removal of Disabilities) Act (1928)</td><td></td></tr>
<tr><td></td><td>Hindu Inheritance Act (1929)</td><td></td></tr>
<tr><td>Indian Partnership Act (1932)</td><td>Hindu Gains of Learning Act (1930)</td><td></td></tr>
<tr><td></td><td>Hindu Women's Rights to Property Acts (1937, 1938, and 1940)</td><td></td></tr>
<tr><td colspan="3">Indian Independence (1947)
Constitution Comes into Effect (1950)
First Independent Law Commission (1955)</td></tr>
<tr><td></td><td>Hindu Marriage Act (1955)</td><td></td></tr>
<tr><td>Income Tax Act (1961)</td><td>Hindu Succession Act (1956),
Hindu Minority and Guardianship Act (1956),
Adoptions and Maintenance Act (1956)</td><td></td></tr>
</table>

as it were between the hands invisible and dead—between the public circulation of capital and the private hoarding of non-circulating wealth. As Birla would put it, Hindu law was caught between 'the utilitarian call to economic progress on the one hand, and the paternalistic imperative of cultural preservation on the other'.

A Neo-Liberal Epitaph for the Rishis

In 1954, on the eve of the Indian parliament's enactment of a series of comprehensive reforms of Hindu personal law, Prime Minister Nehru told the Lok Sabha that colonialism had suppressed the natural evolution of Hindu law.[33] Nehru argued that the only feasible remedy to the 'fossilized', dysfunctional condition of Hindu law was statutory reform.[34]

The Indian parliament passed a series of landmark reforms of Hindu law between 1955 and 1956. The 'Hindu Code Bill' 'was a composite body of laws, made up of distinct sets of legal enactment—the Hindu Marriage Act passed in 1955, and the Hindu Succession Act, the Hindu Minority and Guardianship Act and the Hindu Adoption and Maintenance Act, all of which were passed in 1956'.[35] The effects of the Hindu Code Bill were legion: women were granted greater property rights in their paternal estates, the rules regarding divorce, adoption and marriage were liberalized, and the legal cohesiveness of the joint family estate—the coparcenary—was greatly diminished.[36] The rich diversity of schools of Hindu law—so characteristic of pre-colonial and colonial Hindu law—were elided by a universal, ostensibly progressive body of personal law which applied to those Indian citizens who were neither Muslim, Christian, Jewish, or Parsi. The end result was, as Derrett notes, a system of law that "repudiates in an implied or explicit manner the values and ethos of the ancient background" and that 'has little to do with Hinduism by any possible definition of that term'.[37] Derrett notes that modern Hindu law:

[33] J. Duncan Derrett, 'The British Administration of Hindu Law', *Comparative Studies in Society and History* 4.1 (1961): 10–52, 47, fn 183. Cf. P. V. Kāṇe, *A History of Dharmaśāstra*, vol. 3, 2nd edn (Pune: Bhandarkar Oriental Research Institute, 1973), pp. 820–3.

[34] Of course, some jurists viewed the British influence on Hindu personal law as a positive, progressive development or sought to frame elements of Anglo jurisprudence as inherently India. See S. Venkaṭarāman, 'Influence of Common Law and Equity on the Personal Law of the Hindus', *Revista del Instituto de Derecho Comparado* 8–9 (1957): 156–79; and Rocher, 'Indian Response to Anglo-Hindu Law', pp. 638–42.

[35] Rochona Majumdar, 'Marriage, Family, and Property in India: The Hindu Succession Act of 1956', *South Asian History and Culture* 1.3 (2010): 397–415, 399.

[36] For an overview of the changes ushered in by the Hindu Code Bill, see J. D. Derrett, 'The Codification of Hindu Law', in *Religion, Law, and the State in India* (London: Faber and Faber, 1968), pp. 321–51, and S. V. Gupte, *Hindu Law of Succession* (Bombay: Tripathi, 1972).

[37] Derrett, 'Codification', pp. 321 and 324, citing M. Anantanārāyanan.

> is Hindu in name and contains an occasional and embarrassing reminder of its predecessor, much as a ruinous but ancient building may be pulled down and replaced with a modern structure, which retains the same street-number, some panelling, a decorative window, or even a quaint chimney pot from the old house, alleging a continuity with the past which may appeal to sentiment, but does not deceive the eye.[38]

The uniform Hindu Code Bill constituted the culmination of two trends in colonial and post-colonial Indian social history: (1) the codification, liberalization, and 'modernization' of Hindu personal law; and (2) the creation of a homogenized, racialized, and politically expedient demographic category of 'Hindu'. Contemporary scholars, particularly Donald Davis and Rachel Sturman have argued, persuasively, that the first trend began in 1772 with Hastings' 'Judicial Plan'.[39]

Derrett notes that the reformers, 'large earners . . . jealous of the keenness of their agnates . . . to share their property to the partial or total exclusion of their own spouse, daughter, cognatic relations or friends', 'desire[d] to make property freely transferable' and to 'abolish rules that smacked of antiquity'.[40] Derrett attributes the liberalizing, individuating telos of the Hindu Code Bills to 'an emerging partly-westernized class of well-to-do people, which was to all intents and purposes a caste . . . [and whose members] wanted to intermarry with Muslims similarly placed, not to mention Hindus of equal influence but lower caste'.[41] Of course, for Derrett's cosmopolitan, nuclear-family focused, propertied elite:

> their opponents, the 'orthodox', were people who did not need to contemplate intercaste marriage and suspected the motives of those who did. Religion was attempted to be used as a means of preventing what influential society wanted, and it might have succeeded had not the previous custodians of the Hindu law made out of it, bona fide, so appalling a system, from which anyone would have been glad to escape who cared for his country's prestige.[42]

Many of these reforms are laudable, particularly the full enfranchisement of women, who may now serve as trustee (kartṛ) of the Hindu Undivided Family's

[38] J. Duncan Derrett, 'Statutory Amendments of the Personal Law of Hindus Since Indian Independence', *The American Journal of Comparative Law* 7.3 (1958): 380–93, 382. The final disjuncture of statutory Hindu law from its Dharmaśāstric roots prompted Derrett to pen *The Death of a Marriage Law: Epitaph for the Rishis* (Durham: N.C. Press, 1978).

[39] Donald Davis, 'Modern Legal Framework', in *Brill's Encyclopedia of Hinduism*, ed. K. Jacobsen, H. Basu, A. Malinar, and Vasudha Narayanan (Brill Online, 2014), available from: https://referenceworks.brillonline.com/entries/brill-s-encyclopedia-of-hinduism/modern-legal-framework-COM_9000000166; Sturman, 'Marriage and Family', pp. 89–104.

[40] Derrett, 'Codification', pp. 338–9.

[41] Ibid., p. 348.

[42] Ibid., p. 350.

coparcenary property.[43] At the same time, however, these reforms were accompanied by a disintegration of the joint family (in favour of nuclear families), pre-existing forms of ownership and inheritance (both the paternal coparcenary and maternal strīdhana), and the formal role of religious rites (saṃskāras) in structuring the legal status of individuals.[44] In essence, equality before the law (at least amongst those subject to Hindu law) resulted in a conspicuously homogenous understanding of property, family, and religion—at the cost of the rich plurality of family structures and forms of ownership articulated previously in Sanskrit jurisprudence.

The flattening of Hindu law coincided with a flattening of Hinduism as a religious and ethnic category—alongside similar developments in Islamic personal law.[45] The colonial antecedents of Advaitavedānta's transformation into the representative spiritual tradition of a unified, modern bourgeois Hinduism have been traced in a series of works in recent decades.[46] The jurisdictional category of Hinduism played a decisive role in these transformations. As Davis notes:

> modern Hindu law has expressed in legal form a set of rules and practices that has come to shape the way in which many middle- and upper-class Hindu families understand the 'Hindu' view of inheritance, adoption, marriage, and the like. In other words, for middle- and upper-class Hindu individuals and communities who regularly interact with official governmental institutions and who rely on their predictable legal safeguards, modern Hindu law partially informs who they are as Hindus. Official Hindu law thus protects a restricted sense of Hindu identity and practice that its legislative form helped to create.[47]

[43] For women's progress in obtaining full rights in comparcenary property, see Shivani Singhal, 'Women as Coparceners: Ramifications of the Amended Section 6 of the Hindu Succession Act, 1956', *Student Bar Review* 19.1 (2007): 50–67. See, ***Danamma Suman Surpur vs Amar*** **[(2018) 3 SCC 343]** where the court ruled that the Hindu Succession Act (Amendment) of 2005, in which 'it is the very ***factum of birth*** in a coparcenary that creates the coparcenary, therefore sons and daughters of a coparcener become coparceners by ***virtue of birth***', affords daughters coparcenery rights even if they were born before the passage of the 2005 amendment.

[44] For recent developments in Hindu personal law, see Werner Menski, *Modern Indian Family Law* (London: Routledge, 2013).

[45] Eleanor Newbigin, 'The Codification of Personal Law and Secular Citizenship: Revisiting the History of Law Reform in Late Colonial India', *Indian Economic and Social History Review* 46.1 (2009): 83–104.

[46] See for example, Anand Venkatkrishnan, 'Mīmāṃsā, Vedānta, and the Bhakti Movement' (PhD Dissertation, Columbia University, 2015), pp. 235–7. Also see Brian Hatcher, *Bourgeois Hinduism, or the Faith of the Modern Vedantists: Rare Discourses from Early Colonial Bengal* (Oxford: Oxford University Press, 2008); Brian Hatcher, *Eclecticism and Modern Hindu Discourse* (New York: Oxford University Press, 1999), and Wilhelm Halbfass, *Philology and Confrontation: Paul Hacker on Traditional and Modern Vedanta* (Albany, NY: State University of New York Press, 1995). For a view to the contrary, see Andrew Nicholson, *Unifying Hinduism: Philosophy and Identity in Indian Intellectual History* (New York: Columbia, 2010).

[47] Davis, 'Modern Legal Framework'.

Davis's argument doesn't recapitulate the fashionable fallacy that colonial categories of law and religion created Hinduism as such.[48] Rather, as with Vedānta, the colonial encounter led to a reformulation, or a recalibration of Hinduism. Davis explains that,

> Safeguarding religious identity and practice may have been the ostensible historical reason behind the colonial creation of personal law systems, but modern Hindu law and the HCB have primarily contributed to the creation and protection of a narrow, homogenized political Hindu identity for the modern world.[49]

The broad implications of this narrow identity—with its attendant 'essential religious practices'—for Indian secularism and Hindu nationalist (Hindutva) politics need not be rehearsed, other than to note that it is the formal administrative apparatus of the state (in the form of the Supreme Court) that acts as the privileged arbiter of what is and what is not 'essentially' Hindu.[50]

Out of the Waiting Room of History: Dharmaśāstra and Legal Pluralism

Modern courts' Hindu law judgments contain plenty of Dharmaśāstric 'window dressing'—stray comments from various Dharmaśāstras which have the effect of giving a Dharmaśāstric veneer to a decision reached through statute or binding precedent.[51] These bits and bobbles aside, Dharmaśāstric jurisprudence—the use of the panoply of interpretive techniques to analyse an authoritative body of smṛtis according to the broad conventions of regional commentarial schools—has been relegated to 'the waiting room of history'.[52] One might read Raghunandana Bhaṭṭācārya, Kamalākarabhaṭṭa, or even Jagannātha Tarkapañcānana's writings as evidence for the essence or the history of Indian jurisprudence, but these jurists, like India's great philosophers, are 'not at all considered contemporaries in the way that,

[48] For one such example, see Brian Pennington, *Was Hinduism Invented?: Britons, Indians, and the Colonial Construction of Religion* (Oxford: Oxford University Press, 2005). Of course, Davis does make such an argument with regard to the existence of pre-colonial schools of Dharmaśāstra.

[49] Davis, 'Modern Legal Framework'.

[50] For Indian secularism and its discontents, see Rajeev Bhargava (ed.), *Secularism and its Critics* (Delhi: Oxford University Press, 1998). Also see Smita Narula, 'Law and Hindu Nationalist Movements', in *Hinduism and Law: An Introduction*, ed. Timothy Lubin, Donald Davis, and Jayanth K. Krishnan (Cambridge: Cambridge University Press, 2010), pp. 234–51. In general, the Supreme Court has tended to view Hinduism as a broad, unitary category (to the detriment of various sectarian communities' claims to a non-Hindu status) with an intrinsic ethnic component.

[51] Davis, 'Modern Legal Framework'. See also R. W. Lariviere, 'Justices and Paṇḍitas: Some Ironies in Contemporary Readings of the Hindu Legal Past', *Journal of Asian Studies* 48.4 (1989): 757–69.

[52] Dipesh Chakrabarty, *Provincializing Europe: Postcolonial Thought and Historical Difference* (Princeton, NJ: Princeton University Press, 2000), p. 8. Cf. Venkatkrishnan, Mīmāṃsā, Vedānta, and the Bhakti Movement', 25.

say, Hegel or Marx has become indispensable to thinking about modern democratic politics'.[53]

It is salutary to remember that, until the courts' shift from Paṇḍitas to precedents in the early nineteenth century, Dharmaśāstric jurisprudence was very much a substantive, if unequal, conversation partner with European jurisprudence. Traditional Paṇḍitas including Jagannātha Tarkapañcānana and Bālambhaṭṭa Pāyaguṇḍe actively recalibrated the śāstric arguments of their forefathers in conjunction with British orientalists—whose singular obsessions with uniformity, concision, and consensus no doubt seemed antithetical to the dialogical nature of śāstric intellectualism. Of course, the reform of Hindu law along modern liberal standards—laudable in its efforts to eliminate the graded and often deplorable inequalities enshrined in Dharmaśāstra texts and to foster economic growth through freeing property from the constraints of the joint family—eliminated legal pluralism.

While bemoaning the homogenization of Hindu law, Derrett introduces a possibility, that:

> Without stare decisis, indeed, internal developments within the śāstra (while it lived) were possible. The Digest of Jagannātha translated by Colebrooke already showed signs of such activity, and in the interesting Slavery Case of 1825 the Pandits showed willingness to support 'naturally just' accretions to the śāstra. But by 1864 judicial knowledge of Hindu law was assumed.[54]

Derrett suggests that without the fossilizing forces of *stare decisis*, or of court Paṇḍitas being 'confined to reporting the rulings of long dead authors', then 'hundreds of different systems of customary law would have emerged'.[55] Drawing from Quentin Skinner, Anand Venkatkrishnan argues that:

> one of the benefits of intellectual history is in the vision it provides of alternative historical worlds that, regardless of whether they look different or similar to our own, are in and of themselves salutary reminders of how historically contingent the present is.[56]

The intellectual history of ownership and inheritance in Sanskrit jurisprudence highlights the historical and cultural contingency of liberal, Western notions of property, personhood, and equality. Furthermore, the diversity and regional specificity of Sanskrit jurisprudence calls into question the unitary nature of

[53] Venkatkrishnan, 'Mīmāṃsā', p. 23.

[54] Derrett, 'The British Administration of Hindu Law', p. 47.

[55] Ibid., pp. 47–8.

[56] Venkatkrishnan, 'Mīmāṃsā,' p. 23. Cf. Quentin Skinner, *Visions of Politics*, vol. 1: *Regarding Method* (Cambridge: Cambridge University Press, 2002), p. 6.

property and the jurisdiction of the state—through either its legislative or judicial apparatuses—to define and enforce property rights. Perhaps most radical is the view of the Dharmaśāstrins that religious rites and legal rights ought to be mutually constituted. For Paṇḍitas such as Kamalākara and Raghunandana, relational categories (of son, daughter, wife, brother, Brāhmaṇa, Śūdra, disciple, Gauḍa, Dākṣiṇātya, etc.) defined individuals differently, entailed different ritual obligations and afforded different—though often overlapping—proprietary rights. The intellectual history of ownership and inheritance suggests that in an alternative, or future world in which Dharmaśāstric jurisprudence supplanted Anglo-Hindu jurisprudence, property and persons would look radically different and the law would provide for a justice of a very different nature.

There are of course manifold criticisms of Dharmaśāstric jurisprudence. This monograph, however, militates against the charge that Dharmaśāstra is unchanging, uncompromising, and unable to meet the demands of the modern world. The 2,500 years' worth of texts analysed here demonstrate that although Dharmaśāstra retained a continuity of style—perhaps unmatched in the history of jurisprudence—the jurists of classical and early modern India recalibrated various ideas in the system in dynamic ways. Ownership-by-birth, women's rights to inheritance, the legal validity of property acquired impiously, and divine trusts, are but a few of the novel innovations developed by Dharmaśāstrins whose commitment to the traditional paradigms of the śāstric sciences was of aid, rather than an impediment, to new ideas.

Why should anyone care about the subtleties of a radically communitarian jurisprudence, whose allocation of material resources is based on a deeply unequal religious system of caste, class and gender? What could Varṇāśramadharma possibly have to contribute to contemporary debates about property and political philosophy besides an ultra-orthodox boogeyman? Is the answer simply that Dharmaśāstra's reminder of the contingency of India' liberal political economy is a sign of one progressive product of the colonial encounter? Possibly. Alternatively, one might equally see in pre-colonial Dharmaśāstric jurisprudence a potent rejoinder to Hindu nationalist claims of Hindu law and religion as unitary categories or to the role of property in our current political economy.[57] Advocates of legal pluralism in Europe and America, particularly of communitarian religious arbitration as an alternative to secular state courts, might find common cause with the Dharmaśāstric model of regionally specific schools of law.[58] Indeed, Rowan Williams' infamous endorsement of the 'accommodation' of certain religious legal systems outside of the jurisdictional remit of Britain's

[57] For contemporary debates concerning the nature of property and its relationship to political theology, see the Introduction to this volume.

[58] See, for example, Christian Joppke, *The Secular State under Siege: Religion and Politics in Europe and America* (Cambridge: Polity Press: 2015); Michael Helfand, 'Religious Arbitration and the New Multiculturalism: Negotiating Conflicting Legal Orders', *New York University Law Review* 86.5 (2011):

secular courts, reminds us justice does not always entail equality before the law.[59] Similarly, the Anglo-American concept of private property has come under withering critique in the wake of the globalized free market.[60] The shift toward 'alternative forms of ownership' in progressive law and economics debates might well find conversation partners in the Dharmaśāstric theory of ownership as capable of being held by a multiplicity of ownership simultaneous.[61] Furthermore, advocates of women's financial independence—particularly in rural India, where the gulf between traditional practices and abstract legal rights remains vast—might well find the category of women's property a more productive venue for achieving their laudable goals.[62]

The rise of political Hinduism, the limitations of neo-liberal economics, and the push towards legal pluralism in the West make the investigation of alternative jurisprudences a necessary facet of legal scholarship. Furthermore, some of the most pressing cases before the Indian judiciary involve intricate—and largely unresolved—questions of fiduciary relations in Sanskrit jurisprudence.[63] To cede Dharmaśāstra to religious chauvinists or to blithely accept its caricatured representation by some social activists would consign one of the world's great intellectual traditions to the 'ash heap of history'. Investigating the intellectual history of Dharmaśāstra ought to lead one to enquire about the intellectual future of Dharmaśāstra, even when it forces us to confront difficult questions and moral ambiguities. After all, as Yudhiṣṭhira tells Drupada in the *Mahābhārata*:

> Dharma is subtle, great king, we do not know its course. We follow the path taken by the ancestors, one after another.[64]

1231–1305; Peter Cumper, 'Multiculturalism, Human Rights and the Accommodation of Sharia Law', *Human Rights Law Review* 14 (2014): 31–57.

[59] Rowan Williams, 'Civil and Religious Law in England: A Religious Perspective', *Ecclesiastical Law Journal* 10 (2008): 262–82. For a summary of and response to the many passionate criticisms of Williams' lecture, see Jonathan Chaplin, 'Legal Monism and Religious Pluralism: Rowan Williams on Religion, Loyalty and Law', *International Journal of Public Theology* 2 (2008): 418–41.

[60] For one example of the tension between neo-liberal and indigenous categories of property, see William Coleman (ed.), *Property, Territory, Globalization: Struggles over Autonomy* (Vancouver: UBC Press, 2011).

[61] See, for example, the Labour Party of the United Kingdom's endorsement of this fashionable term: Cheryl Barrott, Cllr Matthew Brown, Andrew Cumbers, Christopher Hope, Les Huckfield, Rob Calvert Jump, Neil McInroy, and Linda Shaw. 'Report: Alternative Models of Ownership' (UK Labour Party, 2017).

[62] See, for example, Srimati Basu, *She Comes to Take Her Rights: Indian Women, Property, and Propriety* (New Delhi: Kali, 2001), esp. pp. 159–90.

[63] The most interesting cases involve religious endowments. See Deepa Das Acevedo, 'Divine Sovereignty, Indian Property Law, and the Dispute over the Padmanabhaswamy Temple', *Modern Asian Studies* 50.3 (2016): 841–65, and Ratna Kapur, 'The Ayodhya Case: Hindu Majoritarianism and the Right to Religious Liberty', *Maryland Journal of International Law* 305 (2014): 305–65.

[64] sūkṣmo dharmo mahārāja nāsya vidmo vayaṃ gatim / pūrveṣām ānupūrveṇa yātaṃ vartmānuyāmahe //1.187.29//

Similarly, Kamalākarabhaṭṭa notes that, 'litigation concerning the division of inheritance befuddles even the great amongst learned'.[65] When we take the time to attend to the complexity of the law, we discover the richness of its ethical possibilities.

Summary of Chapters

This monograph tracked the development of the concept of ownership (svatva) in Sanskrit jurisprudential literature (Dharmaśāstra) and in Sanskrit philosophical literature (Mīmāṃsā and Navya-Nyāya) between the eleventh and nineteenth centuries CE. Charting the relationship between philosophical theories of ownership and juridical models of inheritance formed a novel way of exploring the contested existence of various schools of Sanskrit jurisprudence before the formal establishment of schools of Hindu law by the judicial apparatus of the East India Company in the nineteenth century. Contrary to recent work on the subject, this intellectual history revealed that by 1772, at least three discoverable schools of Sanskrit jurisprudence existed: in Mithilā, Vārāṇasī and Navadvīpa. Furthermore, despite their fundamental misrepresentation of Dharmaśāstra as positive law, colonial administrators such as William Jones and Henry Colebrooke were largely justified in their identification of regionally specific schools of Dharmaśāstra, particularly with regard to ownership and inheritance.

Of course, a 'school of law' is by no means a universal term. In arguments for, and against, the existence of schools of law in pre-colonial Dharmaśāstra, few scholars take the time to explain what constitutes a 'school' and what constitutes 'law'. One does not need to call into question Rocher, Davis and Olivelle's basic distinction between Dharmaśāstra as an expert, meta-legal traditional of jurisprudence and law as positive, statutory codes, but their arguments need to be fleshed out in the context of Indian intellectual history. Ronald Inden's theorization of a 'scale of texts', the patterned ways in which authors situate their writings in relation to previous and contemporary writers, provided a key methodological tool for accepting Rocher and Davis' criticisms of Colebrooke and recasting schools of Hindu law as schools of Hindu legal thought, or of jurisprudence. The point was that thinking of Dharmaśāstra as a primarily intellectual tradition ought to entail reconstructing its intellectual history—replete with the considerations of scholarly lineage, pedagogical technique, and the quest for patronage that made up the social contexts of individual Dharmaśāstrins. Of course, the distinct southern and eastern schools of Sanskrit jurisprudence were themselves the culmination of centuries, perhaps millennia, of intellectual development. The

[65] 'Vivādatāṇḍava (Dāyabhāga Portion)', ed. Herambha Chatterjee, *Our Heritage* 7.2 (1959): 1–23, 1: vivādo yatra viduṣāṃ pramoho mahatām api / **kamalākarasaṃjñena** dāyabhāgaḥ sa ucyate //

story of how these schools came about and of the British encounter with them, told quite a different tale about ownership and inheritance than that which is recounted in existing scholarship.

Chapter 1 examined the development of the concept of ownership in Mīmāṃsā and Dharmaśāstra from the first millennium CE to approximately the fifteenth century CE. The origins of the first discernible school of Dharmaśāstric thought regarding ownership and inheritance—which crystallized the defence of ownership-by-birth in Vijñāneśvara's eleventh- to twelfth-century *Ṛjumitākṣarā*—lay in a Mimāṃsā theory of ownership as an extra-śāstric (laukika) phenomenon. Contrary to Ethan Kroll and Derrett's caricature of Mīmāṃsā theories of ownership as 'deplorable' or 'regressive', Prābhākara-Mīmāṃsā writers including Śālikanātha and Bhavanātha developed a metaphysically detailed and ethically rigorous view of ownership as an extra-śāstrically established fitness for use as desired (lokasiddhayatheṣṭaviniyogayogyatva). Furthermore, the *Mitākṣarā* marked a crucial juncture at which the unsystematic theories of ownership-by-birth that appeared in earlier Dharmaśāstra commentaries (such as Medhātithi's *Manubhāṣya*) were combined with a largely Prābhākara-Mīmāṃsā theory of ownership as an extra-śāstric phenomenon. Vijñāneśvara founded a distinctive school of Dharmaśāstric thought because his scale of Mīmāṃsā Dharmaśāstra texts became the standard way of thinking about the problems of ownership and inheritance. Indeed, the evidence revealed that Vijñāneśvara could be considered to be the founder of a school of thought in the sense that he *consolidated* earlier Dharmaśāstrins' theories of ownership and inheritance and established the parameters for future debate.

Chapter 2 examined the rise of two geographically and culturally specific schools of Sanskrit jurisprudence: the Maithila authors of Bihar, and the Gauḍa school of Navadvīpa, Bengal. Mithilā-based authors, including Caṇḍeśvara, Misarumiśra, and Vācaspatimiśra II, who worked in close association with the Karṇāṭa, Oinīvāra/Kāmeśvara, and Khaṇḍavalā dynasties, developed a scale of Dharmaśāstra and Navya-Nyāya texts that largely ignored the *Ṛjumitākṣarā*'s Mīmāṃsā-inflected theory of ownership-by-birth. These authors accepted the *Ṛjumitākṣarā*'s theory of sapiṇḍa-ship (as a relation of consanguinity), but their juridical models of inheritance focused on limiting fathers' powers of alienation over ancestral property, rather than on promoting sons' pre-partition rights of ownership. These models of inheritance were commensurate with Maithila Navya-Nyāya philosophy, in which ownership's causes *and* incidents are determined by śāstra, rather than by custom (ācāra). Furthermore, these developments in ownership and inheritance occurred in conjunction with a broader coalescence of a self-conciously 'Maithila' Brāhmaṇa identity. This identity was defined politically by the creation of a census of official Maithila Brāhmaṇa lineages (mūlas). This identity was defined textually and culturally by Maithila authors' efforts to identify and to contrast Maithila texts and traditions from those of Bengal (Gauḍa).

A Bengali (Gauḍa), Navya-Nyāya-inflected school of jurisprudence developed at the University of Navadvīpa (founded in 1514) in the early sixteenth century. In many ways, the Gauḍa school, which came to be known in colonial times as the *Dāyabhāga* school, was the antithesis of the *Mitākṣarā* school. The Gauḍas had strong connections to a particular place, utilized the analytical techniques and theoretical presuppositions of Navya-Nyāya rather than Mīmāṃsā, and connected their discussions of ownership and inheritance with a comprehensive scale of Dharmaśāstric texts. This scale covered legal and ritual topics, as well as displaying an obvious desire to surpass a regional rival: the competing centre of Sanskrit learning in Mithilā. Navadvīpan Dharmaśāstrins, including Śrīnāthācārya Cūḍāmaṇi (1475–1525), Rāmabhadra I (1510–70), and Acyutacakravartin (1510–70), and logicians, such as Raghunātha Śiromaṇi (1460–1540), and Jayarāma Nyāyapañcānana (seventeenth century), began to speak of themselves, their ritual practices and their intellectual opinions, as being part of a Bengali (Gauḍa) school of thought.

Navadvīpan jurists recalled Jīmūtavāhana's *Dāyabhāga* from its previous obscurity and used their commentaries on this treatise as a venue within which to build a new, comprehensive theory of ownership and inheritance in opposition to the scholars of Mithilā. Navadvīpan jurists wrote dozens of commentaries on the *Dāyabhāga* in a Navya-Nyāya idiom and dozens of logicians wrote Navya-Nyāya treatises on ownership which defended arguments from the *Dāyabhāga*. The key connection was between various Navya-Nyāya theories of ownership's *causes* as being discernible-from-the-śāstra-alone (śāstraikasamadhigamyasvatva, etc.) and the Dharmaśāstric theory of ownership-by-the-cessation-of-the-ownership-of-the-previous-owner (uparamasvatva) articulated in Jīmūtavāhana's *Dāyabhāga*. Unlike Maithila authors, however, Gauḍa Paṇḍitas argued that, although ownership's *causes* are limited to those mentioned in the śāstra (thereby excluding custom), lawful ownership affords an individual virtually unlimited rights of alienation (the principle of *factum valet*). For the Navadvīpans, the perlocutionary force of their endeavors seems to have been building the reputation and fortunes of their new university.

Chapter 3 explored the reception of the Gauḍa school jurisprudence amongst the predominantly Mahārāṣṭrian community of Paṇḍitas that flourished in Vārāṇasī in the sixteenth and seventeenth centuries. The chapter reconstructed how some of the distinctive features of Indian 'early modernity', the pan-Indian Brāhmaṇa 'ecumene', and the intensively competitive environment of Vārāṇasī inflected the development of the concepts of ownership and inheritance in Dharmaśāstra. The core area of analysis was the Mīmāṃsā and Dharmaśāstra writings of the Bhaṭṭas, the prominent family of Mahārāṣṭrians Paṇḍitas who led Brāhmaṇasabhās in the Kāśīviśveśvara temple. The texts suggest that the Bhaṭṭas recast Vijñāneśvara's *Ṛjumitākṣarā* as a paradigmatic southern, Mīmāṃsā-compliant treatise on inheritance. They incorporated the *Mitākṣarā* and Mīmāṃsā theories of ownership into a comprehensive southern school of jurisprudence and contrasted this school of jurisprudence with that of the Gauḍas. It was probably at this moment that the *Mitākṣarā* and the *Dāyabhāga* moved into each other's orbit and the basic *Dāyabhāga*/*Mitākṣarā*, Gauḍa/Dākṣiṇātya, Navya-Nyāya/Mīmāṃsā division in the jurisprudence of ownership and inheritance was fixed. This suggests that the development of Sanskrit jurisprudence was embroiled in the social politics of early Indian modernity—in squabbles between Paṇḍitas with various regionally and pedagogically-specific lineages, in the marked interest amongst Paṇḍitas for intervening in the caste hierarchies of the northern India, and the increasingly interdisciplinary character of scholastic Sanskrit endeavour.

Chapter 4 tackled one of the central questions in the history of ownership and inheritance in Sanskrit jurisprudence: was Colebrooke's identification of *Dāyabhāga* and *Mitākṣarā* schools of law a 'phony, artificial creation' or a justifiable characterization of the state of Dharmaśāstra *circa* 1800? The answer, unsurprisingly, was a bit of both. In examining the British encounter with Dharmaśāstra in the late eighteenth and early nineteenth centuries, and in tracing the construction of Hindu Schools of Law between 1772 and 1825, a clearer picture emerged. The chapter focused on three digests of Dharmaśāstra that were compiled at the behest of the East India Company and whose English translations were utilized by British jurists in colonial courts: the *Vivādārṇavasetu*, the *Vivādabhaṅgārṇava*, and the *Dharmaśāstrasaṃgraha*. It accepted that the grounding premise of Anglo-Hindu Law—that Dharmaśāstric legal treatises could be read as statutory law—was a distortion of the primarily scholastic nature of Dharmaśāstra. These distortions notwithstanding, however, the colonial-era Dharmaśāstra digests articulated the same discernible, regionally specific schools of jurisprudential thought regarding ownership and inheritance whose evolution was reconstructed in earlier chapters. The *Vivādārṇavasetu* and the *Vivādabhaṅgārṇava*, compiled by teams of Bengali logicians, synthesized and defended the *Dāyabhāga*'s Bengali (Gauḍa) theories of ownership-by-the-cessation-of-the-ownership-of-the-previous-owner (uparamasvatva), ownership as discernible-from-the-śāstra-alone (śāstraikasamadhigamyatva), and *factum valet* against the opinions of Maithila rivals (often utilizing the formal techniques of Navya-Nyāya philosophy). In contrast, the *Vyavahārabālambhaṭṭī*—compiled by a Mahārāṣṭrian Mīmāṃsaka whose intellectual lineage intersected with the Bhaṭṭas—defended the *Mitākṣarā*'s southern (Dākṣinātya) theories of ownership-by-birth (janmasvatva) and of ownership as extra-śāstric (laukika) against the *Dāyabhāga* and logicians identified as Bengali (Prācya, Gauḍa, etc.).

Consequently, it is reasonable to draw a distinction between conceiving of Dharmaśāstra as positive law and positing regionally specific schools of Dharmaśāstric jurisprudential philosophy. In rejecting the first proposition and in accepting the second proposition, it is possible to view Colebrooke's formulation of schools of law—particularly his formulation of Dharmaśāstric theories of ownership and inheritance as rooted in the *Dāyabhāga* and *Mitākṣarā*—as constituting a logical and appropriate understanding of the state of Dharmaśāstra that he encountered directly in the Dharmaśāstra digests compiled for the British and through his collaboration with Bengali, Maithila and Mahārāṣtrian Paṇḍitas. Furthermore, the colonial-era Dharmaśāstra digests substantiated Colebrooke's hypothesis that Navya-Nyāya and Mīmāṃsā theories of ownership lay at the heart of the division of *Dāyabhāga* and *Mitākṣarā* schools of Sanskrit jurisprudence. Davis' argument—that schools of Hindu law were a colonial invention—and Bhattacarya-Panda's insistence that the *Vivādabhaṅgārṇava*'s Navya-Nyāya-inflected theories of ownership were a British interpolation were themselves untenable, artificial distortions of the Dharmaśāstric record. The chapter concluded its criticism of the theory of an epistemic rupture in the śāstric sciences between pre-colonial and colonial India by proposing a new narrative of transformation and transcreation.

Where does this leave us? What work remains to be done? This monograph only scratches the surface of Sanskrit literature on ownership and property. There is a vast archive of Mīmāṃsā, Navya-Nyāya, and Dharmaśāstra texts that exist only in manuscript form and that have never been examined at any length. The colonial archive of Sanskrit digests, Paṇḍitas' vyavasthās, and case law remains an untapped resource for investigating the continuities and reconfigurations of Dharmaśāstric ideas about property in modern India. I hope that in addition to the myriad technical wonders illuminated, this monograph convinces the reader that the Sanskrit jurisprudence of ownership is more varied, more intricate, and of more utility to the future than some quick and current caricatures of it as regressive, pointlessly abstract, or a colonial fantasy might have you believe.

Bibliography

Sanskrit Manuscripts

Bhāṭṭacintāmaṇi by Gāgābhaṭṭa. Ms. Bhandarkar Oriental Research Institute (627/1887–91).

Dānadinakaroddyota by Dinakarabhaṭṭa and Gāgābhaṭṭa. Ms. Bhandarkar Oriental Research Institute 617 (82/1895–8).

Dānakamalākara by Kamalākarabhaṭṭa. Ms Bhandarkar Oriental Research Institute 575 (103/Visrama (1)).

Vibhāgatattvavicāra by Rāmakṛṣṇabhaṭṭa. Ms. Asiatic Society Library 1064.

Vivādārṇavasetu. Ms. India Office Library (1506/3145a).

Vivādasārārṇava. Ms. India Office Library (1505/3145b).

Vivādabhaṅgārṇava. Ms. Bodleian Library No. 720.

Vivādabhaṅgārṇava. Ms. India Office Library (1534/1770).

Vyavahāradinakaroddyota by Dinakarabhaṭṭa and Gāgābhaṭṭa. Ms. Bhandarkar Oriental Research Institute 613 (37/1866–8).

Primary Texts in Sanskrit

Bṛhatī of Prabhākaramiśra with the Ṛjuvimalā of Śālikanātha, vol. 4. Ed. S. Subrahmanyan Shastri. Madras: University of Madras Press, 1964.

Bhāṭṭacintāmaṇi: Tarkapāda. Ed. Sūryanārāyaṇsa Śukla. Benares: Chowkhamba Sanskrit Series Office, 1933.

The Bridge to the Three Holy Cities: The Sāmānya-praghaṭṭaka of Nārāyaṇabhaṭṭa's Tristhalīsetu. Critically ed. and trans. Richard Salomon. Delhi: Motilal Banarsidass, 1985.

Jīmūtavāhana's Dāyabhāga: The Hindu Law of Inheritance in Bengal. Ed. and trans. Ludo Rocher. Oxford: Oxford University Press, 2002.

Dāyabhāga. Ed. Bhāratacandra Śiromaṇi. Calcutta: Vidyāratna Press, 1863.

Dāyabhāga. Ed. and trans. Heramba Chatterjee. Howrah: Saṃskṛta Sāhitya Samāja, 1978.

Dāyatattva. Ed. and trans. Golapchandra Sarkar. Calcutta: Cambray & Co., 1904.

Dharma-Dwaita-Nirṇaya: or Dharmic Alternatives Solved. Ed. J. R. Gharpure. Bombay: Office of the Collection of Hindu Law Texts, 1943.

Dharmaśāstrīyanibandhāvalī. Ed. Śrīrāmacandramiśra & Śrīsiddheśvarabhaṭṭācāya. Darbhanga: Mithilāvidyāpīṭha, 1978.

Kāśikā: Pāṇinīyāṣṭādhyāyīsūtravṛttiḥ. Ed. Arydnera Sharma. Haidarābāda: Saṃskṛtapariṣat, Usmāniyā Viśvavidyālayaḥ, 1969.

Manubhāṣya of Medhātithi. Ed. Ganganatha Jha. 2 vols. Calcutta: Asiatic Society of Bengal, 1932–9.

Manusmṛti: The Laws of Manu with the Bhāṣya of Medhātithi. Trans. Ganganatha Jha. 5 vols. Calcutta: University of Calcutta, 1920–6.

Manusmṛti: with the Sanskrit Commentary Manvarth-Muktāvalī. Ed. J. L. Shastri. Varanasi: Motilal Banarsidass, 1983.

Mitākṣara: With Viśvarūpa and Commentaries of Subodhini and Bālambhatti. Ed. S. S. Setlur. Madras: Brahmavadin Press, 1912.

Mīmāṃsādarśana. Ed. V. G. Apte. 7 vols. Pune: Anandashrama Press, 1929–34.

Mīmāṃsākutūhala. Sarasvatībhavanagranthamālā, no. 12. Varanasi: Sampurnand Sanskrit University, 1987.

Mīmāṃsānayaviveka. Ed. S. Subrahmanya Shastri. 4 vols. New Delhi: Rashtriya Sanskrit Sansthan, 2004.

The Mīmāṃsā Nyāya Prakāśa; or Āpadevī: A Treatise on the Mīmāṃsā System. Ed. and trans. Franklin Edgerton. New Haven, CT: Yale University Press, 1929.

Nirṇayasindhu. Ed. N. R. Ācārya. Mumbai: Nirṇayasāgara Press, 1949.

Sanskrit Documents: Being Sanskrit Letters and Other Documents Preserved in the Oriental Collection at the National Archives of India. Ed. Surendranath Sen and Umesha Mishra. Allahabad: Ganganatha Jha Research Institute, 1951.

Śābarabhāṣya. Trans. Gaṅgānātha Jha. 3 vols. Baroda: Oriental Institute, Gaekwad's Oriental Series; no. 66, 70, 73, 1933–36.

Sārasvatīvilāsa: Vyāvahārakāṇḍa. Ed. R. Shama Shastri. Mysore: Oriental Library Sanskrit Series, no. 71, 1927.

Smṛticandrikā. Ed. L. Śrīnivāsācārya. 6 vols. Mysore: Government Oriental Library, Government Oriental Library series, nos. 43, 45, 48 & 52; Bibliotheca Sanskrita Series, 56, 1914–21.

Tantraratnam. Ed. Ganganatha Jha. 5 vols. Benares: Princess of Wales Sarasvati Bhavan Texts, no. 31, part I, 1930–79.

Vivādacandra. Ed. Ram Krishna Jha. Benares: Vidya Vilasa Press, 1931.

Vivādacintāmaṇi. Ed. Khemarāja Śrīkṛṣṇadāsa. Mumbai: Śrīveṅkaṭeśvara Press, 1955.

Vivādaratnākara. Ed. Kamalakṛṣṇa Smṛtitīrtha. Calcutta: Asiatic Society of Bengal, 1931.

Vivādatāṇḍava: Dāyabhāga Portion. Ed. Herambha Chatterjee. *Our Heritage* 7.2 (1959): 1–23; 8.2 (1960): 25–37; 11.1 (1963): 39–50; 13.1 (1965): 51–8.

Vivādatāṇḍava. Ed. and trans. (Gujarati) M. N. Dvivedī. Baroda: Lakṣmīvilāsa Press, 1901.

Vīramitrodaya. Ed. and trans. G. S. Śāstrī. Calcutta: Thacker, Spink & Co., 1879.

Vyavahārabālambhaṭṭī of Bālambhaṭṭa. Fasc. 5. Ed. Nityanand Pant Parvatiya. Benares: Chowkhambā Sanskrit Book Depot, 1912.

Vyavahāramayūkha. Ed. and trans. V. N. Mandlik. Bombay: Education Society Press, 1880; Ed. P. V. Kāne. Poona: Bhandarkar Oriental Research Institute, Bombay Sanskrit Serial, 1926; Trans. Borradaile. Surat: Mission Press (under the authority of the Bombay Government), 1827; Trans. J. R. Ghārpure. Bombay: Hindu Law Texts, 1921; Trans. P. V. Kāṇe and S. G. Patawardhan. Bombay: Pandurang Vaman Kāṇe, 1933.

Vyākaraṇamahābhāṣya: Paspaśāhnika. Ed. and trans. S. D. Joshi and J. A. F. Roodbergen. Pune: University of Pune, 1986.

Yājñavalkyasmṛti: with the Bālakrīḍā of Viśvarūpācārya. Ed. Gaṇapati Śāstrī. 2 vols. Trivandrum: Government Press, Trivandrum Sanskrit Series; no. 74, 81, 1922–4.

Yājñavalkyasmṛti: with the Mitākṣarā of Vijñāneśvara. Ed. R. K. Panda. Delhi: Bharatiya Kala Prakashan, 2011.

Secondary Texts in English

Bagchi, S. C. *Juristic Personality of Hindu Deities.* Calcutta: University of Calcutta Press, Astutosh Mokkerjee Lecture for 1931 and 1933.

Banhatti, N. D. *Descriptive Catalogue of the Government Collections of Manuscripts Deposited at the Deccan College, Poona.* Bombay: The Government of Bombay, 1916.

Cheryl Barrott, Cllr Matthew Brown, Andrew Cumbers, Christopher Hope, Les Huckfield, Rob Calvert Jump, Neil McInroy, and Linda Shaw. 'Report: Alternative Models of Ownership'. UK Labour Party, 2017. Available from: https://labour.org.uk/wp-content/uploads/2017/10/Alternative-Models-of-Ownership.pdf.

Basu, Srimati. *She Comes to Take Her Rights: Indian Women, Property, and Propriety.* New Delhi: Kali, 2001.

Benke, Theodore. 'The Śūdrācāraśiromaṇsi of Kṛṣṇsa Śeṣa: A 16th Century Manual of Dharma for Śūdras'. PhD Dissertation, University of Pennsylvania, 2010.

Benson, James. 'Śaṃkarabhaṭṭa's Family Chronicle: The *Gādhivaṃśavarṇana*'. In *The Pandit: Traditional Scholarship in India*, ed. Axel Michaels. Delhi: Manohar Publishers, 2001, pp. 105–18.

Benton, Lauren. *A Search for Sovereignty: Law and Geography in European Empires, 1400–1900.* New York: Cambridge University Press, 2010.

Bhargava, Rajeev (ed). *Secularism and Its Critics.* Delhi: Oxford University Press, 1998.

Bhattacharya, Neeladri. 'Remaking Custom: The Discourse and Practice of Colonial Codification'. In *Tradition, Dissent and Ideology: Essay in Honour of Romila Thapar*, ed. R. Champakalakshmi and S. Gopal. New Delhi: Oxford University Press, 1996, pp. 20–51.

Bhattacarya-Panda, Nandini. *Appropriation and Invention of Tradition: The East India Company and Hindu Law in Bengal.* New Delhi: Oxford University Press, 2008.

Billings, Gloria, and William Tate. 'Toward a Critical Race Theory of Education'. *Teachers College Record* 97.1 (1995): 47–68.

Birla, Ritu. *Stages of Capital: Law, Culture and Market Governance in Late Colonial India.* Durham, NC: Duke University Press, 2009.

Blackstone, William. *Commentaries on the Laws of England: Book the Second.* Oxford: Clarendon Press, 1766.

Bovenberg, Jasper. *Property Rights in Blood, Genes and Data: Naturally Yours?* Leiden: Brill, 2006.

Burnell, A. C. *The Law of Partition and Succession: from the MS. Sanskrit Text of Varadarāja's Vyavahāranirnaya.* Mangalore: Stolz, 1872.

Cannon, Garland. *The Life and Mind of Oriental Jones: Sir William Jones, the Father of Modern Linguistics.* Cambridge: Cambridge University Press, 1990.

Cannon, Garland (ed). *The Letters of William Jones.* 2 vols. Oxford: Oxford University Press, 1970.

Chakrabarti, Arindam. 'Introduction'. *Philosophy East and West* 51.4, *Nondualism, Liberation, and Language: The Infinity Foundation Lectures at Hawai'i, 1997–2000* (2001): 449–51.

Chakrabarty, Dipesh. *Provincializing Europe: Postcolonial Thought and Historical Difference.* Princeton, NJ: Princeton University Press, 2000.

Chakrabarty, Dipesh. 'The Muddle of Modernity'. *American Historical Review* 116.3 (2011): 663–75.

Chakravarti, R. M. ' Contributions to the History of Smṛti in Bengal and Mithilā'. *Journal of the Asiatic Society of Bengal* (1915): 311–406.

Chakravarti, R. M. 'History of Mithilā during the Pre-Mughal Period'. *Journal of the Royal Asiatic Society of Bengal* 11 (1915): 407–31.

Chaplin, Jonathan. 'Legal Monism and Religious Pluralism: Rowan Williams on Religion, Loyalty and Law'. *International Journal of Public Theology* 2 (2008): 418–41.

Chatterjee, Nandini. *The Making of Indian Secularism: Empire, Law and Christianity 1830–1960.* New York: Palgrave Macmillan, 2011.

Chatterjee, Nirmal Chandra. 'Patria Potestas in Ancient India'. *Proceedings and Transactions of the All-India Oriental Conference* (AIOC) 2 (1922): 365–77.

Chaudry, Faisal. 'A Rule of Proprietary Right for British India: From Revenue Settlement to Tenant Right in the Age of Classical Legal Thought'. *Modern Asian Studies* 50.1 (2016): 345–84.

Chaudry, Faisal. 'Property and Its Rule (in Late Indo-Islamicate and Early Colonial) South Asia: What's in a Name?' *Journal of the Economic and Social History of the Orient* 68.5–6 (2018): 920–75.

Cohn, Bernard. 'The Initial British Impact on India: A Case Study of the Benares Region'. *The Journal of Asian Studies* 19.4 (1960): 418–31.

Cohn, Bernard. 'Law and the Colonial State in India'. *History and Power in the Study of Law: New Directions in Legal Anthropology*, ed. June Starr and Jane F. Collier. Ithaca, NY: Cornell University Press, 1989, pp. 31–152.

Cohn, Bernard. *Colonialism and Its Forms of Knowledge: The British in India.* Princeton, NJ: Princeton University Press, 1996.

Colebrooke, Henry Thomas. *A Digest of Hindu Law on Contracts and Successions.* 3 vols. Calcutta: Company Press, 1801.

Colebrooke, Henry Thomas. *Two Treatises on the Hindu Law of Inheritance.* Calcutta: Hindoostanee Press, 1810.

Colebrooke, T. E. *The Life of H. T. Colebrooke.* London: Trübner & Co, 1873.

Coleman, William (ed.). *Property, Territory, Globalization: Struggles over Autonomy.* Vancouver: University of British Columbia Press, 2011.

Collingwood, R. G. *An Essay on Philosophical Method.* Oxford: Clarendon Press, 1933.

Cowell, E. B. 'Report on the Tolls of Nudea'. *Proceedings of the Asiatic Society of Bengal* (1867): 86–102.

Cox, Whitney. 'Law, Literature, and the Problem of Politics in Medieval India'. In *Hinduism and Law: An Introduction*, ed. Timothy Lubin, Donald R. Davis Jr., and Jayanth K. Krishnan. Cambridge: Cambridge University Press, 2010, pp. 167–82.

Cumper, Peter. 'Multiculturalism, Human Rights and the Accommodation of Sharia Law'. *Human Rights Law Review* 14 (2014): 31–57.

Curley, Thomas M. *Sir Robert Chambers: Law, Literature, and Empire in the Age of Johnson.* Madison: University of Wisconsin Press, 1998.

Dalmia, Vasudha. 'Sanskrit Scholars and Pandits of the Old School: The Benares Sanskrit College and the Constitution of Authority in the Late Nineteenth Century'. *Journal of Indian Philosophy* 24 (1996): 321–37.

Das Acevedo, Deepa. 'Divine Sovereignty, Indian Property Law, and the Dispute over the Padmanabhaswamy Temple'. *Modern Asian Studies* 50.3 (2016): 841–65.

Davis, Donald. 'Dharma in Practice: Ācāra and Authority in Medieval Dharmaśāstra'. *Journal of Indian Philosophy* 32 (2004): 813–30.

Davis, Donald. 'Intermediate Realms of Law: Corporate Groups and Rulers in Medieval India'. *Journal of the Economic and Social History of the Orient* 48.1 (2005): 92–117.

Davis, Donald. 'Hinduism as a Legal Tradition.' *Journal of the American Academy of Religion* 75.2 (2007): 241–67.

Davis, Donald. 'Law in the Mirror of Language: The Madras School of Orientalism on Hindu Law'. *The Madras School of Orientalism: Producing Knowledge in Colonial South India*, ed. Thomas Trautman. Oxford: Oxford University Press, 2009, pp. 288–309.

Davis, Donald. *The Spirit of Hindu Law.* Cambridge: Cambridge University Press, 2010.

Davis, Donald. 'Modern Legal Framework'. In *Brill's Encyclopedia of Hinduism*, ed. K. Jacobsen, H. Basu, A. Malinar, and Vasudha Narayanan. Brill Online, 2014. Available from: https://referenceworks.brillonline.com/entries/brill-s-encyclopedia-of-hinduism/modern-legal-framework-COM_9000000166.

Davis, Donald. 'Rules, Culture, and Imagination in Sanskrit Jurisprudence'. *Legalism: Rules and Categories*, ed. Paul Dresch and Judith Scheele. Oxford: Oxford University Press, 2015, pp. 29–52.

Derrett, J. Duncan. 'An Indian Contribution to the Study of Property'. *Bulletin of the School of Oriental and African Studies* 18 (1956): 475–98.

Derrett, J. Duncan. 'Prohibition and Nullity: Indian Struggles with a Jurisprudential Lacuna'. *Bulletin of the School of Oriental and African Studies* 20 (1957): 203–15.

Derrett, J. Duncan. 'The Right to Earn in Ancient India: A Conflict between Expediency and Authority'. *Economic and Social History of the Orient*, 1.1 (1957): 66–97.

Derrett, J. Duncan. 'Statutory Amendments of the Personal Law of Hindus Since Indian Independence'. *The American Journal of Comparative Law* 7.3 (1958): 380–93.

Derrett, J. Duncan. 'The British Administration of Hindu Law'. *Comparative Studies in Society and History* 4.1 (1961): 10–52.

Derrett, J. Duncan. *Introduction to Modern Hindu Law*. Oxford: Oxford University Press, 1963.

Derrett, J. Duncan. 'Justice, Equity, and Good Conscience'. In *Changing Law in Developing Countries*, ed. J. Anderson. London: George Allen & Unwin, 1963, pp. 114–54.

Derrett, J. Duncan. 'The British as Patrons of the Śāstra'. In *Religion, Law and the State in India*, ed. J. Duncan Derrett. London: Faber & Faber, 1968, pp. 225–73.

Derrett, J. Duncan. 'The Codification of Hindu Law'. *Religion, Law, and the State in India*, ed. J. Duncan Derrett. London: Faber & Faber, 1968, pp. 321–51.

Derrett, J. Duncan. *Dharmaśāstra and Juridical Literature*. Wiesbaden: Harrassowitz, 1973.

Derrett, J. Duncan. 'The Concept of Law According to Medhātithi, a Pre-Islamic Indian Jurist'. *Essays in Classical and Modern Hindu Law*, vol. 1, ed. J. Duncan Derrett. Leiden: Brill, 1976, pp. 174–97.

Derrett, J. Duncan. 'The Development of the Concept of Property in India, *c*. AD. 800–1800'. In *Essays in Classical and Modern Indian Law*, vol. 2, ed. J. Duncan Derrett. Leiden: Brill, 1976, pp. 8–130.

Derrett, J. Duncan. 'The Relative Antiquity of the Mitāksharā and the Dāyabhāga'. In *Essays in Classical and Modern Hindu Law*, vol. 1, ed. J. Duncan Derrett. Leiden: Brill, 1976, pp. 198–206.

Derrett, J. Duncan. 'Factum Valet: The Adventures of a Maxim'. In *Essays in Classical and Modern Hindu Law: Anglo-Hindu Law*, ed. J. Duncan Derrett. Leiden: Brill, 1977, pp. 1–24.

Deshpande, Madhav. 'Kṣatriyas in the Kali Age? Gāgābhaṭṭa & His Opponents'. *Indo-Iranian Journal* 53 (2010): 95–100.

Deshpande, Madhav. 'Panca Gauda Panca Dravida: Contested Borders of a Traditional Classification'. In *Anantaṃ Śāstram: Indological and Linguistic Studies in Honour of Bertil Tikkanen*, ed. Klaus Karttunen. Helsinki: Finnish Oriental Society, 2010, pp. 29–58.

Deshpande, Madhav. '"Disagreement without Disrespect": Transitions in a Lineage from Bhaṭṭoji to Nāgeśa'. *South Asian History and Culture* 6.1 (2015): 32–49.

Diaconescu, Bogdan. 'On the New Ways of the Late Vedic Hermeneutics: Mīmāṃsā and Navya-Nyāya'. *Asiatische Studien: Zeitschrift der Schweizerischen Asiengesellschaft* 66 (2012): 261–307.

Dirks, Nicholas. *Castes of Mind: Colonialism and the Making of Modern India.* Princeton, NJ: Princeton University Press, 2001.

Dodson, Michael. 'Re-presented for the Pandits: James Ballantyne, "Useful Knowledge", and Sanskrit Scholarship in Benares College during the Mid-Nineteenth Century'. *Modern Asian Studies* 36.2 (2002): 257–98.

Dresch, Paul, and Judith Scheele. 'Introduction'. In *Legalism: Rules and Categories*, ed. Paul Dresch and Judith Scheele. Oxford: Oxford University Press, 2015, pp. 1–28.

Dutta, Manomohini. 'Inheritance, Property and Women in the *Dāyabhāga*'. PhD Dissertation, University of Texas, 2016.

Dutta, Manomohini. 'Upakāra: The Theory of Spiritual Service and Women's Inheritance in the Dāyabhāga'. *The Journal of Hindu Studies* 11.3 (2018): 260–84.

Dutta, Manomohini. '*Dāya*: The Conceptual Understanding of Inheritance and Gift in the *Dāyabhāga*'. *Journal of Indian Philosophy* 47 (2019): 111–31.

Eaton, Richard. 'Temple Desecration and Indo-Muslim States'. *Journal of Islamic Studies* 11.3 (2000): 283–319.

Eco, Umberto. *The Name of the Rose.* Trans. William Weever. New York: Harcourt, 1983.

Eggeling, Julius. *Catalogue of the Sanskrit Manuscripts in the Library of the India Office*, vol. 1. London: Printed by Order of the Secretary of State for India in Council, 1887.

Ellickson, Robert. 'Two Cheers for the Bundle-of-Sticks Metaphor, Three Cheers for Merrill and Smith'. *Econ Journal Watch* 8.3 (2011): 215–22.

Forrest, George. *Selections from the Letters, Dispatches and Other State Papers Preserved in the Foreign Department of the government of India, 1772–1785*, vol. 2. Calcutta, Government Press, 1890.

Francavilla, Domenico. *The Roots of Hindu Jurisprudence: Source of Dharma and Interpretation in Mīmāṃsā and Dharmaśāstra.* Turin: Comitato Corpus Iuris Sanscriticum et fontes Iuris Asiae Meridianae et Centralis, 2005.

Freschi, Elisa. *Duty, Language and Exegesis in Prābhākara Mīmāṃsā: Including an Edition and Translation of Rāmānujācārya's Tantrarahasya, Śāstraprameyapariccheda.* Leiden: Brill, 2012.

Ganguly, Joydev. *Dharmaśāstra in Mithilā.* Calcutta: Calcutta Sanskrit College, 1972.

Ganeri, Joardon. *The Lost Age of Reason: Philosophy in Early Modern India (1450–1700).* Oxford: Oxford University Press, 2011.

Ganeri, Joardon. 'Contextualism in the Study of Indian Intellectual Cultures'. *Journal of Indian Philosophy* 36.5 (2008): 551–62.

Gharpure, J. R., *Sāpiṇḍya, or, The Law of Sapiṇḍa Relationship.* Bombay: Office of Hindu Law Texts, 1943.

Ghose, J. C. *The Principles of Hindu Law*, vol. 2, 3rd edn. Calcutta: S. C. Auddy & Co., 1917.

Ghose, N. N. *Memoirs of Maharaja Nubkissen Bahadur.* Calcutta: Edinburgh Press, 1901.

Giddens, Anthony. *Capitalism and Modern Social Theory: An Analysis of the Writings of Marx, Durkheim, and Max Weber.* Cambridge: Cambridge University Press, 1971.

Gledhill, Alan. 'The Influence of Common Law and Equity on Hindu Law since 1800'. *The International and Comparative Law Quarterly* 3.4 (1954): 576–603.

Goold, Imogen. 'Property Rights in Bodily Material'. In *Tensions and Traumas in Health Law*, ed. Ian Freckleton and Kerry Petersen. Annandale: Federation Press, 2017, pp. 367–83.

Goold, Imogen and Muireann Quigley. 'Human Biomaterials: The Case for a Property Approach'. In *Persons, Parts and Property: How Should We Regulate Human Tissue in the 21st Century?*, ed. Imogen Goold, Jonathan Herring, Loane Skene, and Kate Greasley. Oxford: Hart Publishing, 2014, pp. 231–262.

Grady, Standish. *A Treatise on The Hindoo Law*. London: Wildy and Sons, 1868.

Griffiths, John. 'What Is Legal Pluralism?' *Journal of Legal Pluralism* 24 (1986): 1–55.

Guha, Ranajit. *A Rule of Property for Bengal: An Essay on the Idea of Permanent Settlement*. Paris: Mouton, 1963.

Gupte, S.V. *Hindu Law of Succession*. Bombay: Tripathi, 1972.

Hacker, Paul. 'Dharma in Hinduism'. *Journal of Indian Philosophy* 34.5 (2006): 479–96.

Halbfass, Wilhelm. *India and Europe: An Essay in Understanding*. New York: State University of New York Press, 1988.

Halbfass, Wilhelm. *Philology and Confrontation: Paul Hacker on Traditional and Modern Vedanta*. Albany, NY: State University of New York Press, 1995.

Halhed, Nathaniel. *A Code of Gentoo Laws: Or, Ordinations of the Pundits, from a Persian Translation, Made from the Original, Written in the Shanscrit Language*. London: Printed for the East India Company, 1776.

Hann, C. M. 'Introduction: The Embeddedness of Property'. In *Property Relations: Renewing the Anthropological Tradition*, ed. C. M. Hann. Cambridge: Cambridge University Press, 1998, pp. 1–47.

Hatcher, Brian. *Eclecticism and Modern Hindu Discourse*. New York: Oxford University Press, 1999.

Hatcher, Brian. 'Sanskrit and the Morning After: The Metaphorics and Theory of Intellectual Change'. *Indian Economic and Social History Review* 44.3 (2007): 333–61.

Hatcher, Brian. *Bourgeois Hinduism, or the Faith of the Modern Vedantists: Rare Discourses from Early Colonial Bengal*. Oxford: Oxford University Press, 2008.

Hatcher, Brian. *Vidyasagar: The Life and After-life of an Eminent Indian*. New Delhi: Routledge, 2014.

Hazra, R. C. 'Śrīnāthācāryacūḍāmaṇi of Bengal: His Works and Legacy'. *Indian Historical Quarterly* (1950): 277–92.

Hazra, R. C. 'Śrīnātha Ācārya-Cūḍāmaṇi: A Smṛti-Writer of Bengal'. *Annals of the Bhandarkar Oriental Research Institute* 32 (1951): 34–52.

Helfand, Michael. 'Religious Arbitration and the New Multiculturalism: Negotiating Conflicting Legal Orders'. *New York University Law Review* 86.5 (2011): 1231–1305.

Hezser, Catherine. 'Roman Law and Rabbinic Legal Composition'. In *The Cambridge Companion to Rabbinic Literature*, ed. Charlotte Fonrobert and Martin Jaffee. Cambridge: Cambridge University Press, 2007, pp. 144–63.

Hiltebeitel, Alf. *Dharma*. Honolulu: University of Hawaii Press, 2010.

Hohfeld, Wesley. 'Some Fundamental Legal Conceptions as Applied in Juridical Reasoning'. *Yale Law Review* 23.16 (1913): 28–59 and 26.8 (1917): 710–70.

Honoré, A. M. 'Ownership'. In *Oxford Essays in Jurisprudence*, ed. Anthony Guest. Oxford: Oxford University Press, 1961, pp. 107–47.

Inden, Ronald. *Imagining India*. Oxford: Blackwell, 1990.

Inden, Ronald, J. Walters, and D. Ali. *Querying the Medieval: Texts and the History of Practices in South Asia*. Oxford: Oxford University Press, 2000.

Ingalls, Henry. *Materials for the Study of Navya-Nyāya Logic*. Cambridge, MA: Harvard University Press, 1951.

Jain, M. P. *Outlines of Indian Legal History*, 6th edn. Bombay: Tripathi, 2006.

Jha, Ganganatha. *The Prābhākara School of Pūrvamīmāṃsā*. Allahabad: University of Allahabad, 1911.

Jha, Ganganatha. *Pūrvamīmāṃsā in Its Sources*. Benares: Benares Hindu University, 1942.

Johnson, Peter. *R. G. Collingwood: An Introduction*. Bristol: Thoemmes Press, 1998.

Jolly, Julius. *Outlines of an History of the Hindu Law of Partition, Inheritance and Adoption.* Calcutta: Thacker, Spink & Co., 1883.

Joppke, Christian. *The Secular State under Siege: Religion and Politics in Europe and America.* Cambridge: Polity Press, 2015.

Kāṇe, P. V. 'The Predecessors of Vijñāneśvara'. *The Journal of the Bombay Branch of the Royal Asiatic Society* (1925): 193–221.

Kāṇe, P. V. *A History of Dharmaśāstra*, vol. 5, part 2. Poona: Bandharkar Oriental Research Institute, 1962.

Kāṇe, P. V. *A History of Dharmaśāstra*, vol. 1, part 1, 2nd edn. Poona: Bhandarkar Oriental Research Institute, 1968.

Kāṇe, P. V. *A History of Dharmaśāstra.* vol. 3, 2nd edn. Poona: Bhandarkar Oriental Research Institute, 1973.

Kāṇe, P. V. *A History of Dharmaśāstra*, vol. 1, part 2, 2nd edn. Poona: Bhandarkar Oriental Research Institute, 1975.

Kaplan, Robert. 'Joseph K. Claims Compensation: Franz Kafka's Legal Writings'. *Advances in Historical Studies* 3 (2014): 115–21.

Kapur, Ratna. 'The Ayodhya Case: Hindu Majoritarianism and the Right to Religious Liberty'. *Maryland Journal of International Law* 305 (2014): 305–65.

Kaviraj, Sudipto. 'The Sudden Death of Sanskrit Knowledge'. *Journal of Indian Philosophy* 33 (2005): 119–42.

Khanna, Vikramaditya. 'Fiduciary Principles in Indian Law'. *The Oxford Handbook of Fiduciary Law*, ed. Evan Criddle, Paul Miller, and Rober Sitkoff. New York: Oxford University Press, 2019, pp. 623–42.

Kroll, Ethan. 'A Logical Approach to Law'. PhD Dissertation, University of Chicago, 2010.

Lariviere, R. W. 'Justices and *Paṇḍitas*: Some Ironies in Contemporary Readings of the Hindu Legal Past'. *Journal of Asian Studies* 48.4 (1989): 757–69.

Lingat, Robert. *The Classical Law of India.* Trans. John Derrett. Berkeley: University of California Press, 1973.

Lopata, Benjamin. 'Property Theory in Hobbes'. *Political Theory* 1.2 (1973): 203–18.

Lubin, Timothy. 'The Theory and Practice of Property in Premodern South Asia: Disparities and Convergences'. *Journal of the Economic and Social History of the Orient* 68.5–6 (2018): 803–50.

Mahmood, Syed. *Indian Law Review: Allahabad Series.* Madras: Law Reports Office, 1887.

Majumdar, Rochona. 'Marriage, Family, and Property in India: The Hindu Succession Act of 1956'. *South Asian History and Culture* 1.3 (2010): 397–415.

Marshall, P. J. *The British Discovery of Hinduism in the Eighteenth Century.* Cambridge: Cambridge University Press, 1970.

Mayne, John. *A Treatise on Hindu Law and Usage.* Madras: Higginbotham, 1878.

McCrea, Lawrence. 'The Hierarchical Organization of Language in Mīmāṃsā Interpretive Theory'. *Journal of Indian Philosophy* 28.5 (2000): 429–59.

McCrea, Lawrence. 'Novelty of Style and Novelty of Substance in Seventeenth-Century Mīmāṃsā'. *Journal of Indian Philosophy* 30.5 (2002): 481–94.

McCrea, Lawrence. 'Playing with the System: Fragmentation and Individualization in Late Pre-Colonial Mīmāṃsā'. *Journal of Indian Philosophy* 36 (2008): 575–85.

McCrea, Lawrence. 'Hindu Jurisprudence and Scriptural Hermeneutics'. *Hinduism and Law: An Introduction*, ed. Timothy Lubin, Donald Davis, and Jayanth Krishnan. Cambridge: Cambridge University Press, 2010, pp. 123–36.

McCrea, Lawrence, and Parimal Patil. *Buddhist Philosophy of Language in India: Jñānaśrīmitra on Exclusion.* New York: Columbia University Press, 2007.

Menski, Werner. *Modern Indian Family Law.* London: Routledge, 2013.

Merrill, Christi. 'The Afterlives of Panditry: Rethinking Fidelity in Sacred Texts with Multiple Origins'. In *Decentering Translation Studies*, ed. Judy Wakabayashi and Rita Kothari. Amsterdam: John Benjamin, 2009, pp. 75–94.

Merrill, Thomas, and Henry Smith. 'Optimal Standardization in the Law of Property: The Numerus Clausus Principle'. *Yale Law Journal* 110.1 (2000): 1–70.

Merrill, Thomas, and Henry Smith. 'The Property/Contract Interface'. *Columbia Law Review* 101 (2001): 773–852.

Merrill, Thomas, and Henry Smith. *Property: Principles and Policies.* New York: Foundation Press, 2007.

Minkowski, Christopher. 'Advaita Vedānta in Early Modern History'. in *Religious Cultures in Early Modern India: New Perspectives*, ed. Rosalind O'Hanlon and David Washbrook. Special volume of *South Asian History and Culture* 2.2 (2011): 205–31.

Minkowski, Christopher, and Rosalind O'Hanlon. 'What Makes People Who They Are? Pandit Networks and the Problem of Livelihoods in Early Modern Western India'. *Indian Economic Social History Review* 45 (2008): 381–416.

Minkowski, Christopher, Rosalind O'Hanlon, and Anand Venkatkrishnan (eds.). *Scholar Intellectuals in Early Modern India.* London: Routledge, 2015.

Mitra, S. C. 'Origin and Development of the Bengal School of Hindu Law'. *Law Quarterly Review* 21 (1905): 380–92; and 22 (1906): 50–63.

Morley, William. *The Administration of Justice in British India: Its Past History and Present State.* London: Williams and Norgate, 1858.

Mukherjea, B. L. *The Hindu Law of Religious and Charitable Trusts*, 2nd edn. Calcutta: Eastern Law House, 1962.

Narain, Vishnu. *Jonathan Duncan and Varanasi.* Calcutta: Firma K. L. Mukhopadhyay, 1959.

Narula, Smita. 'Law and Hindu Nationalist Movements'. *Hinduism and Law: An Introduction*, ed. Timothy Lubin, Donald Davis, and Jayanth K. Krishnan. Cambridge: Cambridge University Press, 2010, pp. 234–51.

Nelson, J. H. *Prospectus of the Scientific Study of the Hindu Law.* London: Kegan Paul & Co., 1881.

Newbigin, Eleanor. 'The Codification of Personal Law and Secular Citizenship: Revisiting the History of Law Reform in Late Colonial India'. *Indian Economic and Social History Review* 46.1 (2009): 83–104.

Newbigin, Eleanor. *The Hindu Family and the Emergence of Modern India: Law, Citizenship and Community.* Cambridge: Cambridge University Press, 2013.

Nicholls, George. *Sketch of the Rise and Progress of the Benares Patschalla or Sanskrit College, Now Forming the Sanskrit Department of the Sanskrit College.* Allahabad: Government Press, 1907.

Nicholson, Andrew. *Unifying Hinduism: Philosophy and Identity in Indian Intellectual History.* New York: Columbia University Press, 2010.

O'Hanlon, Rosalind, and David Washbrook. 'Histories in Transition: Approach to the Study of Colonialism and Culture in India'. *History Workshop* 32 (1991): 110–27.

O'Hanlon, Rosalind. 'Letters Home: Banaras Pandits and the Maratha Regions in Early Modern India'. *Modern Asian Studies* 44.2 (2010): 201–40.

O'Hanlon, Rosalind. 'The Social Worth of Scribes: Brahmins, Kayasthas and the Social Order in Early Modern India'. *Indian Economic Social History Review* 47.4 (2010): 563–95.

O'Hanlon, Rosalind. 'Speaking from Śiva's Temple: Banaras Scholar Households and the Brahman "Ecumene" of Mughal India'. *South Asian History and Culture* 2.2 (2011): 253–77.

O'Hanlon, Rosalind. 'Contested Conjunctures: Brahman Communities and "Early Modernity" in India'. *American Historical Review* 116.2 (2013): 765–87.

O'Hanlon, Rosalind, Gergely Hidas, and Csaba Kiss. 'Discourses of Caste over the Longue Durée: Gopīnātha and Social Classification in India, ca. 1400–1900'. *South Asian History and Culture* 6.1 (2015): 102–29.

Olivelle, Patrick. *The Āśrama System: The History and Hermeneutics of a Religious Institution.* Delhi: Munishiram Manoharlal, 1993.

Olivelle, Patrick. *Dharmasūtras: The Law Codes of Āpastamba, Gautama, Baudhāyana, and Vasiṣṭha.* Oxford: Oxford University Press, 1999.

Olivelle, Patrick. 'Introduction'. *Journal of Indian Philosophy* 32.5–6 (2004): 421–2.

Olivelle, Patrick. *Manu's Code of Law: A Critical Edition and Translation of the Mānava-Dharmaśāstra.* Oxford: Oxford University Press, 2005.

Olivelle, Patrick (ed.). *Dharma: Studies in Its Semantic, Cultural and Religious History.* Delhi: Motilal Banarasidass 2009.

Olivelle, Patrick. 'Dharmaśāstra: A Textual History'. *Hinduism and Law: An Introduction*, ed. Timothy Lubin, Donald Davis, and Jayanth Krishnan. Cambridge: Cambridge University Press, 2012, pp. 28–57.

Olivelle, Patrick. *King, Governance, and Law in Ancient India: Kauṭilya's Arthaśāstra.* Oxford: Oxford University Press, 2013.

Olivelle, Patrick. *A Sanskrit Dictionary of Law and Statecraft.* Delhi: Primus Books, 2015.

Pandey, Anushan. 'Recasting the Brahmin in Medieval Mithilā: Origins of Caste Identity among the Maithil Brahmins of North Bihar'. PhD Dissertation, University of Michigan, 2014.

Patil, Parimal. 'The Historical Rhythms of the Nyāya-Vaiśeṣika Knowledge-System'. In *Periodization and Historiography of Indian Philosophy*, ed. Eli Franco. Vienna: Institut für Südasien-, Tibet- und Buddhismuskunde der Universität Wien, 2009, pp. 91–126.

Patra, Atul Chandra. *The Administration of Justice under the East India Company in Bengal, Bihar and Orissa.* New Delhi: Asia Publishing House, 1962.

Pawate, I.S. *Dāya-Vibhāga: or, The Individualization of Communal Property and the Communalization of Individual Property in the Mitakshara Law.* 2nd edn, revised and enlarged. Dharwar: Karnatak University, 1975.

Pennington, Brian. *Was Hinduism Invented?: Britons, Indians, and the Colonial Construction of Religion.* Oxford: Oxford University Press, 2005.

Phillips, Stephen. *Epistemology in Classical India: The Knowledge Sources of the Nyaya School.* London: Routledge, 2012.

Pollock, Sheldon. 'The Theory of Practice and the Practice of Theory in Indian Intellectual History'. *Journal of the American Oriental Society* 105.3 (1985): 499–519.

Pollock, Sheldon. 'The Idea of Śāstra in Traditional India'. In *The Shastric Traditions in Indian Arts*, ed. Anna Dallapiccola. Stuttgart: Wiesbaden, 1989, pp. 17–26.

Pollock, Sheldon. 'The Death of Sanskrit'. *Comparative Studies in Society and History* 43.2 (2001): 392–426.

Pollock, Sheldon. 'New Intellectuals in Seventeenth-Century India'. *Indian Economic and Social History Review* 38.1 (2001): 3–31.

Pollock, Sheldon. *The Ends of Man at the End of Premodernity.* Amsterdam: Royal Netherlands Academy of Arts and Sciences, 2005.

Pollock, Sheldon. 'Pretextures of Time'. *History and Theory* 46.3 (2007): 336–83.

Pollock, Sheldon. 'Is There an Indian Intellectual History?' *Journal of Indian Philosophy* 36.5 (2008): 533–42.

Pollock, Sheldon. 'The Languages of Science in Early Modern India'. *Forms of Knowledge in Early Modern Asia: Explorations in the Intellectual History of India and Tibet, 1500–1800*, ed. Sheldon Pollock. London: Duke University Press, 2011, pp. 19–48.

Potter, Karl. *The Padārthatattvanirūpaṇam of Raghunātha Śiromaṇi*. Cambridge, MA: Harvard University Press, 1957.

Preisendanz, Karin. 'The Production of Philosophical Literature in South Asia during the Pre-Colonial Period (15th–18th Centuries): The Case of the "Nyāyasūtra" Commentarial Tradition'. *Journal of Indian Philosophy* 33.1 (2005): 55–94.

Rao, Velcheru, David Shulman, and Sanjay Subrahmanyam. *Textures of Time: Writing History in South India, 1600–1800*. Delhi: Permanent Black, 2001.

Richards, John. 'Early Modern India and World History'. *Journal of World History* 8.2 (1997): 198–203.

Rocher, Ludo. 'Hindu Law and Religion: Where to Draw the Line'. In *Studies in Hindu Law and Dharmaśāstra*, ed. Donald Davis. London: Anthem, 2014, pp. 83–102.

Rocher, Ludo. 'Indian Response to Anglo-Hindu Law'. In *Studies in Hindu Law and Dharmaśāstra*, ed. Donald Davis. London: Anthem, 2014, pp. 634–42.

Rocher, Ludo. 'Jīmūtavāhana's *Dāyabhāga* and the Maxim *Factum Valet*'. In *Studies in Hindu Law and Dharmaśāstra*, ed. Donald Davis. New York: Anthem Press, 2014, pp. 305–13.

Rocher, Ludo. 'Schools of Hindu Law'. In *Studies in Hindu Law and Dharmaśāstra*, ed. Donald Davis. London: Anthem, 2014, pp. 119–28.

Rocher, Ludo. 'Changing Patterns of Diversification in Hindu Law'. In *Studies in Hindu Law and Dharmaśāstra*, ed. Donald Davis. London: Anthem, 2014, pp. 129–44.

Rocher, Ludo. 'The Historical Foundations of Ancient Indian Law'. In *Studies in Hindu Law and Dharmaśāstra*, ed. Donald Davis. London: Anthem, 2014, pp. 59–82.

Rocher, Ludo. 'Inheritance and Śrāddha: The Principle of "Spiritual Benefit"'. In *Studies in Hindu Law and Dharmaśāstra*, ed. Donald Davis. New York: Anthem Press, 2014, pp. 267–78.

Rocher, Rosane. *Orientalism, Poetry, and the Millennium: The Checkered Life of Nathaniel Brassey Halhed, 1751–1830*. Delhi: Motilal Banarsidass, 1983.

Rocher, Rosane. 'The Career of Rādhākānta Tarkavāgīśa, an Eighteenth-Century Pandit in British Employ'. *Journal of the American Oriental Society* 109.4 (1989): 627–33.

Rocher, Rosane. 'Weaving Knowledge: Sir William Jones and Indian Pandits'. In *Objects of Enquiry: The Life, Contributions, and Influences of Sir William Jones, 1746–1794*, ed. Garland Cannon and Kevin Brine. New York: New York University Press, 1995, pp. 51–79.

Rocher, Rosane. 'The Creation of Anglo-Hindu Law'. *Hinduism and Law: An Introduction*, ed. Timothy Lubin, Donald Davis, and Jayanth Krishnan. Cambridge: Cambridge University Press, 2010, pp. 79–88.

Rocher, Rosane, and Ludo Rocher. *The Making of Western Indology: Henry Thomas Colebrooke and the East India Company*. London: Routledge, 2012.

Rocher, Rosane, and Ludo Rocher. 'Ownership by Birth, the *Mitākṣarā* Stand'. *Journal of Indian Philosophy* 29 (2001): 241–55.

Row, T. A. *Indian Decisions (Old Series)*, vol. 1: *Supreme Court Reports, Bengal*. Madras: Law Printing House, 1911.

Ryan, Alan. *Property and Political Theory*. Oxford: Blackwell, 1984.

Sandel, Michael. *What Money Can't Buy: The Moral Limits of Markets*. London: Allen Lane, 2012.

Sarkar, Bihani. 'The Rite of Durgā in Medieval Bengal: An Introductory Study of Raghunandana's *Dūrgāpūjātattva* with Text and Translation of the Principal Rites'. *Journal of the Royal Asiatic Society Series* 22.2 (2012): 325–90.

Sarkar, Kisori. *The Mimansa Rules of Interpretation as Applied to Hindu Law*. Calcutta: Thacker & Spink, 1907.

Schroeder, Jeane. *The Vestal and the Fasces: Hegel, Lacan, Property, and the Feminine.* Berkeley: University of California Press, 1998.

Schwab, Raymond. *The Oriental Renaissance: Europe's Rediscovery of India and the East, 1680–1880.* New York: Columbia University Press, 1984.

Sen, Ranji. 'The Emergence of a Service Elite in Bengal in the Half of the Eighteenth Century: A New Dimension of Collaboration'. *Proceedings of the Indian History Congress* 36 (1975): 511–22.

Setlur, S. 'The Bengal School of Hindu Law'. *Law Quarterly Review* 23 (1907): 202–19.

Shastri, Haraprasad. 'Dakshini Pandits at Benares'. *Indian Antiquary* 41 (1912): 7–13.

Shastri, Haraprasad. *A Descriptive Catalogue of Sanskrit Manuscripts in the Government Collection under the Care of Asiatic Society of Bengal*, vol. 3. Calcutta: Asiatic Society of Bengal, 1917.

Singer, Joseph. *Property*, 5th edn. New York: Wolters Kluwer, 2017.

Skinner, Quentin. *Visions of Politics*, vol. 1: *Regarding Method.* Cambridge: Cambridge University Press, 2002.

Smith, Henry. 'Property Is Not Just a Bundle of Rights'. *Econ Journal Watch* 8.3 (2011): 279–91.

Smith, Henry. 'Property as the Law of Things'. *Harvard Law Review*, 125 (2012): 1691–1726.

Sontheimer, Günter-Dietz. *The Joint Hindu Family: Its Evolution as a Legal Institution.* New Delhi: Munshiram Manoharlal, 1977.

Sontheimer, Günter-Dietz. 'Religious Endowments in India: The Juristic Personality of Hindu Deities'. In *Essays on Religion, Literature and Law*, ed. Heidrun Brückner, Anne Feldhaus, and Aditya Malik. New Delhi: Manohar, 2004, pp. 15–68.

Strange, Sir Thomas. *Elements of Hindu Law: Referable to British Judicature in India*, vol. 1. London: Payne and Foss, 1825.

Strawson, John. 'Islamic Law and English Texts'. *Law and Critique* 6.1 (1995): 21–38.

Sturman, Rachel. 'Property and Attachments: Defining Autonomy and the Claims of Family in Nineteenth-Century Western India'. *Comparative Studies in Society and History* 47.3 (2005): 611–37.

Sturman, Rachel. 'Marriage and Family in Colonial Hindu Law'. *Hinduism and Law: An Introduction*, ed. Timothy Lubin, Donald Davis, and Jayanth K. Krishnan. Cambridge: Cambridge University Press, 2010, pp. 89–104.

Sturman, Rachel. 'Custom and Human Value in the Debates on Hindu Marriage'. *Government of Social Life in Colonial India: Liberalism, Religious Law and Women's Rights.* Cambridge: Cambridge University Press, 2012, pp. 148–95.

Subrahmanyam, Sanjay. 'Connected Histories: Notes Towards a Reconfiguration of Early Modern Eurasia'. *Modern Asian Studies* 31.3 (1997): 735–62.

Tebbit, Mark. *Law and Philosophy: An Introduction.* London: Routledge, 2017.

Tully, James. *A Discourse on Property: John Locke and His Adversaries.* Cambridge: Cambridge University Press, 1980.

Vajpeyi, Ananya. '*Śūdradharma* and the Legal Treatments of Caste'. In *Hinduism and Law: An Introduction*, ed. Timothy Lubin, Donald Davis, and Jayanth Krishnan. Cambridge: Cambridge University Press, 2010, pp. 154–66.

Vandevelde, Kenneth. 'The New Property of the Nineteenth Century: The Development of the Modern Concept of Property'. *Buffalo Law Review* 29 (1980): 325–68.

Venkaṭarāman, S. 'Influence of Common Law and Equity on the Personal Law of the Hindus'. *Revista del Instituto de Derecho Comparado* 8–9 (1957): 156–79.

Venkatkrishnan, Anand. 'Mīmāṃsā, Vedānta, and the Bhakti Movement'. PhD Dissertation, Columbia University, 2015.

Venkatkrishnan, Anand. 'Ritual, Reflection, and Religion: The Devas of Banaras'. *South Asian History and Culture* 6.1 (2015): 147–71.

Verpoorten, Jean-Marie. *Mīmāṃsā Literature.* History of Indian Literature; vol. 6, fasc. 5. Wiesbaden: Harrassowitz, 1987.

Vidyabhusana, S. C. *A History of Indian Logic: Ancient, Medieval and Modern Schools.* Delhi: Motilal Banarsidass, 1971.

Ward, William. *A View of the History, Literature and Religion of the Hindoos.* vol. 2. London: Kingsbury, Parbury, and Allen, 1822.

Washbrook, David. 'Law, State and Agrarian Society in Colonial India'. *Modern Asian Studies* 15.3 (1981): 649–721.

Williams, Rowan. 'Civil and Religious Law in England: A Religious Perspective'. *Ecclesiastical Law Journal* 10 (2008): 262–82.

Wright, Samuel. 'The Practice and Theory of Property in Seventeenth-Century Bengal'. *Indian Economic and Social History Review* 54.2 (2017): 147–82.

Index

Note: I have listed individual texts under the entries for their respective authors. The exceptions to this are the Vivādārṇavasetu and Vivādabhaṅgārṇava, which have their own entries. Where the primary entry in the index is a Sanskrit term, I have endeavored to add a reference to the corresponding English term (and vice versa). Please note that details of colonial schools of Anglo-Hindu law appear under 'Colonial Schools of Hindu Law', whereas references for pre-colonial appellations such as 'Gauḍa', 'Maithila', etc., can be found under their own respective entries.

For 'Ownership', there are several entries: 'svatva', 'svāmya', 'svāmitva'; and also 'viniyuj', and 'yatheṣṭavinuj' (yogyatva, yojtva, ārhatā, etc.).